HURON COUNTY PUBLIC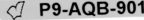

P9-AQB-901

HURON COUNTY LIBRARY

3 6492 00379949 8

HB

THE
ATLANTIC
PROVINCES

THE EMERGENCE OF
COLONIAL SOCIETY

W. S. MACNUTT

THE
ATLANTIC
PROVINCES

THE
EMERGENCE
OF
COLONIAL
SOCIETY
1712-1857

The Canadian Centenary Series

158420

MAY 22 '75

McClelland and Stewart Limited

© McClelland and Stewart Limited, 1965

All rights reserved.
No part of this book may be reproduced
in any form without permission
in writing from the publishers,
except by a reviewer who may quote
brief passages in a review to be printed
in a magazine or newspaper.

The Canadian Publishers
McClelland and Stewart Limited
25 Hollinger Road, Toronto 16

THE
CANADIAN
CENTENARY
SERIES

A History of Canada

W. L. Morton, EXECUTIVE EDITOR

D. G. Creighton, ADVISORY EDITOR

VOLUMES STARRED ARE PUBLISHED

CONTENTS

The Atlantic Provinces

ACKNOWLEDGEMENTS

MAPS AND ILLUSTRATIONS

FACING PAGE 68

Portion of Nicholas Visscher's Map of North America – A prospect of Annapolis Royal in Nova Scotia 1751 – The Siege of Louisburg – The Scene of Strife on the Isthmus of Chignecto – The Harbour of Saint John about 1770 – Charlotte-Town on the Island of St John's 1778 – Cod Fishing in Newfoundland – Grand Pré, Nova Scotia – Sydney in 1785 – Cook's Map of Newfoundland

FACING PAGE 196

HMS *Shannon* leading the *Chesapeake* into Halifax Harbour – Saint John in 1814 – The *Marco Polo* Entering the Mersey – Samuel Leonard Tilley – Charles Fisher – Lumberers on the Miramichi River – Jonathan Odell Joseph Howe – Samuel Cunard – Sir John Wentworth – Hon. Patrick Morris – Hon. James W. Johnston – Charles Inglis, D.D. – Rev. William Black – William Carson, M.D. – Hon. Ward Chipman (Sr.) – Sir John Harvey – Thomas Chandler Haliburton

The Canadian Centenary Series

Nearly half a century has elapsed since *Canada and Its Provinces*, the first large-scale co-operative history of Canada, was published. During that time, new historical materials have been made available in archives and libraries; new research has been carried out, and its result published; new interpretations have been advanced and tested. In these same years Canada itself has greatly grown and changed. These facts, together with the approach of the centenary of Confederation, justify the publication of a new, co-operative history of Canada.

The form chosen for this enterprise is that of a series of volumes. The series has been planned by the editors, but each volume will be designed and executed by a single author. The general theme of the work is the development of those regional communities which have for the past century made up the Canadian nation; and the series will be composed of a number of volumes sufficiently large to permit an adequate treatment of all the phases of the theme in the light of modern knowledge.

The Centenary History, then, is planned as a series to have a certain common character and method, but to be the work of individual authors, specialists in their fields. As a whole it will be a work of specialized knowledge, the great advantage of scholarly co-operation, but, at the same time, each volume will have the unity and distinctive character of individual authorship. The result, it is hoped, will be scholarly and readable, at once useful to the student and of interest to the general reader.

The difficulties of organizing and executing such a series are apparent; the overlapping of separate narratives, the risk of omissions, the imposition of divisions which are relevant to some themes, but not to others. Not so apparent, but quite as troublesome are problems of scale, perspective, and scope, problems which perplex the writer of a one-volume history, and are magnified in a series. It is by deliberate choice that certain parts of the history are told twice, in different volumes from different points of view, in the belief that the benefits gained outweigh the unavoidable disadvantages.

The Centenary History is a series to be written by individual authors; but it is also planned to have a certain common character and to follow a common method. It has been agreed that a general narrative treatment was necessary and that each author should deal in a balanced way with economic, political, and social history. This varied and comprehensive account will, it is hoped, be presented in a scholarly, interpretative, and readable fashion, so that the student may be informed and the general reader interested.

Mr MacNutt in the present book has had a different task from that of his colleagues who have already published other volumes in the Series. Whereas they have studied relatively homogeneous areas, or relatively short periods of time, he has had to bring together the histories of four disparate colonies over a century and a half. This difficult assignment he has discharged with skill and a fine sense of the process of historical growth. What was common in development is emphasized, what was significant in detail is used to confirm; what was vivid in action or in personality is caught by the historian's creative eye. There takes form in the pages to follow a panorama of the emergence of a colonial society, uncertain always of its attachments, drawn to the sea, drawn to the continent, yet achieving a character at once strong and distinct.

W. L. MORTON,
Executive Editor.
D. G. CREIGHTON,
Advisory Editor.

PREFACE

The Atlantic Provinces
The Emergence of Colonial Society

No author could presume to write a specialized study of the history of the Atlantic Provinces. This volume is but a survey of the development of five colonies over a period of a century and a half. A single historian could never make himself familiar with all the original material from which the account is derived. To produce an authoritative version it has been necessary to draw very liberally upon the work of scores of writers and scholars who have given their labours to the history of the Atlantic Provinces. Special reference should be made to the writings of the late Professor J. B. Brebner of Columbia University and of Professor D. C. Harvey of Halifax. In their company the historian can consider himself on firm ground.

Each of the four provinces with which the book deals merits a volume for itself alone to set forth the peculiar characteristics it possessed and the particular forms of development it experienced. The attempt to work the individual provincial histories into a single narrative produced difficulties. But the seas that divided imparted many similarities. It is hoped that the reader, having ruminated upon the diverse and multifold beginnings, will come to the conclusion that a moral emerges : the populations of the four provinces were slowly being fused into a seaward community with attributes basically common to one another. Perhaps dissimilarity recedes as the tale unfolds.

The author is grateful to the Canada Council for a fellowship that enabled him to do research in London and to the University of New Brunswick for a year's leave of absence. For permission to reproduce the portraits of William Carson and Patrick Morris thanks are owing to the Honourable Joseph R. Smallwood and to President Gushue of Memorial University. The illustration of the harbour of St John's in 1770 comes from the generosity of Honourable Chief Justice Furlong, the owner of the original painting. To Mr William Hazen of Lancaster the author is indebted for permission to reproduce the first known painting of colonial Saint John.

The editorial labours of Professors Creighton and Morton have been of inestimable service in the improvement of the manuscript. For various favours and forms of assistance thanks are extended to Dr C. Bruce Fergusson of Halifax, Dr George MacBeath, formerly of Saint John, Mr Allan M. Fraser, provincial archivist of Newfoundland, Professor Gerald S. Graham of the University of London, and to Professors D. MacM. Young and Fred Cogswell of the University of New Brunswick. Essential to the writing of the later Newfoundland sections was the thesis of Dr Gertrude E. Gunn, about to be published in book form by the University of Toronto Press. Very helpful for the latter stage of Nova Scotian history was the thesis of Professor Harvey W. MacPhee of Nova Scotia Teachers' College on the administration of Lord Mulgrave. To the members of the staffs of all the libraries and other institutions mentioned in the bibliography and footnotes the author is obliged for never-failing courtesy and co-operation.

CHAPTER 1

Shore and Sea

One of the most rhapsodic remarks ever made about the islands, seas, and peninsulas that compose the eastern approaches to North America was that they were to the western hemisphere what Greece was to Europe, a conveyor of civilization from the Old World to the New. The Bay of Fundy was likened to the sunlit Aegean.[1] But the comparison might better have been transferred to Europe's northwestern approaches. Many a traveller who visited what are today the Atlantic Provinces of Canada was to be reminded of the bold promontories, rocky coastlines, jagged and treacherous littorals he had seen in Scandinavia. Millions of years before, this whole maritime area had been much higher above sea level, but a long process of subsidence had permitted an invasion by the Atlantic. There was left a complex network of waterways and a myriad of magnificent harbours. Not far from the coastlines the more moderate temperatures of the Atlantic encountered the solid front of the North American winter so that no part of this broken region enjoyed much more than four months of freedom from frost. Many of its seaward approaches were lined by great banks of fog for one hundred days in the year.

By 1712 civilization had come to the region but had made little impression that could be called permanent. Hundreds of shiploads of Europeans had made fleeting visits to this part of America that was nearest to their homelands, but in only one or two small areas had more than a trace of settlement been left. For geographic reasons alone, the region was destined to be passed by or passed through. No great river offered a satisfactory avenue to the interior of the continent. A large proportion of the low mountains and hills, the tablelands and valleys, was unfit for cultivation. The almost barren region of Gaspé denied easy access to the valley of the St Lawrence which, along with the Hudson, was to convey civilization to the unknown interior of the continent. Those who followed Champlain, both French and English, found that the fur trade here offered but moderate

1

returns and that the climate suffered by comparison with that of the settled areas to the southward.

Yet this area of the North Atlantic served as a region of transition from the Old World to the New. Though the terrain of the peninsulas and islands offered little temptation to adventurers, the magnificent fisheries off the shores had attracted Europeans since the early sixteenth century. The shallow waters of the continental shelf, warmed by the sun, produce a great variety of marine organisms known as plankton, which move about with the swirling currents that are formed when the warmer temperatures of the Gulf Stream encounter the colder from Labrador. Smaller fish like herring, squid, and caplin feed on the plankton, following it from one submarine elevation to another. Intense variation in temperature and in the degree of salinity, influenced by fresh water from the St Lawrence and by melting icebergs, affects the supply of all of these minute forms of life. Wherever there are caplin, there are cod and other large fish. Following the voyages of the Cabots and other early explorers, fishermen from Europe came to catch the cod.

By 1712 this North Atlantic fishery was one of the great industries of the West European economy. It was far older than the fur trade of the North American continent. Before Cartier had entered the St Lawrence European sailors were familiar with the cod-producing waters of the region that became known as the banks. Unlike the fur trade, the fishery was a wealth-producing factor for all nations participating in it. "Le Canada n'enrichit pas la France. C'est une plainte comme ancienne que la colonie elle-même."[2] But the seas of Newfoundland were a source of profit to the commerce of London, Rouen, Oporto, Cadiz, Leghorn.

The French, Spanish, and Portuguese had, in the main, anticipated the English, but the defeat of the Armada in 1588 had reduced Spain to a secondary place in the fishery. The French had two great advantages: a large domestic market supplied by an efficient system of river communication from the Atlantic and Channel ports along the Seine, Loire, and Garonne, and a climate that made it relatively easy to produce great quantities of solar salt essential for processing and curing the product. Owing to this second advantage they had, in general, resorted to what was called the wet, green, or mud branch of the industry. Many of their larger vessels never touched shore at all, hastening to the banks early in the spring when the fish were firmer and less perishable, quickly drying them on stagings erected on the decks, covering each daily catch with layers of salt, and, when holds were full, turning home to the shore establishments on the Bay of Biscay where the product was cured for consumption. To a Catholic population, the North Atlantic codfish, "the beef of the sea," had become a staff of life.

Coming somewhat later, the English were stern competitors. Their domestic market was smaller and their supplies of solar salt limited. But the collapse of Spanish and Portuguese sea power opened up to them the markets of southern Europe where Catholic populations abounded. For all of these reasons their establishments on the rim of the fishery tended to become more permanent than did the French. Lacking facilities for the final preparation of the cod at home, they found it necessary to select locations on Newfoundland's shores for the elaborate business of curing and drying. This required a period of five or six weeks. The cod were laid out on stagings, known as flakes, and turned at frequent intervals. Then they were collected into great circular stacks of up to two hundred quintals and covered with brush, or were conveyed to makeshift storehouses to await transportation abroad. Grading was important. The firmest and whitest of the cod were classified for sale in the Mediterranean. The second grade, classified as Madeira, were slightly damaged fish but still salable. The poorest portion of the produce was packed in casks and dispatched to slave-owners in the West Indies.[8]

Since early in the seventeenth century the English fishery had possessed a high degree of organization and political influence. The merchants of Poole and Dartmouth, and of the other ports of southwestern England, who owned the ships and recruited and paid the crews, secured from Charles I in 1634 what they called the Charter of the Western Adventurers, which gave legal force to what had long been called "the customary law." This document stipulated that the first, second, and third captains arriving in each harbour from England should be ranked as admirals, vice-admirals, and rear-admirals for the fishing season, which lasted from March to September. It was the official view that colonizers were transgressors without right to reside within one-quarter of a mile of the shore line.

While the French fishery was dispersed around the shores of the Gulf of St Lawrence, the English were concentrated along the harbours of the Avalon Peninsula where semi-settled communities were formed around rapidly improvised piers and stagings. Cromwell's government strengthened the local authority of the Western Adventurers by giving powers of civil government to his convoy captains and the ordinances of Charles II preserved an official fiction that Newfoundland had no permanent residents. William III's government gave what was considered to be the final sanction to the ruling notion that the island was a great common for the seasonal use of English visitors by an Act of Parliament of 1699, a comprehensive attempt to codify their rights. The Western Adventurers, in staking out an exclusive claim to the use of the Newfoundland littoral as a necessary adjunct to their industry, were sustained by two cogent arguments. First, the fishery was an essential ingredient in the maintenance of British sea power. It trained for the skills and toils of the sea thousands of men who could readily be drafted into the Royal Navy. "The nursery of seamen," it was alleged, was far more important to England than any colony could ever be. The second was that the fishery was an earner of bullion. Very often the ships from the Mediterranean that had unloaded Newfoundland fish in Spanish and Italian ports returned to Devon with their holds in ballast but carrying gold and silver specie that had been paid for their product. To earn gold by achieving a favourable balance of trade was the great commercial object of the times and for this reason alone the fishery came to be regarded as one of Britain's mainstays. To win the balance at the expense of French and Catholic enemies was the ultimate aim. Since the Catholicism of France and southern Europe was the indispensable condition on which the fishery rested, the frequent libations of Jamaica rum partaken of by the Protestant English of Newfoundland were often accompanied by a toast to "the Pope and ten dollars," meaning ten dollars the quintal of fish.[4] The aspirations of the Western Adventurers were very closely attuned to the broader aspects of English commercial policy.

The fishery was not for Europeans alone. Very early in the seventeenth century, when it had been discovered that the cod ran in great numbers off the coasts of Maine and southern Nova Scotia during the spring, the great fishing industry of New England emerged. The Puritans who colonized Massachusetts sustained their slowly growing agricultural economy by making inroads on the sea, and the codfish became for their Commonwealth the symbol of wealth and prosperity. Their "winter fishery," which could be conducted from shore establishments at relatively short distances from George and Sable Banks, launched them into a multitude of sea-going activities. They became familiar with the beaches and harbours of Nova Scotia, acquiring the conviction that Nova Scotia was but a northern extension of their own country. Their own "dry" fishery, conducted in ketches of from twenty to eighty tons manned by crews of half a dozen men, became a power in its own right. Sometimes they sold their fish to English merchants at Newfoundland and added their peculiar ingredients to the quarrels and strifes of that shore. The expansion of their own agricultural hinterland enabled them to supply Newfoundland with foodstuffs. Markets for inferior cod opened in the slave plantations of Virginia. Illegally they sold their fish in the French and Spanish islands of the West Indies and, still more illegally, brought to the English colonies the rum of Martinique and manufactured articles of French and Spanish finery. Skilled in ship-building, they each year became more numerous and more venturesome over the waters of the North Atlantic. This "nest of little peddlers" was a bane to the captains of the Royal Navy who were charged with the strenuous duty of enforcing the Laws of Trade and Navigation. Long before 1712 the New Englanders were a power upon the scene, a strong formative influence in the making of the future Atlantic Provinces.

II

In two sectors of the far-flung, seaward region, settlement had occurred and persisted in spite of the apathy and neglect of the parent states. By 1712 there were nearly three thousand English settlers along the harbours of the Avalon Peninsula. From early colonizing attempts of the seventeenth century slight residues of population had remained and, in spite of English legislation, the fishery slowly added to their numbers. The custom of leaving behind for the winter small groups of caretakers who were charged with the preservation of flakes and buildings slowly increased the roll of those who could begin to think of themselves as permanent residents of Newfoundland. An attempt was made by English ordinances in 1670 to enforce the long-standing custom of annually introducing "green men" to the fishery and ensuring their return to England where they would be available for the purposes of the navy. But many of the "green men" preferred the liberties of the Newfoundland beaches to the restrictions they had known at home and evaded the return voyage. The attractions of the New World were heightened by the New Englanders, who employed every device to bring the "green men" into their own service. Youthful trainees in the fishery were encouraged to encumber themselves with debt and to escape liability by accepting forbidden passage to New England. Newfoundland became a halfway house between the Old World and the New. A later estimate declared that the permanent drain on the English fishery ran as high as fourteen hundred men a year.[5] Smuggling out "green men" of proven capacity in sealed casks beneath the noses of the captains of the Royal Navy for more rewarding service elsewhere provided diversion as well as profit.

In spite of these losses, and in spite of English regulations against "passengers," the shore population of Newfoundland not only maintained itself but became an important by-product of the fishery. West Countrymen of enterprise learned how to gain a livelihood from bases on the shore. Along the shores on which they squatted they even asserted the right to hold private property, daringly and hardily maintained against the visitations of the fishing-admirals who, following the migrations of the cod, landed in whatever harbour they pleased to erect flakes for curing and drying. Some were wealthy and, according to tradition as well as to the records of their travails, lived in stone houses. Masters, who could boast of title derived from the times of John Guy or Lord Baltimore, ruled indentured servants and engaged in the elements of a pastoral and agricultural, as well as fishing, economy. This early strain of English stock had become progressively mixed by the introduction of Irish "boys" or "youngsters" who took ship at Cork or Youghal with Devonshire captains calling for supplies. Society along the shores of the quiet harbours and on the barren estates maintained with difficulty a patriarchal character. Intermarriage and a poor diet, according to contemporary accounts, resulted in a gross loosening of morals and physical deterioration.

Turning their backs on the unknown interior, this shore population found adventure enough and livelihood in the sea. Even by 1675 their "boatmen" were taking one third of the entire catch of fish produced in Newfoundland and, because they were not ocean-going sailors, were accused in Whitehall of bleeding England of her naval strength. Planters were poachers whose presence constituted a legitimate grievance to the Western Adventurers from Poole and Dartmouth, to whom private property was a concept that had no place in the New World. In the nature of things, conflict was indigenous. When Cromwell's government got wind of fishermen fishing "without ships," of boats putting to sea without "ocean sailors," it .was proposed to deport the settlers of Newfoundland to Jamaica. Deportation again became a possibility when the great Restoration merchant, Sir Josiah Child, urged it upon his government. The solution for the difficulty proposed by the highly organized vested interest of the West Country was the deportation of the few women of the shore communities. Small, but stubborn and hardy, the resident population clung to its slight foothold on the island despite the prohibitions of the law and the intimidations of the ship fishermen who outnumbered it ten to one. Disputes among the visitors themselves and between shipmen and shoremen were summarily and casually dealt with by the convoy captains and their deputies. Newfoundland, wrote one of them, was the only English plantation without Church or State.[6] He might modestly have reported that the Royal Navy made voluble, though infrequent, efforts to fill the breach. From Bonavista to Trepassey, the great southeastern arc of the coastline where English influence was dominant, the shore population contrived to endure with the minimum amenities of contemporary civilization. Even at St John's, the heart and centre of the fishery, so admirable for the purposes of the industry in peace and war, such government as there was came from shipboard. On the island itself an only slightly moderated anarchy was suited to the purposes of the Western Adventurers.

On the southern fringe of the region another shore population had come into existence almost as much by chance as by intent. The Acadians, the descendants of the French settlers brought to Port Royal by early entrepreneurs and by the French government when Colbert promoted the colonization of New France, had been greatly augmented by natural increase. By 1712, colonizing groups from overpopulated Port Royal had spread up the Bay of Fundy to Minas and Chignecto. A few families had crossed the bay and entered the valley of the Petitcodiac. Evading the unnecessary task of clearing wooded upland, they had concentrated on the banks of the little rivers that run into the bay, farming the marshlands periodically flooded by Fundy's great tides, constructing dykes of logs reinforced by clay to keep the sea from their fields. Especially at Minas they possessed great herds of cattle and were often reputed to be rich. No reliable figures indicate the size of the population at the time of the British conquest, but this people surely numbered upwards of five thousand.

Following their unfortunate fate in 1755 it became customary for writers to attribute to the Acadians an extraordinary degree of virtue and simplicity. "Really, if ever I knew a people amongst whom the Golden Age as described in History was apparent, it was the ancient Acadians," wrote one of them.[7] If a reason for this primitive innocence must be sought, it is to be found in Rousseau's literary adulation of the state of nature, rather than in the sober facts of history. Society, it is true, had cast few bonds upon the Acadians. The province, in the calculations of Colbert, was to fill the role of supplier of northern products to the French Antilles during the season of winter navigation when the St Lawrence was closed by ice. But France had never pressed this elaborate planning to the stage of execution. The Acadians had been favoured by slack government, for long periods by no government at all. They had learned to ignore corrupt governors and garrisons forgotten by the court at Versailles, had become semi-primitive and unsophisticated in the complexities of the outside world. A purely peasant society had developed. "Every farmer was his own architect and every man of property a farmer."[8] Instead of adding to the wealth of France, their limited commerce was in the hands of the New Englanders. One vexed French governor, attempting to utilize their energies for war against England, declared that they behaved like true republicans, acknowledging neither royal authority nor courts of law.[9] Illiteracy was the common rule. Communal decisions were arrived at by general expression of the public will, achieved in assembly at church doors on Sunday mornings by the guidance of parish priests whose influence could almost always be decisive.

III

These shore communities had survived more than the apathy and neglect, and, in the case of Newfoundland, the hostility of the parent states. Their area of the North Atlantic had for a hundred years been the principal meeting-place and battleground of French and English. For twenty-five years prior to the Peace of Utrecht, war and alarms of war had echoed around them. On the St Lawrence and the seaboard to the south the pattern of settlement had become established. But Newfoundland and Acadia were areas of dispute. Ever since Samuel Argall had in 1613 attempted to enforce the application of the 45th parallel of latitude, which runs through the Bay of Fundy, as the northern boundary of Virginia, Acadia had been claimed by both Crowns. Occasionally the Dutch had joined in the rivalry. Private war had reigned among fur traders and concessionaires. Public war had sometimes occurred even though the powers of western Europe were at peace.

The English primacy in Newfoundland was most severely shaken during the wars of King William and Queen Anne. Since the coming of Europeans to America the waters to the north and west had been Frenchmen's seas, but it was not until 1662 that France established a military, naval, and commercial base at Placentia which was said to offer the best drying-beach in Newfoundland.[10] Here the French not only developed their fishery at an abnormally rapid rate but were in position to seize control of the entire island. Frontenac's sanguinary expeditions had as their grand design the complete control of the fishery on which, it was reasoned, rested the entire naval power of France. In 1696-97 Iberville destroyed all the English establishments at St John's. These were virtually impregnable to attack from the sea but highly vulnerable on the landward side. Carbonear and Harbour Grace were also burned. Yet the fishery continued in spite of massacre, privations of all kinds, the extortions of greedy commanders on both sides, the ruinous diminution of trade. The wage rate rose more rapidly than the death rate. The Peace of 1713 found the planters holding tightly to what remained to them, the character of their remarkable society unchanged in essentials.

The treaties of St Germaine-en-laye, Breda, and Ryswick all confirmed the claim of France to Acadia, but French neglect combined with New England's aggressiveness rendered this possession something akin to a fiction. Since the colonization of Virginia, Englishmen had fished off the coasts of "Accadie or Nova Scotia," as the great region to the south of the St Lawrence was called in the official dispatches of the period. In 1654, when France and England were allies in Europe, the Puritan Commonwealth of Massachusetts had successfully carried its arms against feeble French posts at Saint John, Port Royal, and La Have. This martial flurry very forcefully revealed the intensive interest of New England in the long and broken coastline, an interest which was amplified by Sir Thomas Temple, who was granted the country by Cromwell's government, and by his nephew and heir, John Nelson of Boston. For a long period the French government at Port Royal actually encouraged trade between Acadians and New Englanders. Coal from the interior basin of the St John found its way to Boston. Freely the New Englanders used the beaches of Acadia. Even by 1712 several generations of sea-going men had passed down to their successors the unalterable conviction that this great lone land skirting the maritime approaches to their country was theirs by inalienable right. This did not mean that New Englanders were interested in settling Nova Scotia. Their occupation was merely casual and seasonal. Their vaguely defined purpose was that of the

West Countrymen in Newfoundland – to keep the country unsettled, open and free to the convenience of the fishery on which the prosperity of their ports depended.

This condition of frequent and easy intercourse between the two countries was ended by the Treaty of Neutrality of 1686 between the Crowns of France and England. By it the ports, rivers, and seas of each king in America were closed to the subjects of the other. The war which followed soon afterward brought fierce animosity. When Port Royal became "a nest of pirates," preying on the commerce of New England, the tradition that Nova Scotia was an English land was inflated by pious Puritan enthusiasm and plans for the conquest of Acadia were annually formulated.

The Acadians were to pay the penalty for the cruel triumphs of their Canadian brethren on the western and northern frontiers of New England. Having no Indian allies of account, New England was not organized for reprisal against the overland raids of Frontenac and his successors. She could not strike through the wilderness against Montreal and Quebec. But the short sail of two or three days into the Bay of Fundy made Acadia a victim of her strong urge for revenge. Most of the relatively few English triumphs in the wars of King William and Queen Anne were achieved in the Acadian theatre. Without difficulty Sir William Phips seized Port Royal in 1690 and Nova Scotia was annexed to Massachusetts Bay by the Charter of 1692, a British decision not to be forgotten in Boston until long after the American Revolution. The New England pretension received a setback when, after the Peace of Ryswick, the French not only repelled her fishermen from the harbours of Nova Scotia but claimed sovereignty over the great fishing banks that fronted the coast twenty leagues out to sea.[11] In 1704 the redoubtable Indian fighter, Major Ben Church, seeking vengeance for the Deerfield massacre, the work of the Canadians and their savage allies, descended on Acadia. He ravaged the French settlements on the north shore of the Bay of Fundy, and the fertile villages of Minas. Before Port Royal, however, he was forced to content himself with an ineffectual demonstration.

British conquest of Acadia did not come until Tory influence in Queen Anne's government induced some willingness to support the efforts of the colonists in America. In 1709 elaborate plans for the destruction of the entire French empire in North America fell to the ground for want of co-ordination and because a fleet was sent to Portugal instead of Port Royal. In the autumn of 1710 the grand design received partial implementation. On September 24 a colonial army of five regiments, headed by Colonel Francis Nicholson, a former governor of Virginia, with Samuel Vetch, a Scottish adventurer of great energy and dubious repute as adjutant-general, supported by a British naval squadron under Captain George Martin, besieged Port

Royal. On October 1, Daniel Auger, Sieur de Subercase, a French veteran of warfare throughout the entire region, capitulated with his tattered garrison after a few skirmishes, completely bereft of any hope of support from Old or New France. Port Royal was renamed Annapolis Royal in honour of Queen Anne and this first settled community of France in North America passed permanently into British hands. Simultaneously the British fleet ravaged the French settlements at Placentia.

In all the warfare, from Bonavista to Cape Sable, the French generally had the better of the conflict. As elsewhere in North America, their expeditions were mounted with a quickness and a precision that made the efforts of their more unmilitary opponents from New England seem cumbersome. Their greatest single asset, which more than compensated for their small numbers, was the consistent support of the Indians from whom they learned so much. Micmacs and Malecites were won to their allegiance by the skill and persistence of Jesuit missionaries. Much more important was the devotion to their cause of the great Abenaki confederacy whose power was centred at Norridgewock on the Kennebeck but who served in an auxiliary capacity all the way from Lake Champlain to Newfoundland. French governors had no hesitation in completely identifying the welfare of the Catholic faith with the spread of French imperial power. The ascendancy of the missionaries over the Indians created for the French a third force which was essential to their survival.

In Acadia the rule of France had been weak but that of Britain, for a great many years to come, was to be weaker still. This was largely owing to the menace of the Indians who confined the new and badly maintained garrison of Annapolis to the walls of the decaying fortress. In the last years of the War of the Spanish Succession, Philippe Rigaud, Comte de Vaudreuil, Governor of Canada, desperately sustained the spirit of the savages which gained great impetus from the news of Sir Hovenden Walker's failure at Placentia and his disaster on the St Lawrence. In 1711 a foraging party of eighty British soldiers were ambushed and annihilated within a few miles of the fort. Annapolis Royal, presently to be the capital of a British colony, was little more than a British entry to a hostile country.

IV

In the negotiations preliminary to the Treaty of Utrecht, Matthew Prior expressed the feeling of European diplomats on Newfoundland and Acadia by declaring that industry rather than dominion would determine the ultimate ownership of the region, that a proclamation of sovereignty over territory was immaterial so long as it was not sustained by the industrious occupation of settlers. Because industry was at sea, the control of territory to the westward was of relative inconsequence. For the immediate future all that really mattered was the mastery of the fishery, the only element that could affect the wealth and strength of France and Britain.

The state of war and diplomacy in Europe enabled Britain to put forward strong demands that would, if realized, have completely expelled France from the fishery. The Tory ministers, who in opposition had so violently opposed the European entanglements of the Whigs and had courted the trading interests of the country, were committed to this policy. Utrecht gave to the region a prominence in diplomacy it was seldom to see again. Yet Robert Harley and Henry St John, so eager were they in the end to secure agreement with France, gained for the merchant community of Britain what St John himself described as "in words something, in substance little."[12] They acquired sovereignty over Newfoundland and Acadia. But they allowed the French to retain rights of fishing, curing, and drying around the great northern belt of the Newfoundland shore, from Bonavista on the east coast to Pointe Riche on the west. An equally monumental surrender was the recognition of France's right to retain control of Cape Breton and the other islands in the Gulf of St Lawrence.

The fate of Cape Breton provoked an argument that almost broke up the Utrecht conference. After the preliminary peace was signed, St John repented of his rashness and, prompted by the merchants of London, reopened the question by a proposal that Cape Breton should be shared in common by subjects of both states and that it should remain unfortified.[13] Then commenaced what Prior called "long and sour but civil discourses." The French held hard to "their right by ancient possession" and the earlier commitment of Britain remained unchanged. London never forgave the Tory government for the surrender. Years later one of the principal articles of impeachment against Robert Harley, Earl of Oxford, was that he had consented to it.[14] The Marquis de Torcy, who conducted the negotiation for France, knew the disastrous consequences of complete surrender of the fishery. Thousands of families in the ports of western France were dependent on it for a livelihood. As Newfoundland and Acadia were surrendered to their enemies, French diplomats revived the old designs that had been so prevalent in the days of Colbert. A place of strength on the Atlantic seaboard to compensate for the isolation of Canada during the winter months would have to be held. A northern mart of commerce, open all the year round, would have to be established in order to drive from the French West Indies the ubiquitous New Englanders who illegally had taken over much of the carrying trade in fish, breadstuffs, beef, and timber.

Since an *abri* for the fishery was of greater consequence than thousands of square miles of territory in the interior of the continent, the limits of Acadia were of secondary importance at Utrecht. The commission of de

Subercase, last of the French governors, had included all the territory between the Kennebeck and Gaspé, and, during the negotiations, the Board of Trade had written to St John to urge that the surrendered territory should be so defined. But the plenipotentiaries of the two nations decided that they did not possess sufficient data and deferred the question for the decision of commissioners.[15] In 1719 a gesture was made to honour this agreement. Conferences opened at Paris but the French, who at first professed a sincere interest in delineation, refused to come to account. The two Laws, father and son, who at this time presided over an exciting phase of French colonization, preferred to keep the Acadian situation fluid. The French commissioners, wrote James Pulteney, "give assurances of renewing the conferences but in their private discourse they have no scruple to say they will not bother about it."[16]

To the Utrecht discussions it was the vanquished who reacted more vigorously than the victors. Exhorted by the complaints of Vaudreuil, filled with concern for the future of their North American empire that was now so clearly encompassed, the French government moved quickly to retrieve what it could from the defeat. Already there was circulated from Quebec the doctrine that Acadia "with all its ancient limits" comprised but the settled area of the peninsula, that the great hinterland to the north of the Bay of Fundy remained French territory. Before the summer of 1713 was ended, the garrison of Placentia had been removed to a carefully selected harbour on the eastern coast of Cape Breton, or Isle Royale as the French now called it, where de Costabelle directed the planning of a great French fortress that was to become known as Louisburg, where a new Chateau of St Louis was to symbolize France's determination to defend the eastern approaches to North America. Louisburg became the haven of the dispossessed French fishermen of Newfoundland.

Plagued by the problems of the Hanoverian Succession, the British government was in no humour to press its advantages. So far as Newfoundland was concerned, the Devonshire interests remained dominant in its counsels. Since 1689 a military commander had ruled over a fort and garrison at St John's but he had no authority over the two populations, resident and transient. The Act of 1699 had made no provision for a governor and Devonshire wanted no civil authority ashore. Out of the contrived anarchy the office of governor would have to grow. Placentia saw the coming of a British garrison; and British officers purchased from their withdrawing French counterparts the ownership of the best fishing-rooms in the harbour. Under the new regime the historic complaints of fishermen against the arbitrary conduct of the military were to remain unchanged. The fishery was to be protected but not governed. Placentia was incorporated into the government of Francis

Nicholson, who received the queen's commission for Nova Scotia and commanded the garrison at Annapolis.

No plans were made and nothing was done to consolidate British rule
over the vast Acadian region to which the Treaty of Utrecht had given
title. Off Newfoundland the French fishermen were harassed into a position
of clear inferiority, but in Acadia the initiative was to fall into French
hands. The failure to take decisive measures was most clearly indicated by
the haphazard dealing with the Acadian population. They, by the treaty,
had the right to emigrate to French soil within a year of its signing, taking
with them their movable goods. Their position had been strengthened by a
letter from Queen Anne, granting to them the right to sell their *bona
immobilia*, immovable goods, before migrating.[17] During the critical year
Nicholson did everything he could to encourage their movement to Isle
Royale but, though similarly encouraged by French emissaries, the Acadians
refused to go. The plain fact was that a pioneering life anew on the wooded
and rocky shores of Cape Breton did not appeal to a people accustomed to
the fertile salt marshes of the Bay of Fundy. When the allowed year expired their destinies were legally in British hands but their continued stay
did not ensure that they could become loyal British subjects. Encouraged by
their priests, who were the resolute agents of Vaudreuil, they refused an
unqualified oath of allegiance. In the words of the French governor, the
temporal power could serve as a vehicle for the faith.

Nicholson's determination to be rid of the Acadians did not abate but his
enthusiasm became constrained by the rapid use of Louisburg. The mass
migration of several thousands of industrious peasants with their wealth of
livestock could enormously strengthen the position of the French on Cape
Breton, where already their fortress seemed likely to approach the dimensions of a Gibraltar. The Board of Trade refused to listen to demands for
expulsion. Samuel Vetch, appointed Governor in place of Nicholson when
the Whigs came to power, represented that the little economy of the
Acadians could be integrated with the imperial system of trade. He argued
also that, if the Acadians were expelled, it would be difficult to attract
British settlers to a country completely bereft of population. More pointed
were the dispirited letters of the officers of the garrison at Annapolis who
wanted the Acadians to remain at all costs. They could maintain the ruined
fort with necessary supplies and could serve as a kind of buffer state against
the Abenaki who were murdering English settlers in Maine. By remaining,
declared Major Thomas Caulfeild, the Acadians could prevent an Indian
attack upon Annapolis.[18]

Fear of strengthening the French on Cape Breton was the predominant
consideration. Vetch and his comrades won their case. After the Acadians
lost their right to move to French territory, the British government adopted

the policy of retaining them as subjects of the Crown, of refusing them permission to go to Cape Breton or wherever the French might beckon them.[19]

V

The uneasy peace that settled over the region and lasted for thirty years following the Peace of Utrecht was owing to no diminution of the American rivalry but to the pacific policies of Robert Walpole and Cardinal Fleury in Europe. Having raised her standard on Cape Breton, France allowed colonial animosities to have no part in the making of her national policy. Britain had never planted colonies by expenditure from the national finances and was of no mind to commence doing so in Nova Scotia. On Newfoundland the Western Adventurers reigned supreme. After 1713 the only important element of aggression came from New England, whose expansive energies found a natural outlet in this area of the North Atlantic.

During the quarter-century of war an immense proportion of the trade of Newfoundland had fallen into the hands of the New Englanders. For the hazards of regular transoceanic voyages in the face of French privateering, the merchants of the West Country had come to have an increasing respect. Their larger vessels had given place to the shallops of New England that had become a necessity in the supply of European goods and outside services. Convoy captains irritably reported upon the attempts of the New Englanders to introduce their town meetings and public assemblies to Newfoundland's harbours and beaches, where their presence was usually regarded as a signal for trouble. But necessity compelled the ignoring of the Act of Parliament of 1699 that forbade their voyages to Newfoundland's shores. The return of peace reduced their role to an auxiliary one, for the West Country resumed its former place as chief supplier of beef, flour, and manufactured articles to the fishery. Its larger vessels, now known as "sack ships," appeared on the scene at St John's, taking no part in the catching of the cod and serving primarily as freighters and transporters. Leaving Britain in the spring they would sail for Portugal, load up with salt for Newfoundland, and at the end of the season turn about to sell Newfoundland's produce in whatever southern market seemed most promising. Always there was a race against time, for an early arrival betokened the higher prices that were paid for a superior quality of fish.

Long notorious for their evasion of the British and French laws of trade and navigation, and for their capacity to seduce indentured servants from their duties, the New Englanders began to trade with Louisburg. Their goods were eagerly purchased, as they were by the Acadians of the Bay of Fundy. They also resumed in greater volume the carriage of inferior fish to the West

Indies. But the New Englanders' enlarging trade was still merely complementary to the fishery, which remained the great basis of their economy.
Peace brought hundreds of their shallops to Nova Scotian harbours. The
annexation by the Charter of 1692 had not been forgotten and attitudes of
proprietorship over Nova Scotia in Marblehead and Salem became hardened
and recognizable. A vigorous agitation in 1715 made annexation seem
likely, but other considerations prevailed. Britain was already jealous of
the rapid growth of the New England colonies, and resented their inability
and unwillingness to adjust themselves to the requirements of the imperial
trading system. She could, of course, perceive that the traditional tendency
to disobedience could lead to independence. A report of the Army Commissariat in 1717 gave these cogent reasons for resistance to New England's zeal
for expansion.[20] Already there were regrets for the annexation of "the
district of Maine" to Massachusetts, though this had been made largely
innocuous by the denial to the General Court of the right to make grants of
land.

Massachusetts could not secure control of Nova Scotia but she could
neutralize the efforts of others who sought colonization and development.
After Utrecht the British government received petitions from adventurers of
capital who asked for grants of land and the right to bring out British
settlers. Massachusetts contested all of them by representing that the free
use of Nova Scotian beaches was essential to her seamen. The Board of
Trade again had to consider the knotty problem of whether a land or a sea
population should dominate a colony. On February 5, 1719, when Sir Alexander Cairns, a knight of Kent, petitioned for land in Nova Scotia with a
right to collect fees from fishermen using beaches, he was confronted by
Jeremy Dummer, Agent-General for Massachusetts. The General Court of
that colony pointed out that the beaches of their own country were in
private hands, a great hardship for the fishery which might be avoided in
Nova Scotia by opening the coastline to the common employment of all
His Majesty's subjects.[21] Beaches, Dummer demanded, should be exempt
from any grants of land the Crown might make. When Richard Phillips was
appointed as governor a few weeks later, he was instructed not to permit
grants of land to disturb fishermen within two hundred yards of the shore,
a stipulation sufficient to turn settlers away from a country where the sea
was the principal means of communication.[22] To deter settlement from
Nova Scotia was the object of New England and it is not surprising that in
the colonies to the south this new adjunct to the British Empire quickly
acquired the reputation of a land of bleak and forbidding climate, ruled by
an arbitrary military government and inhabited by a Catholic population.

The conquest produced no ventures in colonization and the area remained
primarily a zone for transients whose industry was centred upon the fishery.

Only on one occasion did there seem an important chance that Britain might exploit her new possession of Acadia. In 1720, when the colonizing and commercial schemes of John Law, the Scottish adviser to Louis XV, were directed against British overseas interests, his attempt to secure from Russia a monopoly of all the produce of the Baltic brought about a counter-proposal in London to give Nova Scotia to the South Seas Company. When a new source for timber and naval stores seemed urgent, Nova Scotia offered a reasonable alternative.[23] But the collapse of Law's colossal projects rendered these speculations void of any important results.

While Britain and France enjoyed peace and prosperity, it was only the men on the spot who attempted to create tension. A military appreciation of 1721 recommended that Britain should construct forts on the southern shores of Nova Scotia and garrison the province with four regiments. It was completely ignored.[24] Rivalry in the fishery and the excitement of Indian warfare on their northern frontiers kept New Englanders on their mettle and in Boston there was an acute sense of the inevitability of a struggle for domination in Acadia. But the imperialism of New England was given no encouragement from the mother country. After her great decision to construct Louisburg. France would enter on no further enterprises of such monumental scale. But the governors of Quebec and Louisburg watched with jealousy every British movement at the approaches to the St Lawrence. With a North American population that was outnumbered by ten to one, Frenchmen had every reason to be grateful for British inertia and to resent any attempt on the part of Britain to improve her position in this strategic theatre.

VI

For half a century the British Newfoundland fishery enjoyed rapid and disordered growth. Foreign invasion had several times come close to destroying it. From that fate it was fortunately to be spared. Driven from Placentia, the French dispersed to the southward and westward. Along the northern shores they were able to exercise their treaty rights of landing for wood and water but they had no place of strength, no rallying point from which cohesion could be imparted to their fishing operations. For the most part they thronged to Cape Breton, though they created a dry fishery, "*une pêche sedentaire*," of considerable consequence off Gaspé and in the Bay of Chaleur. British proposals to settle the Placentia area were defeated by the opposition of the Western Adventurers; and Colonel Samuel Gledhill, the garrison commander, imposed an authoritarian regime over the new fishermen who used the port.

Though subjected to distortions and dislocations, West Country predominance in the Newfoundland fishery lasted throughout the eighteenth century. The first flow of enthusiasm following the peace and the return of thousands of seamen who had abandoned operations during the war was moderated by cold waters prevailing off the coastline for a full six seasons. The poor yields that resulted produced wider dispersal and hardened competition. Planters moved to coves and harbours north of Bonavista where they caught great quantities of fish of inferior value. Abandoning the shore lines of Avalon, others resorted to the Grand Bank in boats carrying up to ten men. Again large yields of low quality resulted. Failure to grade fish gave Newfoundlanders a poor reputation in comparison with that of the French and New Englanders. Yet full prosperity came in 1722 and the larger vessels from Great Britain, which in the good years numbered up to two hundred, regained some of the advantages they had lost to the planters.

Under the favourable conditions of the long peace, the resident population increased from three thousand in 1713 to about seven thousand in 1750. Imperial legislation could not overcome the advantages of a fishery conducted from adjacent bases on the shore over another that was carried on from across an ocean. As the operations of the Western Adventurers became more diversified, they themselves gave encouragement to permanent residence. As they extended their activities from the fishery to trade, as shops and warehouses rose on the harbour of St John's, encroaching on space long and jealously reserved for fishing-rooms, permanence of population became essential. By 1713 St John's was no longer merely a convenient and sheltered base from which the fishery could be conducted. Like Louisburg, it was an emporium for the purchase and sale of goods from all over the seven seas.

As new settlements were opened up, opportunities for individual initiative became greater. Determined men of high character who invested their savings in a by-boat could, by persistent industry over a period of years, look forward to return to England with enough in hand to give competence for a lifetime. But in most cases the hazards, temptations, and difficulties were far too great. The condition determining success or failure was ability to remain free from debt. For the easier circumstances of the fishery after 1713 supplied opportunities also for the merchant-trader who advanced goods prior to the opening of the season and imposed upon fishermen a commercial bondage that was usually never broken. Salt was a commodity absolutely essential to the industry. When it was in short supply, merchants raised the price to exorbitant levels and for delivering it they obliged their customers to take non-essential goods at equally high rates. Back from Spain and Portugal, the skippers of the sack ships would do no business with the planters, unless they would take part-payment for cod in the wines and spirits with which their holds were laden. Payment in goods was the almost invariable rule, for most fishermen seldom saw cash. Ledger books recorded the remorseless two-way profit that merchants extracted from the fishing population. Jamaica rum was so abundant that memorialists claimed the people were being deliberately debauched. It was often said that three or four merchants engrossed the market in St John's but the outports usually endured the rigid monopoly of a single trader. The forcible collection of debts, remarked Captain William Taverner, the surveyor of the south coast, was more ruinous to the fishery than anything else.[25]

Strong men might contend against it but the "truck system," which became entrenched in Newfoundland and later extended itself to the lumbering and agricultural industries of the other Atlantic Provinces, had become the dominant feature of the economy. Simultaneously, after the Peace of Utrecht, the West Countrymen discarded the old system of fishing "by shares" and adopted the payment of wages, usually in truck. This was because they were just as interested in a multitude of trading transactions as in fishing. No longer did "green men" come to Newfoundland in the hope of learning a trade and profiting by their labour. Securing the cheapest kind of help, the factors of Devon placed on shipboard the more degenerate human types of England and Ireland. Poverty, hardship, disease, crime, always familiar to Newfoundland, became more general and intensified as the eighteenth century advanced. Judging from official opinion, the best of these immigrants or "passengers" illegally took ship for the continental colonies. Those who remained were unintelligent, shiftless, wanton.

Still, it was high policy for the British government to maintain the seas and shores of Newfoundland as an enclosure within which no settled authority ruled. The only local jurisdiction derived from acts of Parliament continued to be the seasonal control of the fishing-admirals. Prowse, the historian of Newfoundland, always a partisan of the planters, supplies a vivid description of the kind of justice they dispensed : "In his ordinary blue flushing jacket and trousers, economically besmeared with pitch, tar and fish slime, his head adorned with an old sealskin cap robbed from an Indian, or bartered for a glass of rum or a stick of tobacco," the admiral delivered his opinions "in a fish store, the judicial seat an inverted butter ferkin." Justice might be won by the presentation of a few New England apples or a flowing bowl of calabogus, a favourite drink of the admirals composed of rum, molasses, and spruce beer.[26] The oldest ship fisherman in each harbour was often called "the king," a clear indication of the kind of authority he wielded. This kind of government negated the whole principle of the rule of law and it was the right of the strong that invariably prevailed.

Petitions protesting against outrages upon justice, against finings, trianglings, hangings, frequently came to the Privy Council in London. But the Board of Trade, always conservatively inclined towards Devonshire, would not consider the creation of a shore authority that would give the law to seamen. In 1719, when the whole position was given close attention, the Board's only solution was to remove all the planters to Nova Scotia. In the next ten years the anarchy became intolerable. At St John's a voluble vested interest in landed property had come into existence, property to which the law gave no sanction or protection. Lord Vere Beauclerk, on convoy duty with the Royal Navy in Newfoundland waters, finally drew the attention of the Duke of Newcastle to the monumental ambiguities of Newfoundland; Newcastle, in 1729, insisted that action should be taken. Again the Board of Trade wanted deportation of the residents to Nova Scotia, but the Cabinet would adopt no such rigorous measure. The result was a compromise that effected improvement but only commenced to deal with the problem of government. Captain Henry Osborn of HMS *Squirrel* was commissioned as governor. As commander of one of the king's ships he could not establish himself permanently on shore and his duties were primarily those of an overseer of the fishery. But the novel feature of his authority, as defined by his commission, was that he was empowered to deal with the legal quandaries of the planters by the appointment of justices of the peace and other officers.[27] At the same time Placentia was detached from the government of Nova Scotia and subjected to Osborn's authority.

Osborn tried hard but the exercise of his control was really one of discretion. By the terms of his commission he was ordered not to interfere with the jurisdictions of the fishing-admirals who could always remonstrate that their authority emanated from a source superior to that of his own, an act of Parliament. Men of character, invested with commissions of the peace and presented with law books by the governor, might now make an impact in favour of law and order among the planters all the year round, but the fishing admirals could not be impressed or restrained by these new powers of government that were held by shoremen. As a colony Newfoundland had received formal recognition by a casual exertion of the royal prerogative. But the Act of 1699, denying the legality of a colony on Newfoundland, was still on the statute books.

During the War of the Austrian Succession and the Seven Years' War this civil authority fell into disuse and neglect. For two years, 1745-47, the charge of the Newfoundland fishery was entrusted to the commander of the British naval squadron at Louisburg. Prosperity may have justified this sin of omission. The West Country complained against the inadequacy of convoy protection and the high rates of insurance but the volume of its commerce with Newfoundland consistently increased. The hazards of war merely forced it to become more efficient. The ownership of its vessels passed to a smaller number of firms. Commercial connections, sometimes established by chance, could last fifty years. Poole and Dartmouth traded with Bonavista, Dartmouth and Topsham with Bay of Bulls. Waterford and Dartmouth took the

bulk of the Ferryland cod. To the southward, at Reneuse and Fermeuse, recently settled by Irish immigrants, came ships owned by firms in Dartmouth
and Teignmouth.

As in former times of war the shore population rapidly increased, attain-
ing the figure of 16,000 in 1764. Well might the Privy Council in the following year lament the great contradiction between the aims of official policy
and what had actually occurred.[28] The time for clear decision had long
since passed. What had grown behind the backs of British officialdom was a
Newfoundland colony with a stake in the fishery as great as that of the
Western Adventurers. Still, however, no recognition could be given to the
reality of the change that had taken place over the past fifty years. Still the
Western Adventurers were powerful enough in the counsels of the British
government to deter any attempt that might be made to establish a government on shore and restrict the exorbitant liberties of their own fishermen.
Yet, as population increased, the necessity for such an attempt became more
evident from year to year. The lawlessness that was inherent by reason of
the absence of law became intensified in the years following the '45 rebellion, when newly arrived Irish refused to subscribe to the oaths against
popery and when the authorities inaugurated a crusade against Catholics.
Priests, illegally landed on the island to minister to needy flocks, were
harried away. A series of outrages culminated in the murder of William
Keen, a magistrate of St John's, in 1754.

The absence of law and the slackness of supervision could not obstruct
the growth of the great codfishery. The official figures for 1765 showed that
476,000 quintals were exported. On the Exploits River a prosperous salmon
fishery had developed. A vigorous seal fishery had taken firm root and the
production of train oil, extracted from the livers of the cod, grew in volume
from year to year.

VII

Unlike that of Newfoundland, the Nova Scotian fishery remained a theatre
of sharp rivalry between English and French. By the Treaty of Utrecht the
latter were excluded from the long banks that front the southern shores of
the peninsula. They were also denied the right to fish within ten leagues of
the northeastern coastline, a stipulation made almost meaningless by reason
of the cession of Cape Breton and Isle St Jean. Matthew Prior, in defiance of
the mercantile interests of London, which had insisted on this restriction to
the French, wrote home from Utrecht that he was ashamed to defend it.[29]
Because the fishermen were accustomed to ignore treaties and follow the
migrations of the cod, trespass was certain to occur in the narrower waters of
the Gulf of St Lawrence.

In 1713 three hundred New England vessels sailed northward into the seas that formerly had been perilous and came into quick contact with the French who, according to Admiralty reports, were moving to Cape Breton in very great numbers. Prospects in the Gulf of St Lawrence were so good that a few of the New England skippers erected their stagings on the western shores of Cape Breton and loud cries of trespass ensued. But trouble did not become acute until the islands of Canso came into contention. An ancient meeting-place for fishermen, always in great repute, the islands presented the optimum conditions for prosecuting the industry. Situated at the eastern extremity of the Gut of Canso, they were within easy sailing distance of the best fishing-grounds either in the Atlantic or on the gulf. Behind them was the large Bay of Chedabucto, an admirable haven in tempests, with a long stretch of beach for curing and drying. The channels among the eight or ten islands offered a large number of passages to the inner harbour, so that a vessel could enter when the wind was blowing from almost any direction.[30]

French and English were fishing together from the islands of Canso in 1717 and relations between them were amicable, a situation explained in part by English fear of the Indians. French presence lessened dangers of Indian attack. But this fraternization was offensive to the local powers near-by. Samuel Shute, the Governor of Massachusetts, and St Ovide de Brouillan, the Governor of Cape Breton, each presented claims to exclusive possession. After an unsuccessful exchange of notes, Captain Thomas Smart, acting on Shute's orders, destroyed the huts of the French fishermen in 1718, seized a large quantity of property, and sailed for Boston with the French fishing-admiral as a prisoner and two large vessels as prizes. French reprisal, arranged by merchants on Isle Madame and connived at by St Ovide, took place on August 8, 1720, when English goods to the value of £18,000 were taken in a raid after nightfall. This was the incident that impelled General Richard Phillips, the Governor of Nova Scotia, to decide the issue by military occupation. A company of his regiment was sent to Canso for the following winter, several of the fishing factors from New England co-operating in the construction of lodging and barracks for the troops.[31]

The interior limits of the two empires in America could be left for the decision of posterity, but the contest for a few rocky islands off the coast of Nova Scotia produced a diplomatic incident. James Pulteney and Sir Robert Sutton, the British ambassador at Paris, waited on the Archbishop of Cambrai, chief advisor to Louis xv, with the demand that French fishermen should be restrained to their own waters.[32] The French replied that Canso was theirs, basing their argument on the French version of the Treaty of Utrecht, declaring that the Gut of Canso was one of the mouths or part of the *"embouchure"* of the Gulf of St Lawrence and that the disputed islands lay within it. "M. Rodeau, to support this, declared that the mouth of the river and the gulf were the same thing."[33] Pulteney could get no satisfaction and advised military occupation, the expedient simultaneously decided upon by Phillips. Having planned occupation himself, St Ovide de Brouillan was content to encourage his Indian allies to harass and annoy the New England fishermen.

For twenty years Canso, now firmly in English hands, was the centre of the great New England fishery off the coasts of Nova Scotia. Other commodious harbours, La Have, Chebucto, Port Mouton, were employed, but Canso was the central mart where the rates of exchange were determined. In 1725, the year in which records for the port were first kept, over 56,000 quintals of cod were prepared for market. So great was the New England movement to the north that in 1718 the Board of Trade declared that this fishery probably exceeded in value that of Newfoundland.[34] When Phillips visited Canso in 1723 he thought it would become the greatest port in America.[35] A few families moved in from Newfoundland and sack ships from England began to make regular calls. The posting of a garrison presaged a great expenditure of public money, an expectation that enlarged the enthusiasm of the New England traders. An agitation for a free port, a suggestion sponsored by Phillips, was rejected by the Board of Trade for fear that Canso would become the haven for all the illicit commerce of the American seas.[36] A permanent population quickly formed itself, almost entirely from New England.

Great expectations were not realized but Canso was an important factor in the fishery, subjected to all the fluctuations, hopes, and disappointments of those engaged in the industry. Sometimes the cod were more profuse about Cape Sable and New Englanders could more conveniently carry on operations from their home ports. War and rumours of war with Spain caused grievous downswings and the French profited in consequence. The British government did little to sustain the buoyant prophecies. The company of troops at Canso, augmented by three more from Placentia in 1729, had to be content with huts for barracks and, for protection, a line of palisades raised along a stretch of beach subject to overflow by spring tides.[37] In 1724 it was with difficulty that the Board of Trade secured the promise of a ship of war to guard the Nova Scotian coasts. The Lords of the Admiralty protested that New England should bear expenses of this nature.[38]

The best years were probably from 1729 to 1733. The port records of Canso show that 235 vessels entered the harbour in 1731. Of these, twelve were sack ships from the west of England. Peter Faneuil, the great Boston factor, found his best market here in these years. The rapid growth of the slave population in the West Indies and of the consequent market for refuse fish caused the Canso merchants to look more to the southward. Increasingly they served as middlemen between the French and Spanish West Indies and all the British colonies. Throughout all the northern seas there was a common article of faith, that rum was a commodity essential to existence in a harsh climate. On their newly improvised schooners, the Canso traders supplied the highly favoured product of Martinique, which was denied a market in France owing to the monopoly of the brandy producers, not only to their own fishery but also to that of Newfoundland. Either in the West Indies or at Louisburg it was always possible to bargain with the French, usually by exchanging fish for rum. For the purposes of this illegal traffic Canso was without a peer. Whale-hunting was an important ancillary industry. In 1733 it was said that seventy ships entered the harbour deeply laden with whale oil and that one hundred more were at sea for the same purpose.[39]

After 1734 Canso lost much of its prominence. Marblehead and Gloucester were making strenuous efforts to supplant it as the centre of the New England fishery.[40] In its early years one hundred and fifty permanent buildings had been erected but in 1738 the winter population was reduced to six families. War with Spain in 1739 deprived New England of half its market. The later war with France in 1744 resulted in Canso's immediate destruction. Throughout the long period of peace it was probably the main centre for the entire New England fishery which in most years approached that of Newfoundland in total volume of produce. For the purposes of accurate comparison eighteenth-century statistics are almost worthless, but a recapitulary estimate of 1764 placed its annual value at £180,000, as against £208,000, for Newfoundland.[41]

Annapolis was far removed and impotent, so that the problem of governing this rather ephemeral community of transients was highly complex. The litigiousness common to fishermen, the chronic disputes between skippers and crews, shoremen and seamen, compelled Lawrence Armstrong, the Lieutenant-Governor, to establish a makeshift constitution in 1724. An assembly of fishermen drafted rules against drunkenness, slandering, and sabbath-breaking, for the governance of taverns and the maintenance of order. "A sufficient number of the most knowing men" were appointed as a tribunal before which cases of breach of contract might be brought.[42]

Yet truculence and disorder persisted in spite of Armstrong's elaborate efforts. Desperately he wrote for permission to remove the seat of government from Annapolis to Canso so that the New England demand for a general assembly of the people, after their own custom, might be gratified.[43] Discontent produced the familiar New England complaints against arbitrary government. The garrison commander encroached on the powers of the justices of the peace and, on occasion, the half-abandoned troops infuriated the fishermen by tearing down buildings and stagings for firewood during the winter season. Armstrong was sensitive to the democratic predilections of Canso, "the least appearance of a civil government being more agreeable to the inhabitants than the martial."[44] But his irritation was constantly aroused against those tendencies, so notable among the fishermen of New England, that men from Old England called republican.

VIII

Driven from Placentia and the south coast of Newfoundland, the French after 1713 made themselves more familiar with the remote harbours and beaches of the north and west, finding good fishing-grounds and ample facilities in regions to which the English were complete strangers. This Petit Nord, the region of the coastline to which the treaty allowed them rights, yielded "smaller, whiter and better salted fish" that could command a premium of one dollar a quintal in Mediterranean markets. By custom that was owing to English default, the French acquired a virtual control over the west coast that abounded with good harbours and showed some agricultural possibilities. Not surprisingly it soon became a French point of view that Pointe Riche, named by the Treaty of Utrecht as the southern limit of their treaty rights, was to be identified with Cape Ray, the south-western apex of the island. Amid all these unrecorded activities of the Petit Nord, the Eskimoes of the Strait of Belle Isle were driven to the mainland of Labrador by the Beothuk Indians. These, in turn, quietly and mysteriously disappeared into the interior of Newfoundland to become a cause for curiosity and wonder for succeeding generations.

Along these foggy littorals and on Gaspé, the haunt of sailors from St Malo and Granville, unnumbered hundreds and thousands of French fishermen arrived annually, early in the spring. Erecting their stages for curing and drying, and, in favoured areas, laying in small gardens "for soup and salad," they conducted their vocation from small boats carrying crews of three men. Perhaps two months later came the great ships of St Jean de Luz, Bordeaux, La Rochelle, and Nantes to load the cargoes they prepared. Each ship carried about four thousand quintals, sold at Marseilles at thirty to forty shillings each, or sent onward to a port in the Levant where a considerable proportion of French produce was ultimately consumed. These temporary shore establishments were highly organized on the principle of the division of labour. Experienced men were engaged exclusively in splitting fish and a master-salter with assistants would work with them. Ten hogsheads of salt were required for each hundred quintals of cod.[45]

Though the mud fishery, to which shore operations were only incidental, remained a principal endeavour of the French, another great dry fishery arose on Cape Breton. Louisburg, on the peninsula bordering the ancient resort known as English Harbour, never justified the appellation given to it in New England, "the Dunkirk of America." But its grand cupola surmounting the Royal Bastion, its batteries and magazines, its battlements and casernes, served as the centre for a great entrepôt of commerce and answered one of the purposes intended by its founders. So good were the results of the Cape Breton fishery after 1713 that the French rejoiced in its substitution for Placentia. They had gained, according to a commonplace saying, an ingot of gold in exchange for a bar of silver. Cape Breton was freer of ice-floes than Newfoundland, a condition that guaranteed an earlier commencement of operations and higher prices in Europe. Shore fisheries developed not only at Louisburg but at Isle Madame, St Peter's, Port Toulouse, Port Dauphin, and other harbours across the water from the envied English location at Canso. From France came vessels usually smaller than those that sailed to the Petit Nord, of tonnage fifty to a hundred, whose captains bought boats from the permanent residents and entered into close commercial relations with them. Each captain was something of a shopkeeper, selling nets and other fishing gear, boots and shoes, wines and brandy. In addition to these itinerant vendors there was a large number of mercantile establishments owned on Isle Royale. Many of the proprietors were of Basque extraction and the boast was frequently made that their families had been in the fishing trade for generations. It was often noted that some of these prosperous marts of commerce were owned and managed by widows.[46]

Under French rule monopoly was tried more frequently than under English, but in general it fared ill. This was especially notable on Isle St Jean, the other large island in the gulf which some of the French in 1713 considered superior to Cape Breton for their purposes. Cartier had noted its fine meadows, but France had never summoned the resources to occupy it. In 1719 it was granted to the Comte de St Pierre, first equerry to the Duchess of Orleans, the consort of the Regent, who expected great profits from control of its fisheries. But his inordinate ambitions were coupled with too small an outlay. His failure to introduce settlers and the opposition of the merchants of St Malo who wanted to use the beaches of Isle St Jean without payment of seigneurial dues led to a revocation of the grant in 1725. Port la Joye, the site selected for a capital by French officials in 1720, saw the establishment of a government subordinate to Louisburg and a handful of soldiers as garrison. Later on, in 1731, Jean Pierre Roma made a much more valorous attempt to create a fishing monopoly at Three Rivers on the eastern coast. For thirteen years his fortunes wavered as he fought against the attempts of rivals to entice his people away from him. He resisted the interference of the Abbé Béirne, who represented the spiritual influence of New France's clergy. He fought the plague of field mice that in 1738 consumed even the grass. The enterprise collapsed in 1745 when the New Englanders, fresh from their triumph at Louisburg, looted his property and destroyed his buildings. Until the flight of the Acadians from Nova Scotia, the population of Isle St Jean remained small. At no time did the number of permanent residents reach the figure of five hundred.[47]

It was impossible to establish a monopoly over the entire fishery but a monopolizing spirit was constantly at work. At Louisburg the colonial aristocracy was military, bureaucratic, and commercial. A marriage alliance could open an avenue to increasing affluence, and officers of the garrison, openly or by proxy, entered into business. Society acquired a permanent cast of character. Of the eight army officers who were present at the founding of the colony in 1713, six were represented by sons during the siege of 1745 and nearly all by grandsons at the second defence of 1758. Soldiers were permitted to earn extra pay by working for the fishermen. Their sons, some of whom were enrolled in the garrison at the age of six, enjoyed the same privilege. These close bonds, fixed in the soil at Louisburg, resulted in a sharp spirit of exclusion towards outsiders. Regulations were passed against traders from Old France who wished to remain on the island and sell by retail. Quebec was the capital of New France but the merchants of Louisburg, who resented the necessity of sending specie there to pay for duty on imports, were able to obtain discriminatory legislation against the captains of Canadian vessels. These were compelled to sell their cargoes before leaving port, an ordinance that placed them at the mercy of local buyers. Canadian interference in the widely assorted affairs of Louisburg often gave impetus to the strong spirit of local independence that was rising on the island.[48]

The prosperity of Isle Royale was based, to the great surprise of visitors, on the humble cod. But exports required much more shipping than did the articles of finery imported from Old France, and it was the New Englanders who took up the slack. The British West Indies could consume but one-third of the cod their little ships could carry. In their search for trade, Louisburg exercised upon them an irresistible compulsion. At Canso dozens of their vessels would make legal clearance for Newfoundland but would quickly return, having found cargo much nearer home among the French. Not only cod was taken into their holds, but wines, cloth, linen, sugar, molasses, tobacco were transported wherever ready markets could be found. New England filled the breaches in the walls of the French empire of trade. The very bricks of the fortress of Louisburg had been supplied from the British colonies. Long experience vindicated Sieur de Costabelle, the first governor, who said in a memorial of 1717 that Louisburg could flourish only if it were permitted free trade with the neighbouring English.

The rise to commercial greatness was accompanied by lapses and eccentricities of the French official mind. In spite of the vast volume of trade, legal and illegal, conditions akin to privation sometimes developed. Letters and

memoirs of official persons at Louisburg sometimes remarked on the failure
to provide the garrison with breadstuffs and the feeling of relief in the
springtime when the winter's fare of dried cod was supplemented by provisions from the outside world. If Louisburg failed in the role projected for it
in 1713, it was because of the general failure of the French government to
co-ordinate and develop the resources of its great colonial empire.

IX

Through these prosperous years of the eighteenth century the great cod-
fishery of the North Atlantic was in a state of constant expansion, losing no
part of the important place it held in the economies of France and Britain.
Rebounding from a series of expulsions that followed military defeat, French
fishermen continued to return in greater numbers to engage in the trade.
Off Newfoundland the British fishery, almost completely relieved from the
French military and naval menace, continued its harsh historic development.
The only event that really disturbed its violent and complex growth was the
successful surprise attack of the French on St John's in 1762, an intrusion
that proved to be fleeting.

In spite of the expansion on Newfoundland and the aggressive enterprise
of the New Englanders, it is difficult to resist the conclusion that between
1713 and 1763 the French fishery prospered more mightily than did the
British. In the early 1740's the New England fishery was declining and it
was largely by reason of a growing French pre-eminence that the Louisburg
expedition of 1745 was promoted. All the North American memorials, printed pamphlets, and statistics presented to the British government during the
two great wars argue the clear possibility that the English, of both Old and
New England, could be completely dispossessed of European and West
Indian markets should the French remain in Cape Breton. British aspiration to monopoly over the entire fishery was the only argument of a
solidly commercial kind for the grand ambition of expelling the French
from North America.

Lord Jeffery Amherst was certain of the great commercial consequence of
Isle Royale when, in 1758, he ordered that all its settlements should be
demolished. Owing to "its flourishing state" he was sure that, if the French
were to remain, the number of its inhabitants would in a few years be
sufficient to defend it. In the history of North America the fur trade, which
lured men to the interior and contributed so much to the story of explora-
tion, has been assigned an immense degree of importance. But North
American decisions in the eighteenth century were made by men alert to the
interests of the fishery which held adventurers to the shore. In 1763 the
trade of Canada without the fisheries was reckoned as negligible. It was Pitt's

refusal to allow the French continued participation in the fishery that led to the breakdown of the negotiations at Paris in 1761. Rather than do so he would "lose the use of his right arm" and there is his celebrated dictum that the fisheries were always worth "another campaign or two."[49] The Duc de Choiseul, France's foreign minister, declared that he would rather be stoned in the streets of Paris than surrender France's right in its entirety. Canada could be surrendered without a sense of grievous loss but the fishery was an indispensable element in the livelihood of the French population.

During the long negotiation Choiseul "asked for nothing but a rock that would afford shelter for the barques of their fishermen which they were ready to receive on almost any terms England might prescribe."[50] France was willing to give up Canada but wanted Canso, an island roadstead well suited for a large fleet of vessels. Britain, finally willing to compromise, instead granted her St Pierre and Miquelon. These represented the minimum of France's requirements and were finally accepted by Choiseul under conditions that denied France the right of fortification and permitted close British surveillance. When, following Pitt's resignation, Britain confirmed the rights of French fishermen on the north shore of Newfoundland, granted by the Peace of Utrecht, the commercial community of London violently reacted. The surrender of British monopoly, won by force of arms, was the principal reason for the hostile reception given the Duke of Bedford on his return from Paris.

Responsible for giving advice to the king on measures for increasing the trade of Britain, the Board of Trade had no hesitation in reiterating the traditional opinion on the worth of the fisheries: "The most obvious advantages arising from the cessions made by the definitive treaty are the exclusive fisheries of the River St Lawrence and the Islands in that Gulf."[51] Like the sugar islands of the West Indies, the fisheries of the Newfoundland and Acadian seas meant wealth that was easily obtained. Whatever the great land mass of the continent might have to offer in the far distant future, the fur trade was a bagatelle in the calculations of statesmen, merchants, and bankers in France and Britain.

CHAPTER 2

Fifty Years of Conflict
1713-1763

The peace of Utrecht was much more unkind to the French in North America than the fortunes of war had been, and a brooding disquietude characterized the counsels of Vaudreuil, Governor of New France, when he contemplated what the treaty had left to France. It was taken for granted that peace had brought to New France only a continuation of the struggle, the prolonging of a war that would now have to be waged by clandestine measures against powerful odds. The surrender of Acadia was accompanied by what seemed a malevolent challenge on the other side of the Bay of Fundy, a northward movement of New England's surplus population along the shores of Maine and up the valley of the Kennebeck. This was an expansion that was unplanned but it comprehended the energies of thousands of seekers of new lands. Vaudreuil quickly outlined a policy that seemed essential to the survival of New France and was endorsed by the ministry in Paris. To confine the British to the Acadian peninsula and to substantiate this interpretation of the treaty by reference to ancient maps and writings were to be the principal aims of diplomacy. The little river St George, flowing into the Atlantic from northern Maine, was now declared to be the southern boundary of New France.[1]

The resources of New France were slender but Vaudreuil was not at a loss to find an instrument for his purposes. The Abenaki confederacy had always distinguished itself in the service of France and the missionary priests who served it were exhorted to urge resistance to the northward march of British settlement. Larger funds were set aside to provide gifts for the Abenaki and for the more easterly Micmacs and Malecites. Chapels were erected at St Anne's on the St John River and at Narantsouack in Maine. Sebastien Rasle, the Jesuit missionary who for twenty years had served as mentor to the Abenaki at Norridgewock on the upper Kennebeck, urged the tribes into a general war with the traditional enemy. English pioneers who mocked the savages with the assertion that the King of France had surrendered their country were met by dignified declarations of Abenaki sovereignty and independence. A succession of massacres proved an adequate deterrent to the spread of their settlements. For ten years Vaudreuil successfully employed the fiction of Abenaki independence. How could the King of France, in point of law, cede the territory of the Abenaki to Britain?

On the peninsula as well, the French employed the Indian menace as a deterrent to British occupation. Periodically St Ovide de Brouillan convened the Micmacs on Isle St Jean to foment forays at Canso and along the eastern shores. In 1722, the year in which Massachusetts declared war upon them, they seized over twenty fishing vessels. English reprisal from armed sloops at Canso was effective but the Indians continued to be something more than a nuisance. In the same year they raided an English ship in the harbour at Minas and looted the cargo while the Acadians looked on with indifference, later laughing at official protests and pleading the opportunity to buy goods "à bon marché."[2] In 1724 they crept into the environs of Annapolis and did considerable damage, maintaining well their boast that, though the English might build forts, they did not dare go outside them. When in 1731 the British commander, Lawrence Armstrong, exasperated by his weak position, decided to construct a magazine at Minas, a chief of the Micmacs appeared on the scene to announce "that though King George had conquered Annapolis he had never conquered Minas, that he was king of that country and would not suffer it."[3]

Père Parc, superior of French missions to the Indians, received specific command to order his subordinates to let no opportunity escape for keeping the tribes in a state of hostility. When Père Gaulin, missionary to the Micmacs, counselled peace, he was severely reprimanded and told by both Vaudreuil and the ministry at Paris to modify his conduct. The half-breed Baron St Castine, in his trading-post at Penobscot, found the war bad for business, used his influence against it, and was regarded as a traitor. Yet the vindictive campaigns waged by Governor Dummer of Massachusetts wore the Abenaki down. The sack of Norridgewock and the murder of Rasle before his altar in 1724 went far to break the warlike spirit of the confederacy. In 1727 they came to terms and the peace that resulted was regarded in Canada as still more evidence of British aggression.

The visit of the Governor of Nova Scotia, Richard Phillips, to Annapolis in 1719 accomplished nothing to strengthen the grip of Britain on the province. From the Indians he received the defiant message: Nous voulons avoir notre pays libre. With the Acadians he fared no better. Assured by the Board of Trade of large military reinforcements and an influx of British settlers, he sternly demanded the "oath of allegiance"; the Acadians, in spite of the alarm of their priests, who were prepared to advise migration to Cape Breton, would neither take the oath nor leave the country. Reports from

Cape Breton told of no meadows and no cattle there. Whether the Acadians were a greater asset to France in their homeland or on Cape Breton was a point of debate among the officers of the Louisburg garrison. Yet in either peace or war France could make use of them where they were. Much of the trade of the Acadians was passing to Louisburg – up the Bay of Fundy to Chignecto, over the isthmus to Tatamagouche, and on through the Gut of Canso.

On this occasion the British government was prepared to force the issue, having given to Phillips instructions to expel them should they resist the oath.[4] But reports of intermarriage between Acadians and Indians had made so great an impression on the Board of Trade that, in order to establish peaceful British control, they were willing to give encouragement to the practice and to extend it still further by subsidizing intermarriage between the existing population and British newcomers.[5] These plans for energetic measures came to naught when what seemed urgent in America in 1719 lost its force as Walpole's regime came to ensure the continuation of peace with France. Phillips returned to England, an unruffled absentee.

In 1728 the failure of the white pine forests of New Hampshire to produce masts for the Admiralty resulted in another British plan to colonize Nova Scotia. David Dunbar, a former lieutenant-governor of New Hampshire who was appointed Surveyor-General of the Woods in North America, appeared on the banks of the Kennebeck to execute his commission. His private ambitions were large and, with Thomas Coram, he proposed the establishment of a new colony of Georgia on the lands to the north of that river.[6] Here, in debatable land between Massachusetts and Nova Scotia, he experienced the same disappointment as in New Hampshire. Jealous of their traditional, though dubiously legal, rights, the men of Massachusetts, "as ripe for rebellion as they were in '41," regarded him as an oppressor. One of his deputies was killed by an infuriated New England mob. When he commenced the erection of a fort at Pemaquid, William Taylor, the Lieutenant-Governor of Massachusetts, threatened to demolish it with a force of five hundred men.[7] Many New Englanders who inherited titles to lands north of the Kennebeck, derived either from purchase from the Indians or from grants dating back to the time of Sir Thomas Temple, were prepared to fight.

Simultaneously Governor Phillips was ordered to return to Nova Scotia with the intention of establishing a true "scheme of civil government" and populating the province with a race of mixed lineage. He bought up the seigneurial claims in western Nova Scotia of Mrs Agatha Campbell, who inherited her title from Charles la Tour, and henceforth the Acadians were required to pay quitrents to the Crown.[8] But he could not force from the people an unreserved oath of allegiance. Triumphantly he reported to the

Board that under his own good management the Acadians had made their submission to the King, failing to add that in a separate instrument he had granted them the right not to bear arms on the King's behalf. This arrangement of Phillips in 1730 laid a firm foundation for the Acadian claim to neutrality in future wars. Frequently they spoke of "the treaty" they had made, and throughout British America they were often called the neutral French of Nova Scotia.

The Acadians were becoming too big a problem for Phillips, who was again denied his promised reinforcements from Britain. Enjoying a high degree of material prosperity, they were "like Noah's progeny spreading over the face of the province."[9] At Annapolis they could be intimidated by the guns of the fort. But at Minas they habitually risked governmental displeasure and the more remote settlements at Chignecto were "long under a disobedience to government." Their total number was approaching ten thousand and overflow populations were constantly moving afield to form new settlements. In 1726 a few families, though forbidden to do so by the British government, moved across the bay to found Shepody. The command at Louisburg used every means to encourage the Acadians to look to France for protection, and the reputation of the great fortress gave them reason for doing so. Taking advantage of the clause in the Treaty of Utrecht guaranteeing them the freedom of religion, their priests could face the council at Annapolis with the assertion that they were in Nova Scotia on the business of the French King.[10]

Until the War of the Austrian Succession compelled attention, Nova Scotia, as a British province, continued to be ignored at London. Paul Mascarene, the doughty and conscientious deputy commandant at Annapolis, asserted control as best he could, dealing with the Acadians through their priests as intermediaries, sometimes resorting to a system of elected deputies. The fort and garrison were a show of weakness rather than of strength. So feeble was the garrison that when war came it had to be supplied with firewood from New England.[11] Seeking settlers for her own purposes, New England preferred the use of Nova Scotian beaches free of inhabitants to the real control that could come with British settlement. Phillips had laid out the form of a civil government but soldiers still ruled at Annapolis and the reputation of the country did not improve. Jonathan Belcher, the Governor of Massachusetts Bay, could see see no reason why settlers should go to Nova Scotia when they might live in New England under "an easy, civil government." "By what I heard the government of the petty province of Nova Scotia has been one constant scene of tyranny. God deliver me and mine from the government of soldiers."[12]

II

News of the outbreak of the War of the Austrian Succession came first to Louisburg; the French, though ill-prepared and enduring a period of spring-time semi-starvation, opened the war by capturing Canso, still worse prepar-ed with its garrison of 120 men. François Dupont du Vivier, the commander of this successful expedition, sought complete expulsion of the English from Acadia when in August he summoned Mascarene to surrender the fort at Annapolis. Two ragged armies, led by harassed commanders, faced one another and both were bluffing. Timely arrival of reinforcements from New England enabled Mascarene, without fighting, to last Vivier out.

The ultimate influence which determined the fate of the Acadian region was about to make itself felt. The time for an application of strength in place of a confrontation of weaknesses had arrived. William Shirley, the Governor of Massachusetts, an English lawyer of long standing in the colony who had been able to harmonize its conflicting interests, was about to harness the eager and incipient imperialism of New England. He succeeded in producing a high degree of discipline and organization where previously there had been none and was able, over the next ten years, to persuade the Whigs of the British cabinet, who were engrossed with the diplomatic intrigues of the European continent, to give a new degree of attention to the affairs of North America. It was Shirley who planned and organized the great Louisburg expedition of 1745. Its successful issue projected a series of events that made the North American war a part of a world war, a new concept to the English Whigs, and one that made the Acadian theatre the strategic area in the coming struggle. Colonial governors, both French and English, had for years been writing of a struggle for mastery of the continent. The fall of Louisburg made their prophecies stark reality.

It was not difficult to interest New England in such an enterprise. There were fears of French invasion from Louisburg, but eagerness for employment of the fishermen whose prospects had been blighted by the war, hatred of papists, desire for booty, were stronger motives. The existing New England militia system made recruiting easy. Shirley acquired the assistance of Admiral Sir Peter Warren at New York who agreed, on his own responsi-bility, to blockade Louisburg in the early months of the year so that the French should be deprived of reinforcements and supplies. In England the Duke of Newcastle, Secretary of State for the Southern Department, sent substantial reinforcements of eight vessels of war to Warren when he was informed of the project.

Altogether the colonial general, William Pepperell, an able merchant of Maine without professional experience, had about 4,500 men. With favour-able weather the force achieved a considerable degree of concentration at

Canso during the month of April and the little ships of the colonies beat up along the Cape Breton coast following the receding of the ice-floes. On April 30 the commanders began to disembark their men along the Bay of Gabarus to the west of the fortress. Here there was token resistance only. The French commandant, Dupont du Chambon, at first faint hearted, ordered the evacuation of the Grand Battery, which allowed the New Englanders to bombard the northern and western defences of the town. Still, the outlook was not promising. Several unsuccessful attacks brought discouragement to Pepperell's councils. Morale among the unprofessional soldiers was not high. Their officers freely avowed that only the hope of booty would persuade them to fight resolutely. On May 20 the fleet performed a vital service when the Vigilant, a new sixty-four-gun French man-of-war, was forced to strike her colours after a fierce battle in the approaches to the harbour. Had she managed to make port her crew of five hundred would have doubled the number of the defenders.

It was not until May 26 that Pepperell came to the decision that might earlier have been made with profit. The key to the defences of Louisburg was the Island Battery that guarded the entrance to the harbour and prevented the fleet from taking part in the bombardment. A point of land jutting into the harbour, known as the Lighthouse, was almost exactly a thousand yards off from it, the effective range of Pepperell's largest cannon. After extensive preparations, he occupied this early in June. The Lighthouse Battery of the New Englanders more than neutralized the Island Battery of the French. On June 15, during a furious bombardment from land and sea, the defenders could not stand to their guns. On the 17th, his position had become so hopeless that Chambon sued for capitulation.[13]

The security of all New France was threatened by this new British grip on the St Lawrence approaches and the Marquis de Beauharnois, Governor of New France, quickly submitted his plan for the restoration of French ascendancy in the Acadian theatre. A land force from Quebec should be joined in the spring by a fleet dispatched from France. Annapolis should be taken and the fort dismantled. Real control over Acadia could be established only by occupation of the two great harbours of Chebucto (Halifax) and Lahave, where a new French government should be established.[14]

The strategic importance of Acadia came into remarkable prominence in June of 1746 when a great armament of eleven line-of-battle, twenty frigates, and transports, fireships, and merchantmen left La Rochelle under the command of the Duc d'Anville. Its objects were to recover Louisburg, conquer Nova Scotia, and, if possible, sack Boston. Three thousand veteran troops were on board. From the West Indies Admiral des Conflans, with four large warships, was to join D'Anville at the agreed rendezvous, the harbour of Chebucto. Disaster struck the gigantic enterprise. In the region of the Azores the fleet was dispersed by a great storm. After three months of hard weather on the Atlantic, D'Anville made Chebucto with two shiploads of sick and broken men. Overcome by the supposed calamity to the remainder of his fleet, he took poison and died. Thereafter, as the battered vessels made their way one by one into the harbour, fifteen hundred men died of pestilence, and three warships were burnt owing to a shortage of hands. Divided counsels ruled. D'Anville's successor committed suicide on his own sword. When the Marquis de la Jonquière, who had been appointed Governor of New France, sailed to attack Annapolis on October 13, he picked up some Boston fishermen off Cape Sable and was given information of a British fleet under Warren in the vicinity. Abandoning the whole enterprise, he hastened off to the West Indies. The Chevalier de Ramesay, who for months had awaited the arrival of the fleet at Chignecto with a mixed force of Canadians and Indians, made a demonstration before Annapolis and was easily beaten off by Mascarene.

Annapolis was well sustained with materials and reinforcements by Shirley, who was now attempting to persuade the British ministry to mount a campaign against Quebec. His New Englanders, commanded by Colonel Noble, who occupied Minas, fell victim to the intrepidity and superior mobility of Ramesay. In a blinding snowstorm on the night of February 11, 1747, the Canadian commander attacked and forced a capitulation. But French hopes for this year were dashed by Lord Anson's victory off Cape Finisterre. He captured La Jonquière, who with five vessels of the beaten fleet was bound once more for Nova Scotia. In spite of this success and Shirley's aggressiveness, however, he was commanded to rest upon the defence. Admiral Warren was of the opinion that Quebec was too strong to be attacked and the plan became one of simply strengthening Annapolis and Louisburg. At the same time the Governor of Massachusetts was ordered to prepare a plan of civil government for Nova Scotia along with a scheme of fortification.[15]

As the peace of exhaustion approached in Europe, the British government could not turn their faces from the new implications arising from the late North American events. Shirley's initiative in taking Louisburg and the stake the New Englanders had made for themselves in Acadia commanded respect. If the New England influence were not sufficient, the French had taught the Duke of Newcastle something of its strategic importance by sending D'Anville's fleet to Chebucto. Yet the general state of the war, especially the French victories in the Low Countries, compelled the restoration of Louisburg as peace approached. By the end of 1746 the British were forced to yield it up as the only solid counter for bargaining in the diplomatic game they were playing. The French negotiators at Aix-la-Chapelle were instructed to conclude no peace without the restitution of the fortress that shielded Canada.[16] Commodore Charles Knowles, Governor at Louisburg in 1746, described it as "a bewitching idol" and recommended that it be restored to France. The markets for fish, he argued, were already crowded by the produce of Newfoundland and New England and there could be no increase in production if Louisburg should be retained. The British fishery, he reasoned, could be better protected by establishments on the peninsula.[17]

As restitution became imminent, all the emphasis in London shifted to Nova Scotia. At the close of 1747 a writer in the Westminster *Journal* declared that it was "equal to Canada and Cape Breton together."[18] In 1749 the American pamphleteer, Otis Little, published his *Geographical History of Nova Scotia*, a sure indication of the interest the province now had for the British government and public. Shirley produced his plan for a civil government, placing great weight on a fort at Chignecto, "the Palladium of the Province,"[19] strong enough to be defended against the whole force of Canada and Cape Breton. William Bollan, agent for Massachusetts in London, insisted that such a fort was necessary to destroy intercourse between the Acadians of the Bay of Fundy and Louisburg.[20] In order to mitigate discontent with what seemed a craven and shameless abandonment of New England's interests, Newcastle and the ministry fostered for propaganda purposes the glowing accounts that were current of the importance of Nova Scotia, especially of the commodiousness of the great harbour of Chebucto.

The War of the Austrian Succession did not touch Newfoundland, but Isle Royale's sub-government, Isle St Jean, severely experienced the weight of it. Its little garrison at Port la Joye was included in the articles of capitulation of Louisburg, and Sir Peter Warren, after imposing neutrality upon the inhabitants during his pleasure, planned to deport them to France. Owing to a lack of transports, this proposal was not carried into execution. In September of 1746 a party of British troops from the Louisburg garrison, who had replaced the New Englanders in occupation, was surprised on the banks of the East River by two hundred Micmacs who had been detached from Ramesay's forces at Chignecto. Forty were killed, wounded, or captured.[21]

III

In 1748 there took place a reshuffling of posts in the British government and the responsibility for the new policy in Nova Scotia passed out of the hands of the Duke of Newcastle into those of the Duke of Bedford, who became Secretary of State for the Southern Department. Bedford's part in the formation and carrying out of the policy was not so great as that of Newcastle's satellite, George Dunk-Montagu, Lord Halifax, who became

First Commissioner for Trade and Plantations. The scheme which Halifax, "the Father of the Colonies," presented to the King early in 1749 embodied the ideas of those who had earlier submitted projects – Warren, Shirley, Knowles, Bollan, and Clarke, the Lieutenant-Governor of New York.[22]

The principal idea contained in the new policy was the old one of a Nova Scotian barrier for New England against the attacks and artifices of the French. Extensive fortification and the peopling of the province by subjects loyal to the Crown would be necessary to effect this purpose. Exaggerating the rapid increase in the numbers of the Acadians, Halifax reckoned them to be a factor of the greatest danger. Before it should be too late, English and Protestant settlers should be mingled with them in order that they might lose their identity as a separate people and be made obedient to the royal authority. In addition to this great object, others, equally important, could be served : the procuring of masts for the navy, the enlargement of British trade by the increase of the fishery. French sea power, reasoned Halifax, could be dealt a mortal blow if French fishermen could be restrained from using British waters.

While Admiral Vernon was pleading in the House of Commons for the employment of discharged soldiers and sailors, Halifax advocated that these, to the number of three thousand, should be recruited to form the nucleus of the new settlements. Twelve hundred should be settled at Chebucto, the remainder distributed about the peninsula, specifically at Lahave, White-head, a harbour near Canso, Bay Verte, and Minas. Two regiments should be garrisoned within the province and small sloops of war, rather than line-of-battle, should be employed at sea in order to lessen the hazards of the rocks and shoals of the coastline. Halifax honoured Shirley's demand for a stronghold at Chignecto and proposed blockhouses at Minas and Pisiquid, the heart of the Acadian country, to prevent the propaganda of Quebec from exercising the desired effect on the inhabitants.

The British government acted swiftly. The anger in New England following the return of Louisburg to France was so acute that it was well to give quick assurance of the establishment of the barrier. On March 6, 1749, Bedford received Halifax's plan. By the middle of May Colonel Edward Cornwallis was sailing for Nova Scotia as governor, followed by an armada of transports bearing the settlers and their supplies. His determination was to meet Mascarene at Annapolis, there to superintend the settlement of the province. But, "the wind not serving for the Bay of Fundy," he made the important decision to stop at Chebucto and to keep all the settlers there until the following summer.[23] The proposed settlement of the province became, therefore, the settlement of the Chebucto peninsula, and the new town of Halifax, where three thousand settlers were concentrated, was even more important than its projectors had intended.

The founding of Halifax was a bitter blow to the French. Again, as after the Treaty of Utrecht, they pressed the case for the sovereignty of the Abenaki and the question of "the ancient limits of Acadia" came into prominence.[24] English newspapers announced that the new settlements were to extend to the St Lawrence, and Puyzieulx, the French King's minister for foreign affairs, told Yorke, the secretary to the British embassy at Paris, "Vous nous mal menez dans cette affaire." British assurance that no settlement should be made on territory in dispute exerted an assuaging effect. But Bedford refused a French demand that the old controversy on the ownership of the islands of Canso should be reopened.[25]

While the two governments appointed commissioners for the settlement of boundary and other disputes in the colonies, the men on the spot in America took measures that made negotiations really unnecessary. At Quebec La Galissonière, Lieutenant-Governor for La Jonquière, had come to the conviction that Louisburg left much to be desired as a French stronghold on the sea, that a port on the ocean in communication with New France throughout the winter must be obtained. For this reason he turned to the almost forgotten plan of Colbert for opening a passage to more southerly seas through the St John River country. Indians and small bands of French had long utilized this great river as the quickest route to Quebec from Acadia. During the war which had just ended, a road had been cut from Rivière du Loup to Lake Temiscouata.[26] La Galissonière, therefore, prompted by what the French construed as British aggression, decided to occupy the disputed territory. The settlement at Chebucto, according to one British informant, caused more chagrin to the French in Canada than could the continued occupation of Cape Breton.[27]

What the British called "the French game" immediately commenced. When Cornwallis had landed at Chebucto in June, the Micmacs had flocked to him for presents and he had renewed with them the peace treaty of 1725. A few weeks later they were making small but effective attacks on the outskirts of the new town. This was owing to the influence of Joseph de la Loutre, missionary to the Shubenacadie Indians, whose presence in Acadia was to be a great factor in the reckoning. Against the British he promised "une guerre eternelle," persuading the savages to defend their country against the intruders of Chebucto.[28] Soon the settlers were confined to the palisades. In the autumn, when Cornwallis realized what he was up against, he was forced to assume a defensive role within a small enclave of his new province. When he heard rumours of French forces to the north of the Bay of Fundy, he demanded and received from Whitehall more military and naval assistance to achieve his difficult goal.

As ever, the French were the more mobile. In the winter of 1749-50 the Chevalier de la Corne, with six hundred men from Quebec, took possession of the coveted isthmus of Chignecto. In April, when Major Charles Lawrence arrived to demand French withdrawal and to destroy all fortifications as violations of treaties, La Corne retired across the little river Missiquash, burnt the Acadian village of Beaubassin, and drove the inhabitants with their cattle before him. Hot with anger, Lawrence was confronted with French colours on the dykes and La Corne's declaration that the territory to the north of the river would be defended for the King of France until a decision from the commissioners in Europe should be reported.[29] La Jonquière, now Governor of New France, thereupon laid claim to all the territory to the north of the Bay of Fundy by right of prior occupation.[30]

The British government was quick to understand that the work done in Nova Scotia would be undone should French troops remain at Chignecto. William Pitt, breaking his routine at the Pay Office, wrote of the occupation as another evidence of French intention to seize supreme commercial and maritime power.[31] The Duke of Newcastle was aroused to demand restitution from "the wild French governors in America. This is what they can't justify and what we can't bear."[32] The Duke of Albemarle, British ambassador to France, hastened to Compiègne, where the Court was sitting. There he put the above events before Puyzieulx, who professed to believe that La Corne and La Loutre were land pirates rather than the accredited officers of the king. But when the French government understood the strategic implications of La Corne's presence at Chignecto, it argued in defence of his action. An official memoir alleged that the occupation had been made in self-defence, that the Indians had set fire to Beaubassin, that France could not be held responsible for the conduct of its allies. Cornwallis, it was held, was carrying on a bitter war against Acadians and Indians.[33] Perhaps with deliberate naiveté the two governments referred the affair of Chignecto to the commissioners on the boundary who were about to open their sessions.

In the summer of 1750 Major Lawrence returned to Chignecto at the head of a much greater force, and drove from his landing-place at the point of the bayonet a large number of Indians and French disguised as Indians. He then began on the marshlands the erection of a stronghold to be known as Fort Lawrence. Some three miles to the northward, on higher ground, La Corne was constructing a fort called Beauséjour. British and French in Acadia were now opposed to one another face to face. On this strategic ground warlike incidents occurred, though neither side avowed a state of war. Both offered premiums for scalps. At the end of 1750 a British officer with considerable influence over the Indians, Captain Edward How, was shot and killed while advancing to meet a French flag of truce. For this violation of "the most sacred laws of God and man" the British blamed La Loutre; the French blamed the Indians.[34] At sea the British systematically interfered with the passage of supplies to the garrison of Beauséjour and the small detachment at the mouth of the St John River, seizing vessels on the charge of importing contraband goods into Nova Scotia. "When open force is used, discourses are useless," wrote Des Herbiers, the Governor of Isle Royale, to Cornwallis.[35] While commissioners deliberated in Europe, it was very unlikely that the men on the spot in America could restrain themselves and their forces from open hostility.

During the sinister four years' peace on the isthmus, the French laboured on the defences of Beauséjour. Duchambon de Vergor, the commandant, accepted very literally the advice of his friend, François Bigot, to clip and cut for the ultimate purpose of a purchase of an estate in France. La Loutre kept the Indians on their mettle and supervised the construction of dykes and the establishment of an Acadian settlement to the west of the fort. Britain continued to pour men and money into Acadia. Having voted £80,000 for 1751, Parliament supplied an additional £53,000 to meet the unexpected emergencies. Against the opposition of Bedford and the more pacific wing of the Cabinet, the Board of Trade made its point so that two ships of the line were based at Halifax to neutralize the French squadron at Louisburg.[36]

A diplomatic sham battle in Europe accompanied the increasing mounting of arms in Nova Scotia. The French commissioners for the boundary, La Galissonière and the Marquis de Silhouette, wished to consider as a whole all the points of difference arising out of the treaty of Aix-la-Chapelle. Shirley and William Mildmay, representing Britain, refused to seek solutions by exchange of territory and compromising of claims, insisting instead on a specific interpretation of particular treaties and legal rights. When the French refused to continue negotiations unless "the two great national points," those of Nova Scotia and the West Indian island of St Lucia, should be linked together, the British commissioners deferred to their demand. Having achieved agreement on procedure, they reached a complete impasse on overlapping territorial claims. The French insisted that a line drawn roughly from Canso to Chignecto should be the northern limit of British settlement. In October of 1751 the Grand Committee of the French Council endorsed this stand of their commissioners.[37] Since the French held a loose control over all the territory in dispute, they could well afford to let the talks go on indefinitely.

Tiring of the delay, Newcastle demanded direct negotiations between the two governments, the Privy Council moderating the British requirement to the entire Bay of Fundy coastline and sufficient country to the northward to ensure its quiet possession.[38] Surprisingly, the French agreed that the boundaries of Nova Scotia should be so arranged as to provide the British with communication by land with their colonies to the south. It was stipulated that the Earl of Albemarle and the Comte de Mirepoix should settle the details, but the Earl could never catch up with the French ambassador in his peregrinations about Europe. Diplomatically, France was trifling with Britain and when, in August of 1753, orders were sent from England to the king's governors in America to drive the French by force from their territories, the affair of "the ancient limits of Acadia" became merged in the more general consideration of French or English supremacy in America.[39]

IV

Although the French could not see it as such, this British determination was declared to be defensive in character. The Cabinet, having been voted by Parliament £1,000,000 for American operations, sent a fleet under the command of Admiral Boscawen to Halifax for the purpose of intercepting French troops or supplies of war on their way to Nova Scotia, Louisburg, or Quebec. The instructions to General Braddock, who arrived in America late in 1754 with two regiments of the line, were to drive the French from Chignecto, after reducing all the newly constructed French forts in the valley of the Ohio and elsewhere in the west.[40]

Charles Lawrence, now in command at Halifax, was not content with a plan of campaign that would postpone the operation on which he had set his heart until the end of the season of 1755. Late in 1754 he sent Colonel Robert Monckton to Boston with orders to arrange an attack on Beauséjour for the following spring with Governor Shirley. Newcastle gave encouragement to the plan, urging that the investment should be made so early in the year that the French would not be able to send reinforcements in time from Europe. Animated by the hope of profit from military and naval contracts as well as by the promise of glory, Shirley loyally collaborated.[41] Colonel John Winslow of Plymouth contracted to raise two thousand troops and agreed to serve as second-in-command to Monckton.

Precisely according to plan, a fleet of thirty-six vessels left Boston on May 20, 1755 and sailed up the Bay of Fundy to the mouth of the Missiquash to join five hundred British regulars at Fort Lawrence. Beauséjour was a pentagon of earthworks about 280 feet in width, garrisoned by two hundred French regulars and several hundred Acadians and Indians. On the walls were twenty-six cannon. Underground casemates extended into the wall to provide protection against artillery fire. French valour was not well served by Vergor, the commandant, and Thomas Pichon, the intendant, a paid spy in British service.

On June 4 the British advanced over the low, marshy ground towards Beauséjour. By means of their small boats armed with swivel guns they were able to dominate the Missiquash and the French could impose no obstacle to the march which led to the high ground north of the fort. On June 13 their heavy guns commenced to fire. On the 16th a bomb burst through a casemate thought to be inviolable, killing four men and creating great consternation. As Vergor was informed that no help could be expected from Louisburg, he decided on the capitulation that took place on the evening of the same day. Simultaneously Winslow took possession of Fort Gaspereau, a centre of French supply and communication on Bay Verte.[42]

While Shirley and Lawrence so successfully put their scheme into execution against Beauséjour, the general state of war in North America came clearly into the open. Braddock was marching into the Ohio Valley. Off the banks of Newfoundland, Boscawen, in heavy fog, made contact with a French fleet bearing troops and arms for Quebec and Louisburg. Two great vessels, one the *Alcide*, of sixty-four guns, and the *Lys*, could not escape and, after a severe battle, struck their colours. Eight companies of French troops were brought to Halifax as prisoners.

When Beauséjour, to be renamed Fort Cumberland, fell, three months of good campaigning weather remained. Three regiments of the line were on service in Nova Scotia and Boscawen's fleet dominated the sea. Winslow's two thousand troops from New England were enlisted for a year and, before their time expired, Lawrence determined to put them to use. Within the province but one military factor – and Lawrence could see it as only a military one – jeopardized the security of Nova Scotia. This was the Acadian population whose presence offered invitation to the French to return, and whose disposition he believed to be inveterately hostile. With all his resources at hand, the one thing he could do in July of 1755 was to force obedience upon the Acadians or, if they should refuse obedience, to resort to expulsion, a remedy never remote from the minds of all the British commanders who had served in Nova Scotia since 1713.

Generally the Acadians, a peasant people, abhorred war and preferred to be left out of the military reckoning. At the opening of the previous war some of them had petitioned the Governor of Cape Breton for exemption from French demands for service. "We live under a mild and tranquil government and have all good reason to be faithful to it."[43] Yet, as the raiding parties of Marin and Ramesay traversed the Acadian settlements to attack Annapolis between 1744 and 1747, adventurous young men could not resist the temptation to bear arms for France, particularly at moments when it seemed that French fortunes were high. Much more important than the disposition of the population itself was the determination of the French governors to make use of it and their success in doing so. "All, with the exception of a very small portion, are desirous of returning under the French domination," wrote the intendant, Hocquart, to the Comte de Maurepas in

1745, adding that any Acadians refusing to support France should be dealt with by force.[44] When D'Anville's fleet arrived at Chebucto in 1746 and they were paid in specie for supplies, there was *"une grande joie dans l'Acadie."* The retreating French commanders strove to protect the Acadians against British resentment by issuing them with bogus warrants to supply goods "on pain of confiscation."

The idea of expulsion goes back to Nicholson in 1713 and was fleetingly revived by British commanders whenever they saw necessity for making threats. In 1740 Mascarene had warned the Acadians that, should they continue to show disobedience, "the people of New England would ask nothing better than to take possession of lands cleared and ready to receive them."[45] Traders from Boston had frequently expressed wonder that an alien people on British territory should be permitted to hold such fine lands as those of the Acadians. On several occasions the unguarded utterances of New England officers serving in Nova Scotia seemed likely to throw the nervous Acadian peasants into a general panic. On December 9, 1745 Mascarene had written to Shirley telling him of his hopes of turning the Acadians into good subjects and of how those hopes had been disappointed. Then followed a dispassionate and closely calculated accounting of the factors that would make expulsion possible. The letter closed with the recommendation that his own mild policy should be continued until "such a resolution is judged proper to be effected as most likely tending to the public service.[46]

Shirley's letters to Newcastle during the War of the Austrian Succession contain a persistent series of invectives against the Acadians. He never asked for the expulsion of all because he believed that such an immense operation would not be practical. He did propose expulsion of "the most dangerous" and when an expedition against Canada had seemed imminent in 1746 he suggested that this should be one of the secondary objects of the enterprise.[47] In 1747 he wanted a winter expedition from Louisburg against Chignecto and the deportation of the inhabitants of that most refractory settlement.[48] Commodore Knowles at Louisburg urged the removal of all the Acadians from Nova Scotia and the settlement of Highland rebels on their lands, a proposal greatly deprecated by Shirley who could see himself as Governor of Nova Scotia as well as of Massachusetts with a New England population behind him. Newcastle was convinced that deportation was impossible and feared a general insurrection of the people. Late in 1747 he ordered the postponement of any such scheme but asked that consideration should be given to measures by which it could be carried out at an appropriate time.[49]

Following the Peace of Aix-la-Chapelle the incorporation of the Acadians into an English-speaking Nova Scotia became the object of British policy. By Shirley's direction Captain Charles Morris surveyed the Bay of

Fundy lands in 1748 and laid out estates for fourteen hundred English settlers in the midst of the Acadian countryside. The Governor of Massachusetts now relied on a denial of the episcopal jurisdiction of Quebec, a strict regulation of the priests, the introduction of Protestant refugee clergymen from France, and the promotion of intermarriage between the races as the chief means of turning the Acadians into good English-speaking subjects.[50] In 1748 neutrality, the cherished aspiration of the Acadians, could be but a dream. Pressure from both sides would soon compel a choice. And British pressure now weighed more heavily than that of the French. A London pamphleteer, Argus Centoculis, reflected the official view that, should they persist in their disobedience, they should be made hewers of wood and drawers of water to the natural-born subjects of His Majesty.[51] The American colonial, Otis Little, asked whether or not the British government should continue to tolerate the continued presence of "a colony of French bigots" who could cut the throats of its own people "whenever the priests shall consecrate the knife."[52]

Shirley's compromise program for gradual absorption of the Acadians was completely accepted by Lord Halifax in his plan for the settlement of Nova Scotia. One thousand of the English colonists, the first of many more, were to be settled among the Acadians at Minas and Chignecto. A process of desegregation would have commenced very quickly had Cornwallis, as he planned, gone directly to Annapolis and discharged a proportion of his settlers upon the marshlands further up the bay. Instead he summoned deputies of the Acadians to Halifax and demanded the oath of allegiance. They refused, except on the terms granted by Phillips in 1730, and professed great alarm at the prospect of English settlement among them, inquiring as to whether or not they should be permitted to sell their properties and remove to French territory. Throwing down the mailed gauntlet, Cornwallis told them that they completely misunderstood their situation, that they were by the Treaty of Utrecht subjects of the British Crown, that they had no liberty to go to Canada.[53] To prevent the industry of the Acadians from becoming a military asset to the French was, as in 1713, a cardinal consideration. When the deputies returned to their homes they found a large detachment of British troops at Minas and British vessels cruising in the bay.

The use to which the French could put the Acadians was well demonstrated in the spring of 1750 when the inhabitants of Beaubassin were driven across the Missiquash by La Loutre. Those at Minas were subjected to persuasion falling short of force and the council of Nova Scotia received many petitions for leave to vacate to French territory. The Acadians had as much reason to resent the importunities of their kinsmen as those of the alien British. La Loutre's aim was to move them all, with as much as they could take with them, to Beauséjour, Isle St Jean, and other territories under French control. For the British the expedient of expulsion was always in the wind. But first they should be offered the salutary choice of taking the oath of allegiance. Only when the choice could be forced upon them "in perfect safety," the Board of Trade told Peregrine Hopson, successor to Cornwallis, should decision be demanded.[54]

In July of 1755 Lawrence enjoyed conditions of perfect safety. For the first time in forty years a British governor possessed the power and the opportunity to force the Acadians to compliance with his wishes. After meeting deputies who again refused to take the oath, the Governor and his council decided to deal with the Acadians as subjects of the King of France.[55] Chief Justice Jonathan Belcher, newly arrived from New England, submitted the legal opinion that they should be expelled from the province even if they should agree to take the oath, adding the practical consideration, dominant in the New England mind, that their continued presence would deter British immigration.[56] Late in July the deputies reaffirmed their refusal to become unconditional subjects of the Crown and the decision was taken to deport them to the British colonies to the south. Admirals Boscawen and Mostyn, who were present at the council meetings, concurred in this decision. "Perfect safety" there may have been for the British in Nova Scotia but not elsewhere. Lawrence took great precautions to ensure that first the rumours, later the certain intelligence, of Braddock's defeat in the west should not be circulated among the Acadians.[57]

The victors of Beauséjour, Monckton and Winslow, were charged with the task of rounding up all the Acadian inhabitants and of embarking them on the transports provided by the navy. Charles Morris, the Surveyor General, also a New Englander, drew up a plan for deportation. He recommended that the churches be surrounded on Sunday morning in order that as many Acadians as possible could be captured quickly, and that dykes should be cut and crops burned in order to remove all inducement to return.[58] The St John and Petitcodiac passages to Quebec were closely guarded. Other vessels cruised the approaches to Gaspé and Cape Breton. Tatamagouche, the port of entry to Chignecto from Cape Breton, was destroyed.

As a military operation, the expulsion of the Acadians might be described as reasonably efficient. Circumstances at the three main points of embarkation varied greatly. Annapolis witnessed probably the least confusion and consequent suffering. At Minas the operation was conducted directly under the supervision of Winslow. There he bivouacked four hundred New Englanders in the churchyard at Grand Pré, refusing his soldiers the privilege of playing cards but allowing the liberty of quoits, maintaining a constant vigilance against attacks by the French and Indians. On September 5, 418 males of Grand Pré and vicinity obeyed his summons to meet him in "the masshouse." After their persons were secured they were told that they were the prisoners of His Majesty. The women of the district were permitted to visit their husbands and sons, bearing them provisions. As transports, long delayed, came up the bay to receive the prisoners, they were shipped south-ward according to arrangements made by Lawrence. At Chignecto the ex-pulsion was carried out under circumstances of continuing hostilities. Charles de Boishébert, a Canadian officer and nephew to the Chevalier de Ramesay, organized a force of regulars, Acadians, and Indians in the valley of the Petitcodiac and inflicted a severe defeat on a New England detach-ment under Major Frye who was engaged in destroying the hamlets of that river. On a night in October, eighty-six Acadians confined in Fort Lawrence escaped by digging a thirty-foot tunnel under the south wall. It was the worse, Monckton ruefully remarked, because their wives were still at large in the woods of Shepody, Petitcodiac, and Memramcock.[59]

Owing to the scarcity of transports, the last sailings did not take place until the end of the year. Probably two-thirds of the population were accounted for by the British sailing-masters. A significant remnant from Annapolis became fugitives in the forests of the Cape Sable shore. From Chignecto, still a theatre of war, a large proportion made their way to the valleys of the St John and the Miramichi, and to the Isle St Jean. The dispersal was made the more thorough by the refusal of colonial govern-ments to accept so many shiploads of unwanted Acadians. The House of Burgesses of Virginia sent their quota off to England. They eventually found their way to France and were settled in the outskirts of St Malo.

The French, Lawrence remarked grimly, could no longer be sanguine about occupying a province that was already peopled for them.[60] His work had been signally satisfactory, for the Nova Scotian theatre produced the only good news for Britain in a year of defeats. In London the Board of Trade was startled by intelligence of what had happened, but its reaction was due largely to the heavy financial charges for the work of deportation. Pressing for the complete conclusion of the costly business, the Board describ-ed it as "absolutely necessary for the security and preservation of the province."[61]

V

Owing to the fleet's control of the sea, Lawrence's strong position in Nova Scotia was not seriously compromised in 1756 and 1757, years that were generally so adverse for the British. Halifax acquired an increasingly im-portant role in strategic thinking as the North American war became a world war and as the final struggle for mastery on the continent drew nearer. It had not yet become strongly fortified. When Wolfe arrived in

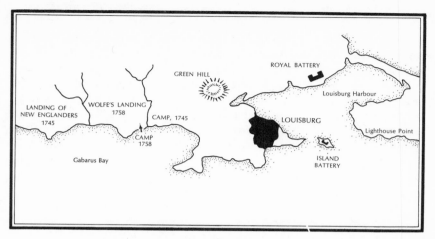

Louisburg

1758 he declared it could not stand an attack for twelve hours.[62] During the spring of 1757 troops under Lord Loudoun's command awaited convoy in Halifax, but his naval colleague, Admiral Holbourne, was slow in getting his fleet across the Atlantic. After he arrived, the season for campaigning was far advanced. When the fleet was dispersed by a great storm off the Cape Breton coast in September, the French naval squadron, safe in Louisburg harbour, missed a great opportunity for seizing a temporary control of Acadian waters that would have permitted a damaging blow at Halifax and unhinged the whole position of strength established by Lawrence.

The French were to have no more such opportunities. In the spring of 1758 General Amherst took supreme British command and a great expedition against Louisburg was in preparation. Land forces amounted to nearly thirteen thousand men, supported by twenty-three men of war, sixteen frigates, and other smaller vessels. This second siege was conducted on lines much more conventional, according to European standards, than that of 1745. During the interval of peace France had garrisoned the citadel with troops of the highest quality from Europe. The walls of the fortress were in an imperfect state, but British appearances in 1757 had caused the French to labour feverishly to improve them. What was of greatest consequence in French calculations and their chief hope for a successful defence, was the construction of fortified entrenchments along the shore of Gabarus Bay, the only possible landing place. The entrance to the harbour was guarded not only by the Island Battery, that had fought so well in 1745, but by four great line-of-battle ships. The commandant, the Chevalier de Drucour, was able and conscientious.

Leaving Halifax on May 29, the great British armament, headed by Wolfe and Boscawen, entered Gabarus Bay on June 2. Fog and bad weather postponed the landing until the early morning of the 8th, when Wolfe himself led the centre of the attack against the well-planned and excellently served defences. Forced to signal a retreat by the fierce French fire, he had the great good luck to perceive a ridge which offered shelter. From this small feature of the shore he organized a successful rush on the French positions. Local French commanders delayed too long in mounting a counterattack against the British beach-head. Many of their troops had been waiting in the trenches for a fortnight. By eight o'clock the 2,300 soldiers manning the western defences and the shores of Gabarus Bay were driven back to the protection of the walls of the town.[63]

Convinced that the outlook was hopeless, Drucour drew in his troops from the eastern side of the harbour, concentrating all his resources within the citadel and its immediate surroundings. This did not mean that the French were giving up the struggle. If anything, they fought harder as the end became more certain, the great consideration being to hold the British as long as possible in order to give Quebec another year of reprieve. Occupying the Lighthouse Battery without resistance, the British quickly moved around the arc of the harbour. Amherst was deliberate, even slow, but Wolfe, charged with the conduct of this long advance, was precipitate. "Wherever he goes he carries with him a mortar in one pocket and a 24-pounder in the other."[64] Relentlessly he advanced his batteries against the French defences, rewarding his men for overtime labour with rum by the half-pint, extra rations of fish, and money. Never was he seriously checked.[65]

Drucour was badly let down by the French admiral. The fire power of four great vessels could have greatly impeded Wolfe's advance from the north but the guns were put to no use. By selecting a position from which she could dominate some low ground at the northern approaches, L'Aréthuse, a frigate commanded by an intrepid officer, Vauquelin, caused more trouble to the British than did the four line-of-battle ships. As capitulation neared, Vauquelin ran the British blockade. L'Aréthuse was badly damaged but, true to form, he brought her safely to France.

By the end of July the Island Battery was completely destroyed and shells were falling into Louisburg from three sides. Only the great French warships sustained the power of effective resistance. On the 21st two of them caught fire and, blazing furiously, drifted ashore completely disabled. On the night of the 25th, British boarding parties stole into the harbour, blew up the third, and captured the fourth. The fleet could now, without reprisal, fire point-blank upon the town. Drucour was forced to accept humiliating terms, to surrender himself and his garrison as prisoners at discretion. In London the news of the victory at Louisburg produced an extraordinary elation. The British were starved for victories and the standards of the French regiments were carried in triumph to St Paul's.

The fall of the great fortress released, for the short season remaining, large British forces for the establishment of complete control over all the Acadian seas. With over two thousand men, Monckton made his way to the St John River in September and reconditioned the old French fort which was in ruins. On the 30th, losing a ship on the rocks of the Reversing Falls, though very alert to the perils of the shoals, he made his way up the river and proceeded as far as Jemseg to capture as many as possible of the dispirited Acadian refugees and destroy their buildings. A smaller expedition under Major Scott did the same work on the Petitcodiac. A garrison of New England militia was left at the new Fort Frederick at the mouth of the St John.[66] During the following winter the New Englanders did not rest quietly. The village of St Anne's had been exempted from Monckton's visitation. On a February night a party of rangers, led by Moses Hazen, fell upon it by surprise, destroyed 147 dwelling-places, and returned to Fort Frederick on reversed snow-shoes, after demonstrating that they were very facile in the barbarities attendant upon warfare with the Indians.[67]

On the Gulf of St Lawrence Wolfe and Boscawen conducted a raid against the slender French settlements on Gaspé, destroying property and breaking up the fishery. Colonel James Murray appeared in the Bay of Miramichi, succeeding in capturing some of the refugee Acadians but missing others who escaped up the river. Before 1758 was out, the settled inhabitants of Cape Breton were deported to France. For the past six years, Isle St Jean had been an important receptacle for refugees from Beaubassin and elsewhere. In spite of its greatly increased population it had never been self-supporting, though a great many accounts, both French and English, gave exuberant estimates of its produce. In November Lord Rollo, detached from Louisburg, carried out the deportation of between two and three thousand people, of whom seven hundred were drowned on the voyage to England. A few living on the western part of the island escaped this and later British attempts to remove them.[68]

By the end of 1758 the British had not only conquered every French place of strength in Acadia; they had also gone very far in carrying out the policy of complete removal of the French population. In February, 1760, following the fall of Quebec, William Pitt, who had organized the North American campaign and imparted such energy to its execution, ordered the destruction of the fortress of Louisburg. His directions to Brigadier Whitmore were to spare the houses but to demolish the walls, making it no longer capable of serving as a protection for the fishery.

VI

Though British victory was assured by 1760, complete peace came slowly to the region of the Atlantic seaboard. About the Miramichi and the Restigouche, Boishébert maintained a strong force of Acadian partisans who, during the summer of 1759, captured no less than seventeen small British vessels. Following the fall of Québec many of them gave up the struggle and surrendered, but Boishébert and what was probably the majority remained in arms, hoping for its recovery. They were witnesses to the failure of France's last hope in the Acadian seas. In the spring of 1760 a large number of store-ships, escorted by several light vessels heading for the St Lawrence, were compelled to enter the Bay of Chaleur when their commander learned that the British fleet had reached the river before him. Landing on the north bank of the Restigouche, he erected batteries and prepared a defence. Commodore John Byron, who commanded the British squadron at Louisburg and gained intelligence of French presence in this region, entered the bay early in July, captured two French vessels, and pursued the remainder of the squadron up the river. As Boishébert and his irregular force helplessly looked on, he easily destroyed the batteries, sank the French vessels or forced them to strike their colours.[69]

Peace negotiations opened in Europe in 1761 and it was the desperate hope of France to retain a foothold on the Atlantic seaboard that brought them to a standstill. She would give up Canada to keep Guadaloupe, but her stake in the fishery could not be surrendered. Her first offer of peace was featured by a proposal that Britain should restore Acadia in return for the abandonment of French interests in Guiana. Then followed her plea for Canso that was followed by the British offer of St Pierre and Miquelon, "more than adequate to any purpose offered by France."[70] But before this offer reached Paris, the Franco-Spanish alliance had been concluded and the continuation of the war assured. Spanish participation in the Seven Years' War was purchased in part by a French offer of readmission of Spaniards to the fishery from which they had been excluded for so long.

The strong determination of France's principal minister, the Duc de Choiseul, to retain a share of the fishery was given poignant witness when he expended the remains of French sea power on an attempt to conquer Newfoundland, a conquest which could be a powerful bargaining counter at a peace conference. Newfoundlanders had thriven on the war. Year after year their harvests from the sea had gone to market almost without disturbance. The only warlike activity they had witnessed was the rounding up of occasional French merchantmen by privateers. They were violently distracted from their peaceful occupations when, on June 24, 1762, a French force landed at Bay of Bulls, marched overland, and took St John's, where there was a garrison of sixty-three men, without a fight. The complacency of the English-speaking world was likewise disturbed. Diatribes against the new ministry of the Earl of Bute appeared in the London press. In Nova Scotia several hundred Acadians who had been brought as prisoners from the northern wilderness and were labouring on the Bay of Fundy lands which now belonged to new masters, displayed such a mutinous disposition that they were marched off to Halifax and shipped on transports to Boston. The general alarm resulted in the dispatch of troops from New York under Colonel William Amherst. Joined by reinforcements from Louisburg and by a small fleet under Lord Colville, he arrived at the narrow entrance to St John's harbour on September 11. The French had but seven hundred troops and were in no condition to carry on sustained operations. After the British landed at Torbay, the affair ended with a sharp encounter at Quidi Vidi and the surrender of the French on Signal Hill.

For France this surprising foray was unnecessary. The pacific British ministry which ruled in Whitehall now that Pitt had resigned was prepared to grant in substance what France desired. The Board of Trade was giving warning of a European dread of British monopoly in the North Atlantic fishery. The Duke of Bedford, leader of the "Peace Party," argued that the exclusion of France was unreasonable and unnatural. In defending itself against its opponents in Parliament, the ministry made a great deal of the definition of French fishing privileges in the Treaty of Paris as "a liberty" and not as "a right." To the British fishing trade, as well as to the French, no importance could be attached to the distinction.

St Pierre and Miquelon, with the French Shore, all that were left to France of its empire in North America, were characteristic outports of Newfoundland. For the past fifty years they had supported a small British population, both resident and transient, and endured the familiar rivalry between planters and ship-fishermen.[71] Now they became French possessions in full sovereignty but were not to be fortified. French planters and fishermen replaced the English, who withdrew to Newfoundland.

Slight as these concessions were in territory or territorial rights, however, they were great in significance. They meant that the French fishery remained as the basis of French Atlantic sea power, and therefore as great a power as before the loss of New France. And they meant also that the Atlantic colonies remained subject as always in the past to the policies and needs of others – of France, of England, and of New England.

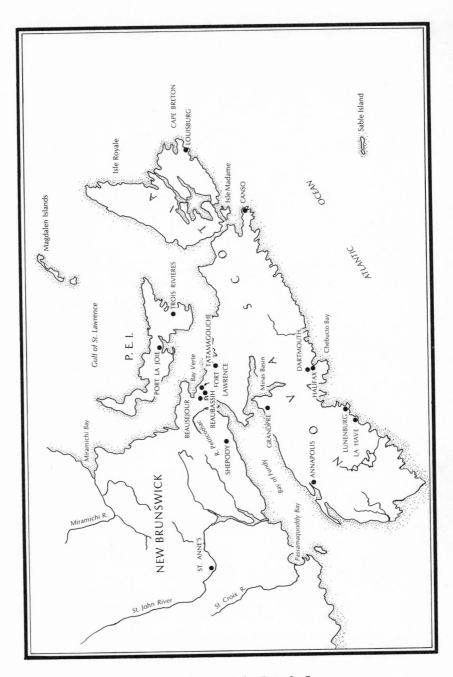

Acadia at the Time of the British Conquest

CHAPTER 3

The Beginnings of Permanence
1749-1775

The year of the foundation of Halifax, 1749, saw the first clear evidence that a British population could lodge itself on Nova Scotian soil. The same year may be taken to indicate that the shore population of Newfoundland, highly favoured and greatly increased by two wars of the mid-century, had acquired a certainty of continuing existence. Nova Scotia was settled as a conscious act of British imperial policy, but Newfoundland was peopled in spite of the axioms of overseas enterprise to which Whitehall was most receptive.

In the truest sense of the expression Nova Scotia was a royal colony. For the first time in her history Britain had established, as an act of public policy, a new community in North America. By careful supervision and the expenditure of great sums she was to sustain Nova Scotia for many years to come. The new departure of 1749 was to cost "this wittol nation," as Edmund Burke was later to complain, the sum of £700,000. But in the making of Nova Scotia, imperial policy, though a factor of great consequence for many years, was responsible for little more than a beginning. Standing at the gateway to the continent, the Acadian region was open to the flow of many peoples, receptive to the impulses of many national cultures. Diversity, rather than uniformity, was to be the rule as the march of events continued.

Halifax changed character within a year or two of its founding. The three thousand settlers brought by Cornwallis turned out to be "the King's bad bargains." Discharged soldiers and sailors were not qualified for clearing the wilderness. The warlike behaviour of the French denied the establishment of outports and of an agricultural hinterland for the new town. The raids of the Indians, the most notable of which halted the growth of the new town of Dartmouth across the harbour in 1750, had a terrifying effect on its settlers. From the outset Cornwallis had been compelled to issue edicts against emigration, without success. The fishery, from which a great deal was expected, died when the bounties initially offered by the government were taken away. Industry languished and virtually disappeared as Halifax became a community completely dependent on the flow of cash from Britain. In 1750 the population approached five thousand. By 1755 it had shrunk to about fifteen hundred.

Considerable numbers of Irish, indentured servants from Newfoundland or Virginia seeking to escape the hard obligations to which they were contracted, made their way to Halifax. Their residence in the town, where they were regarded as a wastrel element, did not improve their reputation.[1] "The common dialect spoke at Halifax is wild Irish."[2] But, amid the decay that attended depopulation, the durable and dominating element quickly became the New Englanders, the familiar traders of the North Atlantic seas who, disappointed by the return of Louisburg to France, were attracted to the new colony by the lavish expenditure of public money. Their great aspiration was a free port and they resisted, without success, the setting up of an imperial customs office.[3] It was not long before the officials of the colony raised a cry against the New England reputation for sharp dealing. Yet since they supplied essential goods and services, their presence could not be discouraged and they soon made themselves known as the only respectable element in the civil population, establishing themselves on the fringes of the royal patronage, becoming owners of property and leaders in public affairs. By buying up all available stocks of provisions, they forced the government to issue a continuous stream of regulations against monopoly. In spite of the attractions of Halifax as a trading centre, they were not minded to abandon their old and lucrative connection with Louisburg. Officials newly arrived from England and unwary of the ways of the New World were outraged to discover that an illicit traffic with the French was flourishing beneath their noses. The New Englanders were an immense asset to Halifax but the official mind could not forgive their hard bargaining and their obvious victimization of "the lower orders" as well as of the Royal Treasury.

At the head and centre of an increasingly important New England connection at Halifax was Joshua Mauger, a Jersey merchant whose family had for several generations fished and traded in the American seas. During the occupation of Louisburg he had held a great many profitable contracts from the Admiralty, and his wealth, gleaned from the West Indian trade, was legendary. By advancing credit to many merchants from New England he made them his clients. In London, it was said, his influence was greater than that of Cornwallis himself. At the highest court of appeal he was capable of obstructing the governor's attempts to halt trade with the French.[4] At Louisburg his commercial position was so powerful that Cornwallis was, on several occasions, compelled to solicit his influence to secure the release of prisoners taken by the Indians. In the second year of the colony he acquired a monopoly over the product that seemed most essential to the life of Halifax when he constructed a distillery that was protected against outside competition by a high customs duty. His financial power was so great that officials as well as merchants came under his control.

Within a year of the foundation, the New Englanders in Halifax secured the introduction of the Massachusetts system of inferior courts in which they entrenched themselves. Their justices, unlearned but persistent, strove to enforce New England precedents, usually at the expense of those who came from elsewhere. "The factious distinction between the New and Old England people" became the most prominent feature of public life. Halifax juries decided innocence or guilt on the test of birth or national origin. Rivalries among members of the Council, the majority of whom were New England men, eased their intrusion to the highest level of administration in the little community. So powerful did this cohesive New England influence become that a charge of peculation could, with impunity, be brought against the Governor's secretary. Assertions of superior morality and godliness did not allay the unpopularity their leaders acquired in other quarters. "They speak the truth with intent to deceive." Political rivalry stemmed from the contests for government contracts. "The parliamentary grant, My Lord, may be compared to a man who tosses a few guineas among a crowd, there is great scrabbling, but the luck happens to those few who have the guineas."[5] After 1755, when war became general, the shower of guineas became more profuse and Halifax was prosperous from the visits of fleets and armies. On great occasions, such as the return of the triumphant expedition against Havana in 1762, high carnival prevailed and the merchants enriched themselves by the purchase and sale of booty. Keeping grogshops for the armed forces was a major vocation. Through these exciting years the sole factor that determined political loyalties was the distribution of public monies by the governor and his council.

Diversity in population became more notable in 1750 and 1751, when a new element, German and Swiss, was brought to Nova Scotia by John Dick, contractor to the British government. They represented only an offshoot of the immense stream of Germans who, since early in the century and in accordance with the policy of introducing Protestant settlers, had been brought to America by agencies of the colonial governments. They were first intended for Minas and Chignecto but, owing to the French and Indian menace, were retained within the palisades of Halifax. Here the presence of fifteen hundred indigent people soon proved to be embarrassing. Huddled together in boarded barracks behind the town, denied what they considered to be the necessities of life, they quickly became an affliction and expense to the authorities. No cleared lands were available to receive them. The tools and instruments necessary to husbandry were not at hand. Security for the enterprises of peace was unknown in Nova Scotia. "Farmers can't live in forts and must go in security upon their business . . . ."[6] Forced to a life of inactivity, they asked for the privilege of supplying food to the colony instead of begging for it.[7]

In 1753 there came an uneasy peace with the Indians and a brighter prospect dawned for "the Palatines," as they were generally known. Because of their mutinous state of mind, Hopson would not settle them among the Acadians of the Bay of Fundy as he was certain that they would desert. He therefore ordered a survey of lands on the Bay of Merligash, on the south shore of the peninsula within easy reach of Halifax. There transports conveyed sixteen hundred people and, under the supervision of Lawrence as *custos rotulorum*, the town of Lunenburg was founded.[8] Military discipline was resented by the Palatines, and when the troops returned to Halifax for the winter an uprising against authority took place. Yet when the news reached the capital, the transports, beached for the winter, were refloated and Monckton with two hundred troops easily restored order. The Germans of Lunenberg were more than a little disposed to seek, as a respite from the alarms of war, a status of neutrality equivalent to that demanded by the Acadians.

For several years Lunenburg sustained itself by sending firewood to Halifax, and the people, by their industry, commended themselves to Lawrence. In 1758 the settlement was almost broken up by an unexpected attack of the French and Indians.[9] But by 1760 the governor was able to report to the Board of Trade that all difficulties had been surmounted and that Lunenburg would soon reimburse the Crown for the heavy expense incurred.[10]

Halifax, it was reported, was a place where there was no thirst for knowledge either useful or speculative. Yet it was upon this stony soil that the seed of Canadian self-government first fell. In the early 1750's Nova Scotia had not shaken itself free from its old reputation as a stronghold of tyrannical military government. The instructions to Cornwallis had commanded him to summon a general assembly of the people, two representatives from each township of fifty or more families. But the distribution of the settlers made it difficult for him to meet the conditions laid down for the calling of an assembly. In his time there was agitation for popular participation in government but, since he was popular, it had taken no persistent form. As settlement beyond the confines of Halifax failed to materialize, as the local war developed into a general war, a popular assembly seemed unsuitable to Halifax's wartime role. A civil government had been proclaimed but, in effect, Nova Scotia was under military rule.

The appointment of Charles Lawrence as Lieutenant-Governor in 1753, as Governor in 1755, brought to the head of affairs a man completely pre-occupied with the conduct of the war, a soldier accustomed to deal sum-marily with the complaints of a civil population. Military efficiency required an aloofness from the commercial community and a dependence on the coterie of officials who made up his council. Under Lawrence the distribution of the parliamentary grant became a cause for swiftly increasing acrimony as lush commissions were refused to the New England merchants, and as the officers of government appeared to become more affluent by reason of their public transactions. Military government was blamed for the decay of trade and the decline in population. Beneath the surface of the sullen commercial community burned a fierce antagonism to "the placemen."

The absence of a popular brand of government bothered the Board of Trade. A general assembly of the people was, in the minds of the British Whigs, the outward sign of a people's free state. Prior to 1754 they had ex-pressed perplexity at the failure of the governor to implement his instruc-tion. The appointment of Jonathan Belcher, the son of a former governor of Massachusetts, as Chief Justice in 1755 offered an opportunity to inquire why the instruction had not been carried out. He arrived with a request to examine the legality of Nova Scotia laws, to determine whether or not the courts should countenance legislation passed by governor and council alone. With "a temper fond of being the first in the community," he startled Hali-fax by the pomp and ceremony of his investiture to office. The scarlet robes and full-bottom wig of Westminster that appeared in the homely little court-house gave offence to the democratic New Englanders who knew not the title of "His Honour."[11]

Belcher did not give the Board the opinion it required. Ignoring the legal aspects of the question he contented himself by observing that, since but one township had the number of freeholders required by the royal instruc-tions for the calling of an assembly, governor and council should continue to legislate independently. Furthermore, he volunteered the opinion that there were no persons in Halifax qualified for the offices of representatives in a lower house of a provincial legislature.[12]

Thoroughly dissatisfied, the Board of Trade passed the problem over to the Attorney General and Solicitor General in Whitehall. In this same year, 1755, an assembly was elected in Georgia, where there were only four thousand white inhabitants; and Belcher's opinion was contrary to the opinions of all those who had traditional views on the subject. The Board's prejudices were endorsed when the legal officers affirmed that governor and council alone were not entitled to legislate in Nova Scotia.[13] The decisive step was immediately taken when Lawrence was ordered to consult with Belcher upon a plan for popular representation. "We cannot see how the Government can be properly carried on without such an Assembly."[14] There could be little doubt that the existing system of government was in fact illegal, and the Governor was ordered to keep his instructions secret until an act of indemnification had been passed for all earlier laws that had been enforced without proper authority.

There was good excuse for delay in 1755 and Lawrence did not consult with Belcher until December. Together they produced a scheme for an assembly of twelve members to be elected by all the people of the province as one electoral body. This was forwarded to Whitehall but appended to it were all the former objections to popular participation in government, along with the historical precedent of Virginia where, in the beginning, legislation by governor and council had alone been valid.[15] But the Board overruled all objections. The Virginia precedent was deprecated as one never repeated "since the Constitution of this country has been restored to its true principles."[16] More than anything that came out of Halifax it was Whig purism that moved the Board. The great principle of the sovereignty of a parliament representative of the people was to be applied in an outpost of the Empire so unimportant as Halifax.

Lawrence procrastinated and came close to prevarication on the subject of an assembly. On various pretexts he ignored the matter through all of 1756. The best excuse for him is that he was a busy man, that the important business in hand had nothing to do with the tender, constitutional scruples of the Board of Trade. It was not until January 3, 1757 that he divulged to the council the nature of his correspondence with Whitehall. Then a new plan for representation was drawn up with Belcher's original as a basis. In addition to the twelve members to be elected by the province at large, five townships were given two members each, providing for a house of twenty-two in all. But, determined to postpone to the bitter end an act which he found so distasteful, Lawrence had not reached the limits of his procrastination. He drew up the writ, left it in the hands of the Lieutenant-Governor, Colonel Monckton, and departed for Boston. By this time most of the proceedings in council were well circulated among the people of Halifax. When they asked Monckton to issue the writ for an election they were informed that neither he himself nor the King believed that the suitable time for doing so had yet arrived.

Now sure of their ground, the enemies of Lawrence came into the open and organized a protest. Malachy Salter, a New England merchant whose activities in trade had on many counts aroused suspicions, led in the drafting of a petition against the Governor and in taking a subscription for legal action in London.[17] Belcher, fearful of sharing in charges of disobedience to the commands of the Board of Trade, abandoned his downright stand of two years before and gave his support to the petition. His was the hand that drafted the affidavit of the merchants, and the London lawyer employed to deliver it to the Board of Trade was his own solicitor in the British capital, John Ferdinando Paris. Three other members of the council protected themselves against displeasure by writing in protest against the Governor's disregard of their advice during the deliberations.[18] At the same time anonymous letters came to London from Halifax, asking for the appointment of another governor, "divested of military and lawless principles." Opposition to an assembly was owing, it was argued, to the fears of "the placemen" that their corruption would be detected. "We are as much slaves here as they in Barbary."[19]

Lawrence prolonged the affair as long as possible. As late as November, 1757 he could still profess to believe that the Board of Trade was in sympathy with his point of view. Early in the following year, when Paris formally presented the petition of the Halifax freeholders, the Board would brook delay no longer. Instructions were at once issued for the calling of an assembly. Yet Paris and his clients made little impression on the Board. There was no sympathy with the more particular charges laid against the Governor and his officials, for Paris had no evidence to sustain them. Indiscreetly the merchants displayed their real motives by presenting a long schedule of accounts for the purpose of showing how much more cheaply contracts for the army and navy could be exectued by themselves than by "the favourites of government."[20]

There was no room left for manœuvre and Lawrence succumbed. On May 20 the council agreed upon a meeting of a general assembly for the following October. A modification in the earlier plan, depriving unsettled townships of representation, was adopted, the proposed assembly to contain a total of twenty members. The effect of this change in the mode of representation was to ensure that the representatives of Halifax, and in effect its merchants, would control the assembly. No matter what the scheme of representation might be, it would serve as a forum for the merchants of Halifax almost exclusively. When it finally met in the autumn, Lawrence was pleased to report that it gave him far less irritation than he had apprehended. In this year of 1758 the Governor's appearances in Halifax were but fleeting. Anticipating an important role in the projected military operations of the following year, he was moving about the province to ensure the consolidation of the triumph at Louisburg.

Lawrence was honest and efficient. It would be difficult to show that the merchants of Halifax, his opponents in the first constitutional struggle of British North America, were superior human types or that they singlemindedly were contending for "the rights of Englishmen." Yet, with the benefit of hindsight, posterity can decree that they were right and Lawrence was wrong. The result imparted to Nova Scotia the strenuous techniques of the town-meeting of New England, ensured a high degree of popular participation in government, and commenced the whole process of the elaboration of democratic government in the future Canada.

II

In the minds of Lawrence and the Board of Trade, the expulsion of the French from Nova Scotia was to be accompanied almost simultaneously by the introduction of large numbers of English-speaking settlers. No longer now would the British government encourage migration from the British Isles and the only source of population was New England, where there was land hunger owing to the erosion of many of the older agricultural areas. In 1755 efforts were made to persuade Winslow's soldiers to settle at Chignecto and consolidate control over the isthmus. New Englanders saw for themselves the rich marshlands that required no manures, dyked and cultivated by the Acadians for generations. They had gone with Monckton up the St John in 1758 when he had written glowingly of the country beyond the rugged bluffs at the mouth of the river. As peace approached, fear of the Indians and the limitations imposed by British imperial policy denied them access to the west beyond the Appalachian Mountains. The tenant farmers and the younger sons of New England were compelled to look northward to find free land. A fixed limit for westward settlement and a determination at London to keep British subjects on the coastline forced surplus population of all the colonies to look to the empty regions of Georgia and Nova Scotia.[21]

So long as the French peril remained, official efforts to promote the settlement of Nova Scotia could yield no results. It was not until January, 1759 that Lawrence issued his proclamation inviting New Englanders to come. By this time he could tell them, perhaps a little sardonically, that they would enjoy the same kind of government with which they were familiar at home, meaning that the calling of a general assembly had finally removed the basis for the charges that the province was groaning under martial law. Freedom of religion for all except Roman Catholics was another promise highly esteemed in New England. Though the migration was opposed by New England's capitalists and landlords, a movement of considerable proportions developed in 1760. The work of persuasion was accomplished by agents of the Nova Scotian government who spread the news from Boston, entered into agreements with associations of prospective settlers, and led their representatives to the province for inspection and survey of the Acadian lands. Free transport and small stocks of provisions were offered. Annapolis and Granville were settled from Massachusetts. From New London there sailed several shiploads of farmers from Connecticut and Rhode Island who established at Minas the townships of Horton, Cornwallis, Falmouth, and Newport. In 1761 settlers from Massachusetts founded Cumberland and Sackville townships on the isthmus. Troops patrolled the marshlands as these New England planters established themselves on Nova Scotian soil, for small bands of armed Acadians and Indians still roamed the woods.[22]

Not only farmers but fishermen also shared in this considerable exodus. New Englanders could now in complete safety take up permanent residence much nearer the great banks on which they had always depended for livelihood. A great increase in transient activity at Canso spread into the waters of the Gulf of St Lawrence, where the French had always been dominant, but the only fishing townships that took form were on the south shore of the peninsula: Yarmouth, Barrington, and Liverpool. A northern thrust of the agricultural movement worked its way into the St John Valley. There a party of settlers from Essex County in Massachusetts established themselves on the fertile intervale area to the south of the Nashwaak and Oromocto. Here were Acadians who had survived and remained despite the destruction of St Anne's, and here the Malecite Indians forbade English settlement to the north of this confluence of rivers. The British government had laid it down as a point of high policy that arable lands won from the French should be reserved for disbanded soldiers and sailors. Conscious of error, the Nova Scotian government employed the good offices of Joshua Mauger at London and the settlers were grateful when told that they would be allowed to remain. The community was named Maugerville.[23] Over one hundred and fifty miles from any centre of civilization, it was kept in touch with the outside world by the trading-post set up at the mouth of the river by the firm of Simonds, White, and Hazen from Newburyport in Massachusetts, which fell within the system of control over the commerce of the province established by Mauger.

About seven thousand New Englanders shared in this immigration to Nova Scotia. It took place in the last years of the war with France but did not gather momentum with the peace. It imparted to the province the character of a northern segment of New England and appeared as the logical completion of the process by which New Englanders had, for generations, come to regard Nova Scotia as their own.

This was in spite of the coming of other elements. Nova Scotia benefited by the introduction of several hundreds of Ulster Irish, one of the main sources of North America's growing population in the eighteenth century, most of whom transmigrated from Londonderry in New Hampshire and were settled about Truro and Onslow. A few, brought directly from Ireland, came to rest about the Lahave River. All of this came about in consequence of the work of Alexander McNutt, an Ulsterman who had encountered Lawrence while on garrison duty at Louisburg and unfolded vast plans for the colonization of Nova Scotia by Irishmen. Though he had wide contacts with North of Ireland people on both sides of the Atlantic, he had far from sufficient resources for putting his projects into execution. His overweening proposals that made the peopling of Nova Scotia only incidental to his own aggrandizement were halted by the British government in 1762 when it was realized that they were accelerating the depopulation of Ulster, already a cause for considerable alarm.[24] The advance-guard of the great immigration of Highland Scots to Nova Scotia did not arrive until 1773, when the *Hector* came to Pictou via Philadelphia. About the same time still another element in the population, farmers from Yorkshire, began to mingle with the New Englanders at Chignecto, brought there by Michael Francklin, the Lieutenant-Governor, who was attempting to establish himself as a great landlord.

The settling of marshy intervale, which was accompanied by a notable disinclination to clear wooded upland, was made the more diverse in pattern by the return of the Acadians, whose wanderings, in some cases, lasted for twenty years. Some had never left Nova Scotia, and their continued presence in the colony had been defended by General Amherst in 1761 when he had remonstrated strongly against the views of the Halifax authorities who wished to continue the deportations.[25] The Board of Trade, when all dangers of French invasions had passed, seconded Amherst by reprimanding Belcher for his attempted removal of Acadians to Boston in 1762 and by expressing the hope that they could become useful members of society in Nova Scotia.[26] Yet these unfortunate people, as they laboured on public works at Halifax or on the newly settled estates of the New Englanders on the Bay of Fundy, were still exposed to the dilemma they had faced all through their history. Choiseul sought to use the Acadians in strengthening the maritime power of France by persuading them to move to the French possessions of St Pierre and Miquelon and to the West Indies. Britain indignantly rejected a French demand that the Acadians be permitted to remove to French territory, insisting that they had been subjects of the Crown since 1713, denying that they were entitled to the same privileges as the Canadians under the Treaty of Paris.[27] The circulation among the Acadians of French agents who sought to move them to St Pierre was another evidence to the British government of France's desire for revenge. The policy dictated to Governor Montagu Wilmot in 1764 was that the Acadians should be settled in detached groups about the province and mingled with English-speaking settlers, if they took the oath of allegiance.[28]

Perhaps to a greater extent than at any time during the war, the Acadians were now moved by a spirit of French patriotism. Almost to a man they would acknowledge no master other than the King of France and, on Isle St Jean as well as on the peninsula, asked permission to leave the province.[29]

The Nova Scotian government had very little intention and certainly not the means of preventing them from doing so. In 1764 over six hundred left for the West Indies, where tropical disease accounted for many lives. Others followed. By 1766 very few remained. In this year, according to Sir Hugh Palliser, Governor of Newfoundland, Miquelon was full of Acadians.[30]

This movement very soon reversed itself. Those who had been seduced away by the requirements of French national policy decided to return and were joined by a great many of the deportees of 1755. By 1767 something like a general return to Acadia was taking place. Some, who had made their way to France and been sent back to St Pierre, found their lot a hard one. Fishing magnates from Jersey, of whom Jacques Robin was a conspicuous example, dressed them in French seamen's slop-clothing and brought them to their stations on the Nova Scotian coast where their skill and experience were put to good use.[31] Canso and Isle Madame drew large numbers. But the largest proportion made its way to the Bay of Chaleur and settled about Caraquet, where the Robin firm kept them employed. Here was an area really beyond the effective range of the Nova Scotian government. George Walker, proprietor of a fishing station and sole justice of the peace all the way from Chaleur to Bay Verte, requested in 1769 a separate governmental establishment for this vast and lonely region. Along the entire coast there were only twenty British families and the interior, he declared, was really under the control of the Indians who did precisely what the French told them to do. An illicit trade was being carried on with St Pierre and, among people of both races, lawlessness prevailed everywhere.[32]

At the same time Stephen Landry, having several times been refused the privilege, led a large number of the deportees of 1755 from Pennsylvania to the intervale land of the Petitcodiac at Memramcook. The vacant spaces of Nova Scotia were now going a-begging for settlers and the administration at Halifax was willing to welcome industrious workers and farmers from any source whatever. Lieutenant-Governor Michael Francklin gave strong assurances to the British government that the Acadians could not be harmful, even though their remarkable return took place at a time when the barren rock of St Pierre was jealously scrutinized as the point from which France might attempt to reassert her former role in North America. In 1768, according to Francklin, large numbers of Acadians on the peninsula were accepting the oath of allegiance.

III

By the Proclamation of 1763 the St Croix was taken as the western boundary of the greatly enlarged Nova Scotia that came into existence with the peace treaty. The provincial government's claims to what the French had always considered to be part of Acadia, the country between the St Croix and the Penobscot, were sacrificed by the Board of Trade to the expansionism of Massachusetts. Resentment in the Bay Colony to the wide extent of Quebec, as defined by the Proclamation, was dreaded in London; and it was hoped that this feeling would be mollified by the cession to her of the entire seaboard up to the St Croix.[33] The assumption that a line of hills divided the valleys of the St Croix and the St John from that of the St Lawrence provided the basis for the much-to-be-debated problem of the northwestern angle of Nova Scotia.

Included within the province were the two islands of Cape Breton and St Jean, in English St John. During the war, officers of the army and navy had made a careful inspection of both, and a multitude of good opinions on their potentialities had reached official circles in London. According to the Board of Trade they were the most important acquisitions that the Treaty of Paris had brought to the Crown.[34] Both were protected against immediate settlement by special arrangements. The granting of land was strictly forbidden but, for purposes of developing the fishery, temporary licences of occupation were allowed.[35] Careful surveys, ordered by the Board, were carried out by Captain Samuel Holland in 1765, and the two islands were each divided into lots of twenty thousand acres.

So great was the interest aroused in London that the nobility and gentry of Britain were led to attempt a revival of the proprietorial system of colonization that had been used in the seventeenth century. The idea that colonial society was developing in a manner harmful to the mother country was well fixed in the official mind and John, Earl of Egmont, produced a proposal for the restoration of true principles. What the colonies needed to maintain the constitutional connection with Britain was a landed aristocracy. To supply the gentry so necessary to the royal prerogative in the new dominions, Egmont asked for a grant of the whole of St John's, over which he should rule as Lord High Paramount. He proposed to divide the lands among such notabilities as Sir Charles Saunders, Sir George Rodney, and Admiral Durell. The boldness of the proposal was accentuated by the request for half of the island of Dominica and permission to move several thousand negro slaves northward to work the plantation of St John's.[36] The urge to establish a new feudalism in the region was further exemplified by the Duke of Richmond's petition for the whole island of Cape Breton.[37]

The Board of Trade was more interested in the development of industry than in "Connection, Order, Gradation and Subordination," and gave short shrift to the petitioners, though it did urge the nobility to take an interest in the settlement of the two islands. It was held that each man in America should hold his land directly from the Crown, but the Board's solution for

St John's was not designed to meet with popular approval in the colonies. In 1767 a group of highly favoured persons who deserved well of the Crown were permitted to ballot for sixty-four of its sixty-seven lots. Reflecting Lord Bute's great influence in the Court, many of them were Scots.

In the following year the new proprietors, expressing great confidence in the future of St John's, petitioned that a separate government should be established there. Michael Francklin, then in charge at Halifax, was accordingly instructed to ensure the preservation of order among the few fishermen along the shores, some recent arrivals from England and the remnant of the Acadians who, neglecting agriculture, lived by accepting employment from transient fishermen. Misinterpreting his instructions, perhaps deliberately, Francklin expended the entire contingency fund of Nova Scotia in establishing the framework of a sub-government and in the initiation of public works. Charlottetown, the capital of the island, was laid out by Charles Morris on a gently rising slope above Hillsborough Bay. A small garrison of troops, miserably clad, was housed at Fort Amherst, constructed on the remains of the French military establishment at Port la Joye. On the whole island in 1768 there were but 271 inhabitants, 68 English, 203 French.[38] The only transient fishing-station of consequence was at St Peter's Bay, where the London firm of Mills and Cathcart conducted operations. Yet, because of the assurances of the proprietors that the quitrents they would pay would provide the entire cost of a provincial establishment, St John's was separated from Nova Scotia in 1769.

The first governor was Captain Walter Patterson who arrived in October, 1770. About one hundred and twenty families had just reached the island from Scotland but they were no harbinger of a great immigration. The only other important movement into the colony in the next two years was that of the Glenaladale Macdonalds who, led by their chieftain, Captain John, settled his estate of Lot 36 at the head of the Hillsborough River. This was the first of the mass movement of Highland Scots into the Atlantic Provinces. Captain Macdonald was one of the first of Scottish landlords to realize the commercial returns from the conversion of his native glens into sheep-runs. Alleged persecution of Catholics by Protestant landlords was another factor explaining the great migration that was beginning. Tenants were compelled to forswear communication with their priests or face eviction.[39] These people were not sophisticated, but they quickly learned to understand the disadvantages of farming on St John's Island. Many of them deserted Captain Macdonald's estate and headed for Nova Scotia, where free land could be had on easy terms.

It soon became apparent that the great majority of the British proprietors had no intention of honouring the conditions of their grants either by bringing settlers to the island or by paying quitrents. In the first ten years of the new governmental establishment, less than twenty of the sixy-four lots were settled. Since there was no payment of quitrents, the officers of government served without salaries. Their distress was from time to time alleviated by drawing on capital sums provided by the British government for the construction of public buildings and churches.

Privations attended the first settlements. To arrive on the island late in the year without large stocks of provisions was tantamount to perishing of starvation. The miserable death of John Duport, the first Chief Justice, has been ascribed partly to this cause. Though there were but a thousand inhabitants Patterson put the royal instructions into effect in 1773 by calling a general assembly. Consisting of eighteen members who represented the island at large and who held their first session in a tavern, it was designated "a damned queer parliament."[40] Not surprisingly, its first important legislation was an attempt to raise revenue by escheating the lands of proprietors who failed to pay the quitrent.

The remarkable experiment on St John's Island was, for the British government, a method of developing a new colony without drawing on its own revenues. Cape Breton was made the subject of no experiment and its progress approximated that of St John's. Contrary to first intentions several companies of troops were maintained at the demolished fortifications of Louisburg. This assured the presence there of a motley community of rum-sellers and peddlers who lived from the soldiers' pay. New England fishermen appeared and disappeared according to their convenience. In 1765 the whole island was organized as the County of Breton and two representatives were sent to Halifax as members of the general assembly, only to be expelled from that body on the highly proper grounds that there were no freeholders on the island. This produced a miniature constitutional conflict, the New England fishermen arguing that they were not liable to the payment of Nova Scotian duties on spirituous liquors since they were not represented in government. As a community Louisburg faded away in 1768 when the troops sailed to Boston. It became a hamlet of deserted dwellings, mostly those which had belonged to the French and been spared in the demolition.

Cape Breton was neglected largely because of its riches. The French had taken much coal from the bituminous outcroppings which were to be found almost everywhere in the vicinity of Louisburg. British troops in garrison extracted what they required for their purposes. Following the peace, the Board of Trade was besieged by petitions for mining concessions. Favourites of the government at Halifax managed to secure temporary licences, to their considerable profit. But the policy of the British government forbade any large and general exploitation, for the coal of Cape Breton could furnish the mainland colonies with the means of manufacturing iron and other goods that could compete with the manufactured produce of the mother country. On general principles Britain locked up not only the coal mines but also the forests of the island that were, in 1774, reserved for the uses of the Royal Navy.[41]

IV

Until the years of the American Revolution, which saw the reappearance of British war expenditure on a grand scale, Nova Scotia languished. As the Seven Years' War ended and as the parliamentary grant was cut in 1762 to something less than £6,000, Halifax dwindled to a peacetime economy of petty commerce. Slow growth characterized the New England settlements of the Bay of Fundy. Virtually all trade was carried on by barter. Credit was strained as the merchants of Halifax extended their coils into the "back parts," keeping open accounts and placing the settlers in their debt, setting the prices for the goods they supplied and the crops they took in exchange. Only the shrewdest and toughest of merchants could survive the scrabbling competition that this kind of business entailed. A vast network of debt permeated the entire structure of commercial enterprise. Imports greatly exceeded exports so that specie and bills on London, any solid assets, were difficult to acquire. The new sedentary fishery, established along the south shore from Yarmouth to Canso, proved to be disappointing. New Englanders came to Nova Scotia to avoid the necessity of the long voyage home for curing and drying; their cargoes sometimes "turned to maggots" when they opened their hatches in New England ports. Yet even in Nova Scotia the New Englanders could not turn out so fine a product for Mediterranean markets as the British Newfoundlanders and Channel Islanders. Their schooners could not perform as efficiently as the off-shore fisheries of Cape Breton. New England itself, in the late years of the eighteenth century, could do better by trade than in the fishery.[42] A little sawn lumber was occasionally produced at the outports for sale abroad, but the total production of commodities of all kinds enabled the people to import only scanty quantities of British manufactured goods.

Politics hinged on this imbalance of trade and the measures proposed to inject some driving force into an economy that could not be made to grow. Successive governors and administrators tried in vain to persuade the British government to spend money as in the halcyon days of the war. Failing to obtain cash from the outside, the merchants of Halifax, who were the voice of Nova Scotia and held nearly all the seats in the Assembly, desperately availed themselves of all the expedients to increase industry familiar in colonies facing the dilemma of debt. They offered bounties to fishermen and agricultural producers. Often, when the treasury was empty, they bought up bounty certificates at high discounts and eventually realized large profits themselves. When the Debtors' Protection Act, passed in 1750 to attract settlers to Halifax, was renewed in 1760, many entrepreneurs of dubious character remained to share in the slim rewards of trade. The old tricks of establishing land banks and loan offices, of issuing paper currency on the credit of the province, came up against the hard rock of British opposition. To enable the government to function, the only method was the acceptance of debt. To honour demands against the public services this became necessary in 1762 and, over the next three years, notes against the treasury amounted to £16,000.

Following the death of Lawrence in 1760 the local rivalries of Halifax became crystallized into one recognizable interest. This was the great ascendancy of Joshua Mauger who, fortified by his great wealth, became Member of Parliament for Poole and strongly entrenched in the counsels of the British government, particularly those of John Pownall, secretary to the Board of Trade. As Lord William Campbell later said of his agent, Michael Francklin, his word became law.[43] It was Mauger who advanced credit to members of the mercantile ring at Halifax, who by private dealings acquired such a control over public deliberation that he could dictate policy. To such an extent was the trading fraternity beneath his sway that it was commonly asserted he possessed a monopoly over the commerce of the province. William Cawthorn, a merchant of London, declared that he was driven from the province by Mauger's associates out of fear of the competition that he would bring them.[44] Mauger regarded Nova Scotia as his own preserve. His recommendations for filling vacancies on the council were accepted by the Board of Trade. As a surety of control he acquired a large proportion of the securities written against the credit of the province.

Mauger's immense influence was first demonstrated in a contest with Belcher, the Chief Justice, who had acquired the additional office of Lieutenant-Governor in 1760. This vain and pompous official showed great disdain from his judicial bench for traders and he made no attempt in 1762 to conceal his delight when the reduction of the parliamentary grant whittled away the opportunities of scrambling for public money. When his legal purism led him to refuse assent to a renewal of the Debtors' Protection Act as "loose and unguarded against frauds and perjuries," he was faced with such a degree of absenteeism in the general assembly that no public business could be accomplished.[45] Mauger, acting as agent for the people of the province in London, presented a petition to the Board of Trade praying that he should be removed from office as "unacquainted and unskilled in the art of government.[46]

Discomfiture came to Belcher on June 20, 1763, when Michael Francklin, Mauger's kinsman and chief lieutenant in the province, wrote a letter to

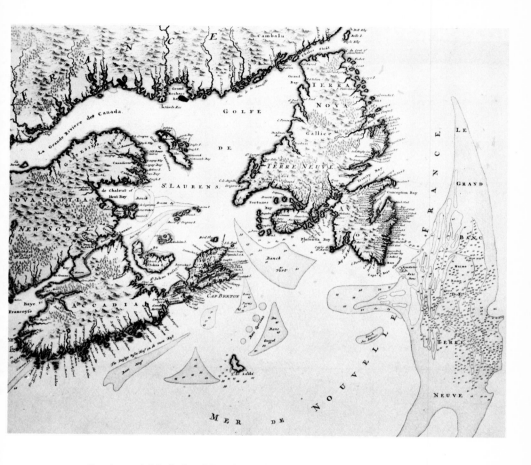

Portion of Nicholas Visscher's Map of North America, late
Seventeenth Century

"A Prospect of Annapolis Royal in Nova Scotia 1751" by Thomas
Chamberlain after J. H. Bastides

The Siege of Louisburg, 1758 (Webster Collection)

The Scene of Strife on the Isthmus of Chignecto, Beauséjour on the left, Fort Lawrence on the right (Webster Collection)

The Harbour of Saint John about 1770 (Collection Chief Justice Furlong)

"Charlotte-Town on the Island of St John's 1778" by C. Randle

Cod Fishing in Newfoundland, from Moll's Map of North America

Grand Pré, Nova Scotia

Sydney in 1785. Frame house on extreme right is that of Governor Des Barres (Webster Collection)

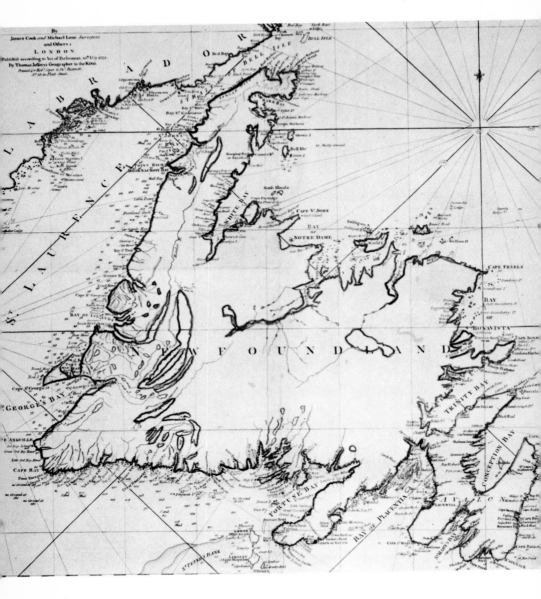

Cook's Map of Newfoundland, 1776 (Courtesy, Memorial University, Newfoundland)

the Assembly announcing that his master had procured sanction for a renewal of the Debtors' Protection Act, that approval of the Board of Trade had been given to other bills to which Belcher had refused assent, and that a very liberal proclamation of Belcher's to the Indians, by which he had given them virtual ownership of the eastern end of the peninsula, had been annulled. In council Belcher blustered a contradiction to this humiliating intelligence. But his humiliation had only begun. A few weeks later his commission as Lieutenant-Governor was revoked and the instructions to the new Governor, Montagu Wilmot, ordered that no chief justice should ever again be raised to executive authority. As if this were not enough, the man who eventually succeeded him as Lieutenant-Governor was Francklin, who had led the agitation against him and brought ruin to his aspirations to the highest office in the province. Commerce triumphed over the legal profession, one of the interesting facets of the affair being that Belcher's promissory notes had found their way into Mauger's hands. Governor Wilmot was a man of no force, and Francklin, sheltered beneath his powerful protector, was the moving influence in Nova Scotia. In later years it was commonly averred by unfriendly critics that he had purchased the high office of the lieutenant-governorship.

By procuring the dismissal of a lieutenant-governor and changing the Board's opinion on the merits of the Debtors' Protection Act, Mauger showed that he was the master of Nova Scotia's government as well as of her commerce. Yet this was but the first of several occasions on which he was to show that he and his well-disciplined Halifax connection could restrain the impetuosities of keepers of the royal prerogative. Lord William Campbell, who arrived as Governor in 1766, could perceive in the all-engrossing activities of the erstwhile smuggler and rum-seller a principal cause of Nova Scotia's failure to progress. The provincial revenue was at a miserably low level, and was inadequate to meet the costs of the roads and bridges that were so desperately needed. It was derived almost exclusively from duties on rum and other imported spirituous liquors. But five-sixths of the rum consumed in the province was produced by two distilleries owned by Mauger at Halifax. They were very adequately protected against outside competition by the tariff impost of five pence per gallon. The consequence was that very little rum was legally imported to the province so that the gross sum realized by the duties was minute.

Arguing the necessity of promoting trade with the West Indies by increasing the volume of imported rum, thereby increasing the revenue, Campbell persuaded the legislature in 1767 to reduce the tariff tax from five pence to three pence. As he saw it, the monopoly enjoyed by the local distillers would suffer but the province would benefit immeasurably. The lobby in London reacted swiftly. Mauger, seconded by Brook Watson and half a dozen others, all holders of provincial securities who reasoned that only the high duties on rum protected their investments, memorialized the Board. To his consternation, Campbell had to cross the ocean to defend the lowering of the duties and was informed that his point of view was "contrary to all true policy."[47] The tariff was raised to its former level and Mauger's monopoly continued to enjoy the principal profits of an economy that was enduring lean years.

Though easy-going and in poor health, Campbell continued to wrestle with the problem of how to accelerate the slow pace of provincial development. His agitation for a tax on land resulted in a law that would indiscriminately tax both resident and absentee proprietors. Whether or not a revenue should be raised from absentee owners became a leading issue in politics and Campbell was on the side of the absentees. Behind the scenes at London, Mauger and his friends continued to snipe at Campbell's notions of how to govern Nova Scotia. When he left in 1773 for the milder climate of the Carolinas he was happy and so were his enemies. His departure was regarded by the Halifax clique as another victory, another evidence of the superior interest they could exert at the Board of Trade.

Such a group of men could not fail to be interested in the possibilities of speculation in land, a form of contagion in the older colonies where the western frontier always offered hopeful vistas. The very great favours of the British government, however, were reserved for outsiders, especially in the years following the peace when eminent soldiers and sailors deserved well of the public. In 1765 practically the whole littoral of the lower St John was granted away to a group of official persons that included Thomas Hutchinson, General Frederick Haldimand, Sir William Johnson, General Thomas Gage, and Charles Morris, the Surveyor General at Halifax.[48] Alexander McNutt, promising a great deal to a credulous Board of Trade, received grants totalling fifteen thousand acres and rights to occupy hundreds of thousands more.[49] Knowing the true worth of lands without settlers, the men at Halifax were more modest and businesslike. Windsor, created a township in 1764 from the old Acadian lands of Pisiquid, was the principal scene of their activities. Here the provincial councillors and other select members of the merchant gentry acquired grants of up to seven thousand acres. Containing the largest block of arable land near Halifax, it became a country seat for the provincial aristocracy. But it was an aristocracy plagued by poverty and debt. Michael Francklin made the understandable mistake by overextending himself by the acquisition of land, trying strenuously to honour the conditions of his grant at River Hébert, "Francklin Manor." The whole province, it was said, was in debt to Francklin, and Francklin, land poor, was in debt to Mauger.[50]

Through this rather dreary testing time of the new Nova Scotia, the New England settlers, primarily occupied with the toil of establishing themselves in a new country, failed to impart to local government and organization the democratic traditions they had brought with them. Centralization of control over local affairs became a fixed idea in the years when the Halifax merchants gained their victory over Lawrence and, in the years following, when Francklin won his ascendancy. In the first year of the general assembly, 1758, incorporation of the town of Halifax was firmly refused.[51] Lawrence's proclamation of 1759 promised to the New England immigrants the same liberties as at home. But on their arrival they discovered that, although there was a township organization, they could not put to work the familiar apparatus of the election of town officials. Spirited protests came to Halifax and there were rumblings of the old complaint that Nova Scotia was a province where government was not free. The fishermen of Liverpool declared that they were deprived of "the right and authority invested in ourselves" to choose their local officers.[52] In 1765 the legislature enacted that town clerks, constables, fence viewers, pound keepers might be nominated by grand juries of the counties but that appointments should be made by the Courts of Quarter Sessions whose magistrates were nominees of the provincial government. This was the barest of concessions to the democratic aspirations of the New Englanders. In practice it meant that the merchants of Halifax, overwhelmingly powerful in the House of Assembly and in the council, possessed ultimate control over the public life of the townships.[53]

To hold local government within the leading-strings of the provincial administration was in keeping not only with the practical interests of mercantile Halifax but with the widely admired example of English justices of the peace – with Virginian precedent rather than with the less respectable ways of life in Massachusetts. From the beginning the provincial capital showed a clear determination to assert domination over all phases of local development. This centralization of authority induced in the people the invariable tendency to look to Halifax for remedies for all their ills.

It was only in Halifax that men possessing the crafts and guiles of politics, the experience of the legislative process and of administrative techniques, were to be found. The earlier governors quickly discovered that it was useless to attempt making their councils more representative. Nominees from the outports seldom showed the necessary esteem for their appointments by appearing at council sessions. The Assembly, too, was compelled to depend on Halifax for the making of a quorum. Rural constituencies often simplified their problem by electing residents of Halifax as members. It was only on rare occasions that a rural offensive against the predominance of Halifax on the floor of the Assembly could be organized. Halifax abounded with lawyers whose daily routine compelled a close surveillance of the work of government. In the countryside they developed associations and interests that could readily project them into the House of Assembly. The merchants of the provincial capital, warily watching the political scene from a point of vantage, understanding the close relationship between politics and trade, were quick to learn the art of turning government to their own purposes.

V

In comparison with Nova Scotia's problems, Newfoundland's were still elementary. Sloping from north to south and from west to east, she turned her back upon the continent and remained aloof from the main streams of colonial life. Even after Halifax became a port of consequence, it was possible to obtain only one or two conveyances each season for Newfoundland. When the colonies of the continent were beginning to examine their relations with the mother country, there was still no official recognition of the fact that a colony existed on Newfoundland at all. The Western Adventurers held sway as before in the counsels of the British government; and still, in the villages of Devon, the great events of the year were reckoned by the Church of England calendar: "Jan! the Parson be in Proverbs, the Newfunlan men will soon be a-coming whome."[54] Document after document that reached the Board of Trade at London referred to the island as "a desolate land," unfit for human habitation, and, in the years following, the British government held to the hard line that the fishery was "a home industry," something like an extension of the coasting trade of the British Isles. "The free fishery" was to be a nursery of seamen, but Newfoundland was not to be a residence for them.

The presence of several thousand planters on the island was a grand contradiction to all the legislation that pertained to Newfoundland and, as in 1728, contradictory measures had to be taken to ensure some kind of order. Colony or not, the permanent residents discovered in 1764 that the limitations of the Laws of Trade and Navigation applied to their community and, to the great distaste of the merchants, a customs establishment appeared at St John's. This was followed in 1765 by a court of vice-admiralty. Colonial status was denied but colonial legislation was enforced, imperfectly as elsewhere.

Captain Hugh Palliser, who arrived as Governor in 1764 and remained on the station for the next four years, was resolved to remove the contradiction. Traditionalist in habit of thought, rigorous in his methods, he was determined to maintain Newfoundland as an instrument for the purposes of the Royal Navy. Systematically his patrols confined the French to their now reduced version of the Petit Nord, but he was equally insistent that the British should respect French rights. The rapid growth of the settled population abruptly halted as he instituted a policy of deportation. Unproductive and wastrel members of the illegal community, hangers-on who had arrived as "passengers" on the sack ships, men who had dissipated their earnings on rum and could not pay the costs of the voyage home, were forcibly removed to the number of something like five thousand. In 1767 he reported that, by the exercise of his strenuous discipline, the number of English and Irish seamen returned in the autumn was double what it had been for sixty years past.[55]

Landlords of fishing-rooms at St John's and of the other desirable stations along the coastline, holding their properties without the surety of legal records, were affronted when Palliser challenged their possession. Those who could boast unbroken occupation since 1685 could, by the statute of 1699, protest on legal grounds, but in 1772 the Privy Council ruled that "the Governors of Newfoundland had no authority whatever to make grants of any part of the Island of Newfoundland."[56] So zealous was the Governor in the enforcement of the Act of 1699 that he seized the property of the seal fishermen on Labrador. This was mostly in the hands of French Canadians and had been in their possession long before 1763. When they appealed to London, the Board of Trade decided that private property could be tolerated in Labrador though not in Newfoundland. The north shore of the Gulf of St Lawrence as far as the river St John was therefore reannexed to Quebec in 1774 and private property continued to flourish.

In 1768, Palliser's last year on the Newfoundland station, the fishery's production was worth £600,000. Twenty thousand men were employed, of whom twelve thousand returned to Britain, Ireland, and Jersey at the end of the season.[57] Here was clear proof of the value of the fishery to Britain and of the need for a rigid enforcement of the traditional policy, and Palliser was the implacable enemy of the colonization of Newfoundland for the rest of his life. Lord North's government was highly receptive to his fixed, mercantilistic point of view, and the Act of Parliament of 1775, which reaffirmed the domination of the Western Adventurers, is remembered as Palliser's Act. More than anything else, it attempted to put an end to colonization by penalizing the masters of ships who failed to bring back to Britain the seamen they had conveyed to Newfoundland. By offering bounties it strove to give fresh spur to the West Countrymen and to reverse the trend of the eighteenth century by which "the free fishery," the source of man power for the navy, had been in decline. Like the Quebec Act of the previous year, it angered the American colonists by denying them access to the trade of Newfoundland. Palliser's Act comprehended the complete suffocation of the struggling settlements of the winter population. They had no voice at London, but their feeling was expressed years later by William Carson when he wrote that the imperial policy was "to keep the

Island of Newfoundland a barren waste, to exterminate the inhabitants, to annihilate property, and to make sailors by preventing population."[58]

Palliser's Act represented the last official endeavour of a strenuous kind to resolve the great contradiction of Newfoundland's history, to write finis to the recurrent theme of conflict between "the free fishery" and the colony. Whatever determination the British government might have shown to execute its provisions literally could not be applied because of the outbreak of the War of the American Revolution. Again, war was to be the salvation of the colony. In 1757, when the French fishery of the Petit Nord had been obliterated, the colonists and by-boatmen had rapidly moved north of Bonavista to take advantage of the good locations there. During this earlier war, the peril of capture by French privateers had brought operations from the West Country to a virtual standstill. Small capitalists, operating off-shore, were able to drive absentee shipowners from the inshore fisheries to the banks. Shore fishermen could commence operations much earlier in the season, could remain at their vocation long after the West Countrymen had sailed for home. While landlordism acquired deeper roots in spite of the law and the operations of trade became more distinct from those of the fishery, while the whale and seal fisheries prospered and the natural process of the division of labour became more firmly established, the technical disadvantages of conducting the Newfoundland fishery from an overseas base became more manifest. Palliser's figures of 1764 showed the new degree of permanence achieved by the colony during the Seven Years' War. Population had increased by three and one-half times the figures of 1751. Of the sixteen thousand people, 8 per cent were classified as masters, 56 per cent as menservants, 5 per cent as women-servants.[59] There were thousands of recent arrivals, new Newfoundlanders who had come to stay in spite of the disciplinary measures of Captain Palliser and the course of imperial legislation.

They composed communities almost anarchic. There were no courts authorized to deal with civil disputes. Courts of Oyer at Terminer, set up by the Governor in 1750 to deal with criminal cases, found their legality called in question. There were few magistrates and none dared offend the powerful monied interests or face the majesty of the fishing-admirals whose authority, stemming from the venerated Western charters, was so highly esteemed among the transients from overseas. Religious strife was becoming normal. As early as 1750 Irish outnumbered English in St John's. The Irish were not always the persecuted. At Harbour Grace, where they were in the great majority, Protestants on occasions were not permitted to bury their dead without fear of assault; and defiance was bidden to the English and Jersey men in the harbour by the appearance of Irish colours on the ensign staffs of vessels.[60]

The irresponsible conduct of many of the shipowners of England in leaving men behind them for the winter was in part responsible for the dilemma of the British government and even in these quarters there was doubt as to what the policy should be. In 1763, after the Board of Trade declared that the Act of 1699 was "the most loose and imperfect that could have been framed" and was a disgrace to the statute books, it asked, in a questionnaire to British merchants, whether or not "a complete and perfect form of civil government was required in Newfoundland." Devon and Dorset, adhering to traditional rigidity, replied in the negative, but Belfast, Waterford, and Glasgow gave an affirmative view. George Milner, a merchant of Poole, produced a dissenting report in favour of organized government because Newfoundland was the scene of "the most lawless rapine, oppression and injustice, dependent on power and numbers only."[61] Palliser's Act, designed to perpetuate the philosophy of keeping government at the indispensable minimum level of the naval commander and the fishing-admirals, was passed in spite of a great deal of humanitarian scruple that wanted Newfoundland to become something more than a "wild west" for the Western Adventurers.

Newfoundland's horizons widened in Palliser's time. He extended protection to the Indians of the Labrador coast, restraining the habitual efforts, not only of his own people but of the French and New Englanders as well, to exterminate them. Captain James Cook surveyed and mapped the really unknown regions of the northeastern and western coasts, and attempted to mark the half-fabulous Pointe Riche, the limit of French treaty rights, just as mysterious to the fishermen as to the diplomats who had written the Treaty of Utrecht. In 1768 the Cartwright brothers, Lieutenant John and Captain George, ascended the Exploits River and became the first white men to see Red Indian Lake. They found whole stretches of river front impounded by fences for the taking of deer. But they could not come upon the elusive Beothuk Indians, who had not really been seen by white men since John Guy had deliberated with them in Trinity Bay early in the seventeenth century. As the Beothuks withdrew and perished, the interior of Newfoundland opened up to the colonists who had so long turned their backs upon it.

CHAPTER 4

Revolution and Reorganization
1775-1785

There is a simple explanation for the failure of Newfoundland and Nova Scotia to participate in the movement of the 1760's that led to the American Revolution. Both were dependent on Great Britain to an infinitely greater degree than any of those colonies that finally accepted the leadership of the Congress at Philadelphia. Officially Newfoundland was not a colony at all. Nova Scotia was not financially self-supporting and her trade was chiefly in British hands. Newfoundland had no experience of democratic action and Nova Scotia had just begun to acquire it. In both, public opinion was largely inarticulate because the interest of those who made it compelled them to shelter beneath the wing of Britain. This simple explanation acquired complexity with the march of events. Had Britain proved lamentably weak, the two communities would have been but as straws in the wind. But since sea power converted this entire region of the North Atlantic into something like a fortress for the Crown, their status as British colonies was to remain unchanged. The Americans impinged on the stability and security of the region, but, after the initial impact of the Revolution, there was little doubt that these colonies would continue within the imperial fold.

In Newfoundland the merchants had reason to grumble as the imperial customs establishment imposed new taxes on trade. But there could be no question of revolt or even of significant protest. Newfoundland was oriented towards the Mediterranean and West Indies, along the lanes of British sea power. Her harbours were annually visited by ten thousand British fishermen, escorted by cruisers of the Royal Navy. She had nothing in common with the continental colonies. New Englanders competed, perhaps too successfully, rather than co-operated in trade; and, though the island had not developed in accordance with imperial precept, it was wedded to British mercantilism. One of the first acts of the Continental Congress, the embargo on trade with British territory, caused suffering in Newfoundland, for the fishery was dependent on New England for breadstuffs, but the consequence was that her ties to the mother country were tightened more firmly.

Nova Scotia was a much more likely candidate for the role of fourteenth insurgent colony. Slight disturbances in Halifax attended the imposition of the Stamp Act in 1765. A town meeting of doubtful authority was convened at Liverpool. Officials and merchants scrambled for confirmation of land grants and payment of fees before the Act, with its greatly increased charges, should go into effect. Not in entire truth, Governor Wilmot reported that there was a complete absence of opposition and obstruction. The reputation for invidious submission gained by the colony in Massachusetts was belied by a report in the Boston Post of October 28 which told of the erection of a gallows on Citadel Hill that bore the effigy of a Stampman. "The friends of liberty" in Nova Scotia, it declared, wanted the patriots of other colonies to understand that only their dependent situation hindered open protest.[1] The settlers from New England, and this meant the majority, wrote Archibald Hinshelwood, the provincial collector of the stamp duties, were indignant with him because he had accepted the office.[2] Strong opposition there was but Nova Scotians were not prepared to fight for a principle. When Mr Speaker Nesbitt received in 1768 the invitation of the Massachusetts House of Assembly to join the other colonies in a united protest, the letter, instead of being presented to the legislature, was passed over the water to London.

Circumstances could easily tip an uneasy balance in Nova Scotia and it seemed quite possible at the opening of the Revolutionary War that a purely local situation might impel the province to adopt a profession of sympathy for the Continental Congress. The British government had enough trouble on its hands without allowing constitutional griefs to appear in still another colony, but its governor at Halifax had decided that Nova Scotia had for years been ruled by a conspiracy of corrupt officials whose villainies must at last be detected and punished. Major Francis Legge was cousin to the Earl of Dartmouth, Secretary of State in Lord North's cabinet. When he arrived in 1773 he at once demanded reform in financial administration, insisting that the cause of debt must be sought out and remedied, and that taxation to remove debt must be introduced. Again the conflict on taxation of absentee landowners arose, but Legge most deeply irritated the Halifax community by social ostracism and unconcealed dislike. Religious susceptibilities were offended by a cynical attitude to the Church. His effrontery to the old and revered rector of St Paul's, Breynton, who, incidentally, was a minor speculator in lands and provincial securities, quickly scandalized a host of enemies.[3] A large proportion of the quitrents had been due for collection in 1772 but the government had done nothing. Legge threw the entire province into dismay by drawing up an elaborate scheme for payment, observing in a somewhat sinister fashion that he "would soon be able to distinguish the grantees who could pay and which could not."[4]

The contest in the making became one of personalities rather than of constitutional principles as Legge commenced an investigation into the public debt. For this the Assembly gave him the excuse he needed. "A retrospection into former abuses might excite a degree of resentment in this House against the individuals who were the cause of bringing these misfortunes upon us."[5] Suddenly a committee of council and assembly, chiefly composed of newcomers who were in sympathy with Legge's animus against the entrenched Halifax clique, commenced to probe into the provincial accounts, going as far back as 1758. As vouchers were demanded the good repute of almost all officers of government was called in question. Legge could perceive in their common reluctance to co-operate the existence of a cabal determined to thwart his efforts for the financial rehabilitation of the province. Behind the cabal was the Lieutenant-Governor, Michael Francklin, of whose great personal influence he was intensely jealous.

The Provincial Treasurer, Benjamin Green, had died two years earlier and been succeeded by his son of the same name. When Legge's committee demanded the public accounts there came the rather astonishing reply that neither the new treasurer nor his widowed mother knew their place of deposit. Despite this evasion, supported by Francklin and most of the officials, the committee in May, 1775 presented a report that showed government officials to be in arrears by eleven thousand pounds. But the committee's findings implicated others beside the official coterie. It proposed that all the loans of provisions, made during the settlements of many years earlier, should be honoured by payment. In this way most of the people of the province, members of the House of Assembly included, were adversely affected. Legge regarded this document as a triumph and appointed one of his newly arrived favourites, James Burrows, to the office of Inspector General of Accounts.

While civil war was breaking out in the British Empire, Legge convened a special court of exchequer. John Newton, one of the customs collectors and a member of council, admitted arrears and paid them. But Jonathan Binney, Newton's brother-in-law and a leading merchant, who in recent years had held the office of chief magistrate and collector of the revenue at Canso, denied charges of withholding sums for his private purposes. A special jury was empanelled and the trial took place before one of the assistant judges, Charles Morris, the sole member of council supporting the prosecution and one of the committee who had investigated the accounts. While the select jury was deciding the guilt of Binney who, with his wife and children, had been thrown into prison, the triumphant governor attended court and caused refreshments to be served to himself and his friends.

These rigorous proceedings closed the ranks of officialdom. Angered by the requirement that he go on circuit, the aged Chief Justice Belcher urged softer measures. The kindly Richard Bulkely, Provincial Secretary since 1749, offended by complaints of incompetence, joined hands with Francklin and John Butler, the agents of Mauger, to implore restraint. In Legge's view the opposition was that of "an enraged party who conjointly for many years have been making spoil of the public revenue."[6] He had little reason to look forward to the meeting of the legislature in 1775. There the influence of William Nesbitt, the Speaker of the House and Attorney General, grew steadily both in debate and in committee. The petition of the imprisoned Binney drew a bill for his relief, not pleading his innocence or denying his guilt, but providing that he make good his defalcations by instalments. The great concern of the representatives of the people became the suppression of any further proceedings of the audit. The Assembly preferred to do its own audit, admitted the shortcomings of officials of government, but exonerated them either in whole or in part.

By the end of the legislative session the struggle against Legge became a scarcely concealed effort to weaken the power of the Crown. The Assembly passed bills to enable the provincial treasurer to make and receive payments without accounting to the governor, to make assemblies triennial, and to authorize the emission of twenty thousand pounds in paper currency. Behind the Assembly was Francklin, the leader of "the inveterate party" who promised "that the debtors should be exculpated and every man's pocket filled with money."[7] Behind Francklin was Mauger, who worked at London for the release of Binney. There the Secretary of State had many more difficult affairs to deal with in 1775. He had commended Legge's energy for proceeding against defaulters but had refused to accede to his request for the dismissal of five councillors.[8] Not until the end of the year, when the British government became aware of the dangers of invasion to Nova Scotia, did the full implications of Legge's energetic actions become visible. Then it was seen that "matters of the most trivial moment respecting merely the domestic economy of the province" had imperilled its security.[9]

At the opening of 1776 the British government ordered the passing of the Binney Act, a clear signal that there would be no more persecution of Halifax officialdom. To deliver the final blows that would ensure the fall of the governor, Francklin left his estate at Windsor for Halifax and organized a battery of petitions seeking his removal. According to his enemies, Legge was forcing the province into the camp of disloyalty.[10] This activity produced prompt results. Another representative of the Crown in Nova Scotia, the third, had been trapped in the coils of Mauger's mystifying connections. Legge was given thirty days to prepare evidence to defend himself against the charges and ordered to sail for England. It must have been some solace to him to inform Francklin, "that turbulent and ambitious head," that his commission as Lieutenant-Governor had been revoked, for the British government had decided not to leave the administration in the hands of his adversary.[11] Commodore Mariot Arbuthnot, commanding the naval station at Halifax, replaced him.

The report of the Board of Trade on Legge's conduct in Nova Scotia recommended that, though he should not be removed from the king's service, he should not return. He was exonerated from all the formal charges laid against him but found "wanting in that gracious and conciliatory deportment which the delicacy of the times . . . demanded." His presence at Binney's trial had been "unwary and imprudent" and "an impropriety."[12]

Nova Scotia possessed the elements that could make revolution possible. Provocation had been given by the kind of conflict that had whittled away the royal authority in many of the older colonies, the confrontation of a well-intentioned but impolitic governor and a local oligarchy. But Legge's assault upon their authority and reputation did not blind the leaders of public opinion to the new vistas opening before them. The Act of Parliament of 1774, which restrained the trade of New England, contemplated the substitution of Nova Scotia for the recalcitrant colonies in the whole orbit of empire trade. Legge urged the British government to make of Halifax what the French had tried to make of Louisburg, the only intermediate point between the colonies and Europe.[13] There was a great deal of wishful thinking upon the mass migration of New England fishermen and Nantucket whalers to the harbours of a loyal province. Parliament offered bounties for the produce of Nova Scotia to fill the empty markets of the West Indies and in 1775 the effects of this great spur to industry could already be felt. New England had forfeited her place in the system of imperial trade and, it seemed to the more hopeful, Nova Scotia could be quickly inflated as a substitute.

The powerful prejudice against Legge, therefore, was not noticeable in the petition of the Nova Scotian Assembly of 1775 to the King, Lords, and Commons of Great Britain. The legislative supremacy of the imperial parliament was acknowledged, together with its right to tax the colonies. But, the petition argued, taxation should be delegated to colonial legislatures so that the cause of requisitions could be publicly shown and understood. In moderate language the historic grievances of North American colonists were stated – the offensive enforcement of the Laws of Trade and Navigation, the inefficient operation of the courts of law, the expensive conditions of land-granting.[14]

The British government accepted the principal proposition offered by the petitioners. On November 29, Sir Grey Cooper moved in the House of Commons that the request of the legislature should be granted, that the amount of duty be 8 per cent on foreign produce imported to the province. In order to develop a great trade between Halifax and the Mediterranean,

Parliament further enacted that wines, oranges, lemons, and other products imported directly to Nova Scotia from the country of origin should be admitted free of charge.[15] When the provincial legislature met in 1776 the first business transacted was the granting to His Majesty of an 8 per cent duty on foreign produce, with the exception of the articles enumerated by Parliament.

II

Militarily, British prospects in the region looked dark as hostilities commenced. At Newfoundland Vice-Admiral Montague had but two twenty-gun vessels and a sloop at his disposal. Every harbour except St John's was open to attack by the rebels. Placentia had been abandoned as a place of defence in 1772. The new Fort Townshend outside St John's had a barracks for three hundred men, but most of the Newfoundlanders who had enlisted were sent to Halifax so that its garrison was reduced to thirty-three. The British plan for the defence of Newfoundland comprehended active resistance on the Avalon peninsula only.[16]

In Nova Scotia the military urgencies were greater and there was the additional burden of a dubious population. In his bitterness Legge condemned the general sullenness and apathy as downright disloyalty.[17] Military men seconded this firm opinion. Cumberland, according to one missionary for the Society for the Propagation of the Gospel, was ready for rebellion; the Minas settlements, according to another, though disaffected, could easily be overawed.[18] If there was a general feeling it was probably that of Lunenburg: "The fire may perhaps not reach our province; but we shall be suffocated by the smoke or scorched to death by the heat that comes from the same."[19] The settlers of Nova Scotia, having achieved a bare competence after fifteen years of pioneering endeavour, wanted to be exempt from the great schism of the Empire. Like the Acadians of twenty years before, they aspired to neutrality. Yarmouth made the request frankly, explaining: "We were almost all of us born in New England, we have fathers, brothers, sons in that country. . . . It is self-preservation and that only which at this time drives us to make our request."[20] Frequent proclamations of the Continental Congress interpreted this naïve desire as favourable to their cause and, for purposes of propaganda, Nova Scotia was sometimes listed among the rebel colonies.[21]

The permanent garrison of Halifax had been sent off to Boston in 1774. In the harbour were the *Cerberus*, a frigate of twenty-eight guns, and a sloop. When rebel privateers broke up the fishery at Canso and scoured the Gulf of St Lawrence for British merchantmen, not a vessel could be spared to halt their activities. Members of the rudimentary government of St John's

Island became the prisoners of two armed schooners and the scant plunder of the fledgling capital of Charlottetown was carried away by their crews. At Halifax successive nocturnal attempts to set fire to the military stores forced their removal to the vessels of war. When Sir William Howe, sorely pressed for provisions at Boston, sent transports into the Bay of Fundy, the people at first refused to supply them. Later, when warships arrived on the scene, they shipped cattle at prices so high that the commissariat was infuriated. The American invasion of Canada at the end of 1775 created a conviction that Quebec was doomed and Nova Scotia would succumb in the spring. During the hard winter that followed, the price of bread doubled as the supply of flour from Quebec was interrupted.

To test the loyalty of the Nova Scotians, at the outbreak of hostilities Legge had enforced a general acceptance of the oath of allegiance. In November, 1775 over seven hundred men attending the sessions of Halifax, King's, and Annapolis counties not only accepted it but also formed associations to uphold the King and the supremacy of Parliament. Yet later in the same month, when the legislature consented to the calling up of the militia and imposed a tax for sustaining it, the country seethed with disaffection. To the people of Cumberland, labourers were wanted rather than soldiers. They were quite firm in stating that they would not march against their friends and relations, but emphatic in their resolution to defend themselves and their property.[22] The Irish of Truro and Onslow adopted the same position.

But if there were any chance that Nova Scotia would slip quickly and easily into the hands of the Americans with the tacit consent of the people, the opportunity rapidly receded. In January of 1776 a regiment of troops arrived from Ireland to garrison Halifax. In March appeared the fleet and army from the evacuation of Boston, and Halifax became temporarily the principal centre of British power in America. Before setting out for his attack on New York, Sir William Howe made the most of his stay in "that nook of penury and cold," strengthening the fortifications on Citadel Hill and building blockhouses on the landward approaches to the town. In spite of two months of strenuous work of this kind and the taking of the *Hannah*, the fastest frigate of the fleet of American privateers that plagued trade, Commodore Arbuthnot continued to regard Halifax as indefensible and doomed.[23]

Both on sea and on land the Americans were capable of only hit-and-run local raids against Newfoundland and Nova Scotia. Released from the earlier restrictions of Congress, their vessels were now conducting general warfare against all territory that remained British. In Maine the men of Machias and vicinity were plotting an invasion of the peninsula by land, a design for which George Washington, requiring all American resources for the main theatre, could find no approval. Nova Scotians, he argued, had not made war on Congress and he could sense in the proposals the desire for booty rather than for a real contribution to victory.[24] But the Machias loggers and fishermen, men who had sought that lonely coast to escape taxation, whether it was British or American, who had scored a bloodless triumph the year before by burning the undefended Fort Frederick at the mouth of the St John, were not to be denied. They were led by Colonel Jonathan Eddy, a fugitive member of the Nova Scotian Assembly, who concentrated his undisciplined forces in the St John estuary and pressed into service a few of the local inhabitants and Indians. Up the river at Maugerville the inhabitants surrendered to his suasion and announced their willingness to accept the authority of the General Court of Massachusetts. A rough road was cut through the forests to the cleared lands of Shepody where boatloads of rebels poled their way up the little rivers to recruit the settlers of Cumberland. These, out of conviction or, as they explained later, out of fear for the destruction of their property, joined the invasion which, in a very half-hearted way, became an insurrection as well.

Guarded by two hundred and fifty regulars under the command of Major Joseph Gorham, Fort Cumberland stood as a barrier to this American infiltration of the province. Late in November when Eddy, under a flag of truce, demanded surrender to "the United Colonies of America" he was indignantly refused. While the rebels wasted their time in dallying. Charles Dixon, a leader of the Yorkshire settlers who remained loyal and whose property was threatened with plunder, made his way to Halifax to inform the authorities. When four hundred reinforcements arrived, the conglomerate rebel army broke up quickly. Its casualties were one American and two Indians.[25] Gorham offered a free pardon to all the inhabitants of Cumberland willing to lay down their arms and very nearly all of them, unwilling rebels, accepted.

In the summer of 1777 British vessels of war entered the Bay of Fundy and cleared the theatre of enemy activity. Fort Howe rose on a great hill overlooking the St John and the firm of Simonds, White and Hazen, sadly harassed by the rebels during two years of occupation, resumed its profitable activities. Colonel Arthur Goold from Halifax enforced allegiance on the truculent inhabitants of Maugerville, some of whom deserted to Massachusetts.[26] A propaganda war was fought for the loyalties of the Passamaquoddy and Malecite Indians. John Allan, a renegade settler of Cumberland who saw his grand project for raising the Indians of Acadia against Britain crumble to ruins, was now sheltering in the woods of the St Croix Valley. Most of the Indians became "Tory" as Michael Francklin, rehabilitated by his appointment as agent to the savages, came to the St John with presents and won their neutrality by a treaty. Pierre Thoma, chieftain of the Malecites, announced that he was "half English and half Boston and would not lift up the hatchet." Later in the year Sir George Collier with a small fleet destroyed the magazine and stores at Machias, dispersing the rebel irregulars to the woods.

In October of the same year the French fishermen at Newfoundland made a sudden and complete departure, taking with them almost all of their equipment. This was in obedience to an order from the Court of France, a muffled warning of the declaration of war that was to come in the spring of 1778. But, however great was Britain's distress elsewhere in the world, her position in the North Atlantic seemed to become more stable and assured. The Comte d'Estaing, in command of a large fleet, considered attacking Halifax and St John's but confined his endeavour to the warmer seas of the Caribbean. The Comte de Vergennes, playing a diplomatic game to keep the United States dependent on France, professed to believe that Canada and Nova Scotia should remain British rather than fall to the sway of Congress. Fearfully the garrison commanders complained of their weakness but the French mercifully stayed away and the Bostonians merely made sham preparations for an attack on Halifax. In 1779, after British forces in this northern theatre were further extended by the occupation of Penobscot, French and American opportunity became the greater but nothing happened.

Alarm and despondency punctuated the closing years of the war but prosperity reigned. With the expulsion of the French from their shore Newfoundlanders again, for five years, enjoyed the monopoly they considered their due. British strength became unassailable as the Governor, Vice-Admiral Montagu, acquired nine ships of war, a garrison of four hundred and fifty regulars in Fort Townshend, and several hundreds of local volunteers who were trained to arms. Almost complete control came when St Pierre and Miquelon, where Yankee privateers had sheltered, were captured and their thirteen hundred inhabitants deported to France. The buildings, erected from timber cut on Newfoundland, a concession granted in the hope of keeping France neutral, were completely destroyed. Although Newfoundland could not be conquered, except at St John's nobody was safe. Privateers were frequently captured, but there were too many of them for the Royal Navy to guarantee complete protection. They haunted the entrances to harbours, daily insulting the inhabitants and burning boats, waiting for the favourable winds that would enable them to sail in and plunder everything of value. The outports clamoured for protection and the government was finally able to supply many of them with the means of self-defence, even cannon. But life was turbulent and, if the experience of Renous in 1780 means anything at all, there was always the chance that transients and wastrels would join the rebels to plunder people of substance.[27] Accounts of great French armaments fitting out at Brest for the conquest of Newfoundland passed many times through the official dispatches. As America became more certain of her independence, her concern for her historic connection with the fisheries became more marked and Henry Laurens, the former president of Congress, captured by ships of the Newfoundland station, bore on his person dispatches that certified an American intention to attack St John's. Yet, amid the dangers that seemed likely to flow from all sides, Newfoundland flourished and the fishery grew. War imposed organization and the regulation of prices of imported foodstuffs became an established practice.

Nova Scotia was similarly preserved for a destiny of her own by British sea power. Often, when the fleet was on the high seas, the privateersmen of New England appeared at the entrance of Halifax harbour and inflicted damaging blows on commerce. The outports suffered similarly and, since plunder was the principal object of the rebels, sympathizers with the Revolution and those who wanted only neutrality incurred losses as well as the loyal. Yet often the common misfortune welded Nova Scotians of diverse origins into a distinctive people. In spite of intense enemy activity at sea, the naval convoys based on Halifax were, as early as 1777, able to provide the fisheries at Canso and Isle Madame with such adequate protection that not a single loss was recorded. A succession of naval lieutenant-governors – Arbuthnot, Sir Richard Hughes (1778-81), Sir Andrew Hamond (1781-82) – succeeded in maintaining this high standard.

As soldiers and sailors in thousands moved in and out of Halifax the merchants fattened on high profits, the old New England nucleus now heavily reinforced by Loyalist Scots who, scenting great opportunities, drifted in from the south. To the refugees from the rebellious colonies Halifax appeared as the entrepôt of a rich and growing trade and its merchants as tycoons. Commodore Arbuthnot observed that it was the wealthy who were most loyal, and it was readily perceived that loyalty could be rewarding.[28] There were some, like a great many other traders along the entire Atlantic coast, who sought profit by trading with both sides. Malachy Salter, who had taken a leading part in the agitation against Lawrence in 1758 and who had held many commissions from government, was charged with conveying intelligence as well as supplies to the enemy, as were John Newton and Jonathan Binney.[29] By charging provincial duties on the rum imported for the army and navy, refusing to apportion any of the revenue to works of defence, the Assembly reduced the public debt from twenty-four thousand to two thousand pounds. As the war came to a conclusion the prospects for Nova Scotia within a greatly reduced British Empire appeared highly promising.

In the townships of the Bay of Fundy the army and navy paid high prices for everything that could be produced. As a result, the Fundy settlements flourished. The new self-sufficiency of these communities coincided with a remarkable effervescence of religious zeal that dismayed and flabbergasted the authorities. In New England the evangelical warmth and glow of the old Congregational Church had been rapidly receding. In Nova Scotia its form and order, its doctrinal rigidity, had little meaning for a pioneering people. Led by Henry Alline of Falmouth, an uneducated boy of self-accusing conscience, New Light preachers assaulted its infant citadels and virtually destroyed it as an institution. Another interesting chapter in the variety of religious experience was chronicled as Alline and his fellow itinerants made their way into every Nova Scotian community from Yarmouth to Maugerville, emphasizing the necessity of conversion. Crowds followed them across the countryside as they travelled, making no demands upon their listeners, often paying their way by labour. Their ascendancy over the feelings and behaviour of the people was so complete that the government feared their imposing power would be harnessed to political activity.[30] Yet, though inspiration was the business of the New Lights, their political beliefs, if any, appeared to be remote from the realities of the great revolutionary conflict that was being waged around them.

III

The Peace of Versailles was concluded under circumstances in which the independent United States held most of the trump cards while France and Britain contended for her future favours. The new British government, headed by Lord Shelburne, who "preferred trade to dominion," was willing to make large sacrifices in order to earn American goodwill. Franklin, Adams, and Jay, the American negotiators, made the most of the situation. Their treaty of alliance with France had included the annexation of all territory remaining British. Congress had considered the acquisition of Nova Scotia an essential requirement.[31] But the complexity of the war induced adjustments in American thinking. The necessity of gratifying a valued ally had raised the possibility of awarding Nova Scotia to Spain.[32] On one thing, however, there was no yielding. John Adams was a New Englander and in negotiating with Britain he was alert to the necessity of enabling New Englanders to continue to participate in the fishery, to go to the northern coasts where they had always gone.

In the preliminary conversations at Versailles it was agreed that the new Nova Scotia, that would now have a foreign state as her neighbour, should have a western boundary on the St John. But, as the war came to a conclusion, the British attitude stiffened. Victory at Gibraltar and in the West

Indies enabled Shelburne to instruct Henry Strachey to press for the St Croix River instead.[33] Having gained their principal points, the Americans yielded. On John Mitchell's map, used by the negotiators, the St Croix appeared clearly as a single stream. From the source of the river a northerly line was to be drawn to "the highlands" that divided the watersheds of the rivers flowing to the southward from that of the St Lawrence. It was reasonable to suppose that "highlands" existed and that a dividing line provided by nature could be found.

The Treaty of Amity and Commerce between France and the United States contained an American recognition of France's claims to an exclusive fishery off Newfoundland. In 1782 France was in a position to retrieve her lost fortunes and her first demand in the negotiations for peace was full sovereignty over the treaty coast of 1763. In addition she asked for islands more advantageously located than St Pierre and Miquelon for the use of her vessels. The result of extended talks was that she had to be satisfied with the return of these former possessions and, by Article V of the definitive treaty, was granted new limits for her Newfoundland fishery, from Cape St John by the north to Cape Ray. This involved a French withdrawal from the coast between Cape Bonavista and Cape St John, where her fishermen had been in close contact with the British, but the total length of her treaty shore, comprehending the entire west coast, was greatly increased. The agreement upon these new limits was relatively easy. Much more difficult was the definition of rights. France demanded exclusive privileges. In substance the British were willing to agree but would not include the word "exclusive" in the treaty. Escape from the difficulty came with a suggestion from Fitzherbert, the British plenipotentiary, that France might be satisfied with a British declaration, made apart from the treaty, *not to molest* the French fishermen on their shore. *Ministeriellement* became the magic word that gratified the pride of France and saved the face of Britain. The French had not acquired an "exclusive" fishery by treaty but by declaration Britain provided them with the essence of one.[34] This remarkable compromise laid the groundwork for all the future troubles of the "French Shore."

The new enemies of Britain as well as the old were admitted to the fishery. The Americans gained not only the right to fish in waters enclosed by British territory, but also "the liberty" of fishing in the inshore waters of Newfoundland and Nova Scotia and of landing on the shore of the unsettled bays and inlets of Nova Scotia, the Magdalen Islands, and Labrador for the purposes of curing and drying. In their eagerness to re-establish themselves on Newfoundland the French were partial to an exclusion of the Americans, so that Britain, to a degree, was able to play off her two enemies against one another and to moderate their demands. But for the Americans, too, the fishing clauses in the Treaty of Versailles gave reason for solid satis-

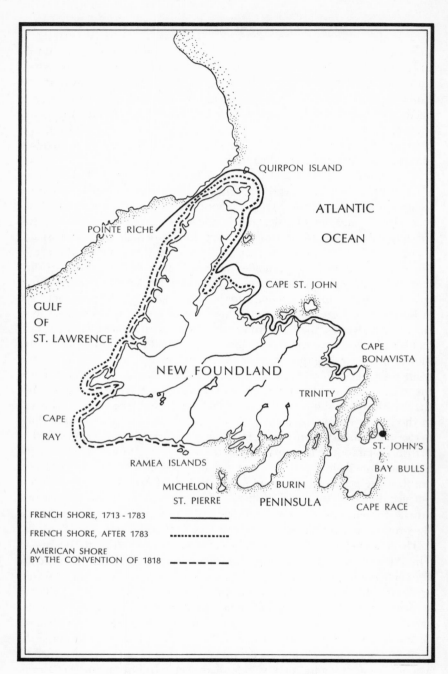

QUIRPON ISLAND

ATLANTIC

OCEAN

POINTE RICHE

CAPE ST. JOHN

GULF
OF
ST. LAWRENCE

CAPE
BONAVISTA

NEW FOUNDLAND

TRINITY

CAPE
RAY

ST. JOHN'S

BAY BULLS

RAMEA ISLANDS

MICHELON
ST. PIERRE

BURIN

PENINSULA

CAPE RACE

FRENCH SHORE, 1713 - 1783

FRENCH SHORE, AFTER 1783 ················

AMERICAN SHORE
BY THE CONVENTION OF 1818 ─ ─ ─ ─ ─

Newfoundland – The French and American Shores

faction. New England could participate in the industry on terms scarcely less disadvantageous than in the days when she had been part of the British Empire.

Newfoundland and Nova Scotia remained British, but the Treaty of Versailles ensured that their region of the North Atlantic should remain a theatre for international rivalry.

IV

For over a year, from the signing of the preliminary peace in September, 1782 until its evacuation by the British troops in December, 1783, New York was the centre of initiative for the affairs of British North America. The casting vote in the fortunes of all the provinces lay with Sir Guy Carleton, who, in winding up the long war from the British side, made decisions that would mould their futures. In this year of strain he was surrounded by American Loyalist leaders, men to whom the issue of the war meant banishment and the liquidation of almost all their worldly property. American Toryism had survived most lustily in the areas where British military power was pre-eminent. At the end of the war New York was the only British position of military strength in the lost thirteen colonies and it was there that Loyalist leaders, bitterly reviewing the lost opportunities of the struggle and their consequent plight, were assembled to make plans for the future.

Around them were fifty thousand American refugees who had made their way into the city and to Long Island in flight from the vengeance of rebel committees. They had remained loyal to the Crown at great cost but this did not save them from the slurs of the British military and the abuse of German mercenaries. In addition to the refugees were the troops of the provincial army, the regiments that had been raised in America to serve the Crown. Brought to New York after the capitulation of Yorktown or drawn into the lines following the opening of peace negotiations, they were suffering from low morale. Many had fought valorously and some of the regiments, such as Tarleton's Legion and the King's American Dragoons, were among the élite corps of the British Army, but the news of the preliminary peace meant there could be no commensurate reward for their services. Shelburne, the British minister who had made such a generous settlement with the victorious rebels, was for them an object of hatred. The treaty promised the good offices of Congress in securing them a safe return to their homes. But the news from the confederated states was that victory had accelerated the persecution of the Tories, that rebel mobs were made the more ungenerous by victory, and that those who had fought against the Revolution were in the category of public enemies.

During the year the strength of the regiments withered away as men took their chances on the uncertain situation behind the American lines. But Sir Guy Carleton discovered that peace increased the number of those dependent on him as more and more refugees, fearful of American fury, streamed into the city. Perceiving the unwillingness of the state governments to respond to the wishes of Congress that the Loyalists should be reinstated in their own country, the British government acknowledged its debt. Loyalist regiments were placed on the permanent establishment of the army, an assurance that their officers would be retired on half-pay, preliminary to the general announcement that other measures of compensation would be offered.

From the beginning of the war Nova Scotia had been an easy and natural place of retreat for fugitive Tories. In 1775 Legge had issued them an invitation to find safety in his province. At the evacuation of Boston in the following year, over one thousand of the office-holders and influential leaders of the pre-Revolutionary society of New England had made a fleeting and unpleasant acquaintance with the chill spring months and high prices of Halifax. Most of them had left the province to become pensioners of the British government, some to acquire office in the reorganized empire of 1783. Other refugees from New England had from time to time found Spartan comfort at Halifax, some in as poor condition as Reverend Jacob Bailey of Kennebeck, who was compelled to face the elegantly dressed ladies and gentlemen of the town in an often-mended pair of blue woollen stockings, black breeches turned a rusty grey and daubed with pitch, and a blue surtout, frilled at the elbows, that had become a coat of many colours.[35] The Toryism of New England lost its leaders early in the struggle and became a scarcely recognizable force. It was the middle colonies of New York and its neighbours that were to supply most of the human material for the great migration to Nova Scotia at the end of the war. At Carleton's side in New York was Brook Watson, Commissary-General to the army and an old business associate of Joshua Mauger, who could inform him in detail on the affairs of the province.[36]

Heralded by agents of Loyalist associations who inspected the country, the vanguard of the immigrants made their appearance in October of 1782. Three hundred were deposited in the valley of the Annapolis, but Halifax, crowded with troops, experienced the brunt of the impact. Thousands were accommodated in warehouses and sheds on the waterfront, under canvas at Citadel Hill and at Point Pleasant, and in the two churches of St Paul's and Mather's. The movement became more precipitate, although Carleton, under pressure to evacuate New York as soon as possible, refused to do so until all the Loyalists could be removed. He was hampered by the scarcity of the shipping that was necessary for all the tasks he had in hand, the withdrawals from Charleston and Penobscot, the continuation of operations in the West Indies, the return of the regular troops and German mercenaries to Europe. Shipmasters unloaded their passengers at the first opportunity and hastily returned to New York. Acting under Carleton's orders, the Nova Scotian authorities at this stage had no detailed instructions from London.

The new governor of Nova Scotia, Colonel John Parr, had come to the colony to enjoy retirement after a long and honourable career in the army. His council, the members of the cabal that had so successfully opposed Legge, contemplated uneasily the onset of new and great developments. Loyalist gentlemen fresh from New York cursed the apparent apathy of the government, contrasted their own sacrifices and fallen fortunes with the opulence of Halifax, and prophesied a quick revolution in the conduct of affairs by the appointment of a Loyalist governor with a Loyalist junta of advisers. To the Loyalists Halifax was a nest of republicans who profited from the king's bounty. Aided by his aged Surveyor General, Charles Morris, and his son of the same name, Parr put his flagging energies to the task of marking off unoccupied areas of the province for Loyalist settlement. These were the harbour of Port Roseway, which he renamed Shelburne in honour of his noble patron, the mouth of the St John River, and the shores of Passamaquoddy Bay.

When the spring of 1783 opened, the transports from New York were assigned to these areas. The two most important were Shelburne and the St John, where new towns suddenly appeared as thousands of civilian refugees were unloaded at each place. Those who came to Shelburne and other harbours of the Atlantic shore were probably the most unfortunate. Excellent harbours could not compensate for the paucity of arable land. Spirits were high in July when Parr arrived on a visit and gave its name to the town which, he told his patron, would be greater than Halifax. At one time population ran to nearly ten thousand, but its ultimate prospects were visible to canny traders who looked in and passed on to other locations. The laying out of hundred-acre lots of rocky countryside along a projected road to Annapolis could excite little expectation of great things to come. On the St John estuary across the Bay of Fundy rose the two towns of Parr and Carleton. The work of establishing the people in these new settlements and of furnishing them with supplies was in the hands of military commissioners. Surveyors of the provincial government appeared on the scene but they were too few and too restricted in their instructions to gratify the impatient demands of an uprooted people for quick rehabilitation.

The great Loyalist migration was made on the strength of solemn British promises. Land for all was one of them, and Loyalist leaders showed great acumen in seeking out the most desirable locations for carrying on trade. On the St John the disposal of water lots fronting the harbour kept a new and rapidly growing community in dissension for over a year. The British government also promised provisions and implements for tilling the soil until the new settlers should become established. This commitment was honoured in general, though great complaints arose concerning details. All knowledgeable men waited in the spring and summer of 1783 for one great assurance. Would the conflict in the British Parliament upon the commercial organization of the remaining empire be decided in favour of the free traders, who wished to admit the Americans to their former privileges, or in favour of the supporters of the historic Laws of Trade and Navigation, who would exclude them from the privileges of British subjects in the West Indies and elsewhere? If the latter should triumph the commercial fortunes of Nova Scotia would be assured, for the Americans would lose the carrying-trade to the West Indies and the supplying of northern products to other overseas markets. These forfeitures, it seemed certain, would fall to the Loyalists.

When the word arrived in August that the mercantilists had triumphed – that the Americans were to be punished for their successful rebellion, that Lord Sheffield, the leader of those who favoured the preservation of the British Empire as a tight commercial monopoly, had dissuaded Parliament from an act of foolhardy generosity – scores of traders from New York to Kennebeck slipped their moorings and sailed north for Nova Scotia. The second great wave of immigration that followed in the autumn, therefore, had a much more commercial character than that of the spring. The main chance for trade now appeared to be in the new British settlements that were developing so rapidly while the Crown continued to pour its treasure into the province. During the wettest September and coldest October on record Sir Guy Carleton dispatched another eight thousand Loyalist to Nova Scotian shores.

Among them came the remnants of the Loyalist battalions and their families. The Carolinians of Tarleton's Legion were the first to land on the desolate harbour of Port Mouton on October 10. They were followed by the headquarters personnel from New York, some Maryland Loyalists, civilian refugees, and emancipated negroes, a total of over two thousand. Subsisting on a pound of salt pork and a pound of biscuit per head per day, they awaited the arrival of the lumber for their new town, called Guysborough. It came in from Halifax at Christmas. Their town constructed, they cut a road through the forest to Liverpool. But all this privation and labour came to nought during a dry month of May when the town was destroyed by fire in a few hours. Some settlers remained behind but the majority departed. A new Guysborough appeared on Chedabucto Bay.

Nehemiah Marks and 280 others sailed for Passamaquoddy where they built the town of St Stephen.[37]

Most of the provincial troops, the remnants of a dozen regiments, went to the St John, following the King's American Dragoons who were settled at Prince William. They occupied blocks of land laid out by Edward Winslow and their agents from Maugerville northward as far as Block Eight, of which Woodstock became the centre. Owing to the late arrival of their transports and the scarcity of shipping on the river, many remained at Parr and Carleton to swell the crowded populations of these new towns. Later in the year there came to Passamaquoddy the traders of Penobscot. Having hoped in vain for the retention of their post in British territory, they crossed the Bay of Fundy with the evacuating British forces and quickly established themselves at St Andrews Point to enter upon the profitable business of carrying American lumber and provisions to the ports of Nova Scotia that were so desperately in need.

On St John's Island, Walter Patterson saw the opportunity he had long been waiting for – finding settlers for the vacant lands of his province, especially for his own estates and those of the officials who supported him in his quarrels. Late in 1783 his agents at Shelburne succeeded in persuading about six hundred Loyalists that the rich agricultural areas of St John's offered much greater promise than the barren and foggy littoral of the Atlantic. Simultaneously in London the proprietors of the lots urged Lord North to move more Loyalists to St John's, asking that they be excused the payment of quitrents for lands on which Loyalists should be settled. Thus the attraction of a considerable group of refugees set in motion the evil consequences of the iniquitous disposal of St John's to a group of absentee proprietors. Loyalists were settled at Bedeque, Pownall, and other places, but, in spite of promises, could not acquire clear title to the lands on which they effected improvement. The injustices inflicted on them by the provincial government and by the proprietors lasted as long as the more general evil that stemmed from the absentee system of ownership.[38]

Until it became known that restrictions on the granting of lands in Cape Breton would be removed no Loyalists came to that island, but early in 1784, when a new provincial government was established, small detachments of settlers commenced to arrive. Abraham Cuyler, a leading Loyalist and former mayor of Albany, made arrangements for the transmigration of three hundred refugees from Canada. Others followed, many of them transient. Most were settled about the new capital of Sydney, established on Spanish River, a decision which speeded the depopulation of Louisburg. Some also went to Baddeck and St Peter's. The figure given by Governor Joseph Frederick Wallet des Barres, three thousand, was grossly exaggerated.[39] Throughout all the new Loyalist settlements dependence on the royal stores was general, but at Cape Breton it was especially noteworthy. Only a sprinkling of Loyalist transients appeared at Newfoundland.

The entire region formerly known as Acadia acquired a totally new appearance in consequence of these large migrations. The population of the peninsula was approximately doubled and hitherto neglected regions became centres of considerable settlement.[40] The lower valley of the St John in 1784 acquired a thin belt of population as the Loyalists, having spent a hard winter in Parr and Carleton, moved out to the lands allotted them. Amos Botsford led a small detachment to the Tantramar where they settled among the New Englanders and Yorkshiremen who were still nursing the animosities of 1776. Sussex Vale, Kingston, Gagetown, and St Anne's became focal points for the new settlements to the north of the Bay of Fundy. There the total number of new settlers was about fourteen thousand.[41] Invariably it was the intervale land that was most sought after and first settled. St John's Island had its population doubled and Cape Breton, for the first time under British rule, acquired a fringe of what could be called a permanent population.

By far the greatest proportion of the newcomers came from New York, New Jersey, Pennsylvania, and the other middle colonies. Southerners from the regiments raised in Virginia, Maryland, and the Carolinas made up a very small quota.[42] New Englanders were to be found chiefly among the leading gentry who had fled their country at the outbreak of hostilities and acquired places of eminence in the Loyalist movement. Quite noticeable was the high representation of minorities in the populations of the lost American colonies, descendants of the Dutch and Huguenots of New York, Quakers from Pennsylvania. Famous names from New York and Massachusetts were to appear in Nova Scotia. The Delancey brothers, Stephen and James, sons of Brigadier Oliver, established themselves at Annapolis.[43] Brigadier Timothy Ruggles, "the father of the many Loyalist regiments that later fought in the war," who from the outset of the Revolution had opposed James Otis and the extremists in the Massachusetts assembly, found repose nearby in the Township of Wilmot.[44] But Loyalist patricians for the most part went to England and remained there or found service elsewhere in the king's dominions. Nova Scotia had but limited opportunity for Harvard graduates. The great majority of Loyalists who came there to stay were middle-class tradesmen, craftsmen, and farmers.

Escheat of many of the great grants of land made ten years before the war had long been in process owing to failure to comply with the conditions and, as the flood of immigrants approached Nova Scotia, the process had to be hastened. Even the great and the near-great had to endure this punishment. Yet the hard lesson of land tenure in the New World was still unlearned by Loyalist leaders who petitioned for large grants in Nova Scotia which, they hoped, would be the means of regaining in the new British Empire the superior places in society they had lost in the old. Aristocracy, they continued to reason, was the instrument by which the Crown could preserve its authority in the remaining British possessions. This familiar political idea acquired coherent form in the request of the Fifty-five eminent Loyalists who, from New York in 1783, asked for grants of five thousand acres in Nova Scotia. Such a protest of jealousy and anger arose among the great body of Loyalists who were awaiting transportation that the British government deferred to it.[45] The new society of Nova Scotia would not be hinged on a landed aristocracy. When Governor Parr received from London his instructions for the granting of lands, the basic allowance was a hundred acres for each head of family, plus fifty acres for each member. The only gradation was a military one. Non-commissioned officers were allowed two hundred acres, subalterns five hundred, captains seven hundred, and field-officers one thousand.

V

Loyalist *amour propre* was responsible for the partition of Nova Scotia of 1784. The long months of confinement at New York produced within Loyalist leaders a determination to gain reward for their sufferings and losses on behalf of the Crown. The idea of a separate and distinct Loyalist haven in the north, ruled by men of proven loyalty and superior intelligence, was an old one long before the transports sailed in the spring of 1783. The idea had almost become a reality in 1780 when William Knox, the under-secretary for the American colonies and the advocate of a re-organized British America, proposed his settlement on the Penobscot, to be called New Ireland.[46]

In 1783 Nova Scotia was the Loyalist haven, but it was governed, so the Loyalists thought, by men whose loyalty was dubious and whose fortunes during the war had been as prosperous as their own had been adverse. As the great emigration commenced and as reports came back to New York from the first arrivals, the impressions that became dominant were those of Parr's indifferent abilities and of the intentions of his advisers to deposit the refugees in the poorest and most barren parts of the province. Through the new settlements ran rumours that the Governor was about to dissolve the House of Assembly, Nova Scotia's Long Parliament that had been sitting since 1770, and call new elections before Loyalists should be qualified for the franchise. In the Loyalist mind distrust of the Halifax authorities quickly became uppermost. It was not long before there were prophecies of the removal of Parr, the nominee of Lord

Shelburne whom Loyalists regarded as an enemy, and the establishment at Halifax of a regime of men whose abilities they respected and whose principles they approved.

This kind of expectation became the more plausible as the Shelburne government resigned, having been defeated in the House of Commons, and the North-Fox coalition took office. Among a host of others Edward Winslow enjoyed high hopes that the influence of Brigadier Henry Fox, the younger brother of Charles James, would be employed to sweep Parr from office along with "the nest of pickaroons" by whom he was surrounded. Just as important were the facts that Carleton at New York was becoming convinced of Parr's incapacity, and that he sympathized with Loyalist complaints against the Nova Scotian administration. On points of controversy he took the part of the men who were by his side. Very fundamental for the future organization of Nova Scotia was the area chosen for settlement of the troops of the Loyalist regiments. Parr wanted them on the coast at Passamaquoddy and elsewhere so that he could easily supervise them from Halifax. Urged on by Winslow, Fox decided that they should be located in the valley of the middle St John and in this he was supported by the commander-in-chief.[47] This decision offended those in Halifax who held grants to great areas of the northern hinterland, and it created a first-class case for the partition of Nova Scotia, of which leading Loyalists, both in the province and at New York, were freely speaking in 1783. Edward Winslow was not alone in believing that the Loyalists, "irritable from a series of mortifications" and military by temperament, could not be mingled with the pre-Loyalist Nova Scotians whose sympathies, though quietly governed, had really been for the rebellion.

Loyalist pride prevailed when still another British government, fresh from an electoral victory early in 1784, found opportunity for a detailed consideration of American affairs. But on the St John Loyalist hopes were at first dashed by the news of the resignation of the North-Fox coalition and the victory of Pitt. With his patron, Lord Shelburne, again in a position of influence, though not of office. Parr was considerably safer from the dangers of Loyalist intrigues. Yet the important fact was that the new government was prepared to accept the advice of Carleton on all the details of British North American policy. When he arrived in London in March to join the host of Loyalist claimants for official favour, he was resolved on partition. The Loyalists, he was certain, were the only means by which the remaining provinces could be kept loyal to Britain. At meetings of the Board of Trade, allegations of disloyalty were made against "the old inhabitants" of Nova Scotia. Partition was resolved upon, with the difficulty of communication between "the back settlements" and Halifax advanced as the principal reason. Partition meant that in large areas of Nova Scotia

Loyalist leaders could acquire office and dignity within new societies of their own fashioning.[48] Superficially it might be remarked that the creation of new establishments of government was a device by which Lord Sydney, the new Colonial Secretary, could dispose of the claims of a large number of eminent and worthy Loyalists who crowded the waiting-rooms of Whitehall and Downing Street.

Decided in the spring, the division was formally ordered on June 18.[49] The importation of American ideas to London in this year was presumably the reason for the disappearance of grandiose plans for making the new settlements more English in form and social organization. William Knox, temporarily restored to influence within the Colonial Office, was compelled to remove from his plan for the new province north of the Bay of Fundy the more authoritarian features of his plan for New Ireland in 1780.[50] The province of New Brunswick, as it was to be called, was given substantially the same framework of government as Nova Scotia. A land-holding aristocracy was, in effect, forbidden by the royal instructions. Surrounded by Americans, Carleton pleaded for the kind of government to which they were accustomed. In only one important respect were his requests denied when the British government insisted on imposing a quitrent, taking effect ten years after occupation, on lands granted to the Loyalists.

The principle of partition was further followed when Cape Breton was simultaneously established as a separate government. Nova Scotia was reduced to the peninsula, bounded on the north by the little river Missiquash, flowing into the Bay of Fundy. Parr accepted the situation gracefully. In spite of Loyalist supremacy at London, he retained his government at Halifax. If his pride was injured, the wounds were made the easier to bear by the stipulation that he should exercise supreme authority both on Cape Breton and St John's Island, while resident in either. Having put the principle of partition into effect, Lord Sydney, who had promised to make of Nova Scotia "the envy of all the American states," did nothing to honour this great commitment. At London all depended on the willingness or unwillingness of Sir Guy Carleton, the hope of the American Loyalists, to accept supreme authority over all the colonies. In 1784 fifty thousand Loyalist expatriates looked to Carleton as to a father. Not only did he honour this confidence by supporting the principle of partition; he was able to dictate the appointment of officers for the new provinces that were coming into being.[51]

VI

The old guard of officialdom at Halifax resented the partition of the province. It was for them a loss of control over extensive territories where their influence had only lightly been extended but which promised much. Loss of the prospects resulting from fresh, incoming populations aggrieved them. They were forbidden to collect fees on the passing of land-grants to Loyalist refugees. They particularly resented the loss of the township of Sackville, now included in New Brunswick, where the commercial connection with Halifax was close and where production during the war had greatly increased. Too late they sent a delegation to London to protest it.[52] Compared with the infant communities around it, Halifax in these years was notoriously, even vulgarly and offensively, rich. In January of 1786 the celebration of the queen's birthday at the Grand Pontac commenced at 8.30 p.m. on the 5th. Following "the splendid array of the Cytherean train," the supper table showed an artificial fountain, obelisks, and monuments, with the temples of Health and Venus. Seven hundred bottles of wines of fine vintage were consumed during the evening and the gentlemen did not conclude the celebration until 11 a.m. on the 6th.[53]

Government came to Cape Breton in November, 1784 with the arrival of the Lieutenant-Governor. Des Barres, a familiar figure in Nova Scotia since 1756 when he had come to America as a subaltern of infantry in the king's service. He had been present at most of the events of the Seven Years' War in the region, and for twelve years afterwards he had been employed in charting the shores of the Nova Scotian coast and in the publication of the Nova Scotian shippers' guide, the four volumes of his magnificent *Atlantic Neptune*. The administration of Cape Breton came as a reward for this latter service, but the exuberant qualities of the Lieutenant-Governor ensured that it would be of short duration. He gained great popularity among the new population by generous dispensations of provisions from the royal stores, but the auditors of the Treasury in London would allow him no credit for generosity. He quarrelled with the leading dignitaries of his small administration. And in the great rivalry among the provinces for the accession of new settlers and new capital, he was too indiscreet in his utterances concerning "the jealousy of Nova Scotia." When he was recalled in 1786 the colonists of Cape Breton seemed but a slender handful of refugees who had been deposited on a desolate shore and forgotten. Sydney, the new capital of what Des Barres promised would be an opulent province, was beginning to look like abandoned Louisburg. Only the presence of troops kept business alive in the town.

St John's Island, in spite of its ranking as a province since 1769, had little more than Cape Breton to show from the benefits of government. A garrison had come to Charlottetown in 1780 and the inevitable stimulation to business had resulted. But during a war when it seemed that nothing British would be left on the other side of the Atlantic, the proprietors did little to speed settlement. Many of the lots fell to new owners at nominal prices. Taking advantage of the prevailing lack of confidence. Governor Patterson in 1781 commenced proceedings of escheat against a number of the absentees. In company with some of his friends and officials he purchased, at well-rigged public auctions, several of the lots declared forfeited. According to his enemy, John Stewart, his whole policy was to legitimize the land-scales of this year, to acquire so much property that he would, in effect, rule even though he should lose the governorship.[54]

Although not ready to spend money to develop their lands, the proprietors were prepared to organize to retain them. In response to their pleas, Lord Sydney in 1784 dispatched to Patterson the draft of a bill that would return the lots to their original owners. The Lieutenant-Governor proceeded to carry out his task with his customary recklessness. Though the community was small and case-hardened, he had already scandalized provincial society by winning for himself the affections of the wife of the Chief Justice. Relying too much on the slowness of communication across the Atlantic, he postponed acting on his instructions on the excuse that London had been misinformed. Dissolving a hostile House of Assembly, he secured a friendly one, at the expense of two thousand pounds, willing to send an address to the Colonial Minister seeking a reversal of the decision.[55] But Sydney, spurred on by the proprietors, recalled him in 1786, appointing in his place General Edmund Fanning, the North Carolina Loyalist leader and former Lieutenant-Governor of Nova Scotia. Even when Fanning arived in November, Patterson continued to pretend misunderstanding in London and did not surrender control until the following spring. Before Patterson left Charlottetown the temptations and opportunities of St John's Island were opened up to Fanning, and the new lieutenant-governor took over from the old the management of the landed interests that had been dubiously acquired by him in 1781.

In November of 1784 the new government of New Brunswick was proclaimed at Parrtown. The Governor, Colonel Thomas Carleton, the younger brother of Sir Guy, was a soldier whose role as a civil governor could never change his military habits of mind and action. His officers of government and the members of his council were for the most part New York Loyalists, men who had advised Sir Guy during the evacuation of that city and who had followed him to London in hopes of gaining the favour of the British government. Conspicuous among them were the Ludlow brothers, Gabriel, given senior ranking in the council, and George, the Chief Justice, who had been so prominent in sustaining the Loyalist cause on Long Island; Reverend Jonathan Odell, one of Sir Guy's most valued secretaries; and the sons of Beverley Robinson, the aged Loyalist patriarch of the Hudson, who preferred to remain in England rather than face the hazards of a new country. There were Massachusetts men such as Abijah Willard, Ward Chipman, and Edward Winslow, who came into a somewhat junior category. In civil matters Carleton was absolutely dependent on advice and for carrying on this kind of business he quickly learned to esteem the assistance of Gabriel Ludlow, Chipman, and Odell, the Provincial Secretary. But his habits were those of command. He regarded his civil role as ancillary to the military. For him his most important duties were directing the tide of settlement high up the St John to the borders of Quebec, establishing new communities under military supervision and protecting them against the Malecites, who could still be considered a nuisance, if not a danger.

Under Nova Scotian management the new settlements of New Brunswick had taken something like fixed form and the new Governor found them in great dissension. The latecomers of the fall fleet had brought serious charges against the Loyalist agents who, through 1783, had disposed of the lots of Parr and Carleton very much to the advantage of themselves and their friends. At Halifax, Governor Parr had sided with the newcomers against the agents and had called them to answer the charges, sending his Chief Justice, Bryan Finucane, to the St John to settle the innumerable disputes. Everywhere there was the disaffection of men who had received considerably less than they had expected – who had endured the privations of a winter and now faced the wilderness of the interior. Carleton's arrival was at first hailed as the end of tyranny, insult, and mismanagement on the part of the Nova Scotian government and the Loyalist agents.

But cleavage and dissension remained among the new Loyalist communities as the new governor accepted the Loyalist agents as his advisors and refused to undo their work. Carleton had little patience with the men of commerce who in great part made up the populations of Parr and Carleton, or with the casual and demanding traders who had come to the St John in hope of making a quick profit from government expenditure. What they needed, he considered, was "a more rigorous police" and this was provided by the charter he granted to the new city of Saint John in June of 1785.[56] Evading the urgings of Lord Sydney to call a general assembly as soon as possible, he organized the new province into counties and parishes, appointing magistrates of his own choosing. Ninety miles up the river, where several tributaries joined the main stream and where the half-pay officers of the provincial regiments were settled on good, arable land, he found a site for his new capital at St Anne's. He was thinking primarily of barrack accommodation for the two regiments he had been promised. Here, it seemed, from the highest navigable point on the river, the great push into the interior could be organized and controlled. In honour of the popular patron of the army, Frederic, Duke of York, the place was renamed Fredericton in November of 1785. In Saint John, where the citizens were not proud of their new charter, the decision to make Fredericton the capital was considered hostile. There the impulse was to look oceanward, rather than inward, to develop overseas commerce by exchange of British for American goods, rather than to make plans for the settlement of the scarcely touched wilderness about Fredericton and the interior of the province.

Having organized the province on the more authoritarian lines of New York rather than those of Massachusetts, where popular participation in government had so often taken the place of "sound principles," Carleton, after a full year of government by order-in-council, issued writs for the election of a general assembly in November of 1785. He got an assembly of the kind of men he wanted, but only by leavening "sound principles" with a degree of trickery and chicanery. The Governor had in fact to overcome opposition in Saint John by dubious methods. The charter, which provided for a mayor to be appointed by the government and for an authoritarian court of law, was denounced as an instrument of tyranny. The proposal to move the capital up the river was regarded as insulting as well as ridiculous and, among the merchants, Carleton's refusal to accept high discounts on bills of exchange made him an enemy. Elias Hardy, the New York lawyer who, the year before, had prepared the protest against the Fifty-Five, organized an opposition party with the clear object of seizing power by means of a majority in the legislature. A riot took place on the night of November 9 when Carleton's supporters were besieged in the Mallard House. When the votes were counted Hardy's party won, but after the sheriff convened a meeting of the candidates to hear a protest, the men on the government's list were declared the winners.[57]

New Brunswick was a unique province. Ninety per cent of its population consisted of newly arrived Loyalists, but dissension broke their ranks upon their setting foot in the new province. Loyalist leaders declared that the proven loyalty of their people made their province the palladium of the British Empire in America, but they brought with them something more than loyalty. It was piously supposed that the fierce fury of public debate, the division of society by political parties, so notable in "the old thirteen," would be exorcised from the constitution of the new province by a spirit of discipline and obedience. Events from the outset showed that such expectations were ridiculous. All the Loyalists had their origin in colonies where public debate was carried on at a high level and where constituted authority was always challenged. It would be almost impossible to find the record of any Loyalist leader of important repute who had approved without reserve the entire policy of the British government towards the American colonies since 1763. The Loyalist refugees on Long Island had been intensely politically conscious, bitterly critical of British military policy during the war, and still more critical during the peace negotiations of the Whigs' policy of surrender. They brought with them to New Brunswick, as to the other colonies, a determination to enjoy the kind of government to which they had been accustomed in their homelands, to concentrate in a popular assembly all the strengths and virtues, the rivalries, intrigues, and ideologies, of an alert and intelligent society.

Five Colonies in a New Empire
1785-1803

As the confusion of the American Revolution and the subsequent Loyalist settlement cleared away, the British region of the North Atlantic displayed a pattern that was remarkable for its irregularity and diversity. Five colonies faced the future under intensely varied circumstances. The base for Nova Scotian prosperity was substantially broadened by the coming of the Loyalists. Newfoundland was still "a fief of the Admiralty," or, in the classic interpretation of William Knox, a great ship moored for the convenience of the British fishery. Nothing had occurred in the course of the war to alter British thinking or to expedite the granting of civil government which the existence of the colony seemed to demand. The remaining three colonies were mere fledglings. Before they could become self-sufficient, new inflows of capital and labour would be required. Hopeful Loyalists blandly assumed that the immense financial expenditure and high degree of parental supervision on the part of Great Britain would be continued, and that the promise of 1783-84 would be honoured by intense British effort to develop the region.

Yet there was to be no continuing policy or plan of action for the second British Empire in North America. Pitt's government, very much under the influence of the *laissez-faire* thought of Adam Smith and of the practical necessity for economizing, was not disposed to anything positive or aggressive. Lord Sydney, the Colonial Minister, having elaborately reorganized the region, proved to be enigmatic and negative. Sir Guy Carleton, Lord Dorchester, coming to Canada as Governor-in-Chief of British North America in 1786, completely failed to support the expectations of the Loyalists, who looked for great things from the man who was so avowedly their hero. He never found the health or leisure to visit the Atlantic Provinces. The visits of members of the Loyalist Commission of 1785 caused confidence and elation, and leading Loyalists received payment of capital sums in token of their losses.[1] British largess to half-pay officers and their dependents was to continue for three-quarters of a century and it became a common saying in the provinces that "Loyalist half-pay officers never died." But, following this preliminary generosity, the purse-strings notably tightened. Small parliamentary grants supported the provincial establishments of government, but no sums were available for the introduction of new settlers or for the consolidation of the work of 1783-84. British policy for the region deteriorated into a grudging assent to the need to meet local and particular urgencies.

As the new settlers of the provinces grappled with the circumstances of a greatly changed world, life became laborious and humdrum. Pioneer travail was not conducive to high thinking, and less praise was given to the bounty of the British government. But one mark of a conscious and articulate imperial policy was the impetus given to the Church of England as an instrument of state. Civil disobedience in the lost American colonies, it was widely considered, had been due to the absence of correct religious principles. Revolution had come because men had not been educated to accept the station in life to which it had pleased God to call them. Obedience to the Crown could be fostered in the new empire by indoctrination in the forms and order of the Church of England. Because of the absence of episcopal supervision and proper means of enlisting an American clergy, the Church had never been able effectively to combat revolutionary propaganda. At New York a critical and militant Tory clergy had won Sir Guy Carleton to this point of view. All the eminent Loyalist leaders had agreed in identifying membership in the Church of England with loyalty to Great Britain. A petition signed by eighteen clergymen asked for the establishment of an episcopal see in Nova Scotia and the founding of a college for the education of candidates for Holy Orders. Windsor, where the gentry of Halifax had country estates, was suggested as a site for the latter.[2]

In response there arrived at Halifax late in 1787 as Bishop of Nova Scotia, with jurisdiction over Canada, Newfoundland, and New Brunswick as well, the Right Reverend Charles Inglis, former rector of Trinity Church, New York. Throughout this vast diocese there were but twenty-four missionary clergymen, all drawing their incomes from the Society for the Propagation of the Gospel, the intermediary of the British government for establishing the Church in the colonies. A few had been in Nova Scotia and Newfoundland for a long time, but most were refugee Loyalists for whom new livings had to be found. Many of these had been ordained as recruits from the disintegrating Congregational Church of New England. Their spirit was latitudinarian but their difficult years as refugees had produced a strong Erastian faith. The consecration of Inglis did not receive unanimous approval among them, and there were a few whose background was so American that they did not want an episcopate at all. To most Americans an episcopate was reminiscent of religious persecution in the seventeenth century and, even among the Loyalists, sentiments of this kind lingered.

The task of Inglis was really to nurture an infant church in the colonies and to make it a dominating force in society. As he stated in a letter to the new Bishop of Pennsylvania, whose task was even more difficult, government was on his side but government expected far too much. The visits he could make to the more remote areas of his charge could be of little more than token character and his work had to be delegated to subordinates. In this, as in civil affairs, the British government was not too late but furnished far too little. Church of England clergymen were too few to bring the ministrations of the Church among the widely scattered settlements. Some of them regarded their missions as being somewhat the equivalent of established English livings. In spite of the honourable record of Bishop Inglis, there is to be discovered in his correspondence a great concern for the rewards of his office that reminds the reader of the more worldly preoccupations of his brother bishops in England during the eighteenth century.[3]

Inglis was able to persuade the Assembly of Nova Scotia to grant £400 annually for the maintenance of an academy at Windsor. This commenced to function in November, 1788. In the following year, after the British government had promised the cost of a college building, he secured from the Assembly another annual grant of £400 for maintenance as well as £500 for the purchase of land. A large building of three stories, 204 feet long, appeared at Windsor, the projected centre of higher education for all of British North America.

It was not difficult to achieve such results at a time when denominational spirit was quiescent and the principle of the union of church and state was accepted by almost everyone. The Church of England had been established by law in Nova Scotia since 1758 and New Brunswick accepted establishment in 1786. Yet Inglis knew his America and his temper was not dictatorial. He understood that, in spite of the great advantage conferred by establishment, his church would have to win its way among the people. For the religious climate was free. Many of the leaders of this embryonic society regarded membership in the Church of England simply as an outward guarantee of respectability. There were certainly a great many infected with the scepticism and cynicism of the age, such as James Putnam, the Assistant Judge of New Brunswick, who many years before had remonstrated with the young John Adams that religion was "a mere delusion."[4] In spite of its acceptance of religious establishment, there was in fact little that was fervently spiritual about Loyalist society. Toleration was an attitude much more generally affected. Nova Scotia was filled with religious dissenters from the Church of England but these, in a vague kind of way, were willing to acknowledge the Church's maternal control. Of these, the

Congregationalists had been the largest group. In 1770 the Congregationalists of Nova Scotia had enjoyed the services of seven ordained ministers, four of whom were graduates of Harvard.[5] The war and the invasions of the New Lights, however, had broken their unity and prepared them to accept the ordained dispensation.

Toleration for Roman Catholics came at the very time when the new religious arrangement was being proclaimed. In the early days of Halifax the penal laws against them had been rigorously enforced. Mass had been tolerated for Acadians and Indians only. In 1770 the Abbé Bailly was ordered to close the door of the barn where he officiated against his Irish parishioners, and had been compelled to use a secluded place six miles outside the town.[6] But in 1783 a petition from the Catholic population resulted in an act of the legislature permitting public worship and a church was opened in the following year.[7]

Newfoundland, too, witnessed a remarkable transformation so far as the climate of religious feeling was concerned. There the Roman Catholic threat to the Protestant Succession had always been taken seriously and as recently as Palliser's time Catholic priests had been hunted like criminals. Catholics in Newfoundland had been subjected to all the disabilities of those in Ireland and, in addition, had been required to pay special taxes. The spirit of persecution that reigned was perhaps most emphatically expressed by an order that children of Roman Catholic parents should be baptized "according to law" by an Anglican clergyman. But in 1784, in consequence of an agreement between the British government and the Vatican, there arrived from Ireland Reverend James O'Donnell as Prefect Apostolic, the real founder of the Roman Catholic Church on the island. Toleration was another example of the manner in which the British government contradicted the tenets of its mercantilist faith, for, as Admiral Milbanke vigorously complained, the construction of churches encouraged the growth of the winter population. On Newfoundland the Church of England had maintained missionaries since 1703. When Bishop Inglis extended his jurisdiction, there were only three and never, during his lifetime, did the island receive the benefit of an episcopal visitation. While Roman Catholic and Protestant dissenting congregations were waxing in numbers and raising new church buildings, the Church of England structure at St John's was in ruins.

Believing that the Church of England must achieve its ends by methods of gradualism, Inglis made only one important effort to effect a drastic change in the colonial way of life. He took violent exception to the marriage laws of Nova Scotia and New Brunswick, objecting to "the trading justices" of the peace in whose hands the power of writing marriage contracts in part resided. The Church of England was established in both provinces. Why, then, were the laws of England concerning marriage not in effect?

But Americans were accustomed to regard marriage as a civil rather than as a religious contract and the two governments refused to strip the justices of their powers. The scarcity of Church of England clergymen was a poignant answer to his complaints. The marriage laws of all the Atlantic Provinces were to become objects of public controversy because they excluded the ministers of the important Methodist and Baptist movements that were now assuming fixed form and direction.

II

Only on affairs of trade did the British government give close attention to the Atlantic Provinces, and the policies pursued continued to be traditional. The decision of 1783 to close West Indian ports to American vessels created fair terms of trade for the shipping interests of Halifax, Saint John, Shelburne, and St Andrews which, while the good fortune lasted, carried on a considerable overseas commerce. But the goods their ships carried were mainly American in origin. Very few of the new settlements, especially in New Brunswick, were able to produce surplus goods for export. Breadstuffs had, in the main, to be imported, and the British Parliament, taking note of necessity, in 1786 made this traffic legal; the lieutenant-governors were given the right to admit American produce by proclamation, a privilege that was to be perennially exercised. Extraordinarily enough, the privilege had later to be extended to include lumber. It was still possible to cut and saw timber more cheaply in Maine than in the two provinces where forests abounded but where there was no large and skilled labour force. Communities were isolated and, for the most part, self-sufficient in food and raw materials. Markets of any size, such as Halifax and Saint John, had to be supplied from the outside. During the war Newfoundland had obtained its flour and beef from Canada. In peacetime this commerce continued to develop, but by an act of Parliament of 1786 the colony was allowed the privilege accorded to Nova Scotia and New Brunswick of importing bread, flour, Indian corn, and livestock from the United States.

The British determination to close the ports of the overseas empire to American shipping produced reprisals in Massachusetts, where traders had a lean year or two in searching for new commerce. But mutual exclusion compelled evasions of the restrictions so that the ships of the provinces and the United States established rendezvous in the anchorages of the Bay of Fundy, or wherever convenience suggested. Trade by barter of British manufactured goods for American foodstuffs and raw materials became a rule of life. American vessels flew their flags in the harbour of Halifax where, as elsewhere, it was not always judicious to enforce the Laws of Trade and Navigation too literally.[8] Especially for the provinces this trade was essential, and the highly developed system of legal evasion fostered smuggling. International trade, in spite of the shipping war, flourished "on the lines," and the Passamaquoddy Islands, by reason of their many safe retreats, became the centre of so great an informal commerce that the statistics of trade were rendered utterly meaningless. The new enterprise in trade of the New Englanders brought tea, citrus fruits, and other products of China and the Mediterranean into British North America by a much cheaper and more direct route than formerly. In orthodox British circles Eastport, on Moose Island, was execrated as the bane of the fair trader and as a nest of criminals and smugglers; but Lorenzo Sabine, the American historian who was brought up there, testifies that many good "Tories" from New Brunswick came to do business.[9]

A few of the irritations of the first empire survived into the second. At the outset the British government was so sensitive to the great constitutional issue of the American Revolution that it withdrew from the royal instructions the requirement that office-holders should take an oath of allegiance to the King in Parliament.[10] In Whitehall there was a great reluctance to take colonial questions, other than those concerning trade, into Parliament at all. At Shelburne many Loyalists took the oath to the King in Parliament, but only on the understanding that the powers of Parliament did not extend to taxation.[11] Loyalists had come to the new provinces bearing in mind the general terms of the surrender in principle, brought to America by the Carlisle Commission in 1778, that the colonies should not be taxed by Parliament. Yet almost as if the Revolution had never happened, the Surveyor General of the King's Woods, Sir John Wentworth, appeared in Nova Scotia bearing the same letter of patent he had employed before the war in the forests of Maine and New Hampshire. There he had been a most industrious prosecutor of those who trespassed upon the mark of the Broad Arrow, which reserved the best pine for the use of the royal shipyards. When he came to Shelburne in May of 1784 his statement of the claims of his office was greeted by angry remonstrances.[12] Appointing deputies in all the provinces, including Canada, he took measures to ensure that the interest of the Royal Navy should be respected by marking off great reserves of pine forest for its purposes. The terms of his commission went so far as to authorize the stencilling of the Broad Arrow on pine of twenty-four inches in diameter standing on private lands as well as public.

Wentworth was a man in the prime of life, still capable of the endurance of his youth, as when he had stalked through the hills of New Hampshire to protect the king's rights. At London he was highly connected and the immense area of his authority enabled him to contest the jurisdictions of colonial governments. Individuals who were developing their new grants of land feared his invasions. The new city of Saint John had to face his challenge for control over projected sites for wharves, booms, and mast-ponds. When forced to a contest he nevertheless shrank from the unpleasant expedient of testing in the colonial courts his authority, which stemmed from the Lords of the Treasury. Colonial lawyers were prepared to show that land-grants were exempt from the visitations of his agents. Yet Wentworth's reservations had a harassing effect on both governments and commerce. He had authority to deny settlement to whole areas of the country.[13]

A completely unexpected intrusion of British policy came in 1790 when, like a bolt from the blue, instructions arrived from London forbidding any further free grants of land in North America. In the great extent of ungranted lands of the Crown, Pitt's government saw an opportunity of redeeming a portion of the heavy expenses incurred by the settlement of Loyalists and disbanded soldiers.[14] The policy of selling land at one dollar an acre had been adopted for the opening up of the western territories of the United States, and Britain was moved by the American example. The British government intended that such a restriction should limit the activities of greedy speculators in land, one of the bugbears of administration in the lost thirteen colonies. Lord Dorchester never put the policy into effect in Canada.[15] But the lieutenant-governors of Nova Scotia and New Brunswick felt compelled to obey the instruction in its entirety. In Nova Scotia it was implemented without noticeable protest. There it was taken for granted that no good land remained for disposal. In New Brunswick it was supposed that the large American claim to the western part of the province, hinging upon a definition of "the true St Croix," was the reason for the summary *mandamus* from London.

This restriction on the granting of land, supposed to be temporary until such time as the British government could work out new arrangements, was actually in effect for seventeen years. It forced the two governments into procedures by which settlers had to be cajoled into tilling the soil without clear title, and by which licensed squatting became the normal state of affairs, especially in areas opened up following the Loyalist arrival of 1783-84. Immigrants who laboured for years on freshly turned lands were compelled to rely on the assurance of "location tickets" that seemed to become more flimsy and specious as the years went by. In New Brunswick, where new immigration was needed to sustain the economy, the effect of the 1790 instruction was stifling. Less than one-tenth of the acreage of the province had been granted. Men of enterprise now had nothing to hope for from government. It was supposed by the British government that land values would rise in consequence of the restriction. The evidence shows that they fell instead and that the policy was contributory to an emigration that became substantial at the turn of the century. At Fredericton, where civil servants subsisted on small salaries with the expectation of high fees for the passing of land-grants, despair became general. As year succeeded year and the announcement of the policy was not followed by any further instructions from London, the impression of British neglect and lack of interest deepened. His Majesty's ministers were too occupied with other matters to set prices for the ungranted lands of Nova Scotia and New Brunswick or to take any measures whatever to render them productive.

Imperial policy, always different for Newfoundland, continued in broad intent to be traditional. Palliser's Act, slightly amended in 1786, provided that the first hundred vessels clearing British ports after January 31 of each year, and carrying crews of which at least three-fourths were British seamen, should receive bounties of £40 each, the second hundred to receive £25 each. These were so successful that European markets were glutted with fish. "Newfoundland," said William Grenville, Secretary of State in 1789, "is in no respect a British colony and is never so considered in our laws."[16] But still the West Country shipmasters deducted forty shillings from the annual wage for the return passage and still left seamen behind. Population continued to grow, reaching 15,000 by 1792. Wrestling with the problems of the unrecognized colony in 1789, Admiral Milbanke allowed himself to be persuaded by his secretary to search his commission for authority to create courts of law. In consequence judges were appointed to dispense the laws of England for civil disputes and to preside over the courts of common pleas that were so desperately needed. But the merchants of St John's who, according to Milbanke, wanted a court "by which they may be permitted, whenever they think proper, to tear to pieces the boatmen and other poor people with impunity," complained to England.[17] The Board of Trade agreed that Milbanke had misinterpreted his instructions and that his courts were illegally constituted. But they had been useful and successful. The new Committee of Trade was convinced by the Governor's accounts of the chaotic state of the judicature on the island and recommended the establishment of a court by Royal Letters Patent.

Delay followed because of the conviction that the Act of 1699 should not be trespassed upon by the operation of the royal prerogative, but finally, in the teeth of West Country opposition, the government in 1791 passed through Parliament an act that gave to Newfoundland a full-fledged supreme court with jurisdiction over both criminal and civil cases. Once again the urgencies of the colony triumphed over the traditionalists. The first Chief Justice, John Reeves, though officiating for only two months of the year during the fishing season, gave to the life of Newfoundland a whole new element of stability and continuity. In 1792 he persuaded Parliament to grant legal status to the surrogate courts of the naval officers, thus ensuring that a degree of justice should come to the outports as well as to St John's. These changes were frankly experimental, but the Act of 1791 was annually amended and improved until, in 1809, it was made permanent.

At the parliamentary inquiry into the affairs of Newfoundland in 1793, honest mercantilists like William Knox and Sir Hugh Palliser continued to fulminate against the Newfoundland community and the institutions provided to give it something more than the minimum of social stability. But the colony had now become so populous and so deeply rooted that it was no longer rational to think in terms of dismantlement and deportation. Newfoundland, moreover, was about to enter upon another phase of the fortunes that had always caused the colony to grow. This was the last and longest of the great wars with France.

III

That conflict, breaking out in 1793 and lasting for twenty-two years, produced over the long run effects on the five colonies that were both stimulating and salutary. Ultimately it generated an economy on something like fixed lines that was stable and prosperous, leading the provinces into the nineteenth century on a wave of surging expansion. It furnished new challenges to the adventurous and its financial inflation gave spur to the industrious. It created a demand for a new staple, timber.

But the effects of the war were dispersed at first, and for the first ten years it could probably be demonstrated that the evil consequences outweighed the good. Nova Scotia and Newfoundland, the more mature economies, gained immediate benefit from the renewed activities of the Royal Navy. The North Atlantic squadron was relatively small compared with that in the West Indies, the normal complement being four frigates and two sloops at Halifax, two frigates and four sloops at St John's.[18] But the ports were frequently visited by other vessels of war of all sizes and the officers of the vice-admiralty courts were to grow immensely wealthy on the booty captured by His Majesty's ships and the privateers. Rising prices brought prosperity to the well-established farmers of Minas and Cumberland, and to all engaged in trade. Sir John Wentworth, the new governor who succeeded Parr in 1792, was to preside over a thriving and vibrant society. After ten years of tolerating the enlarged privileges of the French on their shore, Newfoundlanders again acquired a monopoly of the fishery. Again St Pierre and Miquelon were occupied, by an expedition from Halifax in May of 1793. Though prosperity mounted, the war simply emphasized and intensified the normal processes that kept the fishery going. The great gap between wealth and poverty became wider. Debt became deeper and more widespread.

War also removed any possibility that the British government would regain interest in the growth of its American empire or that new programs of development would be launched. So long as Dorchester remained Governor-in-Chief there was no chance of anything of that nature happening, for he was in profound disfavour with Pitt, Henry Dundas, and other British ministers. To New Brunswick, St John's Island, and Cape Breton, where another effort by government was necessary to reinforce the dubious success already obtained, the situation occasioned gloom. As his two regiments sailed for Halifax and the West Indies, Thomas Carleton at Fredericton witnessed the abandonment of the spacious barracks he had constructed for a thousand men. His plans for the expansion of settlement up the St John had been given impetus by the establishment of the Madawaska settlement in 1789. Several hundred Acadians, gathered from scattered areas in the southern part of the province, had moved there. At Presqu'ile and Grand Falls Carleton had planted garrisons against the Americans who were encroaching from the west, and also against the Malecites who still possessed the capacity to intimidate settlers. The withdrawal of his legions arrested his program for provincial development just as it was getting started and, as elsewhere, the loss of soldiers meant a loss of specie that grievously retarded trade and industry.

In 1787, when Carleton, as commander of all the troops in the Atlantic Provinces, had proceeded on inspection to Halifax, he had been the dominant personality throughout the region, though he failed to receive the respect he thought was his due. The founders of New Brunswick could, with some justice, think of their province as the centre of the renovated empire. But by 1793 complete disillusionment was general. In London Carleton shared the disgrace of his elder brother. Wentworth, highly in favour, was the man of mark, accustomed to give advice to the British government on the affairs of all the provinces. In the war New Brunswick was strategically a backwater and Halifax a place of military strength. Intelligence from London was relayed to Saint John through Halifax so that the merchants of Nova Scotia acquired great advantages, forcing New Brunswick traders to pay high discounts for the forwarding of goods. To the British Admiralty the long voyage around Cape Sable and into the Bay of Fundy was notoriously dangerous. Seldom could Admiral Murray at Halifax find convoy protection for the merchantmen of Saint John, where the overseas trade that had flourished for ten years quickly melted away. In official circles it became customary to think of New Brunswick as a satellite of Nova Scotia. When Prince Edward came to Halifax in 1794 to take command of the troops, this tendency became more pronounced.

St John's Island was completely ignored by the war-burdened British government except on those occasions when the legislature, with the tacit approval of Lieutenant-Governor Fanning, moved to expropriate the landowners who had failed to comply with the conditions of their grants. But the influence of the proprietors at London was able to turn back all such efforts. In 1797, thirty years after the holding of the lottery, not a single settler resided on twenty-three of the townships. On twelve others there was a total of thirty-six families. Nevertheless, in 1798, when the island was renamed Prince Edward after the royal prince of that name, the total population approached 4,400, a tribute to the value of the lands rather than to the effect of the measures of government. Amongst officialdom at Charlottetown there was, following the reckless example of Lieutenant-Governor Walter Patterson, a vested interest that hoped to profit from escheat. But the resistance comprised the proprietors who had honoured the conditions of their grants as well as those who had not. It would be impossible to maintain tenant farmers on one half of the island if the other half should be opened to freehold settlement.

Everybody in Charlottetown, Lord Selkirk was told in 1803 by the loquacious and self-important Chief Justice Thorpe, was asleep. Over the quiet but growing community he found an idle governor surrounded by a "bad" council. The populace was alive to the necessity of escheat and looked forward to the day when free grants would be available, but the Glenaladale Scots, who had come in 1772, continued their improvements on the unwritten promise of leases. The two shire towns, Princetown and Georgetown, were "rotten boroughs" with three houses each. At election time votes could be made by the purchase of their lots. Provisions were scarce and expensive, while farmers looked chiefly to the raising of cattle for income. About four hundred beasts were exported annually to Newfoundland, the returns coming mostly in rum. About seventy small vessels traded with Halifax and Newfoundland. Oats and barley were said to be the best in North America, but the fishery was completely neglected except by the French of the north shore, who were "all farmers and all fishermen." Among the recently arrived English settlers there was a strong feeling against Roman Catholics, who made up two-thirds of the population.[19]

Cape Breton could record virtually no progress during this period. Virulent squabbles distinguished the administration of Des Barres and his successors. In 1800 there were but six miles of passable road on the entire island. Under licence the coal mines were worked by the lieutenant-governors who took a fee of five shillings for each chaldron extracted.[20] The removal of the garrison from Sydney at the outbreak of war threatened to cause the evacuation of the entire population, but three hundred Acadians returned from Miquelon, following its capture, to settle about Arichat. Government could do little to check the illegitimate activities of many transients. Thousands of moose and caribou in the northern regions were slaughtered for their skins, so that the stench of their carcasses could be noticed by the crews of vessels passing along the coasts.[21] Around the shores about Sydney came other interlopers, who cut coal from the cliffs. Like many of the inhabitants of the island, the government of Cape Breton in these years would convey the impression that it had been washed ashore by a great storm and left to its own resources for survival. Sydney, according to an indignant British officer, was the worst place in America. Owing to the economy of Lord Dorchester, the barracks were in ruins. The population consisted of "drunken rascals" who charged a dollar a day for labour. "A gentleman arriving in court and looking at the petty jury held up his hands in amazement that so many criminals should be waiting to be tried."[22]

After ten years the reorganized Atlantic Provinces were completely unable to fill the role planned for them in 1783, of supplying the British West Indies with foodstuffs and raw materials. Only the better and long-established areas of Nova Scotia had beef and flour for export, and the war produced at Halifax a series of prohibitions on the export of food, owing to the requirements of the navy. So far as the carrying trade was concerned, the expectation had been filled to a considerable degree. With the coming of the Loyalists, ship-building had become a familiar vocation and a great deal of American produce, in addition to the home-produced fish, had been carried to the West Indies in Nova Scotian and New Brunswick bottoms. The Americans had poached on the trade, conveying goods to the French and Spanish islands, from which they were re-exported to the British, and smuggling as opportunity offered in collaboration with West Indian planters who preferred their cheaper prices. But at Halifax and Saint John the West Indian markets loomed forth in the minds of the merchants as a kind of promised land where the two provinces would ultimately redeem the extravagant hopes of 1783.

War with France destroyed this prospect. French privateers, operating from New York and the ports of the Chesapeake, intercepted large numbers of provincial vessels, mostly in southern latitudes. At Boston and other American ports unfriendly officials collaborated with the French by selling captured ships and cargoes, sometimes encouraged by mobs wearing the red cockade of the French Revolution. The naval squadron at Halifax succeeded fairly well in keeping the coastlines free from these intruders, but could not supply sufficient convoy protection over the distant sea lanes. For the mast-ships from Saint John Admiral Murray was solicitous, but New Brunswick shipping fared worse than the Nova Scotian. The rise in the rates of insurance was quite sufficient to cause the complete carrying-trade to the West Indies to fall into American hands.

The Treaty of Amity and Commerce of 1794, commonly known as Jay's Treaty, merely set the seal on what the first two years of the war accomplished. To buy the goodwill of the United States and to secure her agreement to restrictions on neutral shipping, Britain admitted her vessels to the ports of the West Indies. When it fell, the blow had moral rather than material repercussions. One of the assurances by which the provinces had been settled in 1783 had been removed and it seemed that Britain had repudiated her faithful subjects in order to give comfort to the rebels. From Halifax vessels under convoy continued to sail to the West Indies. But by and large the overseas trade of the two provinces dwindled to a fraction of what it had been before the war. At the turn of the century it was commonly remarked that New Brunswick had no vessels of any account.[23] In 1799 Liverpool, which once had boasted of a fleet of sixty ships, was reduced to one.[24]

The consequence was that the trade of New Brunswick and Nova Scotia became tributary to the Americans. It was too hazardous and expensive to send large ships to blue water. But little ships, manned by crews derisively termed landsmen by sailors of the ocean, hovered along the coastlines, unloading cargoes of fish into the waiting holds of American deep-sea vessels, especially about the convenient fringes of the shores of Passamaquoddy Bay, the familiar resorts of those who traded "on the lines." This traffic developed new facets as, about 1795, the potentialities of the American market for plaster of Paris, or gypsum, became recognized. In the states south of Pennsylvania it was greatly in demand as a fertilizer, and Phineas Bond, a Nova Scotian merchant, opened a business for importing it to Philadelphia. Dug from the flats of the upper extremities of the Bay of Fundy, it was bartered for tea, tobacco, and other goods that were invariably smuggled into the provinces, the Americans making the prices and terms of trade as they did for fish. While the overseas trade of the great merchants dwindled almost to nothing, little men carried on this thriving trade that made British subjects, as it was often grimly stated, bondsmen to the Americans. Cash balances seldom found their way to the provinces.

The Americans poached upon the trade of Newfoundland, especially on Sundays when they fished in defiance of local laws under the noses of the inhabitants. Their skill in barter and in the acquisition of favourable balances of trade sometimes denuded the shopkeepers of St John's of ready cash. The terms of trade could deprive Newfoundland even of its copper coin to such a degree that the change from a sixpence had to be taken out in "a dram."[25] But the Americans could not fundamentally affect the island's commerce. Owing to the restrictions on neutral shipping and the dangers from Algerian pirates, their large vessels could not convey fish to the Mediterranean. Their cod was sometimes taken to overseas markets in British ships.[26] Still the sack ships came from Devon under convoy but the number of West Country ships engaged in fishing operations steadily dwindled. By 1804 there were only twenty.[27] This was in spite of the fact that the volume of Newfoundland's exports was steadily increasing, the explanation being that the resident boatmen were approaching a position from which they could account for the entire catch. The war and Jay's Treaty could not slow the rapid growth of the colony.

Though apprehensions were great and overseas commerce suffered, hostilities touched very lightly upon the provinces. In 1794 when there was news of the arrival of a French squadron at New York for an attack on Halifax, or St John's, or both, wild alarm rang along the North Atlantic shore. Wentworth called twelve hundred militiamen from the country into Halifax to reinforce the six hundred regulars of the garrison and Carleton erected batteries at Saint John. But the only occasion on which the enemy appeared in force was in September, 1796, when the French Admiral Richery, with seven ships of the line, escaped the British blockade at Cadiz and landed at Bay of Bulls for an attack on St John's. When he discovered that it was strongly garrisoned by the Royal Newfoundland Regiment and that there was no hope of achieving surprise, he contented himself with the burning of a few boats and the taking of a few prisoners. There was great excitement in St John's in 1797 when the fore-topmen of the *Latona*, reflecting the general discontent of sailors of the Royal Navy, mutinied and refused to go aloft. Under the firm leadership of Admiral Waldegrave, the marines and troops combined to restore discipline. Irish difficulties, too, overflowed into Newfoundland. In 1798 an association of United Irishmen, tinged with "the infidel opinions of [Thomas] Paine," formed conspiracies to murder all Protestants as they assembled in church on a Sunday morning, destroy all property, and sail off to the United States. They were forestalled by information laid by Bishop O'Donnell and by the quick action of the garrison commander, Major-General Skerrett.[28]

As the first phase of the great conflict ended in 1801, the prosperity that came with wartime prices was slowly working its way into the back settlements of the Atlantic Provinces. Through the military medium British cash circulated through the countryside as, in 1794, regiments of troops were raised from the colonial population to replace regulars who had gone abroad. This told grievously upon farmers and landowners whose sons marched off to join the colours and forced them to greater exertions of their own. Prosperous agricultural establishments were family affairs with farmers distributing duties among sons and daughters. Almost everywhere the great complaint was shortage of labour. Mingled with the patriotic overtones of the period were the protests of farmers without help and employers in the towns whose production was slackened by enlistments in the army, impressments for the king's ships, and callings up of the militia.

IV

The great immigration of the period was that of Highland Scots who came to Prince Edward Island, Pictou and Antigonish, and Cape Breton, driven from their homeland by landlords who wanted the glens for sheep-runs. In 1790 the Glenaladale Macdonalds were reinforced by new arrivals and in the following year two vessels loaded with immigrants appeared at Pictou. There a segregation on religious lines occurred as Father Angus McEachern crossed from Prince Edward Island to confront the proselytizing activities of the Presbyterian minister, the Reverend Dr McGregor.[29] By his advice most of the Catholics moved along the coast to the eastward. The influx attained something like torrential proportions between 1801 and 1803, when no less than eleven ships arrived.[30] Three of these brought the Selkirk settlers to Prince Edward Island in 1803, discharging their eight hundred passengers on the low shores about Point Prim. Originally destined for St Mary's in Upper Canada, they adjusted themselves so well to the primitive circumstances of the country that Selkirk, over the next few years, sent fresh contingents to join them.

Pictou rapidly became an important centre of population. In 1803 there were five thousand settlers along the eastern shore to the Gut of Canso, the newcomers exhibiting a noticeable preference for living in sight of tidewater. By reason of the presence of two "anti-burgher" ministers, Pictou had already become a town noted for religious and philosophical enthusiasms. The settlers who had come with the *Hector* in 1773 were living comfortably in frame houses as they contemplated wave upon wave of fresh arrivals who subsisted on potatoes for the first year and grew grain in the second. In the harbour the timber trade was thriving but the consumption was provincial and it was said that all the good trees were gone. Selkirk discovered in Nova Scotia that settlers were satisfied with licences of occupation issued by the provincial government. These were generally accepted as good security in lieu of titles which the government was powerless to grant.[31] A great cause of discontent, the grant in 1765 of the entire coast westward to Tatamagouche to the Philadelphia Company, had recently been removed by escheat.

The Gaelic invasion leapt over the Gut of Canso in 1791 when some of the Catholic immigrants settled on the western shore of Cape Breton in harbours as far north as Margaree. From there a few made their way through the forests to the more sheltered vistas of the Bras d'Or Lakes, which quickly became known as the best retreat for prospective settlers. Commencing in 1802, the immigrant ships brought their passengers to Sydney, where they were distributed along the lands bordering this system of interior waterways. Cape Breton became a Scottish enclave where most of the inhabitants could speak only Gaelic and where the fishermen of Skye and other maritime regions of western Scotland found a country well adapted to their way of life.

Small streams of population from other sources entered the provinces in these years. Newfoundland continued to gain its Irish "boys," but lost many of them to the Americans or to other seducers who spirited them away in defiance of the Act of 1699. Faced with the fact of thousands of unchronicled lives and voyages, the historian can fairly infer that the Irish populations of Charlottetown, Halifax, and Saint John came by this route. Of the three larger provinces it was New Brunswick, at this stage, that lagged in the race for population. In contrast with Wentworth at Halifax, Carleton had devised no facilities for immigration. His administration, unlike that of Nova Scotia, had no funds to give encouragement to newcomers. On the St John above Woodstock, where settlement had developed, some of it from across the border, the instructions forbidding land-grants would seem to have had a more damaging impact than in Nova Scotia. This may have been owing to the more Yankee character of the settlers who, in making their improvements, kept in mind the possibility of selling at a profit. They could not do this without clear title. In 1803 New Brunswick had a population of about twenty thousand, a figure not significantly higher than in the year of its founding. The talk was of emigration rather than immigration and the goal was distant Niagara.

At the official level, the tone of life during the years following the Loyalist migration was highly secular, but at the turn of the century religion was fast becoming the great factor in the moulding of the new communities. Religiosity might be a better word to describe the social process as the churches of the Christian faith, both traditional and novel, imparted distinctiveness and a sense of moral purpose to a people who had, to a great extent, been bereft of religious influence. By 1800 the Roman Catholic Church was beginning to face its enormous missionary challenge. Since the conquest it had maintained from Quebec, in spite of great difficulties, a contact with the Acadians that while often interrupted during their wanderings nevertheless remained strong. Many testimonies of missionary priests assert that though the Acadians were sometimes deprived of religious observance for many years, their faith remained unshaken and their lives truly Christian. Especially during the American War and primarily for the purpose of keeping the Indians at peace, the British government had not merely tolerated but actually encouraged the work of the few priests whom the Bishop of Quebec could spare for service in Nova Scotia. At Halifax the abbés Maillard, Bailly, and Bourg held a large congregation together. A few other priests, ranging the forests of northern New Brunswick and cruising the seas of the gulf and Atlantic shores whenever fishing shallops offered convenient passage, extended the benefits of their occasional presence to the far-scattered Acadian communities.

A new departure occurred in 1787 when Reverend James Jones, sent to Halifax by the Bishop of Cork, was made Vicar-General for the English-speaking settlements in four provinces.[32] The Catholic population of Halifax was notoriously Irish and an Irish character was imparted to the jurisdiction. The elevation of Father O'Donnell in Newfoundland to episcopal dignity in 1796 had provided the Church with the framework of an organization throughout the entire Atlantic region. But during this time of intensive immigration from Scotland it was initiative from that country which gave to its work the greatest degree of momentum. Accompanying the Glenaladale settlers to Prince Edward Island in 1772 was Father James Macdonald, who for thirteen years ministered not only to his compatriots but to the Acadians as well. For five years, from 1785 to 1790, the Catholics of the province were without the services of a priest and the Bishop of Quebec was compelled to issue commissions to laymen to perform marriages and administer baptism. This interruption ended with the arrival of Father Angus McEachern, whose journeyings over the entire island by way of forest trails and over the often rough seas to Antigonish and to Judique in Cape Breton really laid the foundations of the Church among its Scottish constituents. Perhaps the most notable English-speaking example among a small group of zealous ministers, McEachern was no doubt able to endure the winter hardships because he learned to know the country almost as well as he knew the people. Continuing the mode of life of a Scottish priest under the religious persecutions of former years, he appeared in public in simple civilian attire. As late as 1812 Bishop Joseph Plessis was shocked by the destitution of the Scottish churches under McEachern's charge. "Only a priest brought up in Scotland would ever think of saying Mass in the like." Exterior symbols of worship such as albs and altar-cloths were absent. Yet the fervour of faith "surpasses all imagination."[33]

The Church received reinforcements when a few Royalist priests, exiled to England from old France, appeared on the scene. The Abbé de Calonne, former Vicar-General of the diocese of Cambrai and brother to the finance minister of Louis XVI, arrived at Charlottetown in 1800 to occupy the farm at the entrance to the harbour on the site of the former Fort la Joye. He strongly upheld the testimony of Anglican and Presbyterian contemporaries that Charlottetown was a wicked place, and found he could make little impact on the habits of the Irish, whom he described as ignorant and drunken.[34] With better fortune, he took refuge among the Acadians in the fishing village of Rustico. To St Mary's Bay there came about the same time Father Jean Sigogne, who established the first permanent mission in the rapidly growing Acadian settlement of Clare.[35] Like the other missionaries he found the first episcopal visitation of Bishop Pierre Denault to the Atlantic region extremely helpful. Amongst this dispersed Catholic community of French, Irish, Gaels, and a few English, discipline was frequently neccessary. The selection of a church site could create profound cleavage. Especially among the Scots, whose church in the homeland was a missionary one, the idea that people should contribute to church maintenance was alien.

As the Methodists and Baptists formed their loosely knit followings into organized churches, religious diversity became more emphasized. Henry Alline had left not even the foundation of a church, but his highly charged evangelistic methods prepared a climate of acceptance for what was to follow. From the Protestant point of view Alline performed a great work merely as a spectacular advocate of liberty of conscience, of the right to preach and to interpret Scripture without the authority of election. The Annapolis Valley seethed with gentle heresies from briefly established creeds. Communities and churches decided for and against the mild Arminianism which Alline had conjured up in defiance of predestinate principles. Compromises were made but seldom lasted, as Nova Scotians became learned in theological high thinking. Out of the mixed groups of Congregationalists and New Lights the Baptists emerged as a cohesive force. The founder of the church at Horton. Theodore Seth Harding, may be taken as a typical product of the theological whirlpools that abounded. He was brought up as a Congregationalist, became a Methodist minister at Horton, was expelled because of his belief in predestination, went to Halifax where he joined the Baptists, and returned to Horton as first Baptist minister.[36]

The old belief in baptism by immersion had come to Nova Scotia with the pre-Loyalist settlers from Connecticut and Rhode Island where it had, in many places, been in the ascendancy. Though long dormant, it had never died and at the turn of the century it became a leading article of faith for many who took part in the evangelistic movement. Realizing the need for discipline in face of antinomian perils, the ancient Christian heresy that sins of the flesh could be tolerated if the spirit was saved, eight ministers met at Horton in 1800 and formed the Baptist Association of Nova Scotia.[37] The model they chose was that of the Danbury Association of New England and it was from New England that they drew most of their doctrinal inspiration and material assistance. Closed communion became a rule. Dogmatic definition and centralized organization imparted power and the zeal for conversion spread rapidly through all of western Nova Scotia and into New Brunswick. Baptist missionaries demanded no financial contributions. Their preaching was eloquent and prolonged. Immersion for the converted offered spectacle to the curious as well as veneration to the devout. In wilderness areas where lonely pioneers had never had the benefit of religious inspiration, the preaching of the Baptists made occasion for communal gathering.

For some years Methodism made equally spectacular progress. Newfoundland, where it was ultimately to make its greatest impact on the Atlantic Provinces, had been the scene of the first Methodist meeting in British North America when Lawrence Coughlan had landed at Conception Bay in 1765. There he encountered a throng of people who gathered not to hear him preach but "to see if he looked like another man."[38] His labour lasted only eight years but he laid the foundation of a continuing Methodist connection that outlasted the quarter of a century in which he had no successor. As elsewhere, Methodist righteousness was called madness and the mercantile community was scandalized. Coughlan had a hard time but when he left there were over two hundred communicants. In the other provinces the history of the movement really commences in 1781 with the conversion of William Black. Black gathered together those who had been under Methodist influence in England and the thirteen colonies, added converts in Cumberland, and opened correspondence with John Wesley and the American Methodist Conference. The coming of the Loyalists and the subsequent appearance of new missionaries, chiefly from the United States, added to their numbers. The first Nova Scotian Conference was held at Halifax in 1786 when duties were divided among five missionaries and the contingent fund was nearly exhausted by the purchase of two horses.[39]

For a few years itinerant missionaries from the United States sustained Methodism in Nova Scotia. When this source of workers was exhausted, the movement lost considerable momentum and was unable to press the opportunities that lay before it, particularly in New Brunswick. Black was favourable to alignment with the American Conference but this body could not render continuous aid. Though Methodism antedated the Baptists it lost its advantage because it could not recruit preachers with the same degree of facile spontaneity. At the turn of the century it numbered eight hundred and fifty communicants and three thousand adherents in the Atlantic Provinces.[40] Yet these figures, like the much smaller ones offered by the Baptists at this period, do not reflect the immense amount of social as well as religious influence the Methodists were able to wield. The inner cells of Methodism radiated to far peripheries.

Bishop Charles Inglis could sense the impending failure of his grand design as these remarkable evangelizing endeavours swept over broad fronts, as Loyalist gentlemen along with the uneducated succumbed to their appeal. Ruthlessly he refused to ordain Methodist missionaries or to allow them to use his churches. His own clergy were too few to fight what he regarded as a contagion of schism and heresy. The Baptists he considered to be frenzied fanatics whose teachers were "very ignorant mechanics and common labourers who are too lazy to work." Their meetings consisted of "groanings, screamings, roarings, tremblings, faintings," where the newly converted called out, "Lord Jesus, come down and shake these dry bones."[41] The bishop, retired to his residence at Claremont, near Aylesford, felt helpless to deal with these old religious phenomena that so devastatingly invaded the new order he was trying to create. As he grew older, the entries in his diary became more despairing.[42]

In attempting to follow a liberal and politic course, Inglis had his troubles, too, with the extreme advocates of the union of church and state. The British government provided an annual grant of £1,000 for the maintenance of King's College at Windsor. The Board of Governors, dominated by Alexander Croke, judge of the Court of Vice-Admiralty, insisted that the statutes of the college should be modelled on those of Oxford, which declared that students should not only adhere to the Thirty-Nine Articles but take an oath to enter no place of worship beyond the establishment of the Church of England. The granting of the Royal Charter in 1802 and the promulgation of the Oxford statute produced a notable decline in registration. Refused by the Governors the right to publish a protest to the offending statute, Inglis called upon the intervention of the Archbishop of Canterbury, but failed to gain substantial amendment.[43] He knew that in an American environment persuasion was the sole means of dealing with religious dissidence, but the Board of Governors preferred to dictate.

Governments composed of sophisticated and educated men who were cynical and apathetic about the more doctrinal elements of faith were not disposed to enter upon persecution in order to sustain the Church of England. Warnings from the Bishop that the levelling doctrines of the Baptists and Methodists could overflow into the domain of civil society seem to have made no impression on men like Wentworth and Thomas Carleton as they issued licences for teaching and preaching to almost all who applied. What they were concerned about was that the royal instructions should be enforced and there were cases in which those who carried on their labours without licence endured some embarrassment and discomfort. The magistracy of King's County in New Brunswick was especially notable for rigorous enforcement of the laws, and a Baptist preacher, James Innes, spent a year in jail for venturing to perform the rites of marriage.[44] Yet those who complied with the royal instructions and the provincial laws concerning marriage received complete liberty. Wentworth and Carleton were surrounded by American advisers who were familiar with evangelizing endeavour of the old frontiers and were sensitive to public opinion. Duncan M'Coll, the Methodist minister at St Stephen, learned to regard Carleton as "a sincere friend."[45] M'Coll was a British subject with an honourable record of military service, perhaps in singular contrast to many American itinerants

of dubious loyalty. He could readily accept the oath of allegiance, a condition demanded by the royal instructions that had the effect of shortening
the stay of a number of his colleagues at a time of high tension in the
relationships of Britain and the United States.

V

Political development in the Atlantic Provinces varied widely. As yet nobody
had thought of the possibility of introducing the proletarian colonists of
Newfoundland to participation in government. Popular feeling was given
occasional expression by acts of violence and lawlessness, or by quickly
silenced protests against the naval courts of law in the outports. But there
could be no forum for the discussion of the affairs of a colony which officially
had no existence. Cape Breton had not acquired sufficient inhabitants for the
calling of a general assembly. Prince Edward Island, with a full-fledged
apparatus of government, could, and did, achieve a strong degree of colonial consciousness in the struggle, now of long standing, against the absentee landed proprietors. The tenantry were persuaded that escheat was
feasible and possible, and old settlers had learned to resent the coming of new
because the case for escheat remained strong so long as the island appeared
to be unpopulated and neglected. At Charlottetown the Stewarts and the
DesBrisays, the families of Peter Stewart, the second Chief Justice, and
Thomas DesBrisay, the Secretary, shared the public patronage, and, in spite
of intermarriage, often quarrelled fiercely with one another.

The legislatures of New Brunswick and Nova Scotia carried on their work
in the advanced political procedures and traditions of the lost thirteen colonies. In spite of all the propaganda that flowed about Lord Sydney at
London, no changes of an authoritarian kind had been made in the structure
and operation of provincial government. Though loyalty and harmony were
watchwords in 1783-84, the provincial governors were to be subjected to the
same strains that had finally destroyed the first British Empire. Loyalists
and pre-Loyalists were indistinguishable from one another in their capacity
for rivalry and dissension, in the scramble for office and patronage under the
new regime. Replicas of the constitutional struggles that had made so large
a part of the histories of New York and Massachusetts were to be the common lot of the two provinces. There was a great deal of talk about the mystic
union between Crown and people, but the British government had produced
no new formula to make the lot of colonial governors easier, no blueprints by
which popular assemblies were assigned limits.

In Nova Scotia the constitutional contest at first took the form of a
struggle between Loyalists and pre-Loyalists, between newcomers and "old-
comers," as the popular prints said.[46] The antagonistic feeling of 1783

welled up to a fight for mastery as the Loyalists gained a bloc of seats in the Assembly during the election of 1785. The British government had promised them preferment in the filling of vacancies to office, but the waiting was long. The attempt to open the way to office was begun in 1787 by two lawyers without office, Jonathan Sterns and Richard Taylor. The two assistant judges of the Supreme Court, Isaac Deschamps and James Brenton, were charged with "irregular and partial administration." Parr and the council dallied with the charges and, as excitement rose, riotings and murder distinguished a Halifax by-election of 1788. Private vendettas mingled with public causes when the House of Assembly met in 1789 and the Loyalist attack was directed against the council. Isaac Wilkins, a leading apostle of moderation in Pennsylvania in 1775 who had asked the House of Assembly to abstain from sending delegates to Congress, urged that the Lieutenant-Governor's "privy council," who were "evil and pernicious," should be removed.[47] Thomas Barclay, a leading Loyalist from New York, spoke equally warmly, pressing British precedents for the dismissal of ministers on address from representatives of the people.[48] In this debate, which vividly anticipated the dilemmas of Durham's era and attacked heavily the Achilles' heel of colonial government, the Loyalists were accused of rebellion.

Until the death of Parr in 1791, the affair of the judges dragged on as the Assembly annually moved for their impeachment. But the coming of Wentworth as Lieutenant-Governor marvellously transformed the troubled scene. Connected by family ties with the great house of Rockingham, he had the talent to capitalize upon them. The exercise of patronage was an art in which he excelled, being able without arousing hostile recrimination to appoint close relatives to high public office in the province. The arrival of Prince Edward, Duke of Kent and later father of Queen Victoria, in 1794 conferred upon Halifax society a distinction and grandeur that were entirely novel, and it was perhaps in keeping with this distinction that Wentworth was raised to a baronetcy. In his time Halifax indulged in effusions of loyalty and patriotism which, says a learned and authoritative writer, genuinely reflected its feelings.[49] Nova Scotians generally took it for granted that Sir John was "The Sovereign's fav'rite and the subject's pride."

> Around his chariot crowding numbers throng,
> And hail his virtues as he moves along.[50]

Tempers seldom flared and there were no suggestions of innovation. It was as if Nova Scotians – for a time – were silenced to complete conformity by the sermon of Bishop Inglis, preached at St Paul's on April 7, 1793, on the news of the outbreak of war with France. His text was, "My son fear thou the Lord and the King, and meddle not with those that are given to change."[51] Beneath the exuberant conservatism lay a solid commercial prosperity. Farmers could sell everything they produced at high prices. After

1795 the fishery was unmolested by French incursions. Sea-going men avenged the losses to overseas commerce; twelve to fifteen provincial privateers, half of them fitted out at Liverpool, were operating under letters of marque.

Thomas Carleton had a much more difficult time in New Brunswick, where democracy ran riot in the Loyalist citadel. Opposition was at first centred in Sunbury County, the home of "the old inhabitants." It soon came to include the merchants of Saint John for whom Carleton had little patience and less liking. It even spread to the Loyalist landowners whose prospects had dimmed from lack of the British subsidies of earlier days, absence of immigration, and decline in the values of real estate. Loyalist gentlemen, having no tenants and no labour to aid them, were mopping their brows in the bush. New Brunswick agriculture was in its infancy and large markets were distant. The marginal economy, supported by pensions and half-pay, promised little cheer for those who had sacrificed so much.[52] Even the officials at Fredericton, slaving on low salaries at a time of rapidly rising prices, were losing heart.

As early as 1792 the Lieutenant-Governor lost the majority that had supported his policies in the House of Assembly. The soul of the growing opposition was James Glenie, a Scot who nursed old grudges against Carleton which had grown out of the unfortunate experience of a court-martial during the Revolutionary War. He was a skilled mathematician turned lumberman, a dark giant of a man who could speak the politics of the bush. To his support came the mercantile representation of Saint John and discontented promoters of agricultural estates. All envied the petty perquisites of the clique of officials who, Glenie alleged, were seeking to engross for themselves all the wealth of the province. At a time when radicalism was in flower elsewhere in the world, though rapidly losing fashion, his opponents called him *jacobin*. There can be little doubt that he was in sympathy with the thinning strands of British thought that favoured the French Revolution. Whatever his principles were, he was prepared to go to great lengths to discredit Carleton's government and to tell the Colonial Office that the Lieutenant-Governor and his officers were stupid, corrupt, ignorant, and uncouth. He had many friends in high places beyond the confines of the province, of whom Prince Edward and Sir John Wentworth were notable examples.[53]

What was in large part a personal vendetta took political form as Glenie's following in the Assembly challenged the council's interference with money bills. Did the council, like the British House of Lords, have the right to alter a money bill? Did the government, like the British cabinet, have the sole right to initiate money bills in the House of Assembly? Nova Scotia was enduring the same controversies, but the New Brunswickers pressed their dilemmas to the logical conclusion, the complete breakdown of the legislative process in the voting of public monies. For four years, from 1795 to 1798, the province was without a revenue. The construction of the badly needed roads and bridges ceased. The indignant assemblymen, who wanted not only the privileges and power of the House of Commons but pay for their services as well, were accused of being the agents of the provincial merchants who, in spite of the suspension of the revenue acts, maintained their high prices for imported goods. The provincial revenue, it was alleged by Carleton's supporters, was going into the pockets of the commercial community.

Whether or not British parliamentary procedure should apply to the legislatures of the colonies was too difficult a problem for the Duke of Portland, Secretary of State in charge of colonial affairs, in the midst of a great war. The answer he gave was that government bills should be given the preference in passing supply, but that private members of the Assembly might also initiate.[54] This merely ensured the continuation of confusion. It permitted the development of two organizations for the expenditure of the scanty provincial revenue, the officers of government appointed under the royal *mandamus* and the system of committees in the House of Assembly. It was all very well for Portland to plead the necessity of harmony. But nobody on either side of the Atlantic was prepared at this stage to consider how harmony could be ensured between a governor appointed from London and an elected assembly of the people. On the more parochial question of whether or not assemblymen should receive daily pay for their services, Portland deferred to the Assembly's request. In both Nova Scotia and New Brunswick pay and allowances to members of the assemblies in these years accounted for one-fourth to one-third of the total revenues available. Few "gentlemen" could afford public service without them.

Glenie could not hold his opposition together for an indefinite period. Patriotic fervour at a time when Britain was in peril made any kind of opposition seem out of place. Owing to a gradual rise in farm prices, landowners began to see brighter times ahead. The poorer people, deprived of the opportunity of working on the great roads that earned them much needed credit, petitioned for the renewal of the revenue acts. In 1799 Carleton regained control of the legislature and secured the passing of a bill for the construction of a province hall at Fredericton, a vote that had been refused for years by the representatives of the seaward counties. Glenie made his last stand in 1802. Carleton's refusal to accept Samuel Denny Street as clerk of the Assembly involved once more parliamentary procedures which differed in Britain and in the colonies – whether or not a popular house of assembly could appoint individuals to public office and pay them by direct vote.

Carleton returned to England in 1803, his nineteen years in New Brunswick having shown little but failure for the grandiose ambitions with which the province had been launched. At the turn of the century the annual revenue was in the vicinity of £2,000, while Nova Scotia's was £20,000. In 1801 Halifax was prepared to subscribe £100,000 for the establishment of a bank and the legislature voted money to pave its streets. Ten years prior to this time, said Sir John Wentworth, it would have been impossible to raise £6,000 for any purpose. New Brunswick had made no such spectacular progress. Any advancement that might have been possible had been halted by the war. Lord Dorchester, regarded as the provincial patron, was retired to England in semi-disgrace. Thomas Carleton had no friends in influential quarters from whom aid could be expected.

The only element of reassurance that came to New Brunswick in the closing years of the eighteenth century was victory in the first round of the long struggle for the border with Massachusetts. The American attempt to establish the Magaguadavic as the "true St Croix," mentioned in the Treaty of Versailles, was halted by the painstaking antiquarianism of Ward Chipman, the British agent to the Anglo-American commission of arbitration. With the help of Robert Pagan of St Andrews, Chipman was able to point to the relics of Champlain's domicile on Dochet's Island as clear proof that the Schoodiac was the true St Croix. The Convention of 1798, signed at Providence, accepted the source of the Schoodiac's northern branch as the point from which the northerly line should run as far as "the highlands" mentioned in the treaty. The settlement opened up a specific approach to the great questions of just where the highlands were, whether or not they really existed, and what the intentions were of the treaty-makers of 1783 who had placed such great confidence in the arbitration of topography.[55] Still the British protested the American occupation of Moose Island where the town of Eastport flourished on the smuggling trade, and the Americans in retort were opening claims against the islands in the Bay of Fundy – Campobello, Deer, and Grand Manan.

In spite of this vindication in part of its western boundary, New Brunswick as a political organism was in a very weak position. Its creation in 1784 had been regarded as a triumph for the Loyalists at the expense of Nova Scotia. But in the 1790's one of the dominant feelings at Saint John and Fredericton was that Wentworth's government and the Halifax commercial community composed a kind of barrier that separated New Brunswick from the patronage of the mother country. As early as 1792, when Lord Dorchester lost favour in Downing Street, the Nova Scotian assembly petitioned for the restoration of the lost portion of the County of Cumberland. Carleton had many enemies and detractors within the gates, especially at Saint John; they argued that if the boundary quarrel should be lost, if one-third of the province should be surrendered to the Americans, the remainder should be re-annexed to Nova Scotia. Sir John Wentworth had such great influence with the British government that he was given the nomination of the commissioner for the St Croix arbitration; and in selecting Thomas Barclay he rewarded a supporter who was doing yeoman service in managing his own legislature. At Halifax an increasingly confident band of administrators and financiers indulged in the possibilities of restoring control over *Nova Scotia irridenta*. By reason of the convenience of communication by sea, Halifax supplied the Miramichi Valley, a region of New Brunswick slow to develop. Halifax's expanding commercial ambitions were translated to political action in 1802 when a memorial came to London urging that the whole eastern side of New Brunswick should be restored to control by the Nova Scotian metropolis.

The five provinces remained, nevertheless, five in all their variety, political and economic, as the great war with France was renewed in 1803.

CHAPTER 6

The Prosperity of War
1803-1815

The second phase of the great war against Napoleon brought a completely new and much higher level of economic prosperity to the Atlantic Provinces. With it came an assurance of competence and a new degree of both local and imperial pride. On the fringes of the conflict, the Atlantic colonies shared in a common experience and morally were knit more closely together. The later extension of the struggle against another hereditary enemy, the Americans, amplified and intensified these consequences. There was exultation over victories in India, Spain, and on the seven seas. Their own shores witnessed frequent reminders of the struggle in which they were largely onlookers, though beneficiaries as well. The urgencies of the economic war against the French and Americans forced the British government to a series of measures that ultimately crystallized in a policy of making the provincial ports the distributing centres for the trade of the North Atlantic.

The end of the peace in 1803 forced the resumption of the close supervision over trade to which merchants and seamen were so accustomed. The North Atlantic squadron of the Royal Navy was never strong enough before Trafalgar to engage a French fleet that might, after breaking the blockade of European ports, descend upon Halifax or St John's. But the Admiralty was sublimely confident that the Halifax command, with the slender forces at its disposal, could perform its task of shepherding the merchant vessels of the colonies to and fro across the Atlantic. This confidence was justified by events, or by the want of them. The plan of action for Newfoundland was based on a strong defence of Signal Hill that barred access to St John's harbour and on the presence of a fifty-gun ship and two sloops of war. Halifax relied on whatever ships the Admiral might have at hand, a strong garrison of regulars, and a large force of militia which, according to the sanguine accounts of Sir John Wentworth, could be embodied quickly and efficiently. Had a French fleet appeared there would have been a sturdy resistance but little hope of averting severe damage. Steadfastly the Admiralty resisted the requests from Halifax for larger forces, keeping its ships on blockade duty in European waters.

Under constant fear of attack, the Halifax command was steadily able to improve the organization and protection of the increasingly large convoys that sailed to Britain, Portugal (the only really free market for fish in Europe), and the West Indies. At the outset of hostilities and for some years after there were grim accounts from Nova Scotia of the shortage of seamen, of the provincial ships that had been trapped by the French and Spaniards in the Caribbean, and whose crews were languishing in dungeons. But as the war continued, the provisions of the Compulsory Convoy Act were rigidly enforced. It was illegal for shipowners to send vessels to sea without protection, the costs of which they were compelled to pay. Insurance warrants were invalid without it. By 1809 six annual convoys, between April and November, sailed from Halifax for England and Europe, the system working with "almost clock-like regularity."[1] The hard-pressed Admiral was able to make provision for New Brunswick vessels as well, especially for the mast-ships that made the difficult circuit of Cape Sable. At Head Harbour, on appointed days, the vessels from St Andrews joined those from Saint John. The south shore of Newfoundland was the rallying area for all convoys passing eastward and westward and there were so many convoy escorts, frigates of up to thirty guns, in this vicinity that the safety of St John's was a factor that caused little concern.[2]

Trafalgar in 1805 removed the threat of invasion, but increased rather than lessened the dangers from privateers as the French were compelled to stake their remaining resources at sea on this spoiling method of waging war. Yet invasion from another quarter became a stark and immediate possibility as the Americans, in 1807, seemed likely to enter the conflict. The conviction of the British government that war with the United States on the issue of impressment was a virtual certainty was fully shared in the Atlantic Provinces. Two regiments of regular troops garrisoned at Halifax were ordered to Quebec, being replaced by one thousand militia. New Brunswick shared the alarm as Gabriel Ludlow, administrator in Carleton's absence as President of the Council, called up a large proportion of the militia of his province. A warlike spirit lasted throughout the winter, but as pay was not quickly forthcoming and the season of spring seeding approached, men deserted in large numbers. As the threat of war receded, employers were the first to complain that so much martial endeavour was unnecessary.

Since 1801 the colonies had been under the administration of the War Office, and the alarm of 1807-8 brought about the establishment of a regime in British North America which was markedly more military in character. Sir George Prevost arrived at Halifax in April, 1808, to displace abruptly the aging Wentworth as Lieutenant-Governor; his most important task was the defence of the Atlantic area. When the Americans failed to declare war he took the large reinforcements he had brought with him to the West Indies for the capture of Martinique. In an equally abrupt way Edward Winslow, now the President of the Council in New Brunswick, was replaced by Major-General Hunter, and New Brunswick became a military district subordinate to Halifax. This "military succession," which became the more emphatic because changes in control of provincial admin- istrationship occurred as frequently as those in the military command, was insulting to the pride of Loyalists like Winslow who, during Carleton's long absence in England, held themselves worthy of the highest office in government.[3]

II

The establishment of the Royal Navy's complete supremacy at sea, so fortunate for the colonies, was accompanied by acts of imperial policy and unforeseen contingencies of war that raised the level of the economy of the region from merely prosperous to booming and buoyant. Goaded by a tem- porary depression as war recurred, the merchants of Halifax under the leadership of William Sabatier, an energetic Maryland Loyalist, organized themselves to face the new challenges. The Committee of Trade of 1804 addressed Lord Hobart, the Secretary for War and Colonies, with the request for "the exclusive privilege of supplying their fellow-subjects in the West Indies with the article of fish on the North American coasts."[4] Their memorial reached Whitehall at a time when the national honour was fret- ting against American encroachments on British trade and when the British government was disposed to stiffen its artificial measures of restraint. Richard John Uniacke, the Attorney General of Nova Scotia, was a good example of a political leader who could go to London in 1805 representing a province that no longer considered itself financially dependent but was conscious of its worth in the struggle for survival against Napoleon. "The lubberly, insolent Irish rebel" of 1776,[5] who had been brought to Halifax in handcuffs from Fort Cumberland, was now the spokesman for a Nova Scotia that sought an imperial destiny of her own. Resenting the extent to which the British colonies had been the victims of American diplomatic pressure and the investment of British capital diverted from the Empire to the United States. Uniacke advocated new measures of control that were adopted over the following years. These were designed to release Nova Scotia and New Brunswick from their commercial role of subsidiaries to the United States in order to win back the carrying-trade that had largely wast- ed away since Jay's Treaty. By his side was William Knox, the aged agent for New Brunswick, who never lost an opportunity of avenging the battles lost to the Americans in earlier days. But it was the more imaginative and practical ideas of Uniacke that exercised the bigger influence on Lord Auckland and the Board of Trade.[6]

The first great decision of the British government to produce salutary effect was the partial withdrawal of the privileges given to American shipping by Jay's Treaty.[7] Lord Sheffield, the champion of British mercantile policy, was again honoured in the provinces for his work in sustaining the vision of a great imperial system of trade. Rather against their will, the legislatures of the West Indian islands were persuaded to grant bounties for the importation of Nova Scotian and New Brunswick fish. Altogether these concessions provided inducements for the provinces almost equal to those given the Newfoundlanders by Palliser's Act. Coupled with the great improvement in convoy protection, they produced immediate consequences. The long-standing connection between the fish-exporting houses of Halifax and the British West Indies really dates from this time, and the maritime tradition of the entire area received immense impetus. Instead of selling their produce to the Americans at poor prices, skippers of little ships brought it for export to merchants of the larger ports who could take advantage of the new and favourable conditions.

This was a shrewd thrust at American control of the carrying-trade, but much more was to follow. It was largely by reason of "the schooner trade" of the Atlantic shore and the Bay of Fundy that the Americans drained specie from the Atlantic Provinces and commanded the multifold transactions of exchange and barter. Since the coming of the Loyalists this illegal commerce had been the bane of the "fair trader"; it had deprived the mercantile establishments of Halifax and Saint John of the opportunity of exporting the produce of their provinces to overseas markets. Canso was a traditional meeting-place for the "rascals" of both nations. In 1786 the British government had commissioned the New Brunswick Loyalist, George Leonard, as superintendent of trade and fisheries there with authority extending to Bay Verte. Later, in 1797, this authority was extended to the waters of the island provinces and to New Brunswick. Leonard was a man of stern principle and indomitable rigour, pursuing American interlopers with religious conviction, prosecuting roguish British customs officials who winked at the illegalities of trade and sometimes collaborated in them. Against the general resistance of traders on both sides of the line he could, in his armed brig *The Earl of Moira*, make a formidable nuisance of himself, but he never came close to suppressing the activities of thousands of seamen in hundreds of little ships.

To combat this American superiority in setting the terms of trade, Uniacke urged the opening of free ports in the Atlantic Provinces. This was an old device which Britain had employed with much success during the commercial rivalries of the eighteenth century in winning the trade of the French and Spanish islands of the West Indies. It became possible to secure the overseas carriage not only of British but of American produce as well, and to force American trade into a British stream, when the Americans, by a minor miracle, unwittingly collaborated. President Jefferson's embargo against British trade in 1808 made the ideas of Uniacke highly relevant. Followed by the Non-Intercourse Act, which really denied to New England traders the right to pursue their livelihood, the American stoppage of trade with England served as a magnificent and quite fortuitous bounty to the shipping of the Atlantic Provinces. Britain retaliated by making Halifax, Shelburne, and Saint John free ports in 1808, St Andrews in 1809. This use of ports free of customs duties, an act of war rendered the more necessary by the urgency of obtaining American supplies for the campaigns just opened in Spain and Portugal, channelled most of the trade of the North Atlantic coastline through the ports of the provinces.

By self-righteously closing American ports to British ships in protest against the restrictions on neutral trade, Presidents Jefferson and Madison sacrificed what New Englanders had won after generations of enterprise on the sea. In his memorial Uniacke declared the Americans dreaded the day when Britain should do something for Nova Scotia. Britain was finally doing something for Nova Scotia but the inspiration was largely American. To enforce his embargo Jefferson was obliged to send his new army into his own seaports. American imports from Britain dropped to 50 per cent of the figure recorded for 1807. But British exports to the United States fell by only 7 per cent. The disparity in these figures was to be explained by the unrecorded and illegal imports via the Atlantic Provinces and Canada. Jefferson's idealistic pronouncements brought ruination to the trade of New England.

Trade had to continue, for, just as Britain was dependent on American foodstuffs, the United States required the manufactured goods of Britain. The coming and going of little ships in the Bay of Fundy was overshadowed by the arrival of larger ones, all British, that carried to Europe the goods illegally moved from American warehouses. It was the British who now set the terms of trade and the prices for fish, gypsum, grindstones. As shipbuilding ceased in New England, as the American government voluntarily, it seemed, forfeited its overseas trade, smaller American ships stealthily sailed from the harbours of Maine to trade with large British vessels. Even though the American government built Fort Sullivan and stationed a garrison of troops at Eastport to enforce the embargo, this citadel of the smuggling gentry was able to double its normal activities. It became a great depot for flour and other dry provisions that were exchanged "on the lines" for British manufactures.[8] Halifax, Saint John, and St Andrews were the bases for British ships that crossed the Atlantic to do business with the smugglers. American shipwrights and carpenters, forced into unemployment by the legislation of their own government, commenced to migrate to the provinces in search of work and encountered the beginnings of a great shipbuilding industry.

The embargo itself lasted only fourteen months, but the character of American diplomacy supplied the momentum that kept the fortuitous trade in re-exports moving in both directions in increasing volume. Sir George Prevost, strongly seconded by General Hunter in New Brunswick, did all he could to encourage the traffic with New England. To a great degree this bland invitation of the Free Ports Act to the Americans to violate their own laws was a necessity arising from strategic thinking, from the general realization that England could not feed herself and that she had to get supplies from the other side of the Atlantic to provide for her armies in Spain and Portugal. Rising prices gave impetus to the traffic. In 1807 the Stars and Stripes showed on the mastheads of fourteen American vessels that illegally unloaded their cargoes in Halifax and were tolerated by the authorities.[9] In the next year, when the traffic was legal in Halifax but highly illegal for the Americans, the number vastly increased. At Washington the statistics showing British purchases of flour, pork, and naval stores, made in spite of the Non-Intercourse Act, appalled the authorities. New England fiercely opposed the embargo and the majority of her seaports, like Salem, were strongly Federalist, taking delight in sending their ships to sea in order to defy it. Marblehead, strongly Republican, supported the government and kept its ships at home.[10]

Saint John and St Andrews experienced rapid increases in population as newcomers from all quarters arrived to share the prosperity that came with the presence of big ships in the Bay of Fundy. The export trade from Halifax to the West Indies between 1808 and 1811 doubled the figures of the previous four years. In 1811 alone New Brunswick doubled its export and import figures in this trade.[11] Capital accumulated in London to the credit of colonial merchants. In Britain there came into existence the British North American Merchants' Association with the object of corresponding with similar organizations in the colonies and fostering trade. Their able memorialist, Nathaniel Atcheson, appropriately conveyed colonial points of view to the British government.[12] A beneficial consequence of the agitation they raised was the consent of the British government to direct voyages homeward from the Mediterranean. Now the ships of the Atlantic Provinces could sell their fish in Spain, load cargoes of oranges, currants, and raisins, and return to Halifax or Saint John without the necessity of paying imperial customs duties at Falmouth in Cornwall – and in time to prevent their cargoes from perishing because of too lengthy a voyage.

With only minor interruptions the War of 1812 enlarged the highly favourable terms of trade. New England was friendly to Britain and commerce was still her life-blood. Though there was no appetite for warlike measures among the Yankee smugglers of Eastport and Passamaquoddy, war could still be profitable. Correctly anticipating British policy, Sir John Sherbrooke, the Lieutenant-Governor of Nova Scotia, offered licences for trading in British ports to American merchants, and Admiral Sawyer, commanding the naval station, ordered his captains not to molest them. The enormous demand for British manufactures offered opportunity for the making of fortunes. Most of the goods which entered the United States during the war came via the ports of the provinces into the hands of these licensed traders, who smuggled them past the often conniving customs officials into the ports of northern Maine. Since the entire American coasting trade was under British blockade, they were distributed along the eastern seaboard by wagon traffic, and Federalist propagandists could write with glee about the fast-sailing mud-clippers that now carried American commerce, about "Madison's nightcaps," the inverted tea-barrels that shrouded the mastheads of the great ships of New England lying idle in Boston harbour.[13] Sherbrooke believed that the licensed trade, so gratuitously sponsored by himself and his junior in New Brunswick, had the effect of further separating New England from the war policy of President Madison.

Sherbrooke's decision to blockade New England late in 1813 did not reduce the great volume of merchandise exchanged by this managed trade. The occupation of the Maine coast to the Penobscot in the next year opened up many more inland routes to the American smugglers. For the duration of the war Sherbrooke estimated that goods to the value of a million pounds sterling passed through Nova Scotia to the markets of the United States.[14] In return American products of comparable value moved to Britain and the West Indies. Under British occupation Eastport carried on a large trade with New Brunswick as vessels of Swedish registry suddenly became numerous. A large section of its populace, cursing the republicans, professed to welcome the British who brought free trade with them.[15]

Between 1806 and 1814 the deliberate machinations of British commercial policy, the eccentricities of American diplomatic action, and the fortunes of war combined to raise the Atlantic Provinces to the status of a great clearing-house for international trade. Along with this transatlantic traffic the petty and local smuggling of the small ships continued to flourish. All the tobacco consumed in New Brunswick except that imported for the king's troops, said a memorial of 1807, was smuggled.[16] Customs establishments, seldom conducted according to the regulations, could not pretend to control the movements of the thousands of fishermen-traders who sailed from the scores of smaller harbours of the Atlantic region. Superficially it might have appeared in 1814 that the commercial expectations of the era of Loyalist settlement had finally been realized, that, after the earlier years of disappointment, the cup of Loyalist hopes had been filled to overflowing, for the New Englanders were now enduring the same kind of commercial bondage that had been the lot of the Loyalists for the first ten years of the Napoleonic Wars. Pamphleteers had conducted many paper wars on the competence or incompetence of the Atlantic Provinces to supply the markets of the West Indies. For a fleeting period the optimists were prepared to believe that they could do so, though the produce they supplied, except for fish, was not their own. As the war came to a close the great question on which merchants and politicians ruminated was whether or not the British government would sustain the high economic level by legislation that would give continued encouragement to an artficially contrived and circuitous trade.

III

Still another fortuitous development occurred in this second phase of the Napoleonic Wars to give immense uplift to the productive capacity of the region. An old ambition of the Loyalists was gratified as the forests at last yielded their abundance of lumber and masts. The rise of the timber trade, destined to produce immense repercussions on the social scene, was rather terrifying to the more morally minded, just as it was satisfying to the materialistic.

A land of virgin forest, upon which settlement had only slightly imping- ed, seemed highly suited to the task of supplying the West Indies with lumber. In the last years of the Revolutionary War the Admiralty, fighting the embargo of the Armed Neutrality of the Baltic, had turned its search for masts and spars to the St John and had been gratified. Not only had the Halifax Dockyard been supplied but there had been a surplus available for export to England.[17] As the Loyalists opened up the valleys of the St John and the St Croix, the most frequent and cheering evidence of industry had been the appearance of scores of little sawmills. Governor Parr had reported upon the same kind of activity in Nova Scotia with absolutely no doubt in his mind that this role of the North Atlantic entrepôt could be adequately performed. Yet when domestic demand for lumber had been filled in the first tumultuous years of settlement, there came the astonishing revelation that the two provinces could not compete in export markets with the Americans. When the greatest and most accessible trees along the banks of navigable rivers were gone, costs mounted. Labour, especially men skilled with the broad-axe, was scarce and capital for organizing and promoting the industry non-existent. A frequent commentary upon the inhabitants of the two provinces was their independence of demeanour, a social trait that was accounted for by the abundance of land. With every man a freeholder none would work for another. The American trade was highly organized with hundreds of workers skilled at squaring timber. As long as the coastal forests of Maine were standing there was a cheap and available source of supply. Their lower shipping costs, derived from the custom of sailing on shares, cheaper insurance, and shorter voyages, gave to the Americans advantages that a new and sparsely settled country could not overcome.

As new settlements were formed at tide-water an occasional cargo of lumber was sent to Britain where the Baltic traders were well entrenched in an expanding market, but most of the shingles and staves were locally consumed. Through the 1790's there were no signs that timber could become a great basic industry to bring sterling, so badly needed for the purchase of British manufactures, into the provinces. It was only the trade in masts, officially sponsored and conducted, that enabled the forests appreciably to add to earning power. Sir Andrew Snape Hamond, who left his lieutenant-governorship of Nova Scotia to become Comptroller to the Navy Board, continued in the search of the St John Valley for the supplies on which the navy desperately depended at a time when the oak groves of England had become completely exhausted and unfriendly Americans sold their cargoes to the French. Sir John Wentworth's Broad Arrow became a familiar mark as his deputies laid out reserves for the navy from the ungranted lands of New Brunswick and Nova Scotia, principally of the former. In 1788 the firm of Hunter, Robertson and Forsyth made a contract to supply great masts for a period of six years, an agreement that was renewed in 1795 when the firm promised to deliver thirty cargoes over the next seven years. These were sent to Halifax, Antigua, and Jamaica, as well as to British dockyards. "Up to 1804 New Brunswick virtually monopolized the naval mast trade."[18] Great activity by men and oxen was to be seen below Fredericton where several small streams fell into the St John, as the inhabitants of Maugerville rifled the woods of the great trees that grew upon their banks.[19]

Though the Atlantic Provinces continued to contribute substantially, after 1804 Canada became the principal source of masts for the navy. The year 1811 saw the greatest export, when the statistics showed 3,151 for New Brunswick, 842 for Nova Scotia, 54 for Cape Breton. Against these figures there were 19,000 for Canada. Standards were high and only masts of twelve inches or more in diameter could be taken. Wentworth encountered many local obstructions. The great reserves he had laid out on the Miramichi, the St Croix, and upper St John were invaded by settlers and the great trees cut down for private use or sale. Settlers were prepared to go to court when the Broad Arrow was stencilled on trees where clear title to land had been granted. Yet, though the Admiralty complained of dry rot in some of the timber, the work carried on under Wentworth's supervision supplied the Royal Navy with its essential requirements of masts and spars until the time of Trafalgar.

The mast trade became of secondary consequence as a great market for commercial timber suddenly opened up. The opposition in Britain to the development of the North American timber trade became negligible in June, 1807, when Napoleon at Tilsit brought Russia, Sweden, and Denmark into an agreement to close the Baltic to British ships. As the price of timber trebled, Parliament imposed duties on the foreign product, thereby assuring colonial merchants of protection for British North American timber for the duration of the war and two years after. Between 1809 and 1812 these duties were progressively increased. Because of this tremendous inducement, timber became the basic element in the economy of New Brunswick and an important element in that of Nova Scotia. As the rapidly growing cities of the Industrial Revolution in Britain offered opportunity for large sales, Scottish merchants emigrated to North America and explored the navigable rivers, to seek out stocks of desperately needed standing pine. Loads of fir and pine timber exported to Britain in 1806 were 7,062 for New Brunswick, 6,781 for Nova Scotia. In 1811 the figures were 75,870 and 17,419, for Cape Breton, 5,800.[20] Fluctuations were violent but through the War of 1812 and after, the spiral moved upward.

The economic and social transformations were greatest in New Brunswick. Though the roads on each side of the river were mere trails, population rapidly moved up the valley of the St Croix. Milltown suddenly became a community of twelve hundred people, with five double and two single sawmills.[21] Charlotte County experienced the first impact of the onrush as the merchants and gentry of St Andrews outfitted parties for work in the woods during the winters and, without compunction, took toll of the reserves Wentworth had laid out for the navy. Profits could be quick and great so that, on both public and private lands, cutting was reckless and improvident.[22] Requirements of the early timbermen were demanding, for a single log was expected to yield a thousand board feet of plank. The smaller trees were ruthlessly slashed and burnt.

A similar and greater onset came to the valley of the Miramichi. Alexander Rankin, who established the firm of Gilmore, Rankin and Company on its north bank in 1812, was a good example of the Scottish factor who, after being dispossessed of his connections in the Baltic, brought his capital, techniques, and knowledge of markets to British North America at this time. Wentworth had established a great reserve on the south bank of the river and the timber-producing potentialities of the valley had been well known since the days of William Davidson, the first English-speaking settler. Now, to join the few fishermen and Loyalist traders of the estuary, came a host of Scottish bosses and skilled labourers, Irish drifters from Newfoundland, farmers from Prince Edward Island looking for work in the winter season, all eager to capitalize on the quick earnings of the timber trade. The forests seemed illimitable and the Miramichi became dedicated to the timber economy. As at St Andrews, Saint John, and almost everywhere in Nova Scotia, ship-building developed as a satellite, though important, industry.[23] To a greater extent than any other region of the Atlantic Provinces, the Miramichi was to ring with the chop of the broad-axe and the shriek of the sawmills.

As long as war lasted the getting out of timber was a patriotic business and the authorities were slow to impose supervision. In New Brunswick, as early as 1810, General Hunter reported to London that the Crown Lands of the province were being looted and future generations deprived of their immense forest resources, but no action was taken.[24] Wentworth and his deputy at Halifax, Michael Wallace, made a token show of preserving the rights of the Admiralty, but the evidence would indicate that their agents made no resistance to the general impulse to cut good timber wherever it could be found and that in some cases they even collaborated, at a price, in evasion of the restrictions. Conventionally minded people spoke and wrote of the lawless, libertine spirit that seemed to sweep over the land as the timber trade boomed. Whatever was left of the Loyalist image of a well-appointed, graded society of gentry whose eminence was based on the ownership of land, supported by a disciplined yeomanry, quickly disappeared. Churchwardens and magistrates, most men of capital, shared in the great enterprise of the timber trade. Lesser men left valuable farm properties to take part in its rewards and hazards.

In New Brunswick official awareness was the greater, for, in the vast wilderness of the interior, forest resources were untouched. Even amongst the generality of the population there was a notion that the Crown Lands might make amends for the disappointments of the past. Nova Scotia had much more widely diffused settlements without such enormous reaches of untouched forest. Almost everywhere axemen had been labouring in its woods for a century. From the beginning there was no inclination to consider timber land as a distinct category so that development in the trade was more piecemeal and less highly organized. Prince Edward Island had no reserve of public lands. In Newfoundland the forest interior was still a subject for speculative enquiry as men exclusively and indomitably sought the wealth of the sea.

IV

The rise to affluence of the Newfoundland fishery was accompanied by a sharpening of lines that brought the problems of the country into clearer relief. Issues of principle were to be settled and others, equally important, arose. In 1803 the total population of the island was on the mark of twenty thousand and, as the war continued and the British "bankers" became fewer, the transients, who only twenty years before had greatly outnumbered residents, shrank to an insignificant minority. Of the permanent residents, twelve thousand were listed as Protestant and eight thousand as Roman Catholic. But in St John's, with a population of thirty-five hundred, Roman Catholics outnumbered Protestants by two to one. Everywhere males outnumbered females, with consequences which caused constant offence to moralists. Judicial records and the reports of missionaries all through the eighteenth century tell of many incestuous marriages. But, as the settled population increased, this great disparity annually declined. The disorder endemic to the colony, for colony it could now be called, was amplified by the continued arrival from Ireland of shiploads of "boarders and dieters" whose stay was often brief. The West Country merchants, whose battle was lost, still propagandized for the depopulation of the island, but the British government appeared to have finally accepted the truth of the words of Chief Justice Reeves that "Newfoundland has been peopled behind your back."[25]

As the great convoys passed and repassed in almost complete safety, the fishery nearly doubled its volume of exports, exceeding a million quintals in 1815. At St John's, now a centre of distribution rather than a fishing depot, merchants were supplied almost entirely by the resident fishermen. The Napoleonic blockade harassed the shippers, but Lisbon always remained open and, as British armies entered Spain, the Mediterranean became a British lake. When the French were able to interfere, neutrals, including the Americans, collaborated to keep markets open. Wages rose so that even common fishermen who were industrious could enjoy comparative affluence. Freed of competition from the French, a largely new population of Newfoundland worked its way up the northeast shore. During the busy season women took part in the work of splitting and curing and sometimes went on such distant voyages that, it is narrated, they were accompanied by midwives.[26] Sometimes in the summer strangers were shocked by the scantiness of their clothing. On this coast the caplin, a small fish of the smelt family, came close to shore, always followed by the cod. Large catches could be had in the month of May only a mile or two from land.

The phenomenal growth of the sedentary fishery at the expense of the Western Adventurers is well reflected by the rapid increase of imports, which in 1815 almost equalled exports. "The nursery of seamen" now sheltered landsmen who only occasionally took to deep water. Judging from the number of desertions from the navy's ships on the Newfoundland and Nova Scotian stations during the war, it could now be argued that the fishery was injurious to the navy's effectiveness rather than a prop for its support. As additional buttresses to the colony and as inducements to the life of shoremen, other industries were fast developing. Ship-building enjoyed a period of expansion, thirty vessels being launched in 1804.[27] The winter and spring seal fisheries in the north employed fifteen hundred men in one hundred and fifty vessels. During January and February the seals of Labrador resorted to the ice-floes in great numbers, bearing their young in the latter month. Winds and currents brought the floes in a southerly direction along the eastern shore. The seals were taken in nets of strong twine two hundred feet long.

As the colony prospered and as the Act of 1699 became so archaic that it lost all relevancy and meaning, a succession of benign governors looked to the improvement of a society where poverty flourished amid great riches. Discovering that the provisions of the English Poor Law could not be enforced in Newfoundland, Admiral Gambier (1802-3), a staunch Methodist, organized voluntary measures of moral and religious uplift. He arranged for the payment of Sunday School teachers and the assembling of the children of St John's for instruction at seven o'clock on Sunday mornings during the summer, at nine o'clock in the winter. The town itself was filthy. Its principal street was at one place only six feet wide. Voluntary measures could accomplish little. Illegally, the resolute Gambier leased eighty acres at the back of the town for the pasturage of sheep and cattle, to help provide food and clothing for the indigent poor. Adopting the philosophy that the chief end of government was "the happiness and good order of the community," he urged upon his return to England, the establishment of a legislative power similar to those in the other colonies. The first suggestion for change leading to self-government in Newfoundland came from a naval governor.[28]

In these prosperous years public order was maintained to a greater degree than ever before, as something like a common conscience prepared to arouse itself in Newfoundland. The novel element of town-planning was successfully introduced in 1805; following a petition from the merchants, many fishing-rooms in the harbour of St John's, reserved for Devon ships but now fallen into disuse, were made available for wharves and mercantile establishments. Two hundred yards from high watermark a road was constructed. Behind it, plots of ground were allocated for dwelling-places. Admiral Sir Erasmus Gower (1804-7), in response to an appeal from the people of Fogo, protected the fishermen from the harsh exactions of the truck system, forcing the merchants to buy fish and sell provisions at previously advertised prices.[29]

In 1805 there came a postal service; in 1806 the first newspaper, the *Royal Gazette*, published by John Ryan, formerly of New Brunswick; in the same year the first charitable organization, the Benevolent Irish Society; in 1811 the first hospital. Local pride became a factor of considerable account in St John's, but a tightly organized movement of the merchants to get rid of a chief justice who baulked their attempts to achieve local improvement was defeated.

With keener tension came still greater changes. The first winter of war with the United States brought exorbitantly high prices for imported food-stuffs and conditions akin to starvation. A new importance became attached to the activities of squatters who kept livestock and maintained market gardens behind St John's. The Act of 1699 forbade cultivation of the soil, but successive proclamations had failed to restrain local enterprise of this kind. A truculent public opinion, roused by the merchants, insisted on rights of holding private property "on a quiet possession of twenty years." Admiral Sir John Duckworth (1810-12), who presented this petition, was in sympathy with its object. While the British fishery prosecuted from the West Country, he argued, had nearly perished, the resident fishery had survived the war and had prospered. It was best, he reasoned, to remove the impediments that hindered its growth.[30] This demand for a fundamental change in high policy was made at a time when the merchants of St John's and sympathizers with the local population were fully aware of the fact that war favoured their cause, that peace could bring back to Newfoundland the ships of the West Country and restore the influence of Poole and Dartmouth at Whitehall.

In June of 1813 Admiral Sir Richard Keats (1813-15) brought instructions to make small grants of land to industrious individuals. In that summer one thousand acres in the environs of St John's were enclosed and the governor boasted of productive and well-cultivated little farms, of hay, potatoes, and vegetables as fine as anything in England.[31] Grants did not exceed four acres and quitrents did not restrain enthusiasm. The British government bowed to the inevitable but would not hasten it. The Act of 1699 remained on the statute-books unamended. Lord Liverpool voiced the official opinion when he declared that it was not proper to hasten a regrettable tendency.[32] In justice to the British government, it must be said that it is easy to understand the reluctance of statesmen to rid themselves of the traditional and naval point of view in an era when, to a greater degree than ever before, sea power had proved to be the sure basis of Britain's strength.

Out of the organization of the merchants of St John's, formed to advance projects in their own interest, there developed a popular movement favouring political reform. To the philosopher, Newfoundland's situation, even at this time of high prosperity, could offer cause only for despair. A community of British subjects was denied that which all true Britons believed to be the basis of freedom – the right to representation in a popular assembly. There was ample occasion for ringing all the changes upon the English, American, and French revolutions, and a political philosopher opportunely appeared on the scene. William Carson, who came to St John's in 1808, was a Scottish surgeon, a native of Kirkcudbrightshire. During the Napoleonic Wars, when any kind of dissent in Britain might appear treasonable, it was in Scotland that the liberal tradition remained most vibrant and Carson brought with him to Newfoundland its questioning, challenging spirit. In temper and in background, in his recklessness of personal consequences, Carson was remarkably similar to James Glenie of New Brunswick, and in Newfoundland there was more to challenge.

To the liberal and philosopher, the conduct of the naval surrogate courts which functioned in the outports provided the most immediate provocation for the tests of reason and morality. An Irish fisherman accused of drunkenness and misconduct could, after being found guilty, be deprived of the whole of his annual wage according to law. But because the employer had given him the liquor and because of previous good conduct, the naval judge deputy would deprive him of merely half his annual wage and the fisherman's face would light up with joy. "The countenances of the fishermen brightened whilst those of the masters fell."[33] This was a comparatively gentle case, for in matters of capital punishment the discipline, rather than justice, of the naval surrogates was as harsh and thorough as aboard the decks of their vessels. For calling in question these methods of administering justice Carson was dismissed from his post as surgeon to the Loyal Volunteers. He was happy in opposition. "The arm of power may humble my mind but cannot subdue it."[34]

It was Carson who inspired the agricultural improvements about St John's. It was he who persuaded the merchants to make a test case of the laws against private property by erecting a building on forbidden ground. The general success of this agitation in 1813 resulted in the circulation of the notion that the British government had been forced to grant reform and emboldened the merchants to press for still greater concessions. From the turn of the nineteenth century the naval governors of Newfoundland were humane men, well disposed to the populace of Newfoundland. At a time of great tension, when projects of reform seemed out of place owing to the perils of war, their dispatches lighted the way to improvement. But Carson's quick, impatient reason would not allow him to wait. He was certain that naval governors, by reason of their habitual exercise of arbitrary authority, were unfit to rule a civil population. Contrary to ancient prejudice, Newfoundland was, he thought, fit to live in. Agriculture was not injurious to the fishery and a settled population should enjoy all the privileges of British

subjects. Carson brought all the existing discontents together into a demand
for a popular assembly. His two pamphlets of 1811 and 1813 constitute
Newfoundland's first literature of reform.[35]

Democracy had beginnings that were both familiar and spectacular. Sir
Richard Keats could perceive in Carson's systematic propaganda the purposes
of wicked and designing men. There was no taxation without representation, but the merchants presented a strong, though unsuccessful, case for
the application to public improvements of the sums realized from the sale
and leasing of property about St John's. Democracy's rank and file, the
tough Irish of the brawling seaport who indulged their fighting spirit on
the Barrens behind the town, were the dangerous and unpredictable allies
of the merchants. Fortunately for the authorities their wrangling was often
dissipated in factional quarrels, gang-fighting, and rough rivalry lightened
by Irish humour. Irishmen of the second generation in Newfoundland
found reason to despise recent arrivals. The Clear Airs of Tipperary, the
Whey Bellies of Waterford, the Dodgums of Cork, frequently combined
against the Doonees of Killarney and the Yellow Bellies of Wexford. So
great were these animosities that they extended to the Church and there is
the account of how Bishop Lambert, a Wexford man, was compelled to
suspend from his priestly functions Father Power of Tipperary.[36] Each
faction had its own quarter of the town and its own general. What fright-
ened the authorities was the dissemination of Carson's doctrines among
these thousands of "the lower orders" whose passions, if mobilized to a
common purpose, could create bloody revolution.

V

The spirit of the times was unfavourable to change but ideas of reform and
readjustment were being circulated in the political laboratories of New
Brunswick and Nova Scotia. In the former province the early and prolonged
period of theorizing upon the true meaning of the British constitution had
ended with the departure of James Glenie. From 1803 to 1815 the men who
dominated its politics had little appetite for the abstract and were more concerned with immediate and practical problems. They were Amos Botsford,
the Speaker of the House of Assembly, John Coffin, a Loyalist patrician and
general in the British Army, James Fraser, an able merchant of Miramichi
who was credited by Sir John Wentworth with bringing about the political
pacification during Carleton's last years in New Brunswick.[37] Meeting
every second year, the legislature appropriated its slender resources to the
construction of the badly needed roads and bridges. Politics were devoid of
great issues; assemblymen concentrated their attention on meeting the
general and insistent demand for local improvements.

Nine times in seven years there were changes in the Presidency of the Council, when the second-ranking officer at Halifax assumed the administration. As the timber trade engrossed the energies of the people, the officers of government at Fredericton, now aging and disappointed men, became resigned to decisions imposed upon the province from other quarters. During the election of 1785 the political history of New Brunswick had commenced with a formal presentation of a great constitutional issue and in the time of Glenie efforts had been made to clarify and define the relationship between mother country and colony.[38] But, during the twelve years prior to the Peace of Ghent, the only issue of principle that provided excitement was a legal one – whether or not the rights of proprietors of the soil extended to low watermark. This concerned the attempt of Simonds, White and Hazen of Saint John to restrain the fishermen of the harbour from carrying on their activities in front of their property at Portland, and was decided against the proprietors.[39] New Brunswick was just beginning to acquire economic substance, and was in no humour to tolerate exercises in constitutional discussion. There was no philosopher such as Glenie or Carson to kindle discontent and to circulate ideas that were novel. The tone of life was homely and materialistic. Nova Scotia had constructed the fine government house which even Wentworth's large salaries could not maintain and had voted the money for an equally fine Province House of stone. There could be nothing so grand at Fredericton.

In Glenie's day the House of Assembly of New Brunswick had been a bear-pit where the factions had quarrelled on the issue of whether or not a money bill introduced by a private member should take equal place with one sent down by the Lieutenant-Governor in Council; whether the power of the purse should be in the hands of committees of the House of Assembly or under the initiative of officials appointed from London. British precedents had produced only interminable argument. Following the ambiguous settlement arranged by the Duke of Portland in 1798, the great debate over principle simmered into quiescence, but the practical consequence of the uncertain decision was that committees of the House of Assembly, eager to serve their constituents, slowly but surely acquired the powers of initiating money grants. American precedents triumphed over the comparatively alien procedures of Westminster. Loyalists might never have read Montesquieu, but nearly all believed in the wisdom and justice of the theory of the separation of powers.

About 1802 this same issue intruded violently into the politics of Nova Scotia and remained central until long after the granting of responsible government. Sir John Wentworth lost his magic capacity to please nearly everybody and with it his dominance in the House of Assembly. The firebrand who did most to destroy his ease was William Cottnam Tonge. The

Naval Officer at Halifax, charged with the regulation of shipping, Tonge was an old enemy whom Sir John had distrusted since 1792, when he had tried to remove him from office. He was a member of one of Nova Scotia's first official families. Entering the House of Assembly, he became a protagonist of the country against the town, working to enlarge the business of the outports by establishment of customs depots, intriguing with other members for increases in the sums for distant roads and bridges, to which the members of the council, all residents of Halifax, were completely apathetic. According to Wentworth, he performed his duty as Naval Officer in an easy-going manner that was satisfactory to his friends in the schooner trade, facilitating false clearances and other irregular practices. In 1805, when Richard John Uniacke was occupied with designs for the reorganization of British North America that included the restoration of Nova Scotia's lost provinces,[40] Tonge temporarily succeeded him in the speakership. Wentworth alleged that he used this position of authority to delay the renewal of the revenue bills so that their operation lapsed, and valuable cargoes of goods owned by his friends entered Halifax without paying duty. One cargo alone, it was said, deprived the province of £1,552.

It was in 1803 that Sir John had first mentioned a highly organized party in the House of Assembly. It was headed by Tonge and ranged against the Governor. In the popular body there was a strong disposition to circulate easy money and a willingness to accept debt in order to improve communications in the agricultural districts. The Council of Twelve, performing both legislative and executive functions, was a citadel of financial conservatism. They now forced the Assembly to provide revenue before making appropriations, but only on the casting vote of the Speaker, Uniacke. Tonge was patronized by the officers of the navy and army, who had no liking for civil administration in Halifax; as they crowded the vestibule of the legislature, Tonge displayed his patriotism and embarrassed the Council by moving in the Assembly that a grant of £10,000 be made to His Majesty for the conduct of the war. This was passed by thirty to two. When the Council professed an uncertainty as to whether or not it would abandon its financial scruples for this great purpose, the Assembly rescinded its motion. This legislative horse-play conjured up among political radicals the question of the desirability of making the second legislative chamber elective.[41]

To the end of his administration in 1808 Wentworth was persistently embarrassed by the hostile party in the House of Assembly. Doggedly the majority held to what they considered to be their rights, the determination of all appropriations in detail. Broadly and constitutionally speaking, this was a continued resistance in the second British Empire to the highly centralized authority of the cabinet in British parliamentary government that had aroused opposition among the American colonists in the days before the

Revolution. Wentworth, for his part, accused members of the House of Assembly, in their efforts to acquire complete control over expenditure, of circulating public money among their political friends, and of squandering the revenues on provisional projects that had no character of permanent improvement. His stand was a metropolitan one. He was supported by the great merchants of Halifax and by his officials, whose influence had been weakened as a result of the sharp work of the legislative committees. A dispute in 1808 illustrates the fundamental character of the contest. Bounties for fishermen were paid exclusively to those who supplied the great ships of the province sailing to the West Indies. In place of the bounty of 1s. 6d. for each quintal of fish so exported, the Assembly wished to substitute a tonnage bounty to all shipowners engaged in the industry, including those who sold to the Americans in the Bay of Fundy. This form of the struggle was a contest between the great ships of Halifax, which so well served the system of controlled imperial trade, and the schooner interests, whose activities were calculated to destroy it.[42]

In his war of attrition with the House of Assembly Sir John did not hesitate to apply to his opponents the label of disloyalty. As this conflict extended, he lost the aplomb of former years and with it his judicial bearing. At the end, his most intimate adviser was Michael Wallace, the Treasurer, whose accounts weathered a storm of vindictive allegations by Tonge and his friends. In 1806 he rejected the election of Tonge as Speaker of the House, exercising a prerogative of the Crown that had not been employed since the Glorious Revolution. In 1807 he suspended him from his functions as Naval Officer, alleging that Tonge was spreading discontent amongst the militia. He created another new precedent in Nova Scotia by denying a judgement of the House of Assembly on contested elections, insisting that his supporter, Thomas Walker of Annapolis, had been rightfully chosen. In this the Law Officers of the Crown in London declared him in error. In 1807 when, through Tonge's influence, meetings throughout the country protested the high fees taken by customs officials, Sir John ruthlessly removed from the rolls the names of the magistrates of Hants and Annapolis who were held responsible for allowing such meetings. Halifax was prepared to suppress local manifestations of this kind.

In an age when the repression of radical opinion seemed essential to national security, nobody called Sir John Wentworth a tyrant. He might be described as one of the best of colonial governors, chosen by virtue of superior education and ability, knowledge of the world, and high connections. As a native American he was highly sensitive to public opinion. If dubious motives are to be attached to his systematic use of patronage, fairness compels an equally critical examination of Tonge and "the democrats." There is every reason to believe that the exercise of patronage was an equally important feature of the system they sought to impose. The historian of democracy in small societies is frequently compelled to ruminate on the relative inconsequence of ideologies and leading principles of belief. In the cases of the smaller societies of New Brunswick, Prince Edward Island, and Newfoundland, the compulsion becomes more powerful.

Wentworth could compromise and he had the capacity to absorb into his intelligent aristocracy able radicals such as Uniacke once had been. Government by men of education and ability was the hallmark of his urbane Tory creed, though there were many abilities he hated and condemned, principally those of arousing public opinion. A much more archaic type of Tory brought the constitutional issue into sharper perspective. Alexander Croke, as senior councillor, took over the administration in December, 1808, when Sir George Prevost departed for Martinique. Croke insisted that he and his government could appropriate the revenues more economically than could committees of the House of Assembly. When the Loyalist Speaker, Lewis M. Wilkins, attempted to remonstrate, the house was prorogued "in a turbulent and violent manner," with no appropriations passed.[43] Croke, whose salary and fees in this era of many prizes were said to treble those of the Lieutenant-Governor, then went so far as to suggest that he was entitled to expend the items on the appropriations list that had been agreed upon by resolutions of council and assembly, even though the passage of the appropriations had not been completed. He was outvoted by his council. In his dealings with Nova Scotian democracy he could perceive what was at issue very plainly. The British parliament, he urged, should increase its grant by £4,000 so that government could be carried on independently of the House of Assembly. To Croke even Uniacke was suspect because, as Attorney General, he drew an annual stipend of £200 by vote of the popular body.[44]

Like the assembly of New Brunswick, that of Nova Scotia was slowly able to impose its authority on the allocation of public funds raised by its own vote. Like other military administrators, Sir George Prevost, for the sake of peace, had not been disposed to quibble about whether or not procedures in colonial legislatures should correspond exactly with those of the parliament of Great Britain. Croke had neither a mandate from the people of Nova Scotia nor the confidence of the Assembly. Yet he attempted to acquire the highly centralized control over financial appropriation held by the British government which owed its power to the House of Commons. Wise and temperate administrators could delay and moderate conflict, but, as colonial self-assertion grew, conflict with an entrenched and conservative administration was inevitable.

A more particular problem created a degree of tension between colonists and mother country. Never in the two provinces had quitrents been collected and landowners, in a bucolic kind of way, had convinced themselves that no demand would ever be made. Yet in 1802 Lord Hobart issued instructions to the two governors to procure from their legislatures the necessary authority to collect quitrents in an orderly manner, the proceeds to be handed over to the provincial treasuries. In New Brunswick Carleton reacted fearfully. He was convinced that landowners were too poor to pay. He was still more convinced that to this area of legislation the power of the House of Assembly should not be extended. He begged for permission to await new instructions and Hobart reluctantly agreed to issue them. Similarly no action was taken in Nova Scotia. It was not until 1807 that the long-awaited instructions arrived, framed by a British government that was not willing to allow the legislatures to participate. The rate of payment was nearly doubled to one halfpenny per acre "every midsummer day forever," and complete authority to collect payment was vested in the Lieutenant-Governor in Council.

Growing old and gradually abandoning hope for a military command in Britain, Carleton desperately strove for permission to postpone the demand for quitrents, arguing that a settler in New Brunswick paid for his land by his labour. Again the Secretary of State yielded and the quitrents became "a subject for future consideration."[45] But in Nova Scotia a more confident government prepared to enforce the demand on a population better able to pay. In three years the Receiver, Crofton Uniacke, collected £643, but of this Sir George Prevost ordered the return of £83 to penurious grantees. In 1811, when the total bill for arrears was about £40,000, discontent turned to alarm and the House of Assembly petitioned for suspension. The reply from Britain proposed a new approach that strongly suggested the influence of Lord Liverpool and Lord Bathurst, notable for their support of the Church. It was to the effect that suspension would be cheerfully granted, provided that the House of Assembly would make proper financial provision for the Church of England. In the words of Bishop Inglis at this time, the Church was in "a deplorable state," but no sympathy was shown for the Church's misfortunes by the Nova Scotia democracy. Punctiliously the house replied that from the time of the first settlement of the province there had been no taxation for the support of the Church of England and attempts to introduce it would create disharmony among other classes of Christians.[46] With that, the whole question of quitrents again fell into abeyance.

The instructions of 1807 with respect to quitrents, however, had brought with them the revocation of the order of 1790 for the suspension of land grants. Settlers could now acquire clear title, at a price, but there was no end to the fluid and uncertain situation governing the granting and occupation of land. By 1815 there were thousands of unlicensed squatters clearing lands in the backwoods of Nova Scotia and New Brunswick, especially in the latter. Sometimes their presence was unknown to government for years. The instruction of 1790 had compelled the two administrations to adopt a lax and tolerant attitude towards these activities. New settlement of any kind was always welcome and there was no disposition to hamper the enterprise of the poor and industrious who entered the wilderness. But after 1807, when regularization was possible, the high fees required for the passing of land grants operated as a deterrent to the acquisition of clear title. In both provinces the continued presence of squatters had to be tolerated.

VI

The War of 1812 with the United States had the effect of lifting the Atlantic colonies to a new feeling of self-confidence and self-importance. The redoubled movements of fleets and armies everywhere provided a martial glamour, swelling provincial revenues and increasing commercial prosperity. The five colonies become more conscious of a British kinship of their own and looked with sympathy to the hard-pressed Canadians as New Brunswick's 104th Regiment, gathered together from distant garrisons, made its celebrated winter march to their assistance.[47] Injurious consequences of the war were casual and unimportant, and, whatever the general result, the feeling was one of victory. Merchants complained of losses at sea, but this was only because the ships of the Royal Navy were blockading New York and the ports of the Chesapeake. American privateersmen were forbidden to land on British shores, so that the coastlines were left almost untouched. The tidings of triumph from Spain swelled the lustre of victory along the frontier of the St Lawrence and the lakes. It was a heyday for Halifax as the prosperous merchants, on these numerous occasions, adjourned to their reading-room across the street from the flat roof of the market-place where bands played selections from loyal airs and marches.

Halifax was the sounding-board for the long roll of savage encounters on the Atlantic. American forty-four gun frigates like the *Constitution, President*, and *United States* enjoyed successes against British frigates of considerably lesser fire-power. But more than ample revenge came on June 6, 1813 when the thirty-eight gun *Shannon* led the much more heavily gunned and manned *Chesapeake* into port as a captive. It was a Halifax lad, Lieutenant Provo Wallis, one of several Halifax men who became admirals in the Royal Navy, who brought the *Shannon* with her prize into harbour as Captain Broke lay wounded in his cabin. This great fight off Boston harbour, in which two hundred and fifty men were killed in thirteen minutes, became a part of Nova Scotian legend. So long as New England remained virtually neutral the American effort at sea could never be more than secondary to that on land. By 1814 British control was absolute and the commercial domain of Halifax extended into New England, where Sir John Sherbrooke, with forces that were not required for the defence of Upper Canada, occupied the coast from Passamaquoddy to Penobscot.

The colonists did more than cheer the accomplishments of the British forces. Privateering was now their historic role. In this they were at a disadvantage compared with the Americans for, while the seas were filled with British vessels, potential American prizes steadily became fewer. Only the Yankee coastal trade offered real chances. Most of the larger vessels that put to sea for overseas ports carried cargoes that were licensed by British consuls at Boston and elsewhere and were destined for British purchase, often in Spain and Portugal. On many an occasion a Yankee ship was brought into the harbour of St John's, Saint John, or Halifax and "monitions" were nailed to her masthead to advise all and sundry that she was under the custody of the Court of Vice-Admiralty. Frequently she was released on the judgement that she was "not a prize." Privateering captains were compelled to obey the law and to co-operate with the Royal Navy, and were held legally responsible for cargoes falling into their hands that were not fair game. Privateers were obliged to fly the Red Jack to distinguish them from the king's ships.[48] Profits could be handsome though not fabulously large. Shipowners had to reckon possible profits against the returns of the carrying-trade, which could be very great. During three months of service the *Sir John Sherbrooke* became famous by taking nineteen prizes, but her owners found it considerably more rewarding to place her on voyages to the Mediterranean.

Altogether there were thirty-seven vessels of the five provinces engaged in privateering during the War of 1812. In addition twelve others carried letters of marque as armed traders. They made 207 recorded captures. The most renowned of all was the *Liverpool Packet*. She was commanded by Joseph Barss, who as a lad of twenty-three and as captain of the *Lord Spencer* had thirteen years before scoured the Spanish Main for prizes. Manned by a crew of forty-five Liverpool fishermen, *Liverpool Packet* took fifty prizes, most of them from the coastal trade of Massachusetts. In Boston she was credited with causing a commercial panic. On a June day in 1813 she came up with the swift, Baltimore-built schooner *Thomas*, twice as large and carrying three times her fire-power. Caught in a light wind, she struck her colours, but the Americans refused to give quarter to the crew of the hated *Packet*. Many fell before the fighting ended. Captured and renamed the *Portsmouth Packet*, the ship again put to sea as an American privateer, only to be recaptured by the Royal Navy and recommissioned under her former name. Under the command of Caleb Seeley of Saint John, she again inspired terror amongst American shipping for the last months of the war.

Thousands of men from the provinces served with the British forces during the war, frequently by impressment, often voluntarily. A certificate of service in the militia was sometimes sufficient to protect a man against impressment, but captains of the Royal Navy created hard feelings by the rigour of their methods. So great was the demand for skilled seamen in the mercantile marine that shipowners were accused of harbouring deserters from the Royal Navy. Workmen of any kind were welcomed everywhere and in all the seaport towns "crimps" and "crimping" became epithets applied to those who seduced soldiers and sailors from their duty.

The military prisons, especially the one at Melville Island at Halifax, were crowded with French and American seamen. The sale of prize cargoes, particularly those of luxury items like Lyons silk, gave boundless opportunity for profit. At one stage thirty American prize ships, roped together, made a bridge across the harbour of St John's, and the clerks of the great mercantile establishments used champagne bottles for target practice on Sunday afternoons. Everything could be disposed of, even in Newfoundland. James McBraire, the Irish ex-sergeant who was famous as one of the shrewdest traders of St John's, caused his friends to wonder why he purchased a prize cargo of twelve hundred grindstones. During the next winter, when provisions were scarce, nobody could buy a bag of bread at his store without taking one for two dollars.[49]

When the news of sanguinary conflicts on land and sea, of delayed arrivals and interrupted voyages, ceased early in 1815 there was a general realization that the end of an era had come. Peace could not sustain the rapid pace of development that the last years of the long war had brought forth. Canny merchants withdrew capital from their ventures and commenced to lower wages. Governments, drawing inspiration from the passing of the initiative to Britain in the final stages of the war with the United States, looked to the evening of old scores. Reverting to William Knox's ideas of a strong British Empire in America, New Brunswick asked for a better boundary against Massachusetts. All could foresee the decline of their infant economies if the West Indies trade should be reopened to the Americans. All resented the immense world trade built up by the United States since 1793 which hindered their growth. Newfoundland wanted the complete exclusion of foreigners from her shores. The fishing clauses of the treaties of 1713 and 1783 deprived Newfoundlanders of what they considered to be their birthright. Though the fishery had become almost entirely sedentary, the merchants of St John's were prepared to use the "nursery of seamen" argument in order to exclude the French and Americans. During the war Newfoundlanders had become familiar with their west coast, "the French shore." Isolated groups of settlers from all points of the compass had established themselves in some of the harbours. If French rights should be restored, the liberty of Newfoundlanders to colonize that coast would be in jeopardy.

Peace brought no victories. Article VIII of the Treaty of Paris in 1814 restored to France all the fishing privileges she had enjoyed on Newfoundland, and she regained possession of St Pierre and Miquelon. Again there arose the spectre of French competition in the markets of Europe, possessed exclusively by Anglo-Americans since 1793, and of the lively competition of the French fishermen in their Petit Nord. Again the promise of 1783, "not to molest," became the cause of frustrating dilemmas. With the Americans very little more than nothing was achieved. An early endeavour on the part of the British negotiators at Ghent to capitalize on their advantage was ruled out by the opinion of the Duke of Wellington, who was convinced that the military position did not justify demands for territorial cessions. The hope, long cherished by the New Brunswick legislature, of making communication with Canada over the Temiscouata portage more secure and of placing the Madawaska settlements beyond American jurisdiction, flickered out. Agreement was reached for the settlement by arbitration of the dispute over the islands in the Bay of Passamaquoddy, particularly Moose Island, where the Americans feared that the British might turn their military occupation into permanent possession. Eastport and its smuggling activities made a *cause célèbre*. It was also decided to set up a commission to run the northern line, agreed upon by the Convention of 1798, as far as the unknown highlands, so plainly specified by the Treaty of Versailles of 1783.

There were gains that seemed significant, though ultimately they were to prove illusory. By going to war the Americans sacrificed "the liberty of fishing" in the inshore waters of the Atlantic Provinces, granted in 1783. This included the liberty of landing on the unsettled creeks, bays, and inlets of Nova Scotia (the unpartitioned province of 1783), the Magdalen Islands, and Labrador. Yankee fishermen had made much of this "liberty." They had seldom scrupled to distinguish between settled and unsettled inlets. There were many accounts of their abuse of the inhabitants and of their destruction of property. The ultra-loyal deprecated the facility given to smuggling and the corruption of British subjects by American habits of mind. The prohibition was at first given some real meaning in 1815 as American interlopers were seized by British warships and brought to courts of Vice-Admiralty.

Jay's Treaty was nullified by the war. The Americans lost their privilege of sending their ships and cargoes to the British West Indies. This was a triumph for the merchants of the Atlantic Provinces who held hard to the principles of the Navigation Acts, "the Palladium of the British Empire." They were still brought up in the belief of the necessity of the old doctrines of exclusion and managed trade. The British government gave them assurance that their strategic entrepôt of imperial control, raised to such undreamed of heights during the war, would continue to be supported. The circuitous voyages, the carriage of American flour, beef, and dry products to the West

Indies through the ports and by the ships of the Atlantic Provinces, would still continue. Again the British government proclaimed a belief that New Brunswick and Nova Scotia could supply the West Indies with all they required, whether the goods were of British or American origin. But there were many straws in the wind to indicate a wavering on essential principles. The West Indian planters clamoured for direct American participation in their trade. The British government admitted American vessels to its East Indian possessions though not to its West. After 1815 the central element in Anglo-American relations was to be the Commercial Convention of 1818. By this relaxation of the Laws of Trade in favour of American goods and merchants, British manufactured goods, conveyed on British ships, could retain their enormous and ever-increasing share of American markets. Even in 1815 it was an open question whether or not Britain, at the risk of losing American goodwill, would maintain the North Atlantic entrepôt by stringent laws of trade.[50] Despite the War of 1812 and its enrichment of the Atlantic Provinces, the major interest of British commerce in time of peace lay in trade with the United States rather than with the limited markets of the British American colonies.

CHAPTER 7

Growth and Growing Pains
1815–1828

The long period of war, from 1793 to 1815, had in the end been beneficial to the Atlantic Provinces, but the societies that emerged during that time had taken little form that was fixed. Rapid transformations of an unstable character had featured their growth. Though native breeds of Newfoundlanders and Nova Scotians had come into existence, and though New Brunswick and Prince Edward Island were making satisfactory progress after slow starts, peoples of different national origins had scarcely begun to be assimilated to one another. The long period of peace that followed 1815 saw the continuation of the process that had been at work, of the rapid introduction of still new immigrants and of their comparatively slow fusing into rudimentary but highly self-conscious communities. For the great formative influence that went farthest to shape the destinies of all the colonies for the next thirty years was the influx of new immigrants from the British Isles. Peace brought to the Industrial Revolution better opportunities for discharging its surplus populations on the shores of British North America.

In all this unplanned, pell-mell development it was the Scots who took the leading part. Those who had earlier settled in the colonies had enjoyed no affluence, but the reports they sent home had the effect of enlivening a spirit for emigration that was already strong. Lord Selkirk's settlement was widely advertised as the most progressive on Prince Edward Island.[1] Those who had come to Pictou and Cape Breton, without supervision or assistance, found, in spite of their privations, that which was necessary to persuade their friends and relations to follow. While demanding landlords extracted higher rents from the poverty-stricken populace of the Highlands and Islands, while the kelp industry languished in the Outer Hebrides, while the unscrupulous agents of shipowners seeking passengers promised freedom from all cares in the New World, the prospect of a hundred acres of free land aroused the desires not only of the young and ambitious but of the aged and infirm.

Throughout this period of upheaval in the Highlands, two or three shiploads of Scots annually stepped ashore at Canso, Pictou, Sydney, or Charlottetown. More emphatically than before, the southern and eastern coastlines of the Gulf of St Lawrence became a Scottish land. In 1826 a large number of Hebrideans, landed by chance at St Andrews in New Brunswick, eventually made their way to Cape Breton, where they knew that their countrymen could be found.[2] Catholics and Protestants continued to dwell severely apart. Pitching upon wilderness land, the black or burnt forest as they called it, they worked with the *cas chreum*, a simple crooked-legged hand-plough, and left few records of their early travails. Visitors to their new country noted a powerful litigiousness, especially upon the boundaries of their holdings, and, among the industrious, an overweening desire to acquire by purchase as much land as possible.[3] They had their share of the improvident and some, though holding to the grim task, could express disillusionment in poetry: "This is the country where there is hardship though the people coming across didn't know it. It was evil they brought on us, those enticers, who contrived through their fairy-tales to bring us out here."[4]

The Lowland Scots were probably as numerous but, unlike the Highlanders, they did not come to British America in groups or clans. Many of them were skilled artisans or tradesmen willing to turn their hands to agriculture, bringing a fair amount of capital that often meant the difference between success and failure. While the Highlanders, speaking Gaelic, long preserved their identity, the Lowlanders, with their broad Scots, could readily mingle with provincial populations. Taking passage at low fares on the returning timber ships, they could be found almost everywhere.

Newfoundland continued to be the principal point of reception for the Irish, though less so than in former years as the timber ships now offered passages for Saint John and the Miramichi. As the post-war depression fell upon the fishery, St John's, crowded with Irish who had been readily absorbed during the last years of the conflict, experienced a swift descent from the height of prosperity to the brink of disaster. From the end of the fishing season in 1815 to the summer of 1818, famine brooded over the island. The winter of 1817-18 was long remembered as the "Winter of the Rals," or the Rowdies. Theirs were the acts of desperate men. In November three hundred houses of St John's were destroyed by fires which were, in the opinion of the authorities, the work of incendiaries. Several hundred men without adequate clothing, reported the Grand Jury, wandered about the smoking ruins at the hour of midnight to seek warmth from the ashes and nourishment from the refuse of the half-burned fish. At Renous a shipload of Irish immigrants left their vessel at the edge of the ice and crawled ashore on their hands and knees to beg provisions from the half-starved inhabitants.[5] Severe cold froze the harbour of St John's so that the town, now bulging with a population of ten thousand, endured its agony in isolation. In the midst of this grief fresh shiploads of Irish immigrants, conveyed under miserable conditions by shipowners from Ireland who were indifferent to the welfare of their passengers, represented impossible additions to the troubles. Some were sent back to Ireland; others, starving and dying, were shipped to Halifax and the mercies of the Nova Scotian government. The only recommendation of the British parliament when it considered the plight of Newfoundland in 1817 was the deportation of five or ten thousand of its people.

The waterfronts of all the principal ports became communal centres for immigrant Irish as destiny determined whether they were to remain as day-labourers, or pass on to the mecca beckoning to most of them, the United States. Unfortunately for the provinces it was the young and self-reliant who could accumulate the passage-money that enabled them to make the second choice. Few were willing to adopt the more difficult expedient of attempting to farm wilderness land without capital. At the ports of the Miramichi, the fastest-growing timber region in the Atlantic Provinces where many of them were landed, the Irish added their own distinctive hurly-burly to a community already noted for disorder and lawlessness.[6]

The few settlements planned and supervised by governments were mainly failures. In 1815 the old problem of what to do with disbanded soldiers again arose, and, in spite of past experience, the British government quickly accepted Nova Scotian suggestions that military settlements should be formed. A leading project was a new road from Halifax to Annapolis that would run in almost a straight line, cutting the distance of the older route through the Minas townships by one-third. At a cost of thousands of pounds to the British government, supported by grants of the legislature, the road was cut through the swamps and forests, and the more stout-hearted of the men of eight or ten regiments, including the Fencibles of Nova Scotia and Newfoundland, accepted grants along its barely beaten course. One or two of these military settlements managed to survive, but most quickly became extinct. Several hundred men were enrolled as grantees. Perhaps fifty lasted out the ordeal.[7] In New Brunswick the veterans of the 104th Regiment did much better on lands of the upper St John where the broad river gave effective communication with the outside world.

Efforts to settle large numbers of blacks on wilderness lands were scarcely more successful. They had come with the Loyalists, both as slaves and as soldiers who had gained their freedom by serving with the British forces. But they had failed to become independent settlers, and their role had become one of honourable domestic servitude. Slavery had ceased to be protected by the law when the courts of both New Brunswick and Nova

Scotia had in 1800 denied the rights of slave-owners to regain possession of lost property. By 1808 both male and female slaves had generally deserted their masters who, in Nova Scotia, made strenuous efforts to enforce their authority by new laws that would prohibit desertions.[8] In Newfoundland an attempt made long before from Bermuda to introduce slavery to the fishery had been boycotted as a threat to white labour.[9] Slaves or not, the blacks had shown themselves, like most whites, to be incapable of farming inferior and stony soil. Yet in 1814, when British warships returned from the southern states of the Union bearing seventeen hundred released slaves, agriculture was the only recourse for these unhappy people, who lacked both capital and skill. They were settled at Hammond's Plains, Preston, and other points outside Halifax. New Brunswick took five hundred, who were settled at Loch Lomond.[10] The British government offered to remove them to Trinidad, but they preferred a northern climate to which they were unaccustomed rather than what they thought would be a return to slavery.

After 1815 the colonial populations and their legislatures would offer little tangible assistance to newcomers. While commerce was unstable, encouragement to immigration was not in fashion. Men of capital were always accorded respect. But most of the Scots and Irish, if not in penury, were on its fringes. Year after year the Nova Scotian legislature, not from policy but from pity, granted small sums of money to aid recent arrivals over their hard first seasons. In New Brunswick financial resources were fewer and the attitude more stringent. Already the slim colonial populations regarded the wastelands as the heritage of their own natural increase. They resented the appearance of strangers who were a charge on the public purse and whose accents of speech and habits of life seemed alien. Already it was said in Nova Scotia that there were no wild lands remaining that were worthy of cultivation. Not since 1800, said a later report of the council, had anybody with capital invested money in them and only those with nothing to lose but their labour would venture to till the wilderness. Official enquiries from England concerning schemes of settlement were met by the response that opportunities in New Brunswick and Canada were much better.[11] The wealthy merchants of New Brunswick, entrenched in the legislature, were likewise disposed to believe that the future of the province depended on commerce rather than on agriculture. Wild lands were valued for their timber alone. The remnants of the "landed interest," those who continued to indulge in the Loyalist belief in the potentialities of great manorial estates, were now without influence as the timber trade extended its ravages into the unexplored forests. Farmers could secure no protection against the importation of the fine American flour which the merchants of Saint John and Halifax sold at good prices. In New Brunswick agricultural endeavour was becoming a mark of inferiority. Occasionally the Nova

Scotian assembly would help immigrants. The merchant-democrats of New Brunswick would do nothing.

In spite of the lack of encouragement from governments, colonization produced in these years rapid increases in population. Between 1817 and 1827 the number of Nova Scotians increased from 82,000 to 123,000. In 1824 the first census of New Brunswick showed 74,000. Though there was no freehold settlement in Prince Edward Island except by purchase, the province had 25,000 people in 1822 and gained 20 per cent over the next eight years. In less than twenty-five years, from 1804 to 1827, Newfoundland, where colonization was opposed to all official policy, trebled the number of her residents from 20,000 to nearly 60,000.[12]

The breaking of the harsh land by an inexperienced people who were accustomed to softer climes was accompanied by calamities that became familiar. Fire, flood, and famine were never remote. Towns were burnt and crops failed, especially in "the cold years" from 1816 to 1818. Minor calamities were normal but a great holocaust like the Miramichi fire of 1825, when one hundred and sixty people lost their lives and eight thousand square miles of forest were destroyed, aroused the conscience of people in all the provinces and in Britain, Canada, and the United States. As if perils by land were not enough, there were frequent tidings of disaster by sea. Each year brought its toll of shipwrecks and bereavements to hundreds of residents of the provinces. Harrowing tales of all kinds of privations appeared in the public prints. Even accounts of cannibalism at sea made their rounds. Not the least of these was that of the 398-ton ship *Frances Mary* that cleared Saint John in January of 1826, her decks loaded with deals to utmost capacity. When picked up in the North Atlantic early in March by HMS *Blonde*, she was a floating hulk. The hearts, brains, and livers of the members of her crew who had died from the hardships of the voyage had been eaten by the survivors, two of whom were women.[13]

II

Religion accounted for the great social phenomena of the new communities that were being shaped. When Bishop Charles Inglis died in 1816, having given the last years of his life to "literary pursuits" at Claremont, the Church of England was completely displaced from the central position that had earlier been assumed for it. In addition to the onset of "the sectarians," internal rivalries weakened its position. After the Bishop had failed to ensure the succession of his able and ambitious son, the British government appointed, according to the petition of the Nova Scotian assembly, Rev. Robert Stanser, rector of Halifax, whom Sir John Sherbrooke described as completely unfitted for the post. For reasons of health Stanser departed for

England in 1816, leaving the immense diocese without a bishop in residence. When the younger Inglis, Bishop John, ascended to the dignity in 1825, the fortunes of the Church were almost beyond repair. Resentful of the neglect of Halifax and reflecting the jealousy of Nova Scotian primacy that had always been notable in Fredericton, the clergy of New Brunswick petitioned for the establishment of a separate diocese in 1819. Doctrinal differences rent its fold. A fair number of the first Baptist and Methodist missionaries were graduates of King's College.

Still the financial support of the Church came almost entirely from England. By the royal instructions lands were reserved for glebes and schools, but these were generally poor and unproductive.[14] Governments quickly learned to fear disfavour if the instructions should be executed too literally. Yet in clerical circles there remained the hope that ultimately the setting aside of valuable lands could make the Church in the colonies self-supporting. Though the Church of England missionaries laboured faithfully, their stipends, however poor, made them independent of the communities they served and very frequently they failed to achieve the common touch that was required for success in frontier regions. Both Bishops Inglis found reason to complain of clergy who offended their parishioners and failed to inspire confidence in societies to which they were complete strangers.

Except for Newfoundland, where the Church of England maintained its position to a much greater extent than elsewhere, it was the Baptists who gave most potent testimony to the eagerness for religious care among pioneer populations. Their zeal may be measured by their willingness in 1814, a time when their constituency consisted largely of the poor and the lowly, to enter the field of foreign missions. A large proportion of their funds was collected by women's mite societies. Refusing to depend on "a hireling ministry" and with only a rudimentary organization, they were able each year to send missionaries into new areas. By 1821 the congregations of New Brunswick could form a separate association of their own. In their great disputations there were often differences of opinion, even heresies. Their entrance to Prince Edward Island encountered some difficulties from contact with a group of Scottish Baptists whose point of difference was that believers should not marry unbelievers. But sentiments of the Spirit almost invariably triumphed over distinctions in doctrinal interpretation. The movement was tolerant enough to endure eccentricities.[15]

For many years it was not unusual for the great and the near great to sneer at the enthusiasm of the Baptist and Methodist denominations. Samuel Vetch Bayard, the commander of the Royal Nova Scotia Regiment, was condemned by his former friends for keeping low company when converted to Methodism. Sir John Wentworth no longer called at his fine house at Wilmot and Lady Wentworth made merry jests at his expense.[16] The new sects were generally regarded as sprung from the ignorance of the poor and uneducated. But, by a fortuitous event, the Baptists received an accession of strength that projected them to the heart of society at Halifax. In 1824, when Rev. Robert Willis of Saint John was presented to the rectorship of St Paul's, a large section of the congregation preferred the more evangelical curate, Rev. William Twining. Thirty eminent seceders, after sampling the merits of other creeds, eventually formed the Granville Street Baptist Church. Among them were the prominent lawyer, Edmund A. Crawley, who was later ordained as a minister, James W. Johnston, soon to be a power in provincial politics, and his brother Lewis, a leading physician.[17] This affair produced unfortunate repercussions for Anglicanism through the provinces as able and educated lawyers and merchants followed the lead of the Halifax group to the Baptist movement. Organized around a hard core of membership, it extended its influence to thousands who were merely on the margin of religion.

Methodism made its greatest imprint on Newfoundland in the years after 1814, endeavouring to fill the vacuum created by the want of clergy in the Church of England which, at the time, had but five missionaries on the entire island. In that year the British Methodist Conference paid special heed to the moral and religious destitution of Newfoundland and adopted the practice of maintaining a dozen licensed workers there. To the outports there came the familiar practice of raising a flag outside the place of worship exactly one hour before service commenced and lowering it at the moment the minister entered the pulpit.[18] The Methodists established a church at St John's despite the displeasure of the authorities, and along three hundred miles of the Labrador coastline took up the declining endeavours of Moravian missionaries with the Indians. As the longer days of late February came to the northern outports, they delivered their "sealers' sermons" to those about to enter upon that hazardous pursuit. Along the newly settled coast of Fortune Bay, westward from St John's, they established a circuit over places where no clergy had ever come. In 1824 active membership in their societies was 1,030, a figure that bore no relationship to the scope of their influence. They encountered many obstacles. Their insistence on observance of the Lord's Day excited the bitter hostility of merchants. By the vulgar their adherents were derisively termed "Crawlers." The growth of the Roman Catholic population and the reported proselytizing activities of the priests aroused the conviction that the Methodists were fighting papistry as well as paganism. The great spate of conversions and "perversions" at this time prepared the way for a generation of religious animosity and violence.

In the other Atlantic Provinces the Baptists filled the religious void before the Methodists were able to send properly licensed missionaries to the more distant fields. But, especially in the provincial capitals, Methodists formed large and influential societies. English missionaries reinforced the native-born circuit-riders, replacing the Americans who had completely disappeared during the war of 1812. English immigrants added to their congregations. Everywhere they made notable conversions, largely from the ranks of the more evangelical Anglicans. Chief Justice Marshall of Cape Breton and two sons of the Anglican minister at Charlottetown might be mentioned as cogent examples, not forgetting the youthful Lemuel Allan Wilmot who, though ambitious for fame and fortune, abandoned the Lieutenant-Governor's levee on New Year's Eve for the watchnight service in the humble Methodist chapel at Fredericton.[19] Another notable convert was Robert Cooney, the historian of the Miramichi, who in his youth had accompanied Father, later Bishop, William Dollard into the Catholic settlements of northern New Brunswick for the express purpose of gathering up anti-Catholic tracts that had been distributed by Methodist circuit-riders. In 1817 a missionary society for three provinces was formed at Halifax and the aging William Black who, when he walked the streets of that city where he was familiarly greeted as "Bishop," could rejoice in a growing and influential constituency. In the newly settled districts excellent local preachers could always be found when circuit-riders failed to appear. But in total numbers the Methodists were exceeded by the Baptists. Their more closely knit organization and higher degree of church discipline could be handicaps in dealing with frontier conditions.

Another force, just as formidable and enjoying a broad base from which to operate, added to the complexity of the religious scene. Presbyterianism in North America had consisted of a few loose strands seldom woven together. In Nova Scotia the first identifiable Presbyterian minister was Rev. James Murdoch of Truro, a Londonderry man like the people he served. The old Congregational churches that did not become Baptist following the New Light movement ultimately gravitated towards Presbyterianism, the most conspicuous being that former citadel of New England dissent, Mathers (St Matthew's) at Halifax.[20] But as the Gulf Shore of Nova Scotia became Scottish and Gaelic-speaking, the Scottish national interest became overwhelmingly paramount. Sent to Pictou in 1786 by the Anti-Burgher synod, Rev. James McGregor was the first to bring the Presbyterian message to the Gulf Shore as far as the Miramichi, to Prince Edward Island, and Cape Breton. Like the travels of other pioneering men of the spirit, his journeys became proverbial for their hazards and hardships. In 1790, when he first visited Prince Edward Island, he was implored to go to the remote settlement of Princetown or Malpeque where men of Cantyre had established themselves twenty years before and had not seen a minister since. To get there he had to make three-fourths of a circle, "sometimes walking, sometimes sailing, sometimes riding." Proceeding up the East River he came to the prosperous settlement of Covehead. From there he walked along the shore for thirty miles, sometimes on expansive beach, often on almost impassable rock. At ferries he took canoes, towing his horse behind him.[21] Wherever he found Scots, he was welcomed by people who had awaited the advent of a Presbyterian minister for years. Some had taken their children for baptism to Parson DesBrisay of the Church of England, but only with great misgiving because he made the sign of the cross and failed to inquire into the moral character of the parents.

The schisms that beset the Church of Scotland in the old land pursued McGregor and his fellow-workers to Pictou. New shiploads of Highlanders brought with them the conviction that only the Established Church of Scotland could properly ordain ministers; and the Presbyterians volubly contributed to the great controversies raging through all the Protestant communities of the Atlantic Provinces as to what was pure Gospel and what was not. Yet in 1817 the Presbyterians of Nova Scotia formed a union with McGregor as their moderator. He had been sent out to make Christians, not Seceders. Still, when tormented by "witches" who kept alive the old differences, he would thunder forth against Erastianism and for the historic doctrine of ministers and elders elected by the people. Enduring their discords and receiving strong support from the Glasgow Colonial Society, the Presbyterians became the principal Protestant group over northern Nova Scotia, Cape Breton, and Prince Edward Island. In New Brunswick they made a belated appearance. St Andrew's at Saint John (1817) became a mother church where the minister, Rev. George Burns, rejected the appellation of dissenter and challenged the Anglican establishment. St Andrew's was given not only a spire but a church bell.[22] Scottish nationalism, encouraged by the presence of the Scottish governor, Lord Dalhousie, at Halifax, would not tolerate inferiority.

Even the Roman Catholic Church was not free from the particularism that flourished in the Atlantic Provinces. The visit of Bishop Joseph Octave Plessis in 1812 to his widespread missions refreshed the morale of the few priests who served him and gave inspiration to their labours. Shocked by all kinds of evidence of destitution, he was at the same time impressed by much evidence of firm faith. His politic deportment excited much respect from the civil authorities. At Charlottetown he persuaded his difficult Irish to construct a church and suggested, perhaps to reassure officialdom, that it should be named for an English saint, St Dunstan.[23] But even Bishop Plessis, handicapped by a grievous shortage of priests, could do little to ease the burden of his workers in this portion of his immense diocese. Irish and Scottish initiative was to move into the great area that Quebec was unable to fill.

A most notable figure in Halifax was Rev. Edmund Burke, remarkable not only for his efforts to improve the Catholic position in the face of the opposition of the civil authorities, but also for the discipline with which he attempted to improve the morals of his Irish parishioners who came in from Newfoundland where they had adopted wastrel ways of life in the fishery. Among Protestants he was unpopular because of his insistent methods in proselytizing the brides selected by his young men. In earlier life he had served the fur trade in Detroit and beyond and had become a British imperialist who could make common cause with Selkirk on his visit to Halifax in 1804.[24] Often he threatened to take his congregation on his back to Canada as part of a plan to fill up the great west with Irish and keep the Yankees out. A man of big ideas, he contemplated with fondness the establishment of an Irish episcopate in Halifax. Negotiations with both London and Rome were necessary, for English law stood in the way. Yet this could be circumvented by the creation of a vicariate apostolic with a non-English title. In 1817 the plan worked out successfully and Burke was consecrated Bishop of Sion.

Realizing the need for still further division but determined to preserve the primacy of Quebec and a considerable degree of centralized authority, Bishop Plessis left for Europe in 1819. The Vatican somewhat anticipated developments by making him an archbishop, but its relations with Britain were amicable and Lord Bathurst's predilection for things ecclesiastical smoothed the road.[25] Consequent upon his elevation, the see of Quebec was allowed four suffragan bishops, one of whom was Father Bernard Angus McEachern of Charlottetown, who took the title of Bishop of Rosen, with jurisdiction over New Brunswick, Prince Edward Island, and Cape Breton. Yet this position proved unsatisfactory to the bishops of the Atlantic Provinces. Quebec still held the authority but would send no aid. Indeed, it sought the reannexation of Nova Scotia in spite of the fact, as Bishop McEachern rather indignantly remarked, that since 1790 it had sent only three priests to the province for limited periods.[26] Allegations of Quebec's neglect and lack of interest became more frequent.

Powerfully aided by Bishop Alexander Macdonell of Upper Canada and by the British government, Catholics of the Atlantic Provinces moved towards the further dismemberment of the Quebec archdiocese. For a long time Rome hesitated because of fears that new dioceses would not be able to sustain themselves financially. But in 1829 Charlottetown became the seat of a see. Amid these gentle ecclesiastical rivalries racial distinctions frequently came to the surface. When Bishop Burke died in 1822, Rome hesitated to fill his place for five years, finally settling upon Rev. William Fraser of Antigonish. Antigonish was to become a great centre of Scottish Catholicism.

As the Christian faith extended over so much newly broken territory, fierce vendettas occurred and recurred between Catholic and Protestant, and between Protestants of different denominations. Yet there were far more examples of Christian charity in which people of different creeds helped one another. Whatever discords arose there was a fellowship in strong drink that brought overtones of jocundity. "What a wonder we did not all become drunkards!" exclaimed David Nutter, a Baptist minister, as he looked back upon the evangelistic efforts of his youth.[27] In 1824 the opponents of Methodism in Saint John prophesied its total extinction when the eloquent James Priestley of the Germaine Street church was charged with too great a susceptibility to drink and read out of the Conference. Cheap spirits offered refreshment during "the protracted meetings" of the Methodists and Baptists, the occasion among all denominations for social intercourse during pastoral calls.

III

All religious denominations contested the establishment of the Church of England. Methodists and Baptists fought the discriminations against their ministers in the Marriage Acts, eventually gaining the desired equality in 1834, coincident with the reform in Britain. Sometimes they sought and received financial grants from government for the construction of churches or grants of land for the support of ministers. Presbyterians of Halifax and Saint John, who maintained a loyalty to the Established Church of Scotland, would have liked legal establishments of their own in the provinces on the same level with that of the Church of England.

It was in the field of education that religious rivalries overflowed into the civil domain. As the religious conscience sharpened, the concern for education became the greater. To ensure a continuing stream of priests, ministers, and itinerant workers, to make the provinces independent of outside aid of this kind, was probably the greatest object. But there was also a widespread concern for elementary education, made the more lively through frequent contacts with Americans. Even the crudest of Yankee fishermen who landed on the coasts, it was noticed, could read and write. Nova Scotia, followed by New Brunswick, had adopted a system of subsidizing local initiative in the establishment of schools. But the sole result of the bounties given was the improvement of education for children already being taught. The effect of the system, it was argued, was to compel the poor to pay for the instruction of children of more well-to-do families in well-populated areas.[28] Probably much more was done for the welfare of the populace at large by the introduction of the Madras or National system of education, so named because of its success in India, which was well advanced by 1820. Supervised and controlled by the Church of England, it made the female teacher a familiar figure, popularized the institution of teacher training, and gave rudimentary instruction to poor children in the towns. Yet even in Nova

Scotia, by far the most advanced of the provinces, education did not reach rural children. Two-thirds of them, declared Charles R. Fairbanks, were growing up in ignorance and vice.[29] In farming communities children were valued for their labour. On Prince Edward Island a wandering Scottish catechist was informed by a pious father that he could not restrain his sons from whittling and playing on the Jew's harp on the Sabbath day. Sons could not be disciplined as in Scotland, for parents were dependent on them.[30]

In the houses of assembly it was generally realized that local and compulsory assessment for the support of schools was the answer to the problem, but majorities invariably came to the conclusion that the country was not ready for it. Since the coming of the Loyalists two generations had grown to manhood under a widespread impression that schooling was an unnecessary luxury. The justices of the peace of Nova Scotia and New Brunswick were often men completely unlettered in the law or in almost anything else.

For superior schooling boys of wealthy families were sent to England or the United States, but by 1820 there was a general conviction that the land was becoming barbarized for want of facilities for higher education. Here the failure of King's College became a subject for considerable concern. For thirty years the institution at Windsor, constructed with British funds and heavily endowed by both British and provincial governments, had been no object of pride. The religious tests, imposed in 1803, excluded four-fifths of possible candidates for degrees in arts. The president, vice-president, and professors had copied the practice of many parsons in England by holding more than one appointment. They sought missionary stations in the adjacent countryside and extra income from the Society for the Propagation of the Gospel. Amongst the small student body discipline had broken down. In this infant institution, expected by the Church and State party to become a replica of Oxford, combinations of young men were organized on "gentlemanly" principles to protect themselves from punishment for evasion of the regulations. Authority could not be imposed even upon the students in divinity. When Dr William Cochran, the aged vice-president, visited the public houses of Windsor at midnight in the execution of his duty, the students, in revenge, wrecked the furniture of his lecture-room and made his life unbearable.[31] In 1827 Bishop John Inglis secured the revocation of "the obnoxious statutes" that excluded dissenters and commenced measures for the restoration of discipline. By then it was too late for King's to fulfil its mission as a university for all British America.

The appointment of Lord Dalhousie as Lieutenant-Governor of Nova Scotia in 1816 brought about a great effort to renovate the lamentable state of higher education. His ideas represented a curious blending of the archaic and the ultra-modern. He believed that the royal prerogative could be beneficently employed after the fashion of his heroes, the first Stuart kings, but that education should be free and open to all, liberally dispensed on a non-sectarian basis. His objective was a college patterned on Edinburgh, an institution to be located in the rapidly growing port of Halifax that would distribute its learning to transient passers-by as well as resident students. After unsuccessfully attempting to procure the abolition of the tests at King's and its removal to Halifax, he proceeded with the execution of his plan in 1818. He had at hand £11,000 derived from customs duties at Castine in 1814-15, which the British government had allocated to local purposes in Nova Scotia. The consequence was the construction, begun in 1820, of Dalhousie College on the Parade.

Dalhousie's liberal and secular ideas on education offered no solution to the problems of the Free Presbyterians of Pictou whose crying need was for more ministers. Rev. Thomas M'Culloch was a man whose whole immense passion was dedicated to the idea that the purpose of education was the proper interpretation of Scripture. From the time of his arrival in 1812, he gave all his energies, along with his quick wit and sardonic pen, to Pictou Academy, which received a charter from the legislature in 1815. He had formidable opposition. Notable Kirkmen, such as Michael Wallace, were opposed to an institution that would enable the Free Churchmen to enlarge their constituency. Bishop John Inglis regarded Pictou Academy as a threat to the privileges of his own institution and to the Anglican establishment. Lord Dalhousie was convinced that a large number of small colleges would hinder rather than advance higher education. Mobilizing support for denominational colleges from other Protestant groups, M'Culloch persuaded the House of Assembly to give financial grants to his academy. But he could not secure permanent endowment. The pursuit of higher learning by all religious denominations could not be subsidized by government. In 1824 the legislative council laid down the principle that financial grants could not be made to denominational schools, that permanent provision for Pictou Academy could be allowed only if its trustees should be appointed by public authority.[32] Another vested interest complicated the problem still further as the Baptists decided that there must be a university for their purposes. Led by the Halifax seceders from the Church of England, they established Horton Academy at Wolfville in 1828 as a step in realization of the project.

The opposing interests that were so violently at work in education merely reflected the dividing forces that predominated in the Atlantic Provinces. Each nationality from which the populations were made up, each geographical region and religious denomination, seemed prepared to enter a destiny exclusive to itself alone. Bishop Inglis had endured many setbacks to his dream that his university at Windsor might be a centre of Anglican thought that might lead all on the appointed way. To add to his griefs New Brunswick now founded a university of its own. Since 1785, when seven Loyalist memorialists had petitioned Governor Carleton to establish a seminary at Fredericton, New Brunswick had shown a manifest desire to make herself independent of Nova Scotia in this respect as in so many others. Poverty had hampered the early beginnings. But in the early 1820's, when the timber trade brought large sums of money into revenues controlled by the Crown, the British government agreed to make from this source an annual grant of £1,000 and to pay for half the cost of the building. In happy unanimity the legislature agreed to provide similar sums.

The rather extraordinary feature of the establishment of King's College at Fredericton, founded by royal charter in 1828, was that the Church of England was given virtual control at a time when sectarian disputes were being violently conducted on broad fronts in New Brunswick as in Nova Scotia. The charter provided for Anglican management and a chair of divinity. One of the principal purposes of the new college was the training of candidates for the Anglican priesthood. British collaboration was purchased at a high price when clerical influence was powerful at the Colonial Office. But the Lieutenant-Governor, Sir Howard Douglas, who prided himself on an ability to make extremes meet, reached a settlement only after he told Lord Bathurst that there could be no college at all unless one of the original stipulations, the subscription by students to the Thirty-Nine Articles, should be withdrawn. With the granting of this concession Protestant sensitivities were mollified.[34]

Education, like constitutional government, lagged in Newfoundland. In 1799 Admiral Gambier had founded the St John's Charity Schools, one for Protestants and one for Roman Catholics, but they enjoyed no continuity of endeavour. At the real commencement, in 1823, Newfoundland's educational policy acquired a rigidly sectarian character when a group of English merchants interested in the Newfoundland trade proposed to found an academy for the training of teachers to be sent to the outports. Their leader was Samuel Codner, who was inspired by the missionary zeal of Lord Liverpool, the British prime minister. To meet the wishes of the people he agreed that religious denominations should take part in its management and, against the wishes of the Governor, the Colonial Office accepted the establishment of the Newfoundland School Society on this basis.[34]

In Prince Edward Island the possibility of creating facilities for higher education received its first serious consideration at this time. When Bishop McEachern applied in 1829 for a grant to pay the salary of a clergyman at his proposed grammar school at St Andrews, he was informed that the legislature would make its educational policy without reference to the requirements of religious denominations.[35] A few years later the Central Academy at Charlottetown, a non-denominational, publicly supported institution, was opened.

IV

External factors continued to bear upon the destiny of the Atlantic Provinces, though not so heavily as in former years. To those who thought primarily of overseas trade, the duel that continued with old enemies, the Americans, was of first consequence, but those who could not lift their eyes to more distant prospects found the Americans remarkably friendly. In 1817, after agreement was reached on the disputed islands in the Bay of Fundy, Britain withdrew her troops from Moose Island and the United States abandoned pretensions to Grand Manan. This revived the dubiously legal trade in plaster of Paris of which Eastport was the centre. Halifax and Saint John, in a determined effort to capture the trade for their larger ships, procured from their legislatures acts to compel the discharge of cargoes in American ports to the south of Boston. The Americans responded with an act forbidding importation except in their own vessels. Smuggling could not be controlled and Nova Scotia capitulated in 1818 when assemblymen from the Fundy counties argued at Halifax that only small vessels could navigate the bays from which the plaster was extracted. New Brunswick had little choice but to follow, yet feeling in Saint John was so strong that a fresh attempt was made in 1820 by imposing a tax on plaster imported into Charlotte County. This struck at the anchorages of Campobello and the other islands where a great many illicit transactions took place, but it proved impossible to enforce when the smugglers showed themselves prepared to resist by violence the officers of the law.[36] The great merchants of Halifax and Saint John could make the laws, but the laws could not control the obnoxious "schooner trade." And the trade in plaster was to become unimportant when new fertilizers were discovered in the American west.

Much to the regret of many in the Atlantic Provinces, the era of shipping warfare between Britain and the United States was coming to a conclusion. The Convention of 1818 on the fisheries indicated the new spirit that was at work in British thinking. Rather than lose the commercial treaty with the United States, Whitehall was willing to restore something of what the Americans had lost by the War of 1812. The idea that Newfoundland was a great buttress to British sea power was now an obvious absurdity. Her resident fishermen produced no recruits for the navy. By this convention the New England seamen were permitted to take fish between Cape Ray and the Rameau Islands and along a large stretch of the western and northern littorals, off the shores of the Magdalen Islands, and on almost the entire coast of Labrador. But the American government was compelled to renounce the "liberty" of the Treaty of 1783 and to abandon the privileges of fishing within three miles of the coasts of the other provinces and of curing and drying on their shores.

There was no government in Newfoundland that could raise objections, but this decision was interpreted as a grievous blow to the entire British Atlantic region, more ruinous than the Treaty of 1783, according to the opinion of the Nova Scotian legislature. Not only did the acquisitive Yankees again appear in Newfoundland waters to break local fishing regulations, but they were given additional means for invading European and West Indian markets from which they had been largely excluded since 1812. Even harsher was the British decision in 1819 to cease the payment of bounties to the ships of the West Country engaged in the Newfoundland fishery. This came at a time when not only the Americans and French, but the Norwegians as well, all subsidized by their governments, were entering upon fierce competition in the traditional markets of the Mediterranean. Newfoundland still belonged to Britain but was no longer a pillar of her supremacy at sea. British self-interest was acquiring new horizons. Though Nova Scotians and New Brunswickers obtained, by the Convention, a monopoly of their own inshore fisheries, they joined in the chorus of denunciation. Even at so early a date as this, Britain seemed willing to sacrifice her colonies in order to enlarge her international commerce.

Yet for several years more Britain sustained the circuitous trading routes that gave ship-building and shipping in the Atlantic Provinces great prosperity. During the first years of peace American traders were at tremendous disadvantage compared with those at Saint John and Halifax, and the overseas trade of the United States fell largely into British hands. Maritime Massachusetts continued to lose seamen and ship-carpenters who emigrated to Saint John and St Andrews. Strongly resenting their exclusion from British American ports, American shipowners were certain to challenge British policy. In 1817 Congress passed an act limiting the importation of British West Indian produce to vessels that were American or belonged to owners in the West Indies. This was aimed at the shipping of both Britain and British North America which, on circuitous voyages of three stages, could earn great profit, especially by conveying American food to the Sugar Islands. In the following year there came a more pointed retort to British mercantilism when an act was passed closing American ports to British ships proceeding from colonies whose ports were closed to Americans. This was directed primarily against the growing trade of Halifax and Saint John which were finding the cold war in shipping very much akin to conditions in the days of Jefferson's embargo and very much to their liking. Washington was determined to break the colonial monopoly in trade. The British

answer was the same as in the days of the embargo, the opening of free
ports at Halifax and Saint John. The act of 1818 "for affording facilities
to the trade of Nova Scotia and New Brunswick" was designed to retain
for the two ports the role of distributing centres for British manufactures in the United States and American produce in the West Indies.[37]
For several years commerce enjoyed renewed stimulation. The Americans
were allowed short voyages to the provinces but re-exportation had to be
in British bottoms.

Enduring continued frustration, the American government, by its Navigation Act of 1820, struck at its own shipmasters who facilitated the British
monopoly by prohibiting the importation of West Indian goods by way of
Halifax and Saint John. This resulted in higher prices of American goods
for the planters of the West Indies. Exchange began to shift from Halifax
and Saint John to the Swedish, Danish, and Dutch islands.[38] At London
a parliamentary battle between West Indian investors and the great shipping interests of Britain resulted in a victory for the former. New legislation
of 1822 resulted in a surrender in principle and the admission of American
ships to the harbours of the British Antilles from which they had so long
been excluded. British diplomacy and commercial acumen had not been able
to overcome the obdurate fact that the West Indies were dependent on
American goods. The Americans had pressed their point to the utmost and,
by an alliance with the West Indian interest and under the leadership of
Senator Rufus King, had won a hard victory.

The ending of the artificial process by which the Atlantic colonies had
been made the apex of a lucrative triangular trade was now in sight, but
American arrogance prolonged it for a few years more. Having won a great
concession, Congress was not willing to allow the ships of New Brunswick
and Nova Scotia to call at American ports on voyages to the West Indies
and no reciprocity was achieved until 1831. Realists had for long admitted
that the provinces could not supply the West Indies. But in 1831 the shipping monopoly, that had become something of a reality, faded into past
vistas as well. Yet the final arrangement, brought about by concurrent
legislation in Congress and in Parliament, opened to shipowners a new
possibility, that of calling at American ports and picking up cargoes for
unloading anywhere in the world.

The so-called British surrender was in accordance with the thinking of the
new era of free trade and substituted competition for protection to shipping
interests. At Saint John, where traditional ideas held hard, there were lamen-
tations and prophecies of doom. Sir Howard Douglas described the British
decision as a cruel blow by a mother to a child of her body. But the feeling
in Halifax was much more optimistic and cosmopolitan. Freedom of trade,
the removal of the last fetters on the commerce of the province that accom-

panied the loss of the special place in the West Indies, produced celebrations that inaugurated new opportunities to "the thinking part of the population." When news of the reforms in colonial trade made in 1825 by William Huskisson, President of the Board of Trade, reached Halifax, "such a day of cheerfulness had not been witnessed in the place for ten years."[39] In New Brunswick, where prosperity in trade depended, or appeared to depend, on British protection against foreigners, Huskisson was no hero.

Under the shadow of great impending changes in British commercial policy in these years, the colonies enjoyed their full share of the world's prosperity. The final impact of the post-war depression, striking hard in 1822, reduced revenues to less than half of those of the year before. In the entire season of construction not a new building rose in Halifax. But upswings as well as downswings were violent. In 1823 the provinces were again on the highroad to prosperity. How important the trade of the West Indies was to Nova Scotia is shown by the Halifax returns from 1819 to 1823. Exports amounted to £621,000, imports to £348,000, the surplus going a long way to enable the province to pay for British and American imports. New Brunswick shipped British and American goods to the West Indies but exported little of its own produce. The whole economy was oriented upon the protected market for timber in the British Isles. Saint John, enjoying ample and easy credit facilities, acquired the reputation for keen and optimistic speculation as ship-building, financed on borrowed money, rose to the rank of a leading satellite industry.

Within the Atlantic Provinces rival commercial spheres of influence were forming. Saint John made great strides in developing its trade with the Nova Scotian side of the Bay of Fundy. As steam began to supplant sail, Digby, Windsor, and the populous places of the Annapolis Valley fell within its expanding orbit. Land transport was difficult and expensive so that Halifax was able to develop its earlier connections with Prince Edward Island and the Miramichi. The slight colonial tariff schedules did not impede the formation of trading zones that transcended political boundaries. Northern New Brunswick, where the coastlines were rapidly filling up with an increasing Acadian population, Irish immigrants, and Scottish timber bosses, was developing a considerable connection with Quebec. Gaspé Loyalists and their descendants were moving to the southern side of the Bay of Chaleur, and, about 1826, the port of Bathurst began to become of consequence.

In the great era of canal construction Halifax and Saint John sought to enlarge trade at one another's expense through the cheap medium of waterways. After a great many years of deliberation the merchants of Halifax secured the incorporation of a company to build a canal along the line of the Shubenacadie lakes and bring the trade of the Bay of Fundy to their own port. The aging and astute Michael Wallace was a leading promoter. The equally astute Simon Bradstreet Robie prophesied ruinous expense and no revenues. Construction was commenced in July, 1826, but subscription for shares fell short and the project collapsed. Halifax was completely uninterested in another venture that originated in Saint John, a scheme promoted by James Glenie as far back as 1800, that would bring the trade of the Gulf of St Lawrence within Saint John's easy radius. This was the construction of a canal across the isthmus of Chignecto. In 1823 a committee of the New Brunswick legislature came to Halifax to interview Lord Dalhousie and Sir James Kempt, but without result.[40]

V

Amid many shocks Prince Edward Island emerged from its stagnant condition and, within its narrow limits, produced a lively political life of its own. Manipulations in the great contest for the ownership of land made it appear a game of skill and patience in which the element of luck could play an enormous part. If the British government had been sufficiently apathetic, two or three individuals of very moderate capital might have acquired possession of the entire island. Lieutenant-Governor Fanning (1786-1805) had played the same game as Patterson, though far more cautiously and discreetly, purchasing the 48,000 acres of his predecessor for £98, arranging by collusion with Chief Justice Stewart and his sons for the escheat of the property of absentee proprietors, whipping up opinion amongst a sullen but alert tenantry in favour of a general confiscation. Discouraging accounts coming to London told of a tenantry that would not labour owing to the grand idea that sooner or later all tillers of the soil would become their own landlords. The proprietors likewise had no enthusiasm. At any moment their lands might be lost by escheat and any investment in them lost as well. Arrears in quitrents at this stage totalled £60,000, more than the island was worth.

In 1803 Fanning had procured authority for the opening of an escheat court and proceedings had commenced against the owners of seventeen lots. But once again, when the issue was really joined, proprietorial influence triumphed and all action was suspended. After nearly twenty years in which Fanning had deceived the British government, had told of glowing prosperity although the amount of tilled land had scarcely increased throughout his long regime, he was recalled in 1805 when Downing Street became convinced that he was a partisan of local interests working for escheat. Absentee proprietorship for Prince Edward Island was bad enough. A greater evil might have been the engrossment of all the land by a lieutenant-governor and two or three official families who were gulling the tenantry with the propaganda that the fight for escheat was being conducted on their behalf.

Des Barres, who made his last official appearance in the history of the Atlantic Provinces as Lieutenant-Governor in 1805 at the age of eighty-three, could never really understand the situation yet strove to grapple with it nevertheless. Turning his back upon the entanglements of the official cabal, whose leader, John Stewart, locally known as Hell-fire Jack, held both imperial and provincial appointments and enjoyed influential contacts in London, Des Barres leaned for advice upon James B. Palmer, an Irish lawyer who was the founder of a new political interest. With William Haszard, the son of a Rhode Island Loyalist, Palmer organized the Loyal Electors, a society that at first was composed of about forty citizens of Charlottetown and gradually extended its influence to the country. Its activities were democratic in character, fostering open discussions of public affairs and inviting criticism of the official coterie. Many of its members were of the Loyalist families who felt betrayed by the failure of the government to honour the promise of 1784 to grant clear title to the lands on which they had settled. "The mere existence of the Society created a panic in the Stewart-Des Brisay-Fanning faction."[41]

As long as Des Barres remained at Charlottetown the Society made itself a formidable force in politics. It won control of the Assembly and Palmer was awarded several public offices by the Lieutenant-Governor. But the discontent the Society aroused created suspicion of more deep-seated intentions. While the cause of political reform in New Brunswick and Nova Scotia was comparatively quiescent, Prince Edward Island had its reformers who were labelled as *jacobin* and levelling. The uncompromising Chief Justice Caesar Colclough perceived in the Society the foes of order and the fomenters of rebellion. While the struggle still raged against Napoleon, political dissent, even in such a small and remote colony, could be interpreted as treason. Supported by the Stewart faction and by the proprietors in London, who professed that the activities of the Society were directed against the rights of private property, Colclough commenced an investigation in 1811. Invective raged and the Society won the election of 1812. But the victory was with the proprietors, who persuaded the British government that tranquillity must be restored. Des Barres was recalled in 1813, Palmer was dismissed from all his offices, and Colclough was transferred to a larger arena of conflict in Newfoundland. The Society was defeated in its intentions and gradually disappeared. But its formal projection of the land problem before the people and its methodical form of party organization prepared the way for the development of democratic government in Prince Edward Island.

The province found its tyrant in Charles Douglas Smith, successor to Des Barres, who seems to have considered that tyranny was essential. Factions ruled the scene at Charlottetown, and Smith, who owed his appointment to the influence of his brother, Sir Sydney Smith, with Lord Bathurst and the Prince Regent, created his own to face them. A son and a son-in-law filled important offices. Without this kind of patronage, he declared, he could enjoy no influence.[42] Local nonentities were raised to the council. Smith's method of defeating public opinion was to ignore it and for four years the legislature was not summoned. During a remarkable session of 1818 the constitutional dilemmas of other colonies were violently illuminated on a reduced scale. When the House of Assembly remonstrated against the veto-ing of road bills, Smith ordered an adjournment. When it refused to adjourn the son-in-law appeared at the bar, allowed it one minute to adjourn, and retired "in a contemptuous manner." Before this scene of fury was com-pleted, the son put his fist through a window of the chamber and was com-mitted to jail by order of the house. The Colonial Office made no attempt to solve this acute constitutional problem.[43]

To ease the situation for the proprietors and to make the collection of quitrents more practical, Lord Bathurst announced in 1816 the cancellation of arrears and a new scale of payments. No longer need estates be settled exclusively by Protestants.[44] But the details of the instructions were marked by obscurities and uncertainties, and Smith was the kind of man who could work out a policy of his own only more or less within the general framework of that of the Colonial Office. In 1818, after giving notice by proclamation, he escheated Lot 55 and divided it amongst the tenantry who were enabled to buy one hundred acre lots on payment of a fee of £5 and an annual quitrent of two shillings. This gave to his regime something of a popular character and encouraged the idea that a general escheat would follow. But there were strange contradictions that prevented the Lieutenant-Governor from emerging as a champion of the toiling masses. Contrary to the express command of the Colonial Office, arrears in quitrents were again allowed to accumulate from 1818 to 1822. Then, early in 1823, escheat proceedings were suddenly launched against several of the proprietors. Judgement was obtained against their lots and they were sold to local officials, including the collector of quitrents and his deputy. Of about £4,000 realized from sales and collections, £3,300 were absorbed in legal expenses, the charges of Smith's friends who were regarded as upstarts by the older families of the island. Not content with flouting local public opinion, Smith blandly ignored re-straining orders of the Colonial Office.

With so many vested interests challenged by a callous disregard for the influential, great demonstrations against Smith and his government developed in 1823. For convening public meetings John McGregor, the High Sheriff of the island, was dismissed.[45] John Stewart was the chief promoter of the agitation and of a petition to the Crown for the removal of the

Lieutenant-Governor. In October he caught a schooner for Pictou just in time to escape arrest by a sergeant-at-arms bearing a writ of attachment for gross contempt and libel of the Court of Chancery. A year passed by before he returned in triumph from London, bearing with him a new lieutenant-governor, Colonel John Ready. Again Stewart had collaborated with the proprietors, of whom Lord Selkirk was a leading agent. His plea of an oppressed tenantry was "a useful shibboleth to get rid of a lieutenant-governor."[46] Smith was the fourth of the lieutenant-governors of Prince Edward Island. All had been recalled by the instrumentality of the proprietors because they had inaugurated or been associated with escheat proceedings.

No solution for the land problem could be obtained. On many an occasion the Colonial Office moved in the direction of escheat but the proprietors always succeeded in preventing action. In 1828, when arrears amounted to £10,000, the familiar arguments against cruelty to defaulters were employed and the British government stopped short of confiscation. It was quite true, as the proprietors alleged, that quitrents had never been systematically collected in any other province. Yet many of them had agents on the island who efficiently and regularly collected rents from the tenantry. The Colonial Office could not summon the resolution to release itself from the binding formula to which it was committed by the lottery of 1767. But the farmers of the island, half-maddened by the necessity of rental payments which precluded them from earning any profit, labouring on lands to which they had no security of continued possession, were excited by politicians to believe that escheat was on the way.

Yet Prince Edward Island was beginning to make very rapid progress. It was easily the most densely inhabited province of British North America. Official accounts reaching London told of an ignorant tenantry that employed primitive methods and implements, but in the early 1820's large numbers of small schooners were exporting root and grain crops to Halifax and the Miramichi. Ready, like his contemporaries in Nova Scotia and New Brunswick, gave stimulus to the formation of agricultural societies, and to the introduction of superior breeds of livestock, which resulted in increased productivity. In the winter seasons young Prince Edward Islanders of the second generation commenced to migrate to the woods of New Brunswick and Maine where they acquired a reputation for being willing to work for low wages.[47]

VI

The fiction that Newfoundland was not a colony continued to live on in the counting-houses of the West Country merchants and among all those who hoped that the transient fishery would revive. But the necessities of a community of forty thousand people forced new recognition of colonial status. A parliamentary inquiry of 1817 into economic distresses brought consideration of the need for creating more conventional forms of government. In consequence Admiral Sir Francis Pickmore, the governor of that year, was ordered to remain on the station for the winter season. Death removed him before he could completely honour the requirement, but a resident governor was the first of several innovations made at this time to show that Newfoundland could not indefinitely be an Ishmaelite in the cluster of British colonies. As material problems became more insistent, it was the more obviously ridiculous to deny the demands of Carson and the agitators for representative government, demands that were given more repute by the earlier suggestions of Chief Justice Reeves and Admiral Gambier.

In 1819 there occurred at Conception Bay the celebrated case of two fishermen, Butler and Landrigan, from which the beginnings of a persistent popular agitation can be dated. In the outports the naval surrogates, assisted by local magistrates, still executed rough justice in the fashion of earlier centuries. Convicted of contempt of court, Landrigan was tied to a fishing-flake and collapsed after receiving fourteen lashes. After a dozen lashes were inflicted, Butler was released on the promise to surrender the property involved in the original action. The subsequent appeal to the Supreme Court was given wide publicity. Early in 1820 Patrick Morris, a thirty-year-old merchant of St John's, born in Waterford, convened a public meeting where not only the action of the surrogates but the absence of legislative power in the colony were roundly condemned. A petition to Parliament, presented to the Houses by Lord Darnley and Sir James Mackintosh, came at a time when a spirit of modernizing and humanitarian reform was in the ascendancy, when the Cabinet and Parliament had their first leisure in thirty years to look closely into the domestic affairs of the colonies.

The British government first contented itself with an order restraining the naval surrogates from inflicting corporal punishment, but it was not allowed to ignore the more fundamental causes of discontent, largely owing to the critical spirit of Joseph Hume and other radicals in the House of Commons. The Governor, Sir Charles Hamilton, admitted abuses but denied the necessity of reform. His influence was more than neutralized by that of Chief Justice Francis Forbes. Since his appointment in 1816 the Chief Justice had irritated the governors by legal decisions that restrained their authority and by liberalizing the obsolete regulations concerning the holding of property. In 1823-24 his advice counted for more than that of Sir Charles Hamilton. The "Act for the Better Administration of Justice in Newfoundland and for Other Purposes" of 1824, often called Newfoundland's Royal Charter, repealed the judicial powers of the fishing-admirals and the naval surrogates derived from the Act of 1699 and subsequent royal instructions to the governors. Two assistant judges were provided for the Supreme Court and the island was divided into three districts where circuit courts were to be held at least once a year. The governor was empowered to create still another court of jurisdiction on the coast of Labrador. Sheriffs and other junior officers were provided.

Sir Charles Hamilton, who advised Lord Bathurst on the details of the Act, showed his dislike for the rising spirit of democracy in Newfoundland by complaining of the presence in the Supreme Court of self-constituted and untrained lawyers who made mischief by agitating public opinion. These he described as "bankrupt merchants." The Colonial Office dealt with the problem by providing Newfoundland with its first attorney general and ruling that all pleading before the new courts should be performed by those who were trained as barristers or advocates in the United Kingdom. But the Colonial Office could not find able men to send to Newfoundland. The quality of the new judges and the attorney general was not such as to ensure that the calibre of legal learning and the character of judicial decisions would show quick and certain improvement.[48]

As an additional recognition that Newfoundland had finally become a colony, the British government, by the same act, gave it the beginnings of constitutional government. Forbes, for all his sympathy with the local population, could not agree that a representative assembly was possible or desirable. Whatever opinion might be at St John's, there was no demand for it in the outports and inability of the smaller communities to produce men fitted for legislative roles was an argument against election urged by all those whose advice was sought. Lord Bathurst, therefore, decided upon the expedient of representation without election. The change came with the appointment as governor in 1825 of Sir Thomas Cochrane, who brought instructions to convene a council. This was to be a purely advisory body, but its establishment implied a sharing of discretion and marked a great step towards the forms of constitutional rule in the colonies. As the reforms came into effect they brought with them an era of courtly display. The Governor seldom appeared in public without wearing his blue uniform fashioned after that of the lords-lieutenant of English counties. All officials, even the constables of the courts, had official dress prescribed. Newfoundland was the most neglected of all the colonies but on official occasions it could make as brave a show of pomp as any. A much greater degree of formality now attended the relationships between the representative of the Crown and the people. No longer would the Governor meet merchants at their whim and choosing, for Cochrane insisted on meetings within given hours. Entertainment became something of a ritual.

During his first years at St John's, Cochrane's personal popularity was immense, as with youthful zest he adopted for himself the role of beneficent father and friend to the people of Newfoundland. Spending public money profusely and putting to work the unemployed poor who were on local relief, he built an admirable system of roads on the Avalon Peninsula and beautified the countryside about St John's. The expenses of his new Government House exceeded the estimate by five times and appalled the Colonial Office. He made valiant efforts to develop agriculture but in the end had to admit failure. There is no evidence that he was able to make progress in a more difficult venture, that of improving the habits of life of the fishermen. During the season, he noted, the rations consumed were four times greater than those of labourers in Britain or of the fishermen of France. Yet these same individuals were, during the winter, a considerable segment (amounting to one third) of the population of St John's. They subsisted on charity, or led miserable and half-starved lives in the outports. Improvidence could not quickly be cured and charity had to be restricted and organized.[49]

Patrick Morris was not the kind of man who would rest content with the mere beginnings of reform. His visits to Ireland brought him into contact with Daniel O'Connell's work for the repeal of religious tests. The civil disabilities of Newfoundlanders were similar to those of Roman Catholics throughout the British Empire; and it was therefore natural that the movement for self-government should draw inspiration and momentum from the cause that was so vigorously pressed in Ireland. The agitation for the establishment of representative institutions was at first almost exclusively Roman Catholic in character – with the added ingredient of Irish dash and drama. Three-fourths of the population of St John's, being Roman Catholic, became unanimously democratic in their ideology. Amidst the happier climate of opinion that Sir Thomas Cochrane had seemingly brought with him, Protestants were opposed to change. Only later, as the Catholic cause in Britain swelled to its triumph, did Protestant merchants and leaders of opinion shift their position in favour of the general appeal for popular participation in government. Political consciousness was sharpened by the soft British policy concerning "the French shore." Since 1815 the French government had slowly but surely been exerting something like sovereign power on the western coastline. Against the easy compliance of Downing Street the St John's Chamber of Commerce remonstrated in vain.[50] It began to appear that only a government in which Newfoundlanders might participate could organize effective resistance to systematic French encroachment.

As the slogans of liberty were voiced in St John's the issue gradually became an open one. The need for the means for more efficient government was glaringly apparent. It was still necessary to appeal for voluntary contributions from public-spirited people to find the funds for local improvements. St John's was in a state of filth but Cochrane's attempts, authorized by the

British government, to secure municipal incorporation were defeated by the obstruction and factional rivalries of its citizens. No taxing power existed within the colony. The increasingly large sums collected by the imperial customs officers were judiciously expended but were entirely at the discretion of the governor and his advisers. The great cries of the English and American revolutions, of no taxation without consent, lay open to the employment of agitators who might care to exercise them.

To ring the changes on the call for liberty was an opportunity that Morris would not miss and his chance came in 1828. Fearing the rising popularity of the appeal for self-government, the merchants of Poole in that year made their last defence of the former state of things that had enabled them to have their own way at the expense of the shore population. A pamphlet they produced argued that Newfoundland was not fit for permanent habitation, that the existing form of government was too expensive, that the naval surrogate justices should be restored to authority.[51] Morris retorted with arguments drawn from the lore of British Whiggery, employing quotations from Charles James Fox, Lord John Russell, and Sir James Mackintosh. "Half a century of freedom within the circuit of a few miles of rock brings to perfection more of the greatest qualities of our nature . . . . " He picked to pieces the principal basis of the Poole complaint, showing that early governors who spent only two months of the year on the island were lavishly rewarded in comparison with Sir Thomas Cochrane, who expended all his modest emoluments on public works for relief.[52] The British Whigs were in opposition but, while waiting for the Tory disintegration that was beginning to seem inevitable, they took heed of the articulate pamphleteer from St John's whose compositions, though not always relevant to the point in hand, were highly literary. Newfoundland was the colony in which the lessons of the American Revolution seemed to have most meaning and Morris, following the example of other British Americans, did not hesitate to threaten that, should London fail to take action, the colony could fall to the young and aspiring republic.

While Newfoundland began to face the adventure of self-government she ignored the mysteries and fascinations of her own interior. In 1822 the apathy was broken when a Scot, William Cormack, made a journey across the broadest portion of the island from Trinity to St George's Bay. After crossing the hilly barrier ringing the eastern shore, he found the central part of the province to be a level plain and predicted that some day it would be good grazing country. His sole companion was a Micmac Indian, but halfway over he encountered a Montagnais from Labrador who was "lord" of all the interior, travelling in an open canoe covered with deerskin and dwelling with his wife "in sylvan happiness" on an island in the middle of a lake.[53]

VII

The democracy entrenched in the legislatures of Nova Scotia and New Brunswick was pre-eminently North American, pre-Loyalist and Loyalist, in character. Political procedures and habits of mind, formed within the traditionally British framework, were derived from the experience of the former thirteen colonies. The new immigrants, Scots and Irish, had not yet acquired the leisure or the educated leadership to make their weight felt in public controversy. In Lunenburg the young people of German descent were only beginning to consider the English language as an acquisition necessary to success in the world.[54] The oldest inhabitants, the Acadians, were not within the broad stream of provincial life. Often isolated in their own settlements, held together in a kind of primitive brotherhood by the pastoral care of their priests, they were generally considered to be beyond the pale of public concern. Contemporary writers described in half-admiring terms their bucolic existence, pitying their ignorance but praising their simple and devout faith and their Old World simplicity. Amidst all the diversity, the settlers of American origin supplied the central strand of political development. In New Brunswick the few inhabitants of the new northern counties looked for leadership to the Loyalist settlements of the St John Valley. In Nova Scotia the Gaels of the east found most of their early leaders in lawyers and merchants who were long established in the province.

Out of the piebald scene that made up the Atlantic Provinces at this time only one simplicity emerged. After thirty-five years of material failure and administrative bedlam, Cape Breton lost its status as a separate colony. Violent factional disputes, suspensions from office sometimes followed by reinstatements, quarrels between civil and military had marked the course of its crude and neglected government. By 1815, in spite of the influx of Scots settlers, population was only in the vicinity of six thousand and many of the inhabitants of the more remote glens in the island's interior were quite unaware of the existence of the shell-like structure of government at Sydney. The last two lieutenant-governors, Generals Swayne and Ainslie, were quite unable to comprehend the eccentricities of the officials and merchants, the leaders of a society completely unaccustomed to regulation and order.

A legal decision brought the situation to the attention of the British government. In 1816 Messrs Leaver and Ritchie challenged the validity of a local Order in Council which charged a duty of one shilling a gallon on imported rum, reasoning that His Majesty, by the Proclamation of 1763 and the royal instructions of 1784, had abandoned the right to tax the inhabitants of Cape Breton without consent of a representative assembly.[55] To the mortification of the local authorities, their case was upheld in the Supreme Court and still further sustained by the Law Officers of the Crown in London. Government by Order in Council at once came under examination and the calling of a general assembly an affair of urgency. All government in Cape Breton since 1784, the judgement implied, had been irregular, if not illegal. To supply regular and legal government, Lord Bathurst considered the possibility of putting into effect the royal instructions for the calling of an assembly but decided against it on the ground that the island did not have sufficient men of competence. Annexation to Nova Scotia was preferred.

Nova Scotia was ready for the acquisition. Its old, irredentist sentiments were powerfully invoked in an address of the legislature to the Prince Regent, praying for a complete re-ordering of the affairs of British North America (the Atlantic Provinces) which would include the reannexation of both Cape Breton and Prince Edward Island.[56] Bathurst himself was certain of his course. Sir James Kempt was instructed to dissolve the council of Cape Breton, reduce the offices of government, and make the island an integral part of Nova Scotia with two members in the House of Assembly. The transformation took legal effect on January 1, 1821. Only the official party at Sydney expressed dissatisfaction, the majority of the inhabitants regarding the change in their state with indifference. Presenting a petition to the House of Commons from the people of Sydney, Joseph Hume, a radical who could champion almost any cause, declared that at the first opportunity the colonists would sever their connection with Great Britain. That conservative and Loyalist partisan of British North America, Sir Isaac Coffin, formerly of Massachusetts, was prepared, should rebellion strike, to knock Cape Breton out in twenty-four hours with a thousand men and a ship of the line.[57]

Opposition to annexation lasted for twenty years but without a firm base. Cape Breton acquired a great industry in 1826 when the Duke of York's mineral rights were taken over by the General Mining Association of London.[58] Smoking chimneys appeared at the northern entrance to Sydney harbour. Markets for coal were quickly found in the United States and Sydney became a coaling station of considerable account for the new steamships of the North Atlantic run.

To the hard-bargaining politicians colonialism continued to be a highly satisfactory condition. The greatness of Britain in the world inspired pride in British citizenship and the yoke of the mother country, if yoke it could be called, was extremely light. Nova Scotians and New Brunswickers boasted of the almost complete absence of local taxation and acquired excessive dependence on provincial governments for local improvements. Provincial revenues were painlessly acquired, so it seemed, from indirect taxation at easy rates on goods imported from abroad. The system of financial appropriation, established against official resistance during the Napoleonic Wars, made the log-roller, the tireless negotiator for the allocation of funds to his neighbours' roads and bridges, the only kind of politician who could enjoy popular favour. This kind of democracy was broad, deep, and practical. "If there bean't a road made up to every citizen's door away back to the woods (who as like as not has squatted there)," said Sam Slick, the voters would reason that the House of Assembly had voted away all the money for great men's salaries. When assemblymen failed to get their failure on "that on the appropriations list they would cunningly blame the failure on "that etarnal Council." All were "up to their croopers" in this kind of politics.[59]

By this time in both provinces there was a tendency to be complacent about the "old and time-honoured" system of financial administration by which the power over the purse-strings was kept firmly in the hands of the representatives of the people. But Lord Dalhousie, angered by the feebleness of the executive powers of government he found at Halifax, was the kind of governor who would challenge this tight-fisted control by committees of the House of Assembly. In Fredericton General Smyth complained about it but he did not challenge. The governor and his officials appointed from London were beyond the control of the House of Assembly. But so far as the workaday routine of government was concerned, the allocation of funds from ordinary revenues for particular purposes, they had no initiative. In the Houses of Assembly there had developed organizations that were executive in character. Precedent might be described as ancient American rather than modern British and the dominating ideas a kind of Yankee Toryism.

Dalhousie charged full tilt against the windmills of legislative management, attempting to introduce British practice in financial appropriation. He was quite satisfied that "his administration" could introduce a more orderly and economical system to provincial expenditure by planning and survey. When he discovered in 1820 that all of the measures he had proposed to the House of Assembly, including a plan for the stream-lining of the militia, had been completely ignored in the appropriations bill, he refused the honours magnanimously voted by the legislature, and left the province for Canada in a humour of dark resentment.[60] "His administration" was able to change nothing. Sir James Kempt and Sir Howard Douglas, two military governors whose careers belied the notion that military men are of necessity autocratic, would seem to have learned a lesson from his failure. To do anything important they realized they would have to work within the legislative framework, not to issue directives from above, to anticipate opinion of the assemblymen and to influence it by gentle and hidden arts of persuasion. Their diplomatic behaviour in Nova Scotia and New Brunswick dulled the edge of controversy and postponed the emergence of sharp disagreement in the relations of the colonies with Britain.

VIII

It was the revenues rising from British legislation which caused acrimony to develop. Of these the customs duties were the foremost. Imperial statutes, designed to regulate trade, had been in force since 1783. Though they were not enacted primarily for the raising of revenue, sizable sums annually accrued at the customs establishments at Saint John and Halifax where the proceeds were paid into the provincial treasuries. On the face of things this was perfectly fair but what irked local democrats was the fact that the provinces gained merely the net proceeds, not the gross, and the expenses of collection usually accounted for three-fourths of everything taken. Customs officials, operating under the direction of the Imperial Treasury at London, assumed for themselves immense discretion. Their salaries, by colonial standards, were very high and these were supplemented by fees that could accumulate to sums greater than the salaries. Henry Wright, the Collector at Saint John, arbitrarily raised rates of duty and emulated his colleague at Halifax, Thomas N. Jeffery, by making exactions on the coastal trade as well as on international commerce. Fees on voyages from one colony to another could be just as high as on transatlantic voyages. In 1820 Jeffery was brought to the bar of the Nova Scotian house and, over the next three years, had to defend himself against the indignant assaults of provincial merchants. He successfully refuted charges of dishonesty, but the revelation of the catalogue of methods by which collectors and controllers might easily and honestly enrich themselves was something more than shocking.[61]

Huskisson modernized the system in 1826. All of the fees allowed to customs officials were swept away, but the British government showed a punctilious respect for vested interests by ensuring that salaries remained high. The officials still appeared as nabobs to the jealous societies of Halifax and Saint John. The surpluses accruing to provincial treasuries still appeared far too low and, following the rejoicings for the coming of free trade in 1825, the revenues failed to increase in accordance with expectations. It was still possible to remonstrate that money was taken from the people without their consent and allocated to privileged officials appointed in London. A dark temper prevailed in both legislatures, and the customs establishment, reformed though it was, remained a target for the invective of the more daring politicians. The olive branch of 1778, by which the colonies were promised freedom from taxation for revenue by the British parliament, was remembered as only one of the historic British liberties that were being violated. Legislatures wanted complete control of customs establishments and the right to reduce salaries to a size commensurate with colonial conditions. Yet, following the great reforms of 1825-26, it was impolitic to press remain-

ing grievances too brashly. Thomas Chandler Haliburton threw a caution-
ary note into the Nova Scotian debate of 1827, reminding the Assembly
that imports exceeded exports by £280,000, that it was English money,
"flowing in a thousand streams" which enabled the province to redeem its
adverse balance.[62] But in 1830 the British government again yielded, granting to the provinces the right to set the salaries of officials.

Other "casual and territorial revenues of the Crown" were of little importance in Nova Scotia. Revenues from the coal fields of Pictou and Cape
Breton had seldom amounted to over £3,000 and this sum was not increased
when the General Mining Association acquired its monopoly in 1826. Timber was taken freely from the forests but revenues from timber were minute.
Yet in New Brunswick it was the politics of timber that made all other issues
very secondary. At the end of the Napoleonic Wars the British government
had been made aware of the spoliation of the forests by private interests, a
process that had developed to full flood about 1808 and had been allowed
to continue unchecked. The result was the establishment of control by the
Lieutenant-Governor and a committee of the executive council in 1819, an
imposition of authority bitterly resented by the merchant democracy of the
House of Assembly. The demand for one shilling a ton on timber taken from
the Crown Lands, which still made up nine-tenths of the area of the
province, was interpreted as a violation of the rights of British subjects, as
another example of taxation without representation.[63] The great areas of
timberland reserved for the navy long before by Sir John Wentworth were
gradually absorbed into the general domain of the Crown.

In New Brunswick "the casual revenues" acquired great importance as
the timber trade, in spite of many gloomy prophecies, moved on to increasingly high levels of production. The revenues gave to the executive government, responsible only to Whitehall, a new independence from the House
of Assembly and a larger consequence in the community. They were carefully expended within the province and new projects, hitherto considered
beyond its means, became feasible – the establishment of a college, assistance
to the Madras Schools, to agricultural and immigrant societies. Smyth was
constantly in trouble with his legislature because he presumed his acts to
be above its critical review, but Douglas faithfully rendered accounts of the
moneys collected and expended, frequently consulting leading members of
the Assembly upon their disposal. The tax was arbitrary and the Colonial
Office held final authority, but the sums realized were expended well in
accordance with the stated wishes of the New Brunswick community.

Had it not been for the appointment of Thomas Baillie as Commissioner
of Crown Lands in 1824. Douglas and a succession of equally politic lieutenant-governors might have softened the acerbities for an indefinite period.
Baillie was the instrument of a policy designed to make the colonies pay for

themselves and for the eventual removal of the civil, military, and ecclesiastical expenses assumed by Parliament. The policy may have been judicious but
the instrument was inappropriate. Virtually independent of the lieutenant-
governor, Baillie proceeded to impose a thorough control over the timber
trade, prosecuting offenders of his regulations, sending his rangers into the
deep recesses of the forests where no control had ever been proclaimed.
Members of the legislature, magistrates, the great and near-great of the land,
fell victim to his stratagems. Arrogant and doctrinaire, he scorned the leaders
of decaying Loyalist families who fiercely resented his high salary and still
greater emoluments. While liberal principles for trade were being promulgated from the Colonial Office, New Brunswick was given sharp and specific
reason for resenting its agencies. Baillie was regarded as a vindictive and
alien public servant whose purpose was to restrain the free enterprise of the
timber trade. Douglas laboured to quiet opinion in the House of Assembly,
but the task was too great. Baillie let it be known that he had come to New
Brunswick to reorganize the entire economy of the province, to raise such
great revenues from the Crown Lands that the whole future costs of government would be assured.[64]

Within his own setting Baillie was a most severe irritant, but in New
Brunswick, as elsewhere, there was no serious disposition to call in question
the status of the colonies or to challenge the control of the mother country.
While British money flowed and while taxation was remarkably light compared with that of the neighbouring American states, colonials continued
to compliment themselves on their fortunate position. Importations of
officials from England were becoming less numerous and the non-responsible
executive councils were filled by wealthy, self-made men who commanded
respect, though the wealthy, being few in number, were closely entangled
with one another by marital alliances as well as by the enterprises of trade.
The whole tone of public criticism was fervently equalitarian. A plenitude
of politicians among small populations found it profitable to encourage
suspicion of learning as well as of wealth. Lawyers were a special target for
representatives of the rural communities. The Nova Scotian bill of 1824
providing that three judges should preside over the inferior courts of the
counties passed by the barest of majorities and was attacked as a measure to
provide sinecures for professional gentlemen. The House of Assembly of
New Brunswick would never agree to provide travelling expenses for judges
of the Supreme Court on circuit, so that justice at the highest level could be
obtained only at Fredericton and Saint John. Justice at the lower level,
dispensed by unlearned local magistrates who encouraged litigation in order
to extract fees, would appear to have been more generally acceptable.
Haliburton's Mr Justice Pettifog was a familiar type throughout New

Brunswick, where magistrates were annually removed from the lists for notoriously culpable practices, as well as in Nova Scotia.

The movement for Catholic emancipation broadened and deepened the social equalitarianism that reigned. Protestants of Nova Scotia were now notorious for their sectarian rivalries that extended into politics. But the comparatively honourable record of toleration for Catholics was well sustained when Lawrence Kavanaugh, a highly respected Roman Catholic merchant of Cape Breton, arrived at Halifax in 1822 to claim the seat to which he had been elected in the House of Assembly. There were differences of opinion as to how the oaths against "Popery" and transubstantiation might be dispensed with, but an address to the Crown brought about the desired result in 1823, with the unanimous approval of both council and assembly.[65] In 1827 the Nova Scotian house reaffirmed this tolerant spirit by petitioning for the removal of the objectionable oaths and in 1829 Catholic emancipation was completely achieved following the passage of the imperial statute. Through the 1820's, parallel with O'Connell's campaign in Ireland, an ebullient spirit was at work among Irish Catholics in the Atlantic provinces. In a few of the more isolated and recently settled regions, such as Gloucester County in New Brunswick, their victory could not be consummated without violent overtones of elation on their own part and of Protestant resentment for the reform which offended so many traditional projudices.[66]

CHAPTER 8

Climates of Reform
1828-1840

Ideas of political reform stirred gently in the climates of colonial opinion as the long era of Tory power in Britain approached its conclusion in the late 1820's. Partly by persuasion and partly by compulsion the Tories were becoming more liberal and the Whigs were professing liberalism with a certainty that time was on their side. Fundamental change was making over the social structure of Great Britain and the political structure was under severe attack. Techniques of criticism and new notions of the dignity and worth of the toiling masses crossed the Atlantic from the British liberals and radicals. In the Atlantic Provinces there were alert democracies, headed by zealous and ambitious leaders who sensed opportunities for putting change to their advantage. In no two of the provinces were circumstances closely similiar, but all were to share to some degree the conviction that government should be taken from the control of the privileged and delivered into the hands of "the people."

Imperial policies rather than local initiative provided the background for the era of reform. Huskisson's commercial changes of 1825 had conferred upon the colonies a new freedom, but it was a freedom resented in many quarters. Defenders of colonial dependence on Britain were nonplussed by the new internationalism in British commercial policy that ran counter to the grain of traditional and Loyalist thinking. The legend of British power was of immense influence, but there were many chilling evidences of British indifference to the colonies. Year after year the radical criticism in the House of Commons of financial votes for colonial establishments became more incisive and, very obviously, the Tory government was becoming sensitive to colonial inroads on the pocket of the British taxpayer. Much of this criticism was ill-informed and abusive. William Cobbett could call Prince Edward Island "a rascally heap of sand, rock and swamp" where sensible Scots would not remain and where only "bed-ridden persons" would take up residence. But while Britain prospered from international trade it was possible to make a fair case for showing that colonies were expensive and unnecessary.

Colonialism began to appear financially less profitable to the colonists as, slowly but perceptibly, British largesse became limited. The reduction of the naval dockyard at Halifax was "a theme for grumbling for years after."[1] A Scottish moralist who visited Nova Scotia and New Brunswick in 1828 emphatically declared that the leaders of the two communities, purse-proud men of great pretensions, would accept their existing status only so long as it yielded financial rewards.[2] Military and naval establishments that enlarged markets remained largely unimpaired for many years, but about 1825 the British government began actively to consider the reduction of civil and ecclesiastical grants to the colonies. Bishop Inglis was exhorted to increase the value of church lands so that the British parliament might be spared the necessity of the annual vote of £8,000 for his diocese. It was decided that Crown assets in the colonies, included in the casual revenues, should be organized and enlarged, and ultimately passed to the control of the colonial legislatures. The general principle coming into favour at the Colonial Office was that each colony should acquire the management of all local revenues in return for a civil list that would guarantee the salaries of imperial appointees and take care of other fixed expenses which it considered important. Philosophically it followed the argument that since colonial trade was free, the colony should maintain the costs of its own government. The British government chose to sever the financial bonds which had been laid upon the colonies. Against the total revenues of Great Britain the sums to be saved were infinitesimally small, but the niggling demands for economy in the House of Commons were barbed and vitriolic.

To build up the casual revenues before surrendering them, the Colonial Office decided to commence the collection of quitrents, abandoned on three separate occasions in Nova Scotian history and never enforced in New Brunswick. An order to impose payment on January 1, 1827 brought powerful remonstrances from the houses of assembly and begging excuses for delay from Sir James Kempt and Sir Howard Douglas. The Colonial Office countered with proposals to abandon the quitrents in return for fixed annual payments from the ordinary revenues of the provinces into the casual revenues of the Crown, but these proved equally unpopular. To colonial populations of the nineteenth century, quitrents, a relic of the unsuccessful administration of the lost British Empire of the eighteenth, seemed archaic and unjust. Rebellion was a word that came, only half jocosely, into common use. Thomas Baillie of New Brunswick, the only official of the two provinces who considered that collection was just and feasible, was threatened with assassination, rather less than half jocosely. Again the sums of money involved were small, perhaps one-twentieth of the

normal revenue of each province. But both provinces contained large proportions of people who would find the annual payment of two shillings per
hundred acres a hardship. To the complaints of the poor could be added the
fears of the wealthy who had speculated in land and were awaiting a rise in
values.

The collection of quitrents became secondary to another device of the
Colonial Office for increasing the casual revenues, that of selling the Crown
Lands. Robert Wilmot Horton, the Undersecretary for the Colonies in
Downing Street, had convinced himself that the system of free grants of land
in British North America had been rendered hopelessly inefficient by local
mismanagement, the jobbing of speculators, and official favouritism. Looking upon the problem from the point of view of a social reformer, he proposed to reorganize the methods by which Crown Lands were alienated
in order to make them the receptacle for the surplus and pauper populations
of Ireland and Great Britain. Sale of public lands had been reputedly
successful in Australia so that "the New South Wales system" could be
introduced to North America. Such a solution seemed simple and rational.
The wages for labour were high and land was cheap. Immigrants could
readily earn the small sums necessary to buy one hundred acres in the wilderness on terms of easy instalments.

Nova Scotians found the proposals for sale of public lands half absurd and
trifling in character. Wild lands were scarcely worthy of offer for sale since
they would not yield the cost of survey. The imposition of such a change,
said a report of the council, was undesirable merely because it would create
unnecessary confusion.[3] But in New Brunswick the change could be revolutionary for the Crown Lands provided the basis for the great staple industry
of the province. Since 1819 the timber trade had chafed and fretted against
a mounting degree of public control. Its merchants drew their logs from
the timber berths which were cheaply leased to them for single seasons by
the Commissioner of Crown Lands at Fredericton. New Brunswickers were
not sufficiently wealthy to buy up the fourteen millions of acres available
for sale. Alien interests, it was feared, would purchase great blocks of the
best timber-bearing acreages and deprive natives of their livelihood. Again
Thomas Baillie aroused the ire of the province's commercial leaders by an
instant willingness to inaugurate the policy of sale and by prophecies that
it would be immensely successful. Contemptuous of the local aristocracy,
he would press imperial claims to their utmost limit and fit the province
into a new pattern of his own fashioning. To his mind New Brunswick
was "an estate" whose harvests he would gather for the general benefit of
the Empire and, only incidentally, for the welfare of the provincial population.

British colonial reformers, contemplating the surplus population at home and the unoccupied spaces of British lands abroad, created widespread alarm by proposals to send tens of thousands of their unwanted poor to North America. In 1827 Colonel Thomas Cockburn, an expert on settlement who had supervised military colonies in Upper Canada after the War of 1812, was ordered to survey 300,000 acres in New Brunswick for the reception of 10,000 immigrants. He recommended the establishment of 2,000 families between the Petitcodiac and the Miramichi, linking the project with one for a great interprovincial highway joining the Atlantic Provinces with Lower Canada.[4] When the British government decided not to pursue the plan, Cockburn asked leave to develop the scheme from his own resources. Ideas of organized settlement such as this roused constant fear that powerful outside interests would take provincial destinies from provincial control. Occasional references to projects for the exportation of British convicts added insult to the fears already engendered.

Priding himself on his knowledge of colonial opinion, Sir Howard Douglas ceaselessly remonstrated against these radical departures in British colonial policy. However rational the sale of land might seem in London, it would never work in New Brunswick and, he warned, the thrusting of all colonial expenses on colonial revenues would result in an abrupt slackening of the feeling of dependence on Britain.[5] Rebellion might not come but the tendency to rebellion would be certain. As if all this were not enough the British government moved in 1831 to reduce the preferences on colonial timber, the bill being defeated in the House of Commons by a narrow majority. While the free trade forces led by Charles Poulett Thomson gathered their strength to bring Baltic timber to Britain on something like equal terms with the colonial, the death of the industry in New Brunswick and the wasting away of the provincial economy were freely forecast. More and more evidence accumulated to strengthen the belief that the enlightened self-interest ruling British policy was exclusively British and not colonial. In January, 1831, when the casual revenues of New Brunswick were taken to pay the expenses of government formerly provided for by Parliament, it seemed that self-support was being forced upon the colony, a self-support that would be accompanied by a new degree of self-assertion.

Lower Canada provided a forum for those who were inclined to speculate upon the relations of mother country and colonies. The recall of Lord Dalhousie in 1828, the subsequent review of colonial administration before the Canada Committee of the House of Commons, the report of the same committee that censured many features of colonial government, gave encouragement to those who believed that revision was required. For those who were out of favour with government the gospel of reform loomed forth as a vehicle for personal aggrandizement. The later remark of Joseph Howe, that up to 1828 the Canadians had been right, represented a broad strand of colonial opinion.[6] Even under the Tories innovation had come so rapidly in Britain that innovation could be a fair cry in the colonies where Toryism had for so long resisted constitutional change. "The Tory species, as known in the British colonies, is nearly extinct in Great Britain."[7]

Yet even among progressive men in the colonies, opinion was fundamentally conservative on the great questions of the age of reform. On the anniversary of Waterloo in 1832 Lewis Bliss, the merchant of Saint John, wrote to his brother in London, Henry Bliss, the lawyer who was so closely involved in the affairs of the British North American Merchants' Association, upon the pleasing but false intelligence that the Whigs had been defeated on the issue of the Reform Bill: "Is the Duke first in the field this day? Joyful news. In this province there are few Whigs. Almost all of us Tories. More than in Nova Scotia."[8]

II

Nova Scotia may have been more liberal minded, but there was little action taken at Halifax that could lead to constitutional reform. Politics were set in a pattern that was essentially democratic. The casual revenues did not provide an important dividing force, as in New Brunswick, between Crown and House of Assembly. Ordinary revenues were disbursed by committees of the house by the now historic and disorderly methods of appropriation, the western counties, which enjoyed a much greater weight of representation, gaining the lion's share of the moneys voted for local purposes.[9] If the council interfered with appropriations, as it did in 1830 when it was roundly rebuked by the result of "the brandy election," the Assembly could majestically cite the precedents of the British parliament.[10] But the tendency was to criticize the personnel of the council rather than to take up an issue of principle by challenging its non-responsible character. According to Howe the Assembly, after its victory of 1831 when the brandy duties were imposed according to its own schedule, was conciliatory and compliant to the highly respected merchants and lawyers who made up the second chamber.

This Council of Twelve, as it was beginning to be called in a sinister kind of way, still conducted its proceedings, which were both legislative and executive, behind closed doors. It was often spoken of as an hereditary aristocracy but its composition had steadily become more commercial in character. Five of its members were partners in the Halifax Banking Company which was based on the great trading concerns of Enos Collins who had made his fortune by financing privateers during the War of 1812. Samuel Cunard was another member who could give testimony to the fact that it was not an aristocracy based upon hereditary privilege. Occasionally it obstructed the Assembly, especially to protect the mercantile interests of Halifax against the outports, but in the main its influence lay in the making of appointments to public office and to the magistracy. Corruption is probably the wrong word but, as the Clockmaker remarked, power induced corpulency. The youthful Thomas Chandler Haliburton called them "twelve old ladies," but they were old ladies accustomed to take their seats firmly. Until Joseph Howe entered politics they kept Nova Scotia, in comparison with the other colonies, in a state of political calm. In 1832 the five banking councillors lost their monopoly when the subscribers to the proposed Bank of Nova Scotia accepted the unlikely condition they imposed, that of the double liability of shareholders, the first occasion on which this safeguard was employed to incorporate a publicly supported bank in British North America.[11]

Nova Scotia was the senior province and opinion in its assembly had usually guided that of New Brunswick. But at this stage the initiative for reform fell to the junior where a palpable grievance, long in the making, appeared to threaten the fortunes of the entire community. Thomas Baillie was adding to the staff of the Crown Lands Office at Fredericton for the purpose of making every tree in his great domain yield its mite to the casual revenues, from which the salaries of the officers of government were now paid. To pay for the costs of surveys that could fasten his grip on the great unexplored areas he proposed an additional tax of threepence on the ton, a suggestion that brought cries of blue ruin from the thriving merchants of the trade. Contrary to custom, he demanded payment for the use of "water lots" on the rivers and harbours where merchants constructed wharves and booms. He inaugurated a policy of reserving blocks of the best and untouched timberlands of the north for the use of great merchants like Joseph Cunard, who could pay for their development. In his estimation New Brunswick could never be developed as long as the Crown Lands Office dealt with large numbers of small entrepreneurs whose wasteful methods had become notorious. His grand objective was to sell the wild lands of the province to outside capitalists of large means, to produce such a great sum that the interest from it could ensure the total cost of government. The success of such a policy would make the Lieutenant-Governor and his officials totally independent of the Assembly. The province could be reshaped and reoriented along new lines without the consultation or consent of the representatives of the people.

Contrary to the predictions of Douglas, Baillie made of New Brunswick the only colony in North America where the sale of land appeared to produce successful results. In 1830 alone he sold land to the value of £60,000. Because, according to the law against aliens, Americans were not permitted to hold land, timber interests of Boston and Maine employed New Brunswickers as go-betweens, displaying an intense interest in the purchase of forest properties. But many of these and later sales were invalidated by the failure to pay second instalments. Capital was sometimes fictitious. Some entrepreneurs found it profitable to pay the first instalment, strip the purchased land of timber, and then to scorn government by refusing to pay the balance. Yet there was much solid evidence to show that the sale of public land was warranted by success. This was because New Brunswick had great stocks of virgin timber and rivers that, compared with those of Maine, were highly navigable. Timber was accessible as well as in vast supply.

Success merely whetted Baillie's ambitions and sharpened the animosity of the Loyalist families on whom he might naturally have leaned for support. Angered by their opposition, he persuaded the Colonial Office to strike from the list of public offices those of the Receiver General and Auditor General, held by members of the important Bliss and Robinson connections. The new Lieutenant-Governor, Sir Archibald Campbell, brought about a reversal of this decision, but the peremptory conduct of the Commissioner, who argued that the offices had become unnecessary because of the increased consequence of his own, enraged the official element at Fredericton. They had always looked to the Crown for support but all the authority and patronage of the Crown now seemed concentrated in Baillie's person. Even the more austere Loyalists who had looked askance at democratic practice in the House of Assembly could see that the only hope of resisting the growing power of the Commissioner of Crown Lands was to ally themselves with the leaders of the timber trade.

The immensity of Baillie's intentions left no room for misunderstanding when he returned from London in 1832 following the organization of the New Brunswick and Nova Scotia Land Company. In the northern part of the County of York, the strategic area of the province that embraced the portage between the St John and the Miramichi, 350,000 acres were sold to this private British company, many of whose shareholders held high places in British public life. The legislative session of that year was comparatively tranquil, but the House of Assembly considered proposals for taking over the Crown Lands. In 1833 public opinion, generated by Baillie's enemies, impelled it to action. An order for collection of quitrents on Midsummer Day of this year ranged the populace behind outspoken assemblymen who were now determined to sweep Baillie from their path. For two years the *Courier* of Saint John had waged a battle against his unpopular policies. The crux of the argument was that however much revenue Baillie might collect from the Crown Lands, most of it was absorbed by the expenses of collection and by the mismanagement of his office. The legislature, it was presumed, could collect the revenues much more cheaply and would cut the salaries of the Commissioner and his "harpies." Political tracts that were reminiscent of the American Revolution began to appear in provincial newspapers, along with more moderate, scholarly articles that told how the domains of the Crown in England had come beneath the control of Parliament.

A constitutional issue added fire to the passions of 1833. For years the British government had been concerned by the criticisms of the councils in the colonies, the juntas of judges and officials who sat in both executive and legislative roles. The logical solution to the problem was the substitntion of two for one – the creation of a smaller executive council and a larger legislative council. This was in accordance with British practice and with the theory of the separation of powers in which British American constitution-alists were steeped. Now the Colonial Secretary, Lord Goderich, put the plan into effect in New Brunswick. When Sir Archibald Campbell published the commission of the new executive the name of Thomas Baillie stood at the head of the list of five. Men such as Richard Simonds and William Black, who had been foremost in government for many years, were relegated to the legislative council of twelve. To bring British practice into effect, observed Lord Goderich, some at least of the members of the small executive should hold seats in the assembly.[12] This presupposed popularity for the new government. But Baillie was contemptuous of popularity and of the elements that create it. His remoteness from public favour was accentuated by his marriage to the daughter of the Provincial Secretary, William Franklin Odell, who had succeeded his father in 1812 and was to keep the office in his family for sixty years. A small family compact was at the heart of power. But against it, in the legislature, was a much more widely spread family compact, composed of the Bliss-Robinson-Simonds connection, soon to be reinforced by a verbose and ambitious scion of the Blisses, Lemuel Allan Wilmot.

Coincident with the demand for quitrents and with the mounting fears of new and arbitrary controls over the Crown Lands, the announcement of the reduced executive council came like a declaration of war. Such a govern-ment, in which the aged Sir Archibald Campbell was overshadowed by Baillie, could command no support in the House of Assembly. As leader of what was now called the cause of the people there came forward Charles Simonds of Saint John, the president of the Bank of New Brunswick which had enjoyed a banking monopoly in the colony since 1820. Embittered by the memory of a prosecution for trespass by Baillie, he regarded the Com-missioner with a deadly hatred. Nova Scotians might say that their own assembly consisted of men of modest means, but Simonds, along with several other popular tribunes, could impart to the New Brunswick house a reputa-tion for wealth.[13] Under his direction a committee on grievances was estab-lished. The passing of eight resolutions based on the report of this committee was directed almost exclusively against the great ascendancy of Baillie in the government of the province. All except one concerned Crown Lands and quitrents. The eighth protested the abolition of the old council of dual function.

To secure control of the Crown Lands and to reduce Baillie to a position of subservience to the timber trade, the House of Assembly sent a delegation to London. A colleague for Simonds was chosen in Edward Barron Chandler who enjoyed great fame as a pleader in the courts of the two provinces. The conservative Whig who presided over the Colonial Office in 1833 was the Rt. Hon. Edward Stanley who was well disposed to the principal purpose of the delegation. Surrender of the Crown Lands and of the casual revenues to colonial control was now a well established principle of British policy in the North American colonies. But the difficulty lay in the price the legislature was willing to pay. Stanley demanded a civil list which would secure the salaries of officers of government at a level considerably beyond what the House of Assembly, whose great purpose was to reduce Baillie's salary as well as limit his power, would accept. The Colonial Secretary furthermore refused to surrender with the revenues the unpaid portion of the Land Company's price of purchase for its holdings in York County. Having failed in an attempt to persuade Baillie to take an office in Jamaica and so rid himself of an immense proportion of the difficulty, Stanley felt obliged to honour the strongly held sense of obligation entertained towards Baillie by Lord Bathurst. This had been created ten years before when the Commissioner had surrendered his claim to a lucrative office in Tunis in favour of another of his lordship's nominees. Baillie preferred to remain in New Brunswick and Stanley reluctantly decided that his interests there had to be protected.[14]

Simonds and Chandler failed in their mission, but they laid the groundwork for an eventual aggreement. They further persuaded Stanley that New Brunswick's Commissioner of Crown Lands possessed a discretion far too comprehensive and secured, in detail, moderating restrictions on certain of Baillie's activities. But, only slightly checked, his office intensified its control over forest resources for the next three years as the boom in timber attained enormous proportions. He reported sales in land of over £153,000 for 1835 and Campbell was able to estimate the eventual accumulation of a capital sum great enough to ensure official salaries forever. In bad temper the legislature bought off the British government's claim to quitrents for an annual payment of £1,000 to the casual revenue. At the same time Nova Scotia paid £1,500. Though all of these revenues were devoted to provincial purposes, the image created in the public mind was that of a niggling and parsimonious British government. Fundamentally the quarrel was one of control. In the House of Assembly the representatives of the people were eager to lay their hands on a new source of revenue and distribute it among their constituents by traditional methods. The

Jonathan Odell

Samuel Cunard

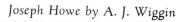

Joseph Howe by A. J. Wiggin

Sir John Wentworth by I. Field

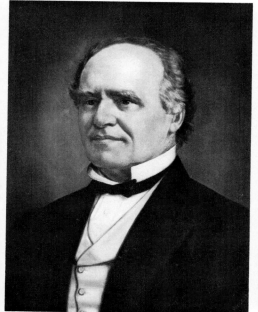

Hon. Patrick Morris
(Courtesy Hon. J. R. Smallwood and
Memorial University, Newfoundland)

"Charles Inglis, D.D."

Hon. James W. Johnston

Rev. William Black

William Carson, M.D
*(Courtesy Hon. J. R. Smallwood and
Memorial University, Newfoundland)*

Hon. Ward Chipman *(Sr.)*

Sir John Harvey

Thomas Chandler Haliburton
(Webster Collection)

officers of government, dependent on the casual revenues for their salaries, feared for their future should the fund be placed at the disposal of capricious politicians. In Nova Scotia the sums were small in comparison with those the Assembly raised by ordinary methods. But in New Brunswick they were monumentally large, a factor alone sufficient to explain the powerful initiative taken by the junior province at this time.

By 1836 the animosities at Fredericton were continuing to deepen. Family and factional quarrels sharpened the constitutional issue as Baillie raised the upset prices for mill-sites offered at public auction, when he insisted that the duration of licences for timber berths should be extended from one year to five. While the value of timber-bearing lands increased, there came a general realization that the refusal of Stanley's offer of 1833 had been a mistake. A disposition came into being to acquire control of the Crown Lands no matter what the price might be. For a dozen years the Colonial Office had been in retreat before the demands of reformers in the colonies. In 1836, while a new and conciliatory secretary, Lord Glenelg, was anxiously reviewing the state of affairs in Lower Canada, the time for action seemed propitious. Although opinion in the House of Assembly was far from unanimous, the procedures of 1833 were repeated. Simonds, though enduring many attacks of a personal nature, again bore the brunt of leadership, but William Crane, a merchant of Sackville, and Lemuel Allan Wilmot were chosen as delegates to go to London.

Harassed by troubles in almost every North American colony, Glenelg was eager to make of New Brunswick a proving ground for his theories of liberal reform. The grievances were specific and the Colonial Secretary found no difficulty in meeting them. He agreed to surrender to the control of the provincial legislature not only the Crown Lands and their revenues but also £170,000 accumulated by Baillie during his twelve years of arbitrary rule. The delegates were not prone to quibble about the price demanded – a guaranteed civil list that would protect the rights of existing civil servants and other interests such as King's College, to whose security the British government had pledged its faith. The agreement, made at London in September, was referred to in later years as a contract. It would be given legal sanction by the passage of a series of acts through the New Brunswick legislature.

To the great displeasure of Glenelg, Sir Archibald Campbell, who, though always nervous of Baillie's wilfulness, regarded the leaders of the Assembly as men of evil, fought a strong rearguard action and professed to be unable to understand his instructions. The winter session of the legislature in 1837 was therefore lost and New Brunswick failed to appear to the remainder of British North America as a docile witness to the wisdom of Lord Glenelg's policies. Campbell and the Odell-Baillie group were playing for time, hoping for a change in British government and the dominance of different policies at the Colonial Office. The House of Assembly petitioned for the recall of the Lieutenant-Governor and hastily dispatched Wilmot and Crane on a second journey to London. But it was not necessary to fight. Campbell anticipated his recall and resigned. Sir John Harvey was ordered from Prince Edward Island to Fredericton to take over the lieutenant-governorship and to hasten through the legislature the bills that would put the agreement into effect. This was accomplished during a summer session of the same year. Suddenly the members of the House of Assembly found themselves masters of large new revenues and of a capital sum of £170,000. By the exercise of a proper moderation and by superbly good timing the politicians of the province had gained everything they had demanded. The acquisition of the Crown Lands was an accomplishment which, at this stage, outstripped all other colonies on the road to reform.

In a more general way New Brunswick led the van of the movement for what was beginning to be called "responsible government." During their sojourns in London Crane and Wilmot pressed for an executive council that could work in harmony with the House of Assembly. Glenelg refused to enlarge the council of five, but wholeheartedly agreed that councillors should enjoy the confidence of the representatives of the people. In accordance with his injunctions Sir John Harvey quickly organized a new executive council. At the head of it was Charles Simonds who had led the struggle for control of the Crown Lands. Lord Durham was to recognize the great progress made in New Brunswick when he declared in his report that "the constitutional principle had been, in fact, fully carried into effect in this province."[15] Imperial magnanimity in New Brunswick could not avert rebellion in the Canadas. But the great scope of the surrender by the Colonial Office made a powerful impression upon the mind of Sir Francis Bond Head in Toronto. The downfall of Sir Archibald Campbell was a forewarning of his own impending "betrayal."[16] Without conceding any principle and without any guarantee for the continuance of the highly popular and satisfactory system inaugurated, the Colonial Secretary had introduced to New Brunswick the essential ingredients of the British system, an executive responsible to the elected representatives of the people.

Yet Durham spent but little time in contemplating constitutional practice in the Atlantic Provinces, or in examining the new dispensation in New Brunswick with which he professed such great satisfaction. Had he looked more closely he would have seen but little of the happy harmony of the British Constitution derived from the fusion of legislative and executive powers to which men so frequently paid lip-service. For private members still introduced money bills and committees of the House of Assembly still voted away the provincial revenues for the creaking and rotten little wooden bridges, for the layers of mud that were draped over forest trails called roads, of the same kind that Sam Slick condemned in Nova Scotia. The government of New Brunswick now enjoyed the confidence of the House of Assembly, but it did not have the elements of financial control that could give it strength and leadership. Centralization of authority was alien to the way of life in New Brunswick where the frontier forces of the rural constituencies were in the ascendancy. In his conversations with Crane and Wilmot, Glenelg had noticed this outstanding contradiction to British parliamentary practice, but had refused to allow it to interfere with the new freedom he granted to the legislature. Working fast against time, against difficulties thrust upon him from all quarters, he preferred to regard it as of secondary importance.[17]

III

Until 1835 the politics of Nova Scotia were comparatively tranquil. Lacking the excitement of the booming New Brunswick timber trade, the economy of the province was in a state of mild depression that was exaggerated by the unsettling effects of a flood of bank paper, principally that of the Halifax Banking Company. In 1834 Alexander Stewart of Cumberland led the popular attack on the secret proceedings of the Council of Twelve. Three years later he was a member of the Council and a prime defender of "the old system." This was in the tradition of Nova Scotian reformers and was to provide a pattern for many a reformer to come.

While New Brunswick was setting the pace, Nova Scotia produced the great orator of reform. Joseph Howe was the son of John Howe, the King's Printer who had left Boston with the great Loyalist migration of 1776. Self-educated in a cottage by the Northwest Arm of Halifax, he became the owner and editor of the *Nova Scotian* at the age of twenty-three. His knowledge was voluminous, but without his powerful constitution and boundless energy this would have been of little account. Slowly, from 1828, his interests transformed his journal from the character of the purely literary to the political. As a young man seeking circulation for his paper, he made himself widely acquainted while riding through the province. He learned to know Nova Scotians and Nova Scotians learned to know his poetry and patriotism, and what was probably more important, his down-to-earth comradeship with the fishermen and farmers. His frailties as well as his merits could carry him a long way. He was a lover of fruit and wine, of the good earth, and, as the ecstatic rigmarole in his diary upon the daughter of Herbert Huntington can testify, of woman.[18] Even in politics he was something of a philanderer. His lustiness had a quality that either attracted or repelled. In the conventional circles of Halifax his private character created contempt and hostility. But this earthiness and love of life which suggested bluffness, realism, and honesty, would appear to have endeared him to the common folk of the province.[19]

Howe enjoyed no favours from the Council of Twelve and, as a young man who had his ear attuned to the new currents of the time, he guided the *Nova Scotian* to a course in sympathy with the swelling sentiments of reform. On January 1, 1835 there appeared in its columns a letter signed "The People." It was written by a friend, George Thompson, but Howe, as the publisher, was legally responsible. It was concerned exclusively with local taxation in the town and county of Halifax, the allegations being that assessments were unjust and that the magistracy improperly derived incomes from collection and expenditure. Though the letter dealt with politics of the town, it was the provincial government, whose nominees filled the magisterial benches, that was under attack. "The system," the whole intricate and closely knit web of privilege by which even the local affairs of Nova Scotia were governed, answered with a libel suit directed against the proprietor of the *Nova Scotian*.

Howe consulted legal friends and was told there was no hope for a successful defence. With the exuberance that was perhaps his most attractive trait of character, he gathered an armful of text, read laws for two weeks, and prepared his own case that was presented before a hostile court and a friendly gallery. Archibald, the Attorney General, could not hold the jury to "the plain rules of law." Everybody who had served on the Halifax magistracy for thirty years, he argued, had been libelled. In his charge Chief Justice Haliburton announced his opinion that the letter was a libel. But after ten minutes of deliberation the jury brought down a verdict of "Not Guilty."[20]

The public jubilation that followed reflected the release of a resentment against the Council of Twelve and its cliques of favourites that had been subdued for years. Howe had established himself as an orator and his success before a court of law was to be extended to another forum, that of the legislature. The astringent influences of good manners and gentlemanly breeding had always restrained the tensions of public debate in Halifax, but the spectacular victory of the young crusader introduced a new element of furore. For it was certain that Howe had challenged and defeated "the system." Nova Scotia had found not only its John Wilkes but also its Charles James Fox.

The young newspaperman, now a politician of mark, entered the House of Assembly in 1836 not only for the purpose of winning municipal incorporation for Halifax, but also to bring about a change in the whole character of government. "The government is like an ancient Egyptian mummy, wrapped up in narrow and antique prejudices – dead and inanimate, but yet likely to last for ever."[21] Quickly he became the leader of the men who were beginning to call themselves reformers. His Twelve Resolutions of 1837, broadly equalitarian in tone, called into question the unrepresentative character of the council, drew attention to its "insulting" and secret deliberations, sought to bring the Church of England down to the level of other denominations in its share of public patronage. Eager to effect change and to gather support, he flirted with the American notion of elected second chambers. But the kernel of the doctrine he preached was the disparity between the constitutional rights of the Briton at home and those of the Briton in Nova Scotia. Public opinion in Nova Scotia was merely the beating of a wind that could not shake the firm fortress of those who were not responsible or answerable to the public. Howe set out to educate Nova Scotians on their constitutional rights. To what extent they understood his ideas is uncertain but there can be very little doubt that they liked the man and that he, so very Nova Scotian himself, liked them.

An address to the Crown, based on the Twelve Resolutions, was passed by the House of Assembly in the session of 1837. It pressed Howe's doctrine of responsibility so plainly that the more conservative members of the New Brunswick house, having achieved their own particular ambition of securing possession of the Crown Lands, found it rather breath-taking and refused to believe that the executive council should be displaced upon losing the confidence of the representatives of the people.[22] The idea was so novel, the implications so pointed, the private as well as public consequences for persons in places of influence so revolutionary, that men could contemplate the new doctrine only with reluctance. Whatever grievances they had in 1837, Nova Scotians, like New Brunswickers, preferred to look to the particular problems of the moment rather than to new theories of government. Yet the declamation and the rhetoric accompanying the Twelve Resolutions had their effect in London. Glenelg, having pacified New Brunswick while attempting to avert trouble in the Canadas, was in sympathy with the spirit of the Resolutions. Straightway he ordered the creation of two councils, executive and legislative, in place of the Council of Twelve, the same reform imposed upon New Brunswick in 1833. He agreed in principle to the surrender of all Crown revenues to the control of the legislature upon the provision of a civil list that would guarantee the salaries of officers of government.

Howe's reform majority in the Assembly, if majority it could be called, was not prepared to follow him to extreme measures in pursuing these great advantages. Rather sanguinely, he believed that the two new councils would contain reform majorities. But in executing the instructions of Lord Glenelg, the Lieutenant-Governor, Sir Colin Campbell, took advice from the men who were in control. Though he went a considerable distance to meet the complaints of the Twelve Resolutions, he left the preponderant party a clear ascendancy in both councils. Howe himself was given no expression of confidence. Delay was in the nature of things as the Assembly of 1838 niggled over Glenelg's price for the surrender of the Crown revenues, as the salaries stipulated for the Lieutenant-Governor, Provincial Secretary, and judges in the proposed civil list were deemed far too high. Indignation over the composition of the new councils waxed high in the House of Assembly, but nobody would take the lead in the obvious constitutional recourse, the refusal of supply. This could harm the assemblymen who controlled it but not the Lieutenant-Governor. The Canadian rebellions rendered extreme measures the more obnoxious. The anger of Howe and the men, many of them lukewarm, who followed him, fell on the head of Campbell. He, they declared, had disobeyed Glenelg's instructions. But they could do no more than protest.

On the subject of responsible government Nova Scotia was the great forum for eloquence, but the multitude of brave speeches produced no action that speeded its coming. Imperial initiative came to a standstill in 1838 as Lord Durham arrived in Canada to survey the affairs of all of British North America. Action was at a pause, but speculation was keen. Enjoying much of the substance of responsible government, New Brunswick was not disposed to quibble about formulas or clarifications. Even among the men who had just won a great triumph there was a general feeling that the whole progress of reform had reached a victorious conclusion. New Brunswick's new government joined with Nova Scotia's more venerable councillors to condemn Durham's proposal for a federation of the provinces and, as the Governor General lost the confidence of the British government at home, the elation of the colonial Tories became more obvious. Accused of radicalism and republicanism, Howe appeared – for a time – as the most conspicuous champion of a losing cause.

The publication of the Durham Report early in 1839 prolonged the uncertainty. Howe felt vindicated and, in New Brunswick, Lemuel Allan Wilmot became its profuse but rather forlorn apologist. While Lord Glenelg failed to declare himself, the Nova Scotian assembly sent a delegation to London to demand the proper implementation of the dispatches of 1837, the chief objective being to force Sir Colin Campbell to select an executive council that could enjoy its confidence. The delegates chosen were William Young and Herbert Huntington, men just as able as Howe, though less spectacular. To present the point of view of the old guard in office, the legislative council chose two erstwhile reformers, Alexander Stewart and Lewis M. Wilkins. Again the Colonial Office endured a barrage of constitutional argument. But on August 31 Lord Normanby, Glenelg's successor, instructed Sir Colin to reorganize his government as a coalition from the contending groups in the legislature. At this stage it would appear that coalition became the formula by which the Colonial Office sought to discard its constitutional problems in all of British North America. Lord John Russell's terse statement that responsible government in the colonies, as proposed by Durham, could not be reconciled with imperial supremacy, excited from Howe the famous *Four Letters*, the most forcefully argued case of all for the reform of colonial government, and, according to the standards of the age, a work of superb literary merit.[23]

Though Russell insisted that the Colonial Office must bear the ultimate responsibility for colonial government, he was resolved to break the power of the factions that ruled gubernatorial councils. His dispatch to Sir John Harvey of August 16, 1839 introduced a completely new concept to the administration of the provinces. New appointees to public office would no longer hold their places for life or "on good behaviour." The tenure of appointment was to be "during pleasure," or on a political basis, so long as a lieutenant-governor should find the individual useful to his purposes. In advancing to meet the wishes of a House of Assembly, a representative of the Crown need no longer be encumbered by officials who were opposed to his policies. Sir John hailed his new accession of power joyously. Like Bolingbroke's Patriot King, he, as a Patriot Governor, would smash confederacies of entrenched officialdom and lead the people in a happy harmony of unanimity. Reflecting the views of the conservative group at Halifax, now known as the Tories, Sir Colin Campbell was perplexed by the discovery that a public office was no longer a piece of private property.

To the defenders of the old order the Russell dispatch created a greater sense of shock than anything that followed in the accomplishment of responsible government. In later years there were many willing to argue that responsible government was really introduced in 1839. It was a measure of the men and of the policies now in the ascendancy at Downing Street that they could take the whole problem of colonial government out of the orbit of constitutional hyperbole, where Howe and a few others were so much at home, and govern in accordance with the generally expressed wishes of colonial peoples without laying down definite limits, or indulging in precise clarifications. Henceforth a colonial governor would be valued by his capacity to keep his legislature in good humour.

IV

The progress of the reform movement in Nova Scotia and New Brunswick created excitement, but similar stirrings of opinion in Newfoundland brought strong elements of danger. The exalted and ennobling doctrines of the new political liberalism seemed merely to accentuate social and religious differences. Violence frequently came to the surface of the scene and was

never far beneath. Newfoundland was not quite ready for any important degree of self-government. But premature experiment could teach lessons of
moderation and restraint.

Only on the eastern side of the Avalon Peninsula and on the north
shore of Conception Bay, where over half of the 60,000 inhabitants were
concentrated, was there a degree of political consciousness. Though Carson
and Morris contributed to the literature of colonial emancipation as ably
as leaders in the other colonies, their demands were nourished on the ruling
idea that since Roman Catholics made up the largest religious denomination, they should acquire control of government. The new sense of self-re-
spect that accompanied the passing of the Catholic Relief Act in 1829
enabled voluble Irish leaders to press this notion to extremes among their
own people. Bishop Fleming and his clergy, not always able to exercise
proper restraint, gave latent support to the rising political consciousness of
the Irish assemblies of St John's. The irate Sir Thomas Cochrane, sensing new
and great dangers on the scene, could inform the Colonial Office that a conspiracy was brewing to bring Newfoundland under Catholic and clerical control.

There were no politics among the new settlers of the south coast which,
since the Napoleonic Wars, had seen the occupation of almost every cove
and inlet. Even the high cliffs of the southwest had acquired a small quota
of fishermen and along the treaty shore there were those who disputed the
tightening grip of the French on the best locations and destroyed French
property in the off-season of the winter. These new communities showed
the same hardy but improvident ways of life that Avalon had seen in the
seventeenth century. The settlers maintained shacks on the shores for the
fishing season, but retired inland for the winter in order to be closer to the
caribou hunting grounds where they erected more durable "tilts." Chimneys were lined with wood, in very great contrast to the "tilts" or shacks
of the more civilized regions of the east which had much longer life because
of the use of tin. A society close to a state of nature is indicated by missionary accounts of naked women smoking corn-cob pipes.[24] Such people
worsened Newfoundland's growing inability to sell fish by providing the
French of St Pierre, who received a government bounty, with cheap squid
and herring for bait. They sometimes sold their own cod to the French for
less than the equivalent of the bounty. Success in smuggling brought occasional glimpses of prosperity. So far as the people of St John's were concerned, these dwellers of remote and little known places were out of the
political reckoning.

Sensing the new possibilities arising from the climate of political change
in Britain, William Carson returned to the fray in 1828. The fishery was in
a state of comparative torpor and among the merchants of St John's and the

outports there was developing a feeling that self-government might provide a remedy for the ills of commerce. Petitions from the outports began to shake the conviction of the Colonial Office that the demand for a representative assembly was the product of Irish agitators in St John's. Yet the basic facts of Newfoundland life still appeared to outweigh these revelations that favoured change. The Colonial Office was moved only by the changes that occurred at Westminster. The British Reformers, who now commanded a majority in the House of Commons, could not ignore the distant echoes of their own trumpets. The plea for "liberty and equality" was trenchantly reinforced by the declaration of George Robinson, member for Worcester, England, who as a merchant had long resided in Newfoundland and knew its problems, that, if the colony were given a legislature of its own, Britain would never again be compelled to pay a farthing towards the cost of its civil government.[25] Yet even the liberal Colonial Secretary, Lord Goderich, had qualms. Society in Newfoundland appeared to be so broken by social and religious divisions that it would be incapable of parliamentary deliberation. As a compromise plan James Stephen, legal adviser to the Colonial Office, submitted a scheme of government that advised the omission of a legislative council, always in the colonies a cause for "democratic hostility," and the establishment of a joint assembly of elected representatives and appointed officials.[26] But Goderich felt that such a constitutional novelty, known only in Demerara, could best originate in Newfoundland itself.

Enthusiasm in Parliament for colonial reform could not, however, be checked by technical and constitutional objections. On the day that Britain's great bill for parliamentary reform received the royal assent, Lord Howick, amid the applause of Joseph Hume and the radicals, introduced another to grant the prayer of the Newfoundland petitions. The new commission to Sir Thomas Cochrane of March 2, 1832 was in no important respect different from that of the representatives of the Crown in New Brunswick and Nova Scotia. The assembly to be elected would be compelled to endure the same obstructions and frustrations from a legislative council as those of the more advanced colonies. The colony was given control of virtually all revenues in the hands of the Crown and the surrender was accompanied by the familiar requirement for a guaranteed civil list that would provide for office-holders, in this case £6,550 per annum. The protests of Cochrane and the official ring at St John's were sympathetically heard but, amid the flow of liberal enthusiasm in Westminster, had to be rejected. Like a voice from the past, the merchants of Poole also objected, but found no sympathy.[27]

The first appeal to the people of Newfoundland, conducted late in 1832, resulted in the election of fifteen members representing nine constituencies. Rather unaccountably the newly settled regions of the south and west were completely ignored in the scheme of representation. The novelty passed over the colony in a generally peaceable manner, but in St John's there were ugly forebodings of violent disharmonies for the future. A Protestant merchant, William B. Row, was threatened with "dire consequences" should he persist in offering himself as a candidate for election. So seriously did he regard the threat that he withdrew. The real conflict lay within the Catholic or "liberal" party. Bishop Fleming supported his brother-in-law, John Kent, and William Carson. But a more "conservative" Catholic group, violently resisting what they thought was the undue influence of the more recently arrived clergy and their adherents, insisted on opposing Carson.[28] Their candidate, Patrick Keough, was victorious, and the man who had been the author of reform ideas in Newfoundland, who for a quarter of a century had led the van of the attack on the old order, was excluded from the first session of the legislature for which he had so long contended. The by-play of politics among the Irish factions, the hostility of "the Wexford Yellow Bellies," the trickery of "the tallies" defeated him.[29]

The more intelligent of the democratic politicians who were so new to glory realized that they were merely at the beginning of a long struggle. "The young upstart" of 1832 was John Kent, who was convinced that Newfoundland must follow the well-marked trail of constitutional struggle that other colonies had begun. "Oligarchical principles," he declared in an electoral speech, must be overthrown.[30] Threatened with a complete loss of power the official and mercantile classes drew more closely together. Members of the council, composed exclusively of Church of England men, were resolved to lose no further ground. To a very great degree the legislative struggle that began was one of Catholic versus Protestant, but it was a class war as well. There were only two classes in Newfoundland, said Chief Justice Tucker, the suppliers and the supplied. The attitude of this legal gentleman was one of frenzied opposition to the representative institutions "which had been foolishly requested and unfortunately granted."[31] After a brief career of pompous and learned obstruction, he resigned his office in protest.

From January 1, 1833, when the first session opened, the new era proved to be one of humiliations and failures. Fish catches declined and famine faced the outports. Enthusiastic democrats without sources of revenue were confounded by the responsibilities of governing the colony. Since all agreed that new taxation could not be borne, nothing was done to improve the condition of the people. Council and Assembly waged ceaseless war and, in what the historian of Newfoundland calls "mild outbreaks of legislative insanity," personal vendettas replaced the profession of principles.[32] Impatient assemblymen belittled the financial concessions made by the British government and sought to reduce the civil list which protected officeholders. Gradually there came the sobering realization that Newfoundland could not be self-supporting. The more radical demanded from Britain the reimbursement of ten thousand pounds in customs revenue collected in the years before the assembly had been granted the power of the purse. Understanding the demand and from long experience being well prepared for it, the British government agreed to pay the entire costs of administration until April 1, 1834.

The frustration already inherent in the new representative system entered a phase of chronic violence when Carson was sent to the Assembly in a by-election late in 1833. Sponsored by Bishop Fleming and the less moderate Catholics, he conducted in the *Patriot* a vitriolic campaign against Sir Thomas Cochrane and the whole mechanism of executive government. When the *Patriot* alleged that Cochrane refused to employ Catholic servants, though seven of thirteen of his domestic staff were of that faith, the Lieutenant-Governor sued for libel. Before the case came to court Rev. Father Troy, chaplain to Bishop Fleming, announced himself to be the Junius of Newfoundland and the author of the objectionable article. Religious controversy became a normal feature of the public prints. The *Public Ledger*, the leading "Conservative" organ, could fight back with vigour just as great and with as little restraint.

According to Cochrane, the Irish of St John's were instructed by their clergy to employ physical force.[33] On Christmas Day, following more than the customary libations of "morning," a mob attacked the home of Henry Winton, the editor of the *Public Ledger*, with the intention of burning it and destroying his press. Quickly the magistrates requested the calling out of the small garrison and Cochrane complied. The soldiers used great restraint but, according to official accounts, bayoneted several persons in order to protect themselves. A public meeting on December 27, chaired by Carson, protested the appearance of the military and awarded the accolade of peacemaker to Bishop Fleming. A circular letter of the Bishop to his parishioners announced Cochrane's disapproval of "the base and abusive purposes" of the *Public Ledger*. But Cochrane, in a reply to the Bishop, placed the blame for the riots on Christmas Day on the Catholic clergy. Just where Cochrane stood amidst the increasing tension of religious strife is perhaps best revealed by the plea of the Colonial Office to the Foreign Office, as early as July of 1833, that the Vatican should be asked to ensure that its clergy in Newfoundland should be made "more exemplary and more like their behaviour elsewhere in British colonies."[34]

Yet the Colonial Office was not certain as to how it should deal with the troubles in Newfoundland. Contrary to his expressed wishes, Cochrane was recalled in the autumn of 1834. For eight years he had given all his energies to the progress of the colony, the kind of progress that could be inspired by authority in high places. Opponents as well as friends had agreed that he was Newfoundland's "best governor." But on the day of his departure he was insulted and stoned by an extremist mob. His exit was rendered the more humiliating by the prophecy, made by Carson in the *Patriot* a year before, that the newspaper and its cause would be the instrument of an eventual recall. The coming of representative government produced something more than a violence of feeling. In May of 1835, as the editor of the *Public Ledger* was descending Saddle Hill, on the rough road between Carbonear and Harbour Grace, he was knocked from his horse by a blow from a stone and set upon by a gang of ruffians who beat him to insensibility and cut off his ears.[35] "Worse than Harry Winton got" became a familiar threat as religious discord sharpened.

In accordance with the new democratic aspirations the legislature passed a quadrennial act so that the new Lieutenant-Governor, Captain Henry Prescott, was compelled to dissolve the House of Assembly in 1836 while religious antipathies were still rising. The elections that followed fully justified his fears. A parade of five hundred "brave lads" from Carbonear routed "the Tories" of Harbour Grace and nobody was allowed to vote without sash or hatband of green. Carson and his colleagues sustained the tempo of excitement in St John's, winning easily. There the "mad-dog" or "Orange" Catholics lost custom at their places of business, were condemned from the altar, and, according to the dispatches to Downing Street, were, in effect, excommunicated. The mark by which they could be distinguished was subscription to the *Public Ledger*.[36] Triumphant on the Avalon Peninsula, "the Liberals" could easily dominate the new house.

For four years more the legislature of Newfoundland followed the maze of constitutional conflict that was familiar to the more mature colonies. Revenue bills were tossed from one house to the other without passage. Chronic poverty of colonial resources, the religious rancours and the feuds of the parties, stripped the conflict of any parliamentary decorum it might have had. In 1837 the road bill was passed thirty-one times in the Assembly and on as many occasions the council amended it, the Assembly giving each amendment the six-months' hoist. In the same year Lord Glenelg gave a decision in favour of the council's right to amend the details of money bills, but this brought no peace. Unsuccessfully the Assembly invaded the area of executive power by nominating road commissioners. John Kent, the most inflammatory of the younger "Liberals," had his nose pulled on the streets of St John's by Doctor Edward Kielly. Kielly was brought to the bar of the House of Assembly and, refusing to make an apology, was arrested and jailed. This spirited quarrel caused more excitement than any of the graver causes of constitutional disagreement. It was taken to the Privy Council, where it was decided that a colonial assembly did not possess the same privileges of parliament as the House of Commons of Great Britain.[37]

Against the violent tirades of Carson, Kent, and Patrick Morris, the Tory defence was inept and ponderous. Henry John Boulton, who deserves a prominent place in a list of eccentric chief justices of Newfoundland, brought from Upper Canada a determination to preserve the obsolescent forms of colonial government in a community that was much more turbulent and divided. Ignoring the Lieutenant-Governor, he pompously announced a series of changes in the nomenclature and procedures of the legislative council over which he presided, attempting to make it as much as possible like the council at Toronto and therefore similar to the House of Lords. Not to be outdone the House of Assembly referred to its sittings as those of the Commons and there were frequent references to sessions of "Parliament." All of this brought stern denials from the Colonial Office. There was something more than propriety and pomposity in the methods employed by the Supreme Court to restrain the victors of 1836 and to exclude Catholics from the lists of grand jurymen. Undoubtedly it was "the Liberals" who were immediately responsible for Newfoundland's climate of riot and disorder. Yet it can be strongly argued in their defence that the whole machinery of the lawcourts as well as the patronage of the executive government was used against them in a violently partisan manner.

Boulton, who earned the soubriquet of "hanging judge," affronted the populace at large by fundamental changes in his interpretation of the historic laws of attachment which prohibited the seizure of boats and equipment of fishermen during the season. Traditionally "current suppliers" had been given the preference in seizing the assets of debtors. Boulton ruled that preference should go to creditors of long-standing account. The whole operation of the fishery was violently disturbed by this revolutionary decision. When a petition praying for his removal, subscribed by thousands of signatures, resulted in success in 1838, almost all Newfoundland was in jubilation. The Privy Council rejected the specific charges brought against him, but condemned the Chief Justice for participating in the politics of the colony. Yet the verdict was hailed as a triumph for all the causes he had opposed. "Victims of judicial tyranny, persecuted priests and people! all Newfoundland, lift up your hearts in thankfulness to God! Boulton is convicted! condemned!! sentenced!!!"[38]

As the legislature did little but serve as a clearing-house for social and religious acerbities, the experiment of 1832 again became an open question. An election riot at Carbonear late in 1840, when "the priest's party" fought it out with Catholic opponents, resulted in the loss of lives and destruction of much property. Prescott was censured by Lord John Russell for his tardiness in dispatching troops to the scene. As the Tories offered awkward questions in the House of Commons the British government became convinced that Newfoundland was not ready for even a limited degree of self-government. A last abortive session in 1841 ended this experimental phase in the colony's political development when the House of Commons appointed a committee to investigate the working of the constitution and the two branches of the legislature sent delegates to London to offer evidence.

V

While Newfoundland faltered on the road to reform, New Brunswickers rejoiced in what was accepted as the essence of internal self-government. In Nova Scotia, where very little change had up to this point occurred, the great cry was that responsible government had not been conceded in principle. There was no uniform pattern for constitutional progress, and British statesmen, though eager to remedy colonial grievances, avoided catch-all definitions and declarations of high policy. Smallness did not disqualify Prince Edward Island from following in the path of the larger colonies and sharing in the adventure of seeking greater popular participation in government. Already it was fashionable at Charlottetown not only to denounce the policies of the Colonial Office but to behave independently of the other colonies. But reform of government was secondary to the reform of the land-holding system. For many years constitutional change was sought as the instrument for expropriating the land of the absentee owners.

Nearly one third of the occupiers of land now held title by freehold.[39] But this merely aggravated the problem in the minds of the tenantry at large. Those who paid a £5 annual rental per hundred acres, plus other assessments, could compare their lot with that of the fortunate dwellers of Lot 55 who paid the mere two shillings of quitrent and who had been delivered from their landlord years before by a court of escheat. Few of the landlords were descendants of the original grantees of 1767. Most had purchased their holdings on speculation, having "gambled on the forbearance of government at low prices."[40] Some, with agents at Charlottetown, gained good income. Others hoped to gain by neglect, trusting to the labour of their neighbours for improvement in valuation. Two great consolidated estates, the Worrell and Selkirk, comprised hundreds of thousands of acres and Sir Samuel Cunard was gradually building up an estate of 212,000 acres. All were regarded as tyrants. With the coming of the Irish, squatters became a formidable element, there being over seven hundred in 1840. In remote areas of the bush they were organized and half-embattled. As Robert Harris, the artist, discovered twenty years later, surveyors were unpopular and sometimes took their lives in their hands. The wail of the conch horn, brought from the West Indies by schooners importing rum and molasses to the island, could mobilize twenty or thirty burly and hairy Irishmen to the protection of primitive clearings that were staked out by the roots of trees.[41]

The wavering course of the Colonial Office produced maddening reverberations amongst the tenantry. Escheat had often been indicated by its policy and promised by local politicians but always denied. Representatives of the Crown had given impetus to the idea and the Loyal Electors had brought it to the dimensions of a political platform. In 1832 an Escheat Party was formed. Its leader was William Cooper, an estate agent who had been disappointed in his ventures and resigned his post to become a tribune for the tenantry. Also prominent in the movement was Alexander Rae, who was adversely described as "an obscure country schoolmaster of no fixed abode."[42] At Hay River, in the northern part of King's County, where Cooper possessed great influence, a large meeting of the tenantry in 1836 agreed to resist the payment of rents and the exercise of proprietorial authority. The movement spread rapidly to other parts of the province. Prince Edward Island was divided by a class war of a virulence almost equal to that of Newfoundland. As a member of the House of Assembly, Cooper extended his activities to the winning of a majority by working to the utmost limit the burning issue of the land question. He was signally successful. Twice he was committed to the custody of the sergeant-at-arms for refusing to apologize to the House. But in the election of 1838 the Escheat Party won eighteen of twenty-four seats. The proprietors and their agents were mildly terrorized. The officials of government at Charlottetown, several of whom were agents themselves, feared revolution. Even a liberal minded lieutenant-governor like Sir John Harvey regarded Cooper's declamations as "treasonable."[43]

The Colonial Office was comparatively unaffected by all of this. In 1836 it made a slight concession to reform when it authorized the sale of small acreages that had been reserved for church and glebe purposes. The position of the lieutenant-governors, Sir Aretas Young, Sir John Harvey, and Sir Charles Fitzroy, was extremely difficult. While urging action upon Downing Street, they were compelled to uphold the rule of law and the rights of private property. In private Fitzroy pressed the case of the people and the island government against the proprietors. In public he urged "the deluded tenantry" to cease their agitation for escheat.[44]

Leading an overwhelming majority and becoming speaker of the House of Assembly, Cooper secured, in 1839, the passage of resolutions, termed absurd and wild by the proprietors and their supporters, in favour of escheat. The executive and legislative council, consisting of members of a few closely related Charlottetown families, easily the best edition of a family compact the Atlantic Provinces could offer, had no choice but to oppose his extremist demands. Cooper's retaliation was to seek a wider degree of democratization in provincial government through the familiar formula of an elected legislative council.[45] The first check to his victorious progress came later in the same year when he went to London to interview Lord John Russell.

Holding the view that such communications would be improper, the Colonial Secretary refused to receive him. The convenient attitude developing in Downing Street upon the land question was that both parties were "too unreasonable."[46] In fact Prince Edward Island benefited by the reform already applied to New Brunswick and Nova Scotia, the dismemberment of the old council, the equivalent of Nova Scotia's Council of Twelve, and the formation of separate executive and legislative bodies. Power became more widely dispersed and an important step towards the adoption of British practice was taken when Sir Charles Fitzroy raised two members of the House of Assembly to the executive.[47]

Lord Durham's castigation of the proprietors and of their influence at London resulted in permission for the provincial legislature to tax all lands on the island. But Cooper's failure to make impact on the Colonial Office was the first clear signal to the tenantry that the program of escheat was not acceptable to Whitehall. With passion and aplomb democratic action had been tried and the results were negligible. The populace at large had to face the realization that they were at the mercy of the law and their landlords.

Civil strife did not keep people away. In six years, from 1827 to 1832, the population rose by one-third. The census of 1841 showed a figure of over 47,000, of whom more than half were settled in Queen's County. Charlottetown, with over 4,000 people, was beginning to have the semblance of a capital as plans were drawn up for its provincial building. The intense preference for living close to tidewater lost importance as new settlers moved into the inland regions. Scots continued to arrive but proportionally they lost strength as English and Irish, particularly the latter, appeared on the scene. The most neglected area, that of the extreme west, began to be filled up by Acadian overflow and new Irish.

As Prince Edward Island stood on the threshold of a great reputation for agricultural production, exportable surpluses slowly arose. Oats, so favoured by the Scots, and potatoes were the principal items. Only the Acadian settlements persisted in the attempt to make of wheat a staple product. The quality of farm animals was rapidly improving. Writing in 1828, John McGregor stated that the pigs of the island resembled greyhounds as much as the better types of hogs. But by 1840, owing to the work of Colonel Ready and a number of English gentlemen-farmers, the province was noted for the excellence of its livestock, especially for its large and strong horses, many of which were sent to the timber camps of the Miramichi and the Restigouche. Strangely enough, the townships, particularly those in eastern Prince County, which were especially noted for the "high farming" that was coming into favour and for superior yields, held hard to the employment of oxen. As in government, so in farming, the Atlantic Provinces combined new ideas with older methods.

CHAPTER 9

New Light and New Shadow
1840–1848

On July 17, 1840, when the RMS *Britannia* arrived in Halifax after a passage of thirteen days from Liverpool, it seemed that the era of steam navigation of the Atlantic would bring multifold advantages to the four colonies.
It was all owing to the vision and energy of a native Haligonian, Samuel
Cunard, who had been obsessed for twenty years by the idea of "an ocean
railway." A self-made man of impoverished background, he had distinguished himself by his industry in the Navy Yard, and had, according to common
repute, established a business of his own from the handsome profits of the
purchase of a prize vessel during the War of 1812.[1] The list of subscribers for
shares in the *Royal William,* constructed at Quebec for the run to Pictou
but immortalized as the first vessel to cross the Atlantic by the exclusive
employment of steam, showed his name at the top. In 1838, when the Admiralty called for tenders for the establishment of a steam packet service for
the carriage of mail to Halifax, no British firm bid for the contract but
Cunard seized upon the opportunity. The British North American Mail
Steam Packet Company, of which he was the inspiration and founder, enjoyed a virtual monopoly of steam navigation of the North Atlantic for the next
ten years. A man who was prominent in church, politics, and the militia,
Cunard might be regarded as only one of many Halifax merchants who made
their port a great place for trade and whose widespread activities betokened a
prosperous future for the entire region of the British North Atlantic.

Though at Sydney the General Mining Association ran coal-cars over six
miles of rail, propelled by locomotives that had replaced horses in 1836, railways were still the promise of a future era. Still the fastest means of travel
was the stage-coach, a development that had commenced in 1816 when a
journey from Halifax to Windsor, a distance of forty-five miles, required
only nine hours by coach. The general improvement of roads in the 1820's
resulted in faster transit. The change made in mail routes by the Imperial
Post Office in 1817, from the Annapolis-Saint John to the Amherst-Dor-
chester-Saint John route, led to the extension of postal service into eastern

New Brunswick. By 1836 stage-coaches ran regularly from Amherst to Saint John and the Miramichi. Governmental subsidy was an indispensable condition. New Brunswick's roads were notoriously superior to Nova Scotia's and in 1840 the average speed was eight miles per hour. On the upper Saint John, along the historic route by which the mails had been carried to Quebec in the winter season, great improvement had resulted from the road-building operations of British troops in garrison at Temiscouata. Sectional jealousies, however, hindered development in some areas. Anticipating the rapid passage of news from Europe with the coming of steam navigation, the Saint John Chamber of Commerce in 1839 invited Halifax to co-operate in establishing a daily stage service via Digby, but Halifax refused.[2] In spite of such inter-city rivalries, stage-coach travel continued to develop until the construction of railways became general.

Progress came rapidly to the Atlantic Provinces as they passed into the vibrant and hungry forties of the nineteenth century, but according to North American standards, it could be reckoned as slow. Progress had become a slogan, but progress was insufficient to ensure any lead over the development of the interior of the continent that was now beginning to become so important. A cruel blow fell in 1845 when Cunard, seeking a renewal of his prosperous contract, selected Boston as the sole western terminus for his line of steamships. Poor roads from Halifax to Pictou and Amherst made transit of the mails slow and cumbersome. Halifax could not assemble sufficient bulk cargo to make the calls of large steamships worthwhile and profitable. Nova Scotia's economy was highly unspecialized, many of the farmers being fishermen as well. Most of her surplus beef, poultry, vegetables, and coarse grains were handily taken care of by coastal shipping that sailed to nearby markets, chiefly Newfoundland. That the Atlantic colonies were not to share in the surging expansion of the continental interior and were, to a considerable extent, to remain apart from it, was vividly illuminated by the fleeting importance of "the pony express" of 1849. In January of that year, when Saint John was connected by telegraph with Boston, New York newspapers sent representatives to pick up the latest European news from the mail steamers as they halted at Halifax. In eight hours, relays of fast riders carried their dispatches to Digby where they were ferried across the Bay of Fundy to Saint John. News arriving at Halifax in the morning could be published in New York evening journals. But this spectacular means of communication was lost at the end of the same year when Halifax and Saint John were connected by telegraph.[3]

Population increased at a steady rate. By 1848 Nova Scotia's exceeded 276,000 and New Brunswick's 220,000. But in the two mainland provinces the statistics of population growth were often confused and uncertain so that at times it seemed that emigration exceeded immigration. In the border areas of New Brunswick and in western Nova Scotia men acquired the roving habits of the Americans, constantly on the lookout for an opportunity to sell newly improved lands at a profit and migrate westward where the fields seemed greener. A grievous loss of younger and able men became more noticeable in 1849 when California commenced to take its toll from the provinces.

Industry acquired no new important areas of development. The General Mining Association, having expended £300,000 of capital and paid no dividends, discovered by 1842 that its hopes of illimitable American markets for coal were destroyed by prohibitive tariffs. An almost complete dependence on the restricted markets of British America became the palpable fact this great enterprise had to face. Even here it suffered from the competition of British coal that was imported as ballast on the returning timber ships.[4] In Newfoundland, where the annual production of cod approached one million quintals, better times were recorded through the 1840's. The great growth of the seal industry changed the character of life in many of the outports during the winter season, providing employment for the outfitting and repair of vessels and contributing to the development of what might be called a middle class. Large vats for the manufacture of seal oil were to be seen at Fogo, Twillingate, Greenspond, and Trinity, and in the ports of Conception Bay. Each spring, as the seal fishermen sailed off, the toast of "Bloody decks to 'em" was a hearty one and on the ice-floes of the north these skilled and hardy men shot or clubbed to death each season up to 600,000 seal.[5] Until the entrance of steam vessels concentrated the management in fewer hands, this industry was a steadying and wealth-producing factor in the economy of Newfoundland. During the forties St John's acquired gold bullion in considerable quantities, brought by Spanish vessels arriving to purchase fish and helped to do so by the preferential duties of their government. Prince Edward Island was achieving a remarkable degree of self-sufficiency, but a vigorous export trade was able to pay for the imports of a society that consisted, to a great extent, of recently arrived immigrants. Eighty-five per cent of her exports were taken casually, in home-produced little ships, to the markets of the neighbouring provinces. For a time lumber was an item of consequence but as the forests were felled it lost importance. Oats forged to the front as the principal earner of credit. Queen's County and the port of Charlottetown still accounted for over half of the province's population and trade, but Georgetown, Souris, Malpeque, and Cascumpec Bay were important shipping centres. All contemporary accounts of the island's fishery are disparaging.[6]

In New Brunswick the timber trade continued on its exciting upward curve of increasing production, though shocks were always imminent. A reduction in the British preference of 1841 brought conditions akin to panic, for speculators were convinced that all the fortunes of the trade depended on the vagaries of British economic thinking, in which the free traders led by Cobden and Bright gained increasing influence. Bankruptcy and unemployment became general in Saint John. There followed a flight of skilled carpenters and mechanics to hitherto unwanted wooded upland, for many were now willing to heed the traditional exhortation that the only real safety lay in agriculture. Contrary to the prophets of New Brunswick's doom, complete recovery came in 1843 and the timber trade resumed its upward ascent – rather to the dismay of those who hoped for a revival in agriculture and increased valuations for agricultural lands.

The continued fierce assault on New Brunswick's forests, tolerated and even encouraged by a legislature that was really under the control of the timber merchants, was a principal reason for the final settlement of the boundary with Maine in 1842. The establishment of Maine as a state in 1821 and the fierce spirit of local patriotism within it had rendered a settlement favourable to New Brunswick infinitely more difficult to achieve. Surveys carried out in consequence of the Treaty of Ghent weakened and stultified the British argument that "the highlands" were to be found in the vicinity of Woodstock. Topography inexorably reinforced the literal American reading of the treaty of 1783, that the northerly line from the monument established in 1798 should extend almost to the St Lawrence. Negotiations broke down in 1822 and, following a flurry of border incidents, the case was referred in 1828 to the arbitration of the King of the Netherlands. His award, a 55-45 compromise in favour of Maine, was rejected in 1832 by the American Senate, owing to the intransigent stand taken by the politicians of the sovereign state, who severely embarrassed the efforts made by the federal government to achieve a reasonable settlement. Almost every year there was an incident on the blurred border, especially in Madawaska where Maine's patriots attempted to win the Acadians and French Canadians from their British allegiance. But, by reason of its superior communications along the St John River, the government at Fredericton was able to preserve a strong controlling influence.

The entry of New Brunswick timbermen in 1838 to the valley of the Aroostook, searching for the ever more elusive big trees, provoked the short-lived and bloodless "Aroostook War" of 1839. By the truce between Sir John Harvey and General Winfield Scott, Maine powerfully impinged upon New Brunswick's dominating position when she was given civil control of a temporary nature over this valuable part of "the disputed territory." But strong pressure from Washington forced her to accede to a settlement between Daniel Webster and Lord Ashburton in 1842. The ensuing treaty granted to New Brunswick what was considered to be the indispensable minimum – retention of the Acadian settlements to the north of the St

John and communication with Quebec by way of the Temiscouata port-age. The northerly line was halted very far north but not so far as to satisfy the fervent patriots of Maine, whose grievances were mollified by payments from the federal treasury at Washington. Lord Ashburton, in sublime disre-gard for the illogical bulge of American territory that almost separated two British provinces, could assure his government that essentials had been preserved and that the territory itself was valueless.[7]

II

As they waited the decisions of the British government on the questions arising from the report of Lord Durham, no simple statement could define the positions of the reformers of the four colonies. In New Brunswick Sir John Harvey presided over a harmonious legislature that lavishly dispersed the new revenues that accrued from the Crown Lands. Nobody was prepared to listen with much attention to the elaborate expositions of the new doc-trine of responsible government that came from Lemuel Allan Wilmot, and they were benignly ignored. Newfoundland had disqualified itself for respon-sible government. Only with the publication of the Durham Report had Prince Edward Islanders commenced to think about it. Early in 1840 Nova Scotia was the only province where the reformers were to make responsible government, the application of British cabinet procedure, a central issue of principle. A legislative battle of four years came to a head in February when James Boyle Uniacke resigned from the executive council and joined Howe's party. There followed an address to the Crown for the removal of Sir Colin Campbell which was carried by a narrow majority. Throughout the country the minority organized meetings of protest and, before an immense throng in Halifax, Howe enjoyed his first confrontation with his great opponent of the future, James William Johnston.

All questions of colonial government awaited the solutions of Lord Syden-ham who visited Halifax and Fredericton in July. In New Brunswick the Governor General found all to his liking. Sir John Harvey was "a pearl of civil governors" who serenely and with dispatch swept troubles away by rul-ing with the aid of a council whose members enjoyed the confidence of the people's representatives. Charles Simonds, the senior executive councillor and Speaker of the Assembly, was labelled by his few opponents as a dicta-tor, but the opposition, the adherents of the dispossessed Odell-Baillie fac-tion, could not effectively challenge the popular character of the govern-ment that had been established. Sydenham had harsh strictures for "the abominable system" of financial appropriations which he found in the lower provinces, but did nothing about it. Enough problems of an abstract and constitutional nature were already to be encountered in British North America. To calm trouble without raising new issues was the injunction of Lord John Russell and this Sydenham was able to do.

At Halifax it was relatively easy to arrange a compromise from which a strong government could emerge. A lieutenant-governor who had divided Nova Scotia on party lines could never succeed in restoring harmony and, on Sydenham's advice, Sir Colin Campbell was recalled. Triumph was so sweet to Howe and his supporters that they were easily captivated by Sydenham's blandishments. In the interest of good government four of the reformers, Howe, Uniacke, Archibald, and McNab, were willing to accept a vindication only in part of their principles and agreed to serve in a coalition administration with Johnston and four other opponents. Government had to be made to work from a broad basis of support in the House of Assembly. The idea of government by a single party was foresworn, although Howe was made more aware by the reproaches of his friends than by the sneers of his opponents of a sacrifice of the principles for which he had contended. Sydenham left Halifax in complete confidence that the new Lieutenant-Governor, Lord Falkland, would have no trouble, for the ablest representatives of the old Council of Twelve and of the upstart reformers were "captured" together in the administration he had been able to organize. Government by party had always been advocated by Howe, but party spirit was now to be deprecated. Howe's sole condition for entering the coalition was incorporation of Halifax as a city, a reform which was enacted in 1841.

The design of Sydenham, maker and patron of coalitions, lasted for many years in New Brunswick, where the junta of leading politicians eventually became known as "the compact," being composed of merchants and lawyers of historic Loyalist families. When Sir John Harvey was recalled in 1841 for an indiscreet inattention to Sydenham's resolve to be firm with the Americans in Madawaska, Simonds lost his pre-eminence. His place was taken by a trio of influential legislators, Hugh Johnston, a merchant of Saint John and Gagetown, Edward Barron Chandler, and Robert L. Hazen, a lawyer of Saint John. To their all-embracing control the new Lieutenant-Governor, Sir William Colebrooke, ultimately and reluctantly was compelled to surrender.

Colebrooke came to New Brunswick with all the zest of a reform-minded English Whig, convinced of the impurity of its politics and of the need for revitalizing public life at the municipal level. His reform program – to take the financial initiative out of the control of legislative committees and pass it to the executive council, in keeping with British procedures, and to incorporate counties and parishes so that local improvement could come by direct taxation – was aimed at the immense ascendancy in all public affairs enjoyed by members of the House of Assembly. Their proceedings in all matters concerning money he regarded as organized corruption. Against this program the politicians of the province banded themselves together and in the elections of 1843 Colebrooke failed miserably. A still more remarkable disruption of local political practice which caused him to be generally execrated was the appointment of his son-in-law, Alfred Reade, an Englishman, as Provincial Secretary in 1845. The influential members of his government resigned and rebellion reigned in the House of Assembly. There came some sharp speculation on the meaning of responsible government, but quiet was restored when the Colonial Office vetoed the appointment. Although there were no fixed precepts of colonial government, Lord Stanley was nevertheless affronted by a lieutenant-governor who so brashly and unnecessarily could arouse such a violent degree of colonial discontent.

New Brunswick had but two eminent theorists who pressed for responsible government, Lemuel Allan Wilmot and Charles Fisher, the junior member for York. Both owed their political success to their more businesslike qualities that became manifest in the allocation of supply in the House of Assembly and, by the exercise of patronage, the building up of powerful local interests in their constituency. There were no organized parties in the House of Assembly and the general aim of the executive council was to govern in accordance with the wishes of the majority of the House. Government at the executive level was, of necessity, weak and vacillating. What was needed was a firmly disciplined majority party in the Assembly through which the executive council could rule with authority, but New Brunswickers, in these years, liked to compliment themselves upon their freedom from the party quarrels that had become so notorious at Halifax.

In the Nova Scotian capital, Sydenham's coalition lasted only three years. As a member of the executive council and Speaker of the House, Howe enjoyed his new importance. His busy brain and vivid imagination were conjuring up new schemes for the reorganization of the British Empire on the liberal principles he had so eloquently expounded. His pride in the Nova Scotian achievement prompted him to suggest to Sydenham that he go to Canada and, by establishing a newspaper, teach the Canadians the true meaning of British constitutional principles. His ambition was to make of Nova Scotia "a normal school for British North America."[8] But the suave and adroit Johnston was making greater headway into the confidential counsels of Lord Falkland. The exuberance of Howe could repel as well as attract and Falkland was a stickler for what were beginning to be called the correct standards of gentlemanly deportment. Johnston, the leader of the increasing and voluble Baptist denomination, abounded in respectability. Howe had no religious affiliations and he was "the friend of publicans and sinners . . . the hero of a hundred scandalous stories, and the known father of an illegitimate child.''[9] Both were men of great ability but, to the convention-ally minded, Johnston was much the safer of the two.

The incipient rivalry came to open quarrel on the question of higher education. Three colleges, sponsored by religious denominations, drew sub-sidies from the provincial government. A fourth, Dalhousie, originally in-tended to be non-sectarian, had come in part under the control of the Presby-terians. Largely because one of their eminent divines, Dr Edmund Crawley, had not been appointed to the faculty at Dalhousie, the Baptists, as already noted, had extended their activities at Horton and opened Acadia College. At Halifax the Roman Catholics were planning for St Mary's, and both of these new institutions opened negotiations for provincial assistance. The idea reigned that "one or two professors" could make a college and that each religious denomination was entitled to public support.

According to William Annand, a friend of Howe and with him founder of the *Morning Chronicle*, it was not higher education but "bitter sectarian jealousies" that throve on a multitude of small financial grants. With char-acteristic vigour Howe led the agitation for "one good college." Contempt for the small, undernourished institutions that were in course of develop-ment underlay the logic of his appeal for a provincial university and, for the moment, it was the Baptists who became his principal target. "If we are to have a pope I would as soon have one at Rome as at Horton; if persecution is to be tried, it may as well come under solemn pontificals as under a black coat and tights."[10] Acadia was sustained, he said, by contributions of "gold rings, yarn stockings and shingles," and the youth of Nova Scotia would be just as safe in a metropolitan university on the Grand Parade at Halifax as "imbibing a sour sectarian spirit on a hill in Horton." A militant and democratic group such as the Baptists could only fight back with the same vigour. Howe and Johnston became estranged.

When Lord Falkland accepted Johnston's advice and dissolved the House of Assembly late in 1843, Howe fully understood that he had been thrust to the fringes of the administration. In the following January, when the Lieutenant-Governor appointed Johnston's brother-in-law, Dr Mather Almon, an executive councillor, he could no longer resist the impulse to re-sign in order to gain the freedom openly to attack those whom he now con-sidered to be his enemies. Coalition, he decided, was not the proper principle on which to bring self-government to British North America.

Single-party government now became a fixed idea so far as "the Liberals," as Howe's following now called themselves, were concerned. To their oppo-nents, the old guard who had ruled before 1840, and the hesitating members of the Assembly who favoured reform but were in no hurry to obtain it, the Conservative or Tory label was attached. These denied that there were two parties, affirming that even if there were, there was no difference between them. A vindictive opposition in the Assembly led by Howe clarified its aims, however, with a thoroughness that now startled the traditionally minded. The idea that the executive should be acceptable to the majority of the representatives of the people was no longer novel. That the members of the executive council should hold public offices, that the departments of administration should be apportioned to the men who could master the Assembly, was revolutionary to those trained in the political and social procedures of the colonial past. That the holding of an office would be dependent on the vagaries of electoral opinion, or on the caprices of a popular assembly, gave pause to a populace that was essentially conservative in character. Responsible government, as defined by Howe, implied a rather terrifying degree of concentration of power and patronage in the hands of relatively few individuals.

Howe could envisage his own forum in Nova Scotia as no less respectable than that of the Parliament of Great Britain and in this great aspiration he was encouraged by the advice of Charles Buller, the Radical reformer in London. But for several years he laboured in vain to persuade the Nova Scotian assembly that British political and administrative practice should be introduced. Johnston, now without challenge as the Conservative leader, was an able tactician as well as a capable debater, and held control of the House of Assembly by narrow majorities. Old reformers who had always pressed for self-government were firmly on his side and had been rewarded by office. In his frustration Howe, through the columns of the *Nova Scotian*, deluged his opponents with abuse and ridicule, moderating his rancour by employment of the florid and full-blown constitutional argument, always on a high plane, in favour of the doctrines of Lord Durham. He was the victim, in return, of the same kind of ridicule and abuse, although it was not so clever. His resentment of Lord Falkland for the preference given to Johnston over himself in 1843 received free and frivolous expression in his pamphlet, *The Lord of the Bedchamber*.[11] It set Nova Scotia laughing, but did not topple Johnston's administration. At the opening of the legislature in 1846, in the Speech from the Throne Falkland rather imprudently referred to a certain railway company as made up of "reckless and insolvent men," an organization with whom the Young brothers, William and George, sons of Agricola and leading Liberals, had intimate connections. In reply, Howe even more imprudently threatened "to hire a blackfellow to horsewhip a lieutenant-governor." His political and social ostracism from Government House, followed by Johnston's easy sway over the deliberations of the House of Assembly, reduced him to a state something akin to despair and rendered him capable of harsh and uncompromising pronouncements such as this.

The party spirit in Nova Scotia, said one of the legislators at Fredericton, was "a disgrace to civilization."[12] After 1844 the Assembly of Nova Scotia was a battle-ground for two teams of impassioned politicians, the spoils of public office being the prize of victory. The traditionally minded deprecated the fierce rivalries that had become the new fact of life, but they had to be shown that the disciplined political party was a necessary instrument if Halifax was to have its Parliament of Westminster in miniature. The party required a sacrifice of independence, a devotion to the leadership of a single individual, a concentration of authority, which were alien to political experience in the Atlantic Provinces. This is why the plea for responsible government brought with it the fear of political revolution.

III

While Nova Scotia entered its maze of constitutional debate in 1840-41, the era of constitutional experiment in Newfoundland seemed indeed to have ended. Lieutenant-Governor Prescott refused to issue writs for a general election. Government was being carried on by warrants for expenditure, Prescott trusting that a later act of indemnity would relieve him of charges of illegality for paying out sums of money which council and assembly, during the last legislative session, had not disputed, even if they had not voted them. Carefully watched by the Tories in opposition, the British government set up its Parliamentary Committee on Newfoundland which received evidence from all who presumed to think themselves informed on the subject of the island. Lord Aberdeen presented the petition of the St John's Chamber of Commerce which asked for a change in the constitution to guarantee "security to property and protection to life." Many of the signatories were merchants who in 1832 had favoured the establishment of representative government. Firing his last gun, Sir Thomas Cochrane declared that Newfoundland was simply "a great ship with stages lying around her," arguing that she had no need for the normal modes of colonial government.[13] Delegates from the council and Assembly arrived too late to give evidence to the committee, but their cases were heard by the Colonial Secretary, Lord Stanley, who took office with a new Tory government.

Officialdom was completely convinced that Newfoundland was a distinctive community and therefore required an unusual form of government. Sir James Stephen, who in 1832 had favoured the idea of a single united legislative chamber of elected representatives and nominated officials, had now reversed his opinion, but his new chief took it up with enthusiasm. The Newfoundland Bill, which Lord Stanley introduced to the House of Commons in May, 1842, proposed an amalgamated legislature for four years, consisting of fifteen elected and ten appointed members. Representative government was not abandoned, but it was subjected to a thorough chastening.

A new lieutenant-governor was on the scene, chosen by the Whigs before they went out of office for his skill in "the art of conciliation." Sir John Harvey had exonerated himself from culpability following his summary recall from New Brunswick early in 1841 and in September of the same year arrived in St John's. "Handsome Harvey," as he was called, honoured the confidence. Socially he was a charmer and Newfoundlanders of all parties liked the bluff and genial manner in which he shrugged off difficulties. He made only one enemy of note in Chief Justice Bourne, who denounced the "reciprocal favours" in which he allegedly indulged with James Crowdy, the colonial secretary, charges which ended in the Chief Justice's dismissal.[14] Harvey's private financial affairs were notoriously in disrepute and the extension of "reciprocal favours" might be taken as a very good description of the methods by which he had acquired great adulation in New Brunswick. Yet a keen political sense lay behind the easy-mannered exterior which disarmed extremists. His refusal to identify himself with any party carried Newfoundland to a degree of tranquillity she had not known for many years.

In addition to these amiable personal qualities, he was fortunate. During his term of six years Newfoundland was prosperous and abundant revenues provided for a progressive legislative program. Harvey was imbued with a sense of the importance of Lord John Russell's dispatch of 1839. He resolutely refused to allow his officials to dominate the executive council and take a strong line of any kind against the Liberals in the legislature, whose fierce aggressiveness was transformed into a grudging compliance with his policies. Perhaps of equal importance with anything else was the provision in the Newfoundland Act of 1842 which assigned to the lieutenant-governor the power to initiate financial appropriations in the legislature. The British government had introduced this practice into the legislature of United Canada. Sir William Colebrooke had sent to London harrowing accounts of the corruption of legislative committees in New Brunswick. In spite of its impressive literature of reform, Nova Scotia showed no disposition to forswear the log-rolling intrigues of assemblymen that Sydenham had denounced in 1840. The introduction of the British system of expending public money imparted to the lieutenant-governor of Newfoundland a power commanding respect that was absent from his colleagues in the adjacent mainland colonies.

As success and harmony attended the efforts of the amalgamated legislature, public satisfaction reigned. Carson, Morris, and Kent were members of the executive council so that, although there was still a war of the printed word conducted by editors who found the tranquillity not to their liking, the elements of Irish turbulence and mercantile conservatism were loosely yoked together. Perhaps sobered by a visit to Rome, Bishop Fleming took no further part in politics. Divisions of authority in local affairs were made on a religious basis that was determined by the faith of the local majority. In Newfoundland, Sir John Harvey was Sydenham's ideal governor. His coalition had been made, in great part, by act of the British parliament. Nearly always he had his way. By reason of his responsibility to the Crown and to the people he could ignore his officials and discipline his assembly – always with great charm.[15]

Yet the satisfaction became less notable as the experiment of the amalgamated legislature wore on to its conclusion. However successful it may have been, it offended the bright idealism of the age. Richard Barnes, a Methodist member of the legislature, found political apathy as difficult to bear as the political terrorism of former years and called the experiment made in Newfoundland "a badge of disgrace upon its forehead."[16] Speculation on the action of the British government at the end of the four-year period became rife. The weight of all official and mercantile opinion was that Newfoundland was still unready for representative government. But John Kent, yearning for the day when his Irish followers would again become embattled, insisted that it was. As responsible government became a louder cry in Nova Scotia, from which Howe was in correspondence with him, Kent raised his sights. Forced to give an opinion to the Colonial Office, Harvey declared that he did not want responsible government for Newfoundland. As in New Brunswick, there were not, in his opinion, sufficient men of ability to make a two-party system work. But the draft bill he offered to the Colonial Office provided for a legislature wholly made up of elected members.

Again Harvey was fortunate. Newfoundland was about to enter a period of renewed and violent party politics, as the great fire of June, 1846 destroyed two-thirds of St John's, including two thousand buildings and sixty mercantile establishments, the first of a series of disasters. The always lucky soldier was called from the ruins to Nova Scotia where "the art of conciliation" was greatly to be desired.

IV

At Halifax, Johnston was still firmly in command and the province was enjoying a boom-time in trade consequent on the expansion of commercial credit in Britain and the United States. But the whole political climate was changing, for the Whigs had returned to power in Britain. The announcement of new trade policies that would free Britain from the commercial preferences given to the colonies logically implied a greater degree of freedom for the British communities overseas. While the last bonds of the old commercial empire were being severed, there could be no reason for a continued close control over the internal affairs of the colonies. As the reformers of British North America awaited the changes that seemed certain to come, Howe, though always fervent in his British loyalty, was moved to declare that if the new Whig government should not grant responsible government, the colonists would in a few years be compelled to fight for it.[17] Yet belligerent expressions of opinion were, for the reformers, unnecessary, since the new Colonial Secretary was Earl Grey, brother-in-law to Lord Durham. Theorists like Howe and Lemuel Allan Wilmot, who for years had clung to the principle of Durham's great report and had endured ridicule and abuse in doing so, suddenly felt vindicated. Sir John Harvey was an old Whig himself and one of his first actions on reaching Halifax was to send for Howe and assure him of his favour.

In New Brunswick an election was held in the autumn of 1846, too soon to be influenced by the great changes that were at work in British colonial policy. Hard-headed men of business, who knew that elections were not won by appeals to abstract principles of progress, openly scoffed at "Responsible Nonsense" and the Johnston-Chandler-Hazen control of the legislature was strengthened. Again Wilmot, who had resigned from the government during the Reade affair of 1845 on the principle that the office of Provincial Secretary should be made political and responsible, was isolated in the Assembly with only one or two devotees to keep him company.[18] But in Nova Scotia an election was imminent during the summer of 1847 and Sir John Harvey, after ten years of experience as a colonial governor, had no liking for the employment of his own discretion in the choice of executive councillors should a substantial change occur in the composition of the House of Assembly. Wanting a blueprint for constitutional conduct, he applied to Earl Grey in January, allowing ample time for a specific reply. His favourite method of forming a government was by coalition "of individuals of talent and influence of all parties," but in Nova Scotia coalition was scarcely possible.[19]

Sir John took the trouble to secure the written views of both parties concerning the procedures to be followed. The case of Johnston and the Conservatives was one that was mellowed by all the experiences and prejudices of the colonial past in America. The British system of government by a cabinet composed of heads of departments they regarded as being entirely unsuited to the administration of a colony. A self-made man of comparatively humble background, Johnston could consistently declare that government should be carried on in accordance with "the generally understood wishes of the people." He agreed that the executive council should resign upon losing the confidence of the House of Assembly. But it seemed almost nefarious that the heads of public departments should of necessity hold seats in the Assembly, be placed in a position that would enable them to dominate its deliberations, be exposed to all the temptations and pressures that were incident to political warfare. This was the essence of Tory resistance to the doctrine of responsible government as enunciated by Howe and the Liberals. It can easily be construed as a desperate and selfish attempt to retain office and patronage for their following, but its reasoning was based on historic American attitudes, above all the idea of the necessity for separation of the executive and legislative powers. It seemed imperative that public officers should be men of ability and probity whose politics should be kept within bounds. How reasonable was it to expose them to the errant caprices of public opinion and the urgencies of private interest by enabling them to control the making of policy in the legislature?[20]

The argument that the mere holding of office did not constitute the essential business of government, that office and government could remain separate from one another, supplied the basis of resistance to responsible government in New Brunswick and Prince Edward Island as well as in Nova Scotia, where the issue was voiced most articulately. Charles Simonds, the erstwhile reformer of New Brunswick, could see the introduction of British practice as the beginning of tyranny, as the end of an era in which American legislators could keep "placemen" under rigid control. There was reason in Howe's allegation that "the Tory system" was republican and not British. Yet there was one feature of traditional American practice which the enthusiasts for responsible government did not choose, at this stage, to remove. As Johnston and his colleagues reported, the financial initiative "in the most emphatic manner" was not with the government.[21] Charles Fisher made a bid for executive control over appropriations in New Brunswick, but without success. Howe favoured it but could not sway his comrades to see the necessity for it. Responsible government might come, but legislative committees would continue to dominate the vital fields of taxation and expenditure. Governments and office-holders might change, but assemblymen would hold the purse-strings.

Grey's reply to Harvey was a blueprint not only for Nova Scotia but for all of British North America. If the people should change the composition of the House of Assembly, the executive council should be changed in accordance with the principles of the majority party. There was nothing novel about this but Grey, expressing a belief that the distinction between the Conservative and Liberal points of view was superficial rather than fundamental, pointedly instructed Harvey to award a limited number of public offices to the party victorious in the election. In principle, therefore, his dispatch of March 31 represented a victory for Howe and the Liberals who, however, were to fight their battle in ignorance of its contents. The only condition, something of a stickler to a society where levelling prejudices were in the ascendancy, was that the permanent officers to be replaced, generally considered as wealthy in consequence of long years of service to the public, should be compensated by pension for their loss of income and security.

The legislative session of 1847 brought deadlock and the house was dissolved in the knowledge that an election would be held during the approaching summer. Cheered by the favourable auspices of the visit to Halifax of Lord Elgin, the new Governor General and a son-in-law of Lord Durham, Howe conducted a whirlwind campaign, addressing sixty public meetings throughout the country in three months. In New Brunswick the few reformers were acquiring an appetite for victory and Lemuel Allan Wilmot was educating the Assembly on the principles of "the new, old system" that would surely come.[22] But responsible government, being a great issue of principle, was not overworked in the Nova Scotian election. Much of the material employed for propaganda was drawn from the history of earlier years. The Liberals raised the economy cry, alleging that the high-salaried officers of government were enjoying their privileges wrung from the toil and sweat of the people. The politics of the civil list and the arrears of the casual revenue received traditional treatment; Howe and his party emphasized the determination to gain control of the Crown Lands but refused to pay the price asked by the British government. All official salaries, including those of the judges, they argued, should be reduced. Because they were in office the Conservatives knew and understood the full implications of Grey's dispatch. Realizing the possibility of a fundamental transformation on the official and social scene at Halifax, they fought back the more fiercely. Personalities figured prominently and much was said to justify the allegation that the struggle was not for principle but for the material rewards of office.

That something more than a great constitutional principle was at stake was shown when a new element violently intruded into politics. Religious discord had been common in Nova Scotia and very frequently had marked off political alignments. Perhaps it was in Pictou County, where Kirkmen and Secessionists were always at odds, that this politico-ecclesiastical rivalry was most notable. The dispute over Pictou Academy had led Kirkmen to support the old Council of Twelve and contending ministers of religion had given political speeches in taverns. In 1845, to keep the factions apart, the sheriff had built a barrier ten feet high across the main street of Pictou.[23] But in 1847 it was the Roman Catholics of Halifax, vividly reminded that though they composed one-third of the population, they held less than one-fiftieth of public office and patronage, who became organized into a political phalanx. Their publication, The Cross, exhorted them to band together as one man and vote Liberal.[24] Another journal, unofficial in character and produced exclusively for the election, the Irish Volunteer, had harsh words for "the rude, thistle-faced disciples of Knox" and "the degraded followers of the worse than reptile Calvin."[25] This frank avowal of partisanship raised among the Conservatives a cry of warning of the dangers of Catholic ascendancy. Much propaganda was derived from Howe's presence at a service at St Mary's Cathedral on St Patrick's Day, and from the marriages of various candidates, both Liberal and Conservative, to Catholic wives. The *Christian Messenger*, the organ of the Baptists, planted itself firmly on the side of the poised and sophisticated yet austere Baptist leader, Johnston. Howe continued to be remembered as the foe of denominational colleges and he enjoyed sniping at the tattered plumage of the Church of England establishment. His outspoken and impolitic secularism is appropriately illustrated by the remark ascribed to him that he would be happy to have the political Baptists if Johnston would keep the religious ones. A superficial impression might be that the Tories consisted almost exclusively of Baptists and Anglicans.

Political excitement attained dimensions never before experienced in Nova Scotia as the elections were held on August 5, one of Johnston's last acts having been the passage of a bill to provide for simultaneous polling in all constituencies. The results indicated but did not assure the return of twenty-nine Liberals and twenty-one Conservatives. Though party spirit was strong, several of the successful candidates had not completely committed themselves to either allegiance. The Liberal victory in Halifax City and County was regarded by the Conservative *Morning Post* as owing to a solid Catholic vote for Howe and his colleagues, an opinion privately reaffirmed in a dispatch to Earl Grey from Sir John Harvey, who declared that both the Irish Roman Catholics and the Free Presbyterians had voted Liberal to a man.[26] In almost every constituency majorities were slender.

Johnston held to a hopeful Conservative attitude that the outcome of the election would not be clear until the meeting of the legislature in the winter and did not resign. The situation was so fluid that Harvey indulged his passion for dabbling with thoughts of coalition, but the Liberals were assured and united. Though irritated by the delay, they could afford to wait for the palm of complete triumph. When the legislature met in January, 1848, there was no uncertainty. Their choice of William Young as Speaker was confirmed by a majority. On the 25th Johnston submitted to a vote of confidence and was defeated. His resignation and that of his government came two days later.

Nova Scotia thus became the first province of British North America in which the system of responsible government was formally conceded and given effect. James Boyle Uniacke became the leader of the new Liberal government with Howe as Provincial Secretary. Almost immediately the complicated quarrel over the civil list was settled when the reform-minded

Assembly secured control of the Crown Lands and mineral resources in return for a guarantee of annual payments of £8,440 for the maintenance of the principal public offices.[27]

Although Nova Scotia acquired the accolade as leader in the movement for reform, it lagged, in this rather important instance, eleven years behind New Brunswick. There the transformation came without public' excitement and comparatively without notice. A new Lieutenant-Governor, Sir Edmund Head, equipped with Harvey's blueprint, reformed the government in March on "departmental lines." Since an election had been held but little more than a year before, he could see no reason to consult the people. Strength in the legislature was his guiding objective and the familiar coalition his method. He could make no mistake by leaning heavily on Edward Barron Chandler, now the politician of greatest influence amongst "the compact party" which had ruled for ten years. To avoid obstruction he destroyed the unity of the incipient Liberal party by bringing into the administration as Attorney General Lemuel Allan Wilmot, whose talent for embarrassing a government in the House of Assembly was greatly feared. The coalition consisted of six designated Conservatives and two Liberals, though many would have denied that two parties existed in the New Brunswick legislature.[28] There was little enthusiasm, but rather a reluctant compliance with the change among the men who, priding themselves upon their roles as tribunes of the people dominated public thought. When the House of Assembly voted on February 24 upon whether or not to approve of the principles laid down by Grey's dispatch to Harvey of the previous year, eleven members voted against them. These were "country members," men of the equalitarian rural counties who feared that the discipline of public officers and party leaders would destroy their historic independence.

The transformation was technical rather than fundamental. Self-government in the colonies had been advancing steadily for twenty years. British obstruction, when it occurred, had been owing to bad advice and information given by colonial governors and their local oligarchies. Since 1830 successive colonial secretaries had urged governors to enlarge popular support for their administrations in the houses of assembly and to govern in accordance with "the generally understood wishes of the people." Rebellion in the Canadas had merely hastened this process. The significance of the Nova Scotian events of 1847-48 was the triumph of the British system of party government over the more disorderly and antiquated American methods that had long been jealously guarded. The leading public offices, torn from the control of previous holders, became political, but it would be difficult to argue that Nova Scotia became intensely more democratic in spirit and in temper in consequence of these changes alone.

Responsible government, as it was understood by the politicians of the two provinces, was not so great a boon that they could, with exuberance, pay the full price demanded by Grey. It was only with great difficulty that the Nova Scotian assembly would agree to provide a pension for Sir Rupert George, whose family had held the provincial secretaryship since the time of Sir George Prevost. There was so much feeling in the New Brunswick assembly against the payment of pensions to public servants that it preferred to retain the services of Thomas Baillie as Commissioner of Crown Lands rather than have his office become immediately political in accordance with the doctrine of responsible government. Not until 1851 did Sir Edmund Head succeed in freeing the department of its incumbent by persuading the legislature to agree to the payment of a pension. By doing so he made it available for a salaried political officer who could strengthen his government in the legislature.

V

The *laissez-faire* policies of the Whig government that were so notable in 1847 and 1848 carried Newfoundland to its former status as a colony with representative government only. In the first of these years there was a poor fishery, and famine threatened when the potato crop failed in the outports. In line with traditional practice during times of distress, the merchants reduced their orders for winter supplies and hoarded what they had already imported into the colony. Harvey's successor as lieutenant-governor, Sir Gaspard LeMarchant, could find among the poor only a disposition to accept relief and, among the rich, a great determination to evade taxes. In spite of these adverse circumstances, the Newfoundland Act of 1847 restored the constitution of 1832 with some trifling restrictions concerning the franchise. Any remaining impulse to continue the nomination of officials to the House of Assembly was stifled. This was another resounding defeat for the colonial Tories of 1847-48. Had moderation really come, asked the *Ledger*, in quizzical and disappointed humour.[29] This question quickly gave place to another as John Kent and his following raised the query : Had self-government really come?

Attempting to raise the colony from a slough of political apathy, the Liberals convened a great meeting at St John's on May 24, 1848. Their object was to acquire a constitutional government like that of Nova Scotia, whose example they regarded with envy. A cabinet government of departmental heads, another mirror of Westminster, became the aspiration of those who sought to raise Newfoundlanders to the status of their fellow-subjects in British North America. For Grey's recent concession, however gratifying it may have been, merely emphasized their inferiority. From the merchants there came hostility to the ambitious proposal, open in the colony and behind closed doors in London. LeMarchant, unsure that Newfoundland was worthy of representation in a general assembly, was certain that the establishment of responsible government was thoroughly unsound. As the democratic process was restored and as a quiet election took place early in 1848, a new crusade commenced to give assurance that tranquillity and apathy would not long remain.

The plea of liberalism could not go completely unanswered at the Colonial Office in 1848, but Grey and his colleagues were not yet prepared to believe that the refinements of the constitutional procedures of Westminster could be allowed to Newfoundland. To make responsible government work in any society, they believed, the presence of a large body of financially independent and educated men was a necessary condition. The society of Newfoundland was almost completely lacking in this necessary ingredient. They were the more sure of their correctness of judgement as they compared Newfoundland with a still smaller society, that of Prince Edward Island. There the land question was slowly being displaced as the sole public issue of importance. The year 1842 was a decisive one in which the British government finally gave absolutely clear assurance that it no longer considered a general escheat to be feasible. Disillusioned by the failure of the fair promises of Cooper and the other escheat politicians, the tenantry abandoned the more violent techniques of resistance and began to come to terms with their landlords. In the elections of that year the number of escheaters in the House of Assembly dropped from eighteen to six. But the more settled scene still echoed with the violent discords of ten years earlier. In March of 1843 the Scottish tenantry of Lot 45 forcefully reinstated a dispossessed tenant on his farm and destroyed by fire the home of the landlord's agent. Troops were sent from Charlottetown to East Point to restore order. Feeling amongst the population became so acute that Father John Macdonald, who ministered to the Roman Catholic parish of St Margaret's and was himself a landlord of the Glenaladale estate in Lot 36, was finally compelled to abandon his charge on suspicion of sympathy for the government. John MacIntosh, member of the House of Assembly and one of the most violent of the escheaters, created a great public sensation and opened a complicated suit at law when, early in 1844, he interrupted the church service at St Margaret's to demand a hearing for the cause he represented.[30]

Politics acquired a complex pattern as they commenced to centre upon the eccentricities of the Lieutenant-Governor, Sir Henry Vere Huntley, who arrived in 1841. Deriving great satisfaction from Lord John Russell's dispatch of 1839, he would appear to have believed that the principal duty of a lieutenant-governor was to cow and subdue a local aristocracy. Like some of his predecessors, he organized a faction of his own to combat the

Charlottetown family compact (the expression had a literalness of meaning that was unknown in other provinces). For this purpose he drew on leading elements of recently arrived immigrants whom he described in his dispatches as being of an intelligence superior to the natives. The prevailing point of view amongst the Compact, he declared, was that "only a backwoodsman knows how to legislate for a backwoodsman."[31] Irked by the refusal of the Compact, which after the elections of 1842 had a firm control in the Assembly, to add to his salary and allowances, the Lieutenant-Governor allowed his relations with the dignitaries of the capital to deteriorate so grossly that he withdrew his patronage from educational, agricultural, and other associations designed for the advancement of the province. He was depicted as a tyrant and, because the ascendancy of the Compact, like that of Johnston and his party in Nova Scotia, rested on a strong basis of popular assent, his name became opprobrious throughout the province.

Yet behind the verbosity and strong passion of Huntley there was a great deal of resource, and he had the opportunity to put it to work in 1846 when the electoral results shattered the ascendancy of the Compact in the House of Assembly. Thirteen of the twenty-four members elected were new to political life. The leader of the Compact was Joseph Pope, a member of an English West Country family prominent in the shipping and trade of the Bedeque region since the turn of the century, whom Huntley now dismissed from the executive council. This peremptory action, unjustified by his instructions, resulted in a reprimand from the Colonial Secretary, William Ewart Gladstone.[32] But, still enjoying the struggle, Huntley turned for support to those who were now speaking of responsible government as the solution for the island's problems. A seat in the executive council was offered to Alexander Rae. He, however, deferred to the superior merits of George Coles who, during the session of 1846, had come to the fore as the leader of the Prince Edward Island reformers. Coles was a man of practical bent who combined the management of several agricultural enterprises with those of brewing and distilling. In his youth he had travelled extensively in England and the United States and had come to the conviction that superior education was required before a just solution to the land question could be found. He looked to responsible government as the instrument by which better educational facilities could be provided, by which a more enlightened population might eventually be produced. Entering the legislature in 1842 in close association with the escheaters, he had exerted a moderating influence upon them following their defeat, persuading them that free land could be won by methods of gradualism. In 1846 he had led the legislative attack upon the Compact, had distinguished himself as an able debater, and had been accused by the Popes, Palmers, and Havilands of appealing to the gallery of the legislative chamber rather than to the rulings of Mr Speaker. In that year, according to Huntley, the legislature resembled a theatre rather than a parliament.[33]

Coles and his colleagues carried resolutions favouring responsible government through the new house of 1847. But there could be no simplicity in the approach to a project of reform that was technical in character. As carried, the appeal was merely for an executive council partially composed of the majority party in the House of Assembly, four out of eight. An amendment of the Compact, proposed by Francis Longworth, created confusion in the reform ranks and attracted nine votes. It declared that true responsible government could be achieved only by keeping the principal public offices non-political, though forcing their holders to support the measures of the executive council.[34] This idea of government by executive councillors without salaried offices and by permanent salaried officials was the substance of Johnston's cry in Nova Scotia and of "the country members" in New Brunswick. The notion that electoral contests should result in new dispositions of salaried offices was, to the conservatively minded, novel and distasteful. It had a more lasting appeal in Prince Edward Island than in any other colony.

Huntley's nomination of Coles to the executive council infuriated the Family Compact. The populace of a British colony was now presented with the curious spectacle of an executive councillor appealing for endorsement in a by-election and being fiercely opposed by his colleagues. Coles was condemned by T. W. Haviland as "an ignorant and uneducated man," as "a working butcher" who laboured with his hands.[35] When "libellous placards" against him were distributed among the voters of First Queens, Coles demanded the dismissal of Haviland and other public officers, citing the 1839 dispatch of Lord John Russell which authorized the lieutenant-governor to discipline those who opposed his policies. The Compact pressed the argument of guilt by association against Coles, holding him responsible for the revival of the hopes of the escheat party that had been so disastrously crushed in the election of 1842. They blamed him for the Belfast Riots of 1847, an affair of Irish Roman Catholics and Scots Presbyterians in which lives had been lost, an electoral quarrel in which the old passion for escheat had been allegedly fanned into new flames by the reformers.[36] But victory for Coles in First Queens gave Huntley a triumph over the Compact whose ascendancy he had resolved to break. Government House, it was charged, was illuminated to more than the usual degree when the customary torchlight procession through the streets of Charlottetown wended its way there in celebration. Windows were broken in the homes of leaders of the Compact and a bill of indictment for damage was brought against Coles by the Grand Jury at the following session of the Supreme Court. To break the power of the Compact, Huntley was leaning on the doctrine of responsible government. The cry of the Compact was that "Mr. Coles has sold himself to Sir Henry V. Huntley for self-aggrandizement."[37]

This remarkable alliance of the Lieutenant-Governor and the reformers against the local oligarchy continued to strengthen itself as Huntley appointed James Warburton, another reformer of recent arrival, to a seat in the executive council. But his acceptance of the doctrine of responsible government was unacceptable to the Colonial Office; and, after the Compact sent a delegation to London seeking his recall, his plea for a second term of office in Prince Edward Island, where he seemed to enjoy his stormy tenure, was rejected. In vain the reformers sought an extension of his stay. At St Peter's Bay a meeting of four hundred persons endorsed his policies. The petition sent to London to oppose the allegations of the Compact was headed by the names of Coles and Edward Whelan, a young journalist who was a product of Howe's printing establishment at Halifax and who now, in the *Examiner*, was conducting a hard war of propaganda against the Compact.[38]

At the Colonial Office Earl Grey decided to refer Prince Edward Island's claim to responsible government to the new Lieutenant-Governor, Sir Donald Campbell, who, after six months of consideration, came to the conclusion that the grant would be "dangerous and impracticable." Only in Charlottetown, he was certain, were the people ready for the new mode of government. There were no other towns and there were no enlarged views. In the rest of the province, from East Point to West Point, there were not twenty men capable of participating in the scheme of government advocated by the reformers.[39] Upon the consequent refusal to initiate responsible government, the Compact established an uncertain ascendancy in the House of Assembly. Edward B. Palmer, who had resigned his seat on the executive council in protest against Huntley's conduct, was reinstated and became recognized as the leader of the Conservative party which grew out of the Compact.

The views of Earl Grey and Sir Donald Campbell on the parochial character of government on the island at this time were confirmed by an unfriendly writer who could find no enlightenment in Charlottetown. The politicians were depicted as "the forty thieves" who beguiled "the greedy and cunning tenantry" with promises of escheat. Familiar sights about the town were "the Prime Minister" emerging from his tavern and the executive councillor descending from his load of dried cod-fish.[40]

VI

The thrust for emancipation from imperial control was given impetus by the trading policies of the British government to just as great an extent as by the local movements for responsible government. In cutting the colonies adrift by repealing the Corn Laws, reducing the timber preferences, and abolishing the Navigation Acts, Whitehall produced a mixed reaction that was, for the most part, gloomy and angry. There were great differences of opinion in Nova Scotia and in New Brunswick. The more diverse economy of the older colony made it comparatively independent of the changes in British economic thinking, for no staple industry was gravely menaced. But New Brunswick was almost completely dependent for the earning of foreign exchange on the sale of timber in British markets and on the endeavours of the shipbuilders whose livelihood was intertwined with that of the timber merchants. Nova Scotia could accept the changes with equanimity. New Brunswick regarded the performance of the British Whigs as a betrayal and, as the protests reached their climax in 1848-49, opinion in that colony changed from apprehension to panic.

Nova Scotia might glory in the achievement of responsible government as recognition of the quasi-independence that had been long enjoyed, but the same kind of independence for New Brunswick appeared to be coupled with commercial ruin. The "liberal" attitudes of Grey and Elgin came as pale, political facets of a ruthless economic policy which could depopulate the colony and destroy a great industry that had grown by reason of imperial preference. In 1847-48, while Nova Scotians were quarrelling over forms of government, New Brunswickers were painfully contemplating the decline in their commercial fortunes. For years the belief had solidly prevailed that the great timber industry could survive only so long as the British government would sustain the preferences. As Parliament systematically cut away the last bonds of the old colonial system, meetings took place in every city, town, and hamlet of New Brunswick to consider new departures. Even so cool and farseeing a lieutenant-governor as Sir Edmund Head accepted the general belief that the whole character of society would have to endure a fundamental transformation, that the population would have to convert itself to an agricultural and fishing community. Anticipating the worst, merchants and shipbuilders reduced operations. Skilled workmen abandoned Saint John for Australia and New Zealand or, in mood of desperation, again formed associations for the opening of farming areas in hitherto neglected forest upland. To the merchants of Saint John it seemed bitterly unbelievable that American shippers could now contend for the carriage of British trade although the government at Washington would offer no reciprocal privileges. As proprietors of a great ship-building centre they looked with covetous eyes upon the fast growing coastal trade of the United States. Their prime ambition was to gain American registry for their vessels and participation in the rich north-south seaborne commerce. While Nova Scotia endured crop failures and a slight shrinkage in the volume of her trade that followed the world-wide contraction in banking credits, Joseph

Howe could speak with satisfaction on the sound state of the province. Across the Bay of Fundy there was "scarcely a solvent house from Saint John to Grand Falls."[41]

In making a complete break with past commercial policy, the British Whigs thrust upon the colonies a freedom for which they were generally unprepared. Yet for ten years, all the signs and portents in British public opinion had indicated that Britain no longer considered the colonies important, and that she sought to withdraw the privileges she had so long conferred upon them. The British Possessions Act of 1846 had enabled colonial legislatures to reduce or repeal the imperial customs duties to which they were still subject. In the same year the timber preferences were reduced. In 1848 Britain withdrew from the administration of colonial customs establishments and it was certain that the Navigation Acts would be repealed in 1849. Colonists had to weigh the advantages of the new freedom against the privileges that were gone or about to go. Nova Scotians were not dismayed but New Brunswickers saw blue ruin ahead. The impact of all these measures on Newfoundland and Prince Edward Island was scarcely noticeable, but the new climate of commercial freedom had the inevitable effect of sharpening commercial speculation and directing opinion towards new political horizons.

Against the uncertain commercial vistas of the future the cheers for responsible government were only halfhearted. In many quarters sullenness and resentment against what many called British betrayal were the most prominent attitudes. The withdrawal of privileges so long given seemed like discrimination against the colonies. As the British government improvidently relaxed the provisions of the Passenger Act to permit uncontrolled Irish immigration to colonial shores, this resentment became intensified. Halifax, Saint John, and many of the lesser ports witnessed scenes of acute misery. Four hundred sick and half-starved Irish landed at Charlottetown, after taking ship in Ireland for "Charleston, near Baltimore."[42] The last great exodus from Ireland, caused by the potato famine of 1846-48, was the most tragic of all and in the colonies it was unwanted. Local authorities were put to great expense in extending the existing and inadequate facilities for relief. Not until the British government agreed to pay for a large proportion of the costs incurred did anger commence to abate.

Responsible government was merely the outward sign, not the cause, of a new era in the development of the Atlantic Provinces. By 1848 emigration from the British Isles on a great scale had come to a conclusion and an increasing proportion of colonial populations was native born. Forced to make important choices of their own, provincial governments suddenly realized that they were dependent on their own exertions. The spirit of the United Empire Loyalists still burned brightly, but those who had been most fervent in looking to Britain were now most mortified by what they regarded as a deliberate and almost traitorous severing of the imperial tie. Pro-Americanism, never respectable but always on the fringes of political speculation, became more bold. Those who surveyed the scene from a blatantly commercial perspective became more vociferous in pointing to the attractions of the enormous and ever increasing market of the United States that was protected by high tariffs. Yet the Americans had a bad record for driving hard bargains and the disunited British colonies had little with which to bargain.

However advanced the colonies of the Atlantic area were and however fit or unfit they may have been for responsible government, they were mere fledglings in comparison with the great forces and mature societies which encircled them. There was to be no choice in 1848. All of them, it became clear, were forced to set their courses by expediency and this was to take the form of greater co-operation with one another and with Canada. This distant colony, whose recent growth had made it something of an envied enigma, was much disliked for its record of rebellion, and seemed strangely alien because of its bi-racial character. But it had been thrust into the same quandary as the provinces of the Atlantic region. It was in this mingling of light and shadow that the first gleam of a new nationality could be perceived.

CHAPTER 10

The Ending of the Colonial Era
1849-1857

In 1849 four governments faced the challenge of what was to be a new era. Freed from the closely controlled system of imperial trade, the Atlantic colonies were to enjoy eight years of almost complete self-government before a new set of forces would seek to engulf them in a new political and economic system. Howe's imagination had never been confined to the narrow limits of his own province and the Liberal government of Nova Scotia was eager to show its mettle. But the chief complaint came from New Brunswick where the new problems possessed an urgency unequalled in the other three.

A Canadian intrusion into the affairs of the Atlantic Provinces set the course of intercolonial communication in motion. When the grain preferences in the British market were lost, William Hamilton Merritt, the canal-builder and capitalist of Canada West, could see only one future for his enterprises – free entrance of agricultural and other natural produce into the United States. Corresponding with William Young and Lemuel Allan Wilmot in 1849, he persuaded the government of New Brunswick to initiate the calling of an intercolonial conference on trade at Halifax.[1] There, for the first time on their own volition, Canadian leaders exchanged views on an official basis with those of the Atlantic Provinces. Reciprocity was the word in fashion and the dominating idea of the conference was to win access for fish, lumber, and farm produce to the United States, where the new industrialism of the eastern cities created an extraordinarily high demand. Under the influence of the merchants of St John's, who feared that commerce with the United States would destroy their monopoly of imports to the island, the government of Newfoundland ignored the advice of Sir Gaspard Le Marchant and refused to send delegates to the conference. Nevertheless, there as elsewhere, reciprocity became a slogan full of promise for future prosperity. Especially in New Brunswick, where trade had dwindled to a third of its normal volume, there was a feeling that, since

Britain had deprived the colonies of an assured market for their products, she should be compelled to find another by negotiating a treaty with the Americans.

The best bargaining counter that could be offered to Washington was the inshore fisheries of New Brunswick, Nova Scotia, and Prince Edward Island, from which the Americans were legally excluded by the Convention of 1818. Yet the provinces had taken very little advantage of the wealth of the sea. Halifax exported fish in considerable quantities to the West Indies, but elsewhere the trade was conducted on a seasonal and irregular basis. High tariffs in the United States denied American markets to British fishermen. American bounties to the sea-going men of Massachusetts continued to make competition hopelessly unfair. Most of the fish caught by New Brunswickers and Nova Scotians in the Bay of Fundy was sold "green" to the Americans, who marketed it at high prices. This was the long-standing practice of the international fraternity of the Bay of Fundy where it was customary to claim both British and American citizenship. Fish caught in British waters was sold tariff-free in Boston, where bounties were paid with no questions asked. American goods, paid in barter, continued to be smuggled into the provinces. Still this immense segment of the British Atlantic fishery, all the coastal waters of Nova Scotia and New Brunswick, was tributary to the Americans. Prince Edward Islanders openly rejoiced in the subservient role. Their own fishery was of little account, but the Americans were welcomed to their shores for the goods they brought in exchange for the provision of bait and other services. This feeling was so dominant that in 1849 the island legislature petitioned the Queen to relax the operation of the Convention of 1818 and admit American vessels to the inshore fisheries. At Charlottetown the cry for reciprocity was taken up with vigour.

Yet there was no unanimity. At the time of the Halifax conference, feeling in New Brunswick ran so high that its government was willing to sacrifice almost anything in order to attain free entry to American markets. The public mind, according to a minute of council, would soon seek relief "by incorporation with the neighbouring republic" unless this purpose were realized. The province was entirely willing to give up its exclusive title to the inshore fisheries in return for reciprocal free trade and privileges for its coastal shipping, along with the withdrawal of the American bounties to fishermen.[2] But Nova Scotia was not nearly so desperate and a much larger proportion of her population drew its livelihood from the sea. She refused to move very far towards accepting a policy of abject surrender. In the legislature Johnston and the opposition were declaiming upon the historic heritage of the coastal waters. Altogether apart from more practical considerations, the government did not dare adopt the drastic expedient advocated by

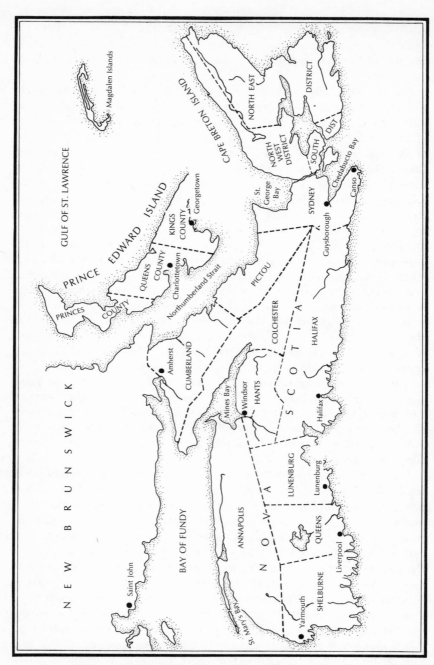

Nova Scotia and Prince Edward Island in 1851

New Brunswick. The Halifax conference could reach no specific conclusions. But its resolutions announced the necessity of maintaining the British connection and of closely co-operating with one another, something that was portentous for the future. All through New Brunswick associations were formed to consider new departures for provincial trade, one of which was to be the development of closer connections with Canada. They were ridiculed by Fenety's *Morning News* for refusing to consider another, annexation to the United States. Shame for the surrender of time-honoured monopoly and anger for Britain's adoption of free trade dominated political and commercial speculation in Saint John. Annexation was one of the topics of discussion in the mysterious Reform Club of Dr John Livingstone, whose meetings were attended only by the more daring and unorthodox.[3]

Having neglected the fishery all through their history, the Atlantic Provinces now set out to make it a worthwhile stake in bargaining with the Americans. An insistence rapidly developed that American vessels, according to the Convention of 1818 but contrary to all custom, should be excluded from the inshore area. There was a good legal justification for this course. On many occasions the British government had declared that the Bay of Fundy was a British sea and in 1844 had announced that the three-mile limit was a line drawn from headland to headland rather than one following the indentations of the coast. Provincial temper now demanded that these limitations should be rigidly enforced and the vessels of the Royal Navy at Halifax became an object of greater attention. Following her conversion to free trade, Britain, it was reasoned, owed her colonies a great deal. A part of the debt could be paid by protecting colonial rights in the fishery and forcing the Americans to yield a goodly price for their surrender. While axes lay idle in the forests and all other industry seemed in a state of paralysis, politicians orated upon the heritage of the sea. It seemed certain that the people would have to enter upon its hazards with more zest and enterprise, and might, in return for the new benefits of reciprocity, sell a portion of it to the Americans.

Stock-taking of ideas on the state of the colonies in the era of free trade was expedited by other ominous realizations. The Atlantic Provinces were closer to Europe than any other part of North America, admirably located to serve as a connecting link between the New and Old Worlds. But they contemplated uneasily the rapid development of the interior of the continent, for they were enjoying little part of it. To the north the St Lawrence River had become a great avenue for international commerce. To the south the port of New York was engrossing the ocean-borne commerce of the United States and much of British America as well. By these great sea-lanes the quickly unfolding interior was being supplied with European goods. Halifax and Saint John were by-passed. Immigration dwindled to a trickle. Almost everywhere else immense progress was manifest and the great cities of the eastern United States were being linked by railways. By the sheer onrush of the progress in communication elsewhere, the Atlantic Provinces were becoming isolated from the life of the continent.

Railways were the wonder of the age and it was to railway construction that Atlantic leaders looked for improvement in this rapidly deteriorating situation. For years men had seen visions but no important action had been taken. St Andrews had pioneered the grand idea of bringing the trade of Canada to the Atlantic in the winter season. But the energy of the capitalists of that town had been brought to no purpose by the unfavourable decision upon the disputed territory through which it was proposed to run a railway to Quebec, and by the failure of shareholders to honour their commitments.[4] In 1846 the legislatures of New Brunswick and Nova Scotia had petitioned the Queen for the construction of a railway along the line of the projected military highway between Halifax and Quebec, a route that for strategic reasons would run from the Nova Scotian capital over the Cobequid Hills and up the eastern and northern shores of New Brunswick. Since funds for a survey could not be raised from local resources, the British government had commissioned Major W. H. Robinson, a scion of the Loyalist family of Fredericton, to do the work. His report, published late in 1848, revealed no technical obstacles to construction and created a new flurry of speculation, a narrow gleam of hope amid the gloom of that year. Vociferously it was pointed out, again with special vigour in New Brunswick, that the cost of such a railway, optimistically estimated at £3,000,000, should be entirely absorbed by Great Britain as atonement for the predicament in which she had placed the colonies. The maintenance of British authority in the colonies, it was stridently asserted, depended on construction of "the Intercolonial."

Such an intercolonial railway, paid for by the mother country, became a popular and exciting idea. But support for the expenditure of local capital could be mobilized only for projects that were more immediate and less imperial. In March of 1848 Howe had successfully introduced to the Nova Scotian assembly a bill that pledged £330,000 to the construction of a railway between Halifax and Windsor, but it had been fiercely attacked as a modern manifestation of the capital's historic determination to draw off the trade of the Bay of Fundy outports. Local pride became schooled to advertise every small community that looked on the sea as the terminus of a great railway. In New Brunswick, Saint John could not, at this stage, quite muster sufficient strength in the legislature to attract provincial support for its local ambitions. The rage there was for railway communication with the Gulf of St Lawrence, for the distribution of the produce of the gulf fisheries and agricultural surpluses of Prince Edward Island, now becoming impressive, in the markets of the eastern United States to which Saint John was linked by steamship communication with Boston. The defeat of a bill to provide heavy financial support for a railway between Saint John and Shediac by the legislative council in 1849 saw Saint John's despair reach its lowest ebb. It gave inspiration to new schemes for political reform, especially for a legislative council that should be elective.[5]

The grand scheme for the linking together of British North America by rail communication rallied the declining pride of British patriotism. But the inevitable premise was that Britain should pay the cost of "imperial" projects. Colonial legislatures would contemplate the allocation of their own revenues only for construction sectional in character. The numerous projects studied were almost entirely oriented towards American markets in which such great faith was placed in 1849.

II

Railway construction, so optimistically regarded as the high road to prosperity, was henceforth persistently pursued as the great aim in life for New Brunswick and Nova Scotia. Speed was the preoccupation of the age and it seemed elementary that the great termini of North American railways should be located as far as possible to the eastward so that the slow and cumbersome transatlantic voyages to Europe should be reduced to a minimum. When Earl Grey's dispatch of June 1850 dispelled all hopes that the British government would pay for the Intercolonial, the two provinces entered upon a period of seven years in which, after a series of innumerable false starts and compromises, fragmentary results were achieved.

Immediately following Grey's refusal, pressures to bring the provinces into the economic orbit of the United States gained obvious strength. John Alfred Poor, a railway promoter of Bangor, Maine, whose ambition was to contest the southward movement of railway traffic to New York and to make Portland the great entrepôt for the trade of the northern United States and Canada, came forward with his project for the European and North American Railway. Running eastward from Bangor, it would traverse the populous parts of New Brunswick and Nova Scotia. The general reasoning was that Saint John and Halifax were a thousand miles closer to Europe than New York, and that they, as well as Portland, would share in the overseas transit of North America's produce. There were ancillary proposals for a railway running into Cape Breton that would be joined by train-ferry with still another running along the southern shore of Newfoundland. A great convention held at Portland on July 31 heralded this grand scheme with a blaze of pageantry and a profusion of oratory. Both governments sent delegations which gave enthusiastic support. Attempting to bring his native

Annapolis into the scheme, J. W. Johnston did not succeed in gaining support for the passage of the European and North American by train-ferry over the Bay of Fundy. This international concord seemed to promise a highly effective and more profitable substitute for the Intercolonial. For New Brunswick it was especially satisfactory since it accommodated itself to Saint John's requirement for a line to Shediac. Since the plan for the Intercolonial by-passed Saint John, its popularity at the outset had rested almost solely on the postulate that Britain would pay.

Rather regretfully the British government approved the Portland plan and it appeared that "the national scheme" of the Intercolonial had gone into the discard. Yet suddenly it came to renewed life when Howe went to London in November of 1850 and in the following March secured from Grey an offer to guarantee the interest charges on capital raised for an intercolonial line. This meant that money could be borrowed in London at 4½ per cent, a rate far lower than in any North American market, and gave a new lustre of practicality to the project. Ever since he had entered politics, Howe had found Nova Scotia too small for his aspirations; the role he had chosen was not merely intercolonial, but imperial, and he did not shrink from forcing the hand of Grey, who did not come to decisions easily.

Yet there was much missionary work to do on his own side of the Atlantic. Nova Scotia was by no means unanimous in agreeing to assume the financial obligation for another railway into Halifax. In New Brunswick the legislature, having pledged a great deal of credit to the European and North American, baulked at Grey's requirement that interest payments on the Intercolonial should be a first charge on the revenues. But in the northern counties, which had become railway-conscious, there was enthusiasm for the Intercolonial. In the summer when Howe visited Edward Barron Chandler at Fredericton, where he was able to overcome a prejudice that Nova Scotia was interfering in the affairs of the other provinces, he encountered the demand that the route of the Intercolonial should be shifted to the valley of the St John. It became clear, too, that Canada supported this position. Howe resisted but eventually concurred. New Brunswick became a willing partner in the venture when it seemed possible that "the great national scheme" could be harnessed to the southern and international projects that were so popular in Saint John, where it was glibly assumed that the British guarantee would include the New Brunswick section of the European and North American. Formal approval for the construction of the Intercolonial was given by the three governments at a conference in Toronto during July.

Very late in the same year the blow fell that brought to a conclusion the hopes for a quick execution of the scheme. On December 29 Grey wrote to say that Howe had misinterpreted the intentions of the British government, and that no guarantee could be given for a route that deviated so widely from Major Robinson's survey. The indispensable condition was that the Intercolonial should be as far as possible from the American frontier. In the Colonial Office it was taken for granted that the European and North American was an American railway. Howe had, indeed, given a new meaning to the consent he had won from Grey during the previous winter and there was, on his part, a curious reluctance to believe that the Colonial Secretary had meant exactly what he had said. On his side, Grey was guilty of a lack of precision that enabled the exuberant Nova Scotian to lead all British North America along a winding path that ended only in disillusionment. Howe's enemies made all they could of the fiasco and his reputation as a man of practical business, something he was not, was considerably deflated. Canadian sincerity came into question when Francis Hincks gave public expression to the widespread conviction among politicians of his province that the Intercolonial would never pay. Howe was strongly inclined to blame the entire failure on the sinister influence at the Colonial Office of John M. Jackson, a principal in the great firm of railway builders that was seeking North American contracts. From the outset Howe championed public construction and ownership, a point of principle that aroused many antagonists.

In the summer of 1852 an attempt to salvage the plan was made at a conference in Halifax. But Howe sullenly refused to build for thirty miles beyond the Nova Scotian border to the Bend of Petitcodiac, a feature of the original design. Still licking his wounds, he was too busy to go to England in the autumn with Hincks and Chandler, who were refused the guarantee for the greatly revised Intercolonial, just as downrightly by the British Tories as by the Liberals a year before. But by 1853 the prophets of doom had been completely confounded and the two provinces felt competent to finance their own projects. Prices for lumber had risen to twice those of 1849. As a result of the repeal of the Navigation Acts, foreign vessels appeared at Saint John but New Brunswick shipping throve as never before. Now capable of taking a more independent course, Chandler was able to pledge the credit of his province to the European and North American, and to enter upon a contract with the British contractor, Jackson, of the firm of Jackson, Peto, Betts and Jackson, for the construction of 214 miles of line. A few months later, with the Nova Scotian economy simmering to a peak level of production, Howe went to England and borrowed £1,000,000 for his lines from Halifax to Truro and Windsor.

Together the two provinces entered upon railway construction in 1853. Forced by pressure from Charles D. Archibald, the agent of Jackson in Nova Scotia, and his friends and clients within the Liberal party, as well as by the representatives of the outports in the legislature, Howe relinquished the great principle of public ownership to which he was passionately attached. Later, as the Crimean War increased the strain on credit, Jackson lost interest and public ownership became a necessity. Cheerfully Howe abandoned other governmental duties to preside over the Board of Railway Commissioners. The line to Truro was completed in 1857. Gradually it became apparent that it represented the maximum effort of which Nova Scotia was capable. According to the estimate of the able engineer James Laurie, construction was satisfactory but maintenance was ruinously expensive. Owing to Howe's long absences from the province, the railway became a gigantic fleshpot for political patronage. Gross receipts were pocketed by conductors and station agents. Much of its revenue came from "piggy-back" freights as vehicles of all descriptions were mounted on flat-cars for the quick run into Halifax.[6]

Public ownership was forced upon New Brunswick as well. Encountering a variety of unexpected difficulties, Jackson abandoned his contract in the spring of 1855. The capital in the European and North American Railway Company of Saint John was really fictitious. Warned by the unhappy experiences of American investors in railway shares, the public could not be persuaded to support the enterprise to which so much lip service was paid. Poor and the Bangor promoters, who had initiated the whole scheme at Portland, had done nothing towards building a railway to the New Brunswick border. Capital in Maine, too, was largely fictitious. Borrowing £800,000 from Baring Brothers, the government took up the stock and vigorously pressed on with the work of construction. The Bend of Petitcodiac became Moncton and a railway centre of consequence. Connection between Saint John and Shediac was finally completed in 1860. This, too, was a labour of exhaustion. New Brunswick had no financial resources to gratify the demands of the northern and eastern counties for railway construction which continued to rage unchecked although it was realized from the start that the Saint John-Shediac line could yield no profit. Taxed to pay for the southern lines, the north kept up a strong agitation for the Intercolonial. By 1857 the private promoters of the St Andrews-Quebec Railway, now more realistically designated the St Andrews-Woodstock, had constructed only thirty-four miles of line.

Publicly financed railways, which brought the provinces into the international money markets, impelled them to a greater degree of budgetary efficiency. While legislative committees controlled the details of appropriation and expenditure, it was difficult to inspire money-lenders with confidence in provincial credit. Pressures emanating from London slowly accounted for the reluctant abandonment of the ultra-democratic, loose, and disorderly procedures which had been inherited from the long-lost American colonies. For years colonial governors had expressed sharp disapproval of the under-the-table bargains by which assemblymen had traded favours and acquired patronage for their constituencies. To the more rigorously schooled of the colonials, politics had become a dirty game. Gingerly the Colonial Office had employed the slender methods at its disposal to work a change towards the British practice. In 1857 the government of New Brunswick, by resolution of the House of Assembly, acquired the initiative in financial appropriation. Nova Scotia followed suit in 1860. Now the two governments had finally acquired the strength necessary to initiative in all phases of administration.[7] The British government had forced the same change upon Canada on the occasion of the Union in 1840 and upon Newfoundland in 1842.

III

The movement to achieve reciprocity continued, but with more measured tread. To demonstrate their eagerness several of the colonies, in 1849 and 1850, passed acts to provide for free trade in natural products with the United States that were to go into effect as soon as the Americans returned the favour. But as trade revived in 1850 and as new levels of prosperity were attained in 1852, the urge to gain reciprocity lost its edge and the colonies were in a humour to bargain more sharply. In New Brunswick, where the urge had been by far the greatest, the experts, who had forecast complete expulsion of its timber from the British market, were confounded by the sale of quantities greater than ever before on the Clyde and Mersey. In 1853 producers were able to dictate to merchants the prices they would accept for their wares. Cash, rather than truck, was offered as payment, a novelty that suggested the coming of a new era. In Newfoundland the feeling was one of complacency. A good fishery in 1849 left the colony untouched by the maladies that were so general elsewhere. But the prospect of acquiring free entrance for fish to the American market, the most appealing feature of a proposed pact for reciprocal trade, awakened the interest of the Liberal party in the legislature so that the cry for reciprocity took second place only to that for responsible government. While Frenchmen and Americans enjoyed treaty rights on their coasts, Newfoundlanders were not disposed to haggle over additional privileges for the Americans in the inshore fisheries.

Earl Grey regarded a reciprocity agreement with the United States as absolutely necessary to halt annexationist movements in Canada. He was therefore willing to surrender the inshore fisheries as an element of little account. The Conservative government of Lord Derby, responding more warmly to the plea of the Atlantic Provinces, was resolved to make of them a prize for which the Americans would be willing to pay a great deal.

Following a truculent demand of the Nova Scotian legislature for greater naval protection, Sir John Pakington, the Colonial Secretary, announced in May of 1852 the dispatch to Halifax of a fleet of small vessels of war. Though Nova Scotia had provided the chief inspiration for his decision, all of the colonies joined in the game of forcing Britain to take action. During the summer there were six seizures of American schooners, all poaching within the three-mile limit. To protect their nationals the Americans, in considerable exasperation, sent their own warships into the Bay of Fundy and Gulf of St Lawrence. But this gentle exertion of force by Britain had an impact on American opinion and the British government had made its point. The Americans were summarily reminded of the importance of the Convention of 1818. Owing to the good sense of the local British and American naval commanders, no unpleasantness resulted. The British were happy to force the issue as easily as possible, for the results they wanted were merely diplomatic. At the same time the Americans were given firmly to understand that the inshore fisheries could not be made the subject of a separate negotiation, that they would have to be included in a general agreement comprehending the lowering of their own tariffs.

Following the presidential election of 1852 the situation at Washington became greatly simplified, and reciprocity became an issue to which all American politicians were willing to give close attention. Before it could acquire any prospect of success, the Northerners had to be persuaded that closer trade relations with British North America would herald political union, the Southerners that a new prosperity in the provinces would render annexation unlikely. In 1853 detailed items for a proposed treaty came under general discussion, and Pennsylvania and Maryland opposed the placing of Nova Scotian coal on any list of free items. Convinced of the necessity of securing the inshore fisheries, the American government in September sent Israel D. Andrews to Halifax and Saint John for the purpose of allaying opposition in the legislatures of the two provinces. To create good will he made payments totalling $20,000 in strategic quarters. But the United States would not consider as feasible the most specific requirement of Nova Scotia and New Brunswick, the admission of their vessels to American registry and to participation in the American coastal trade. Rather than do this, Washington would abandon negotiations.[8]

At precisely the right moment Lord Elgin went to Washington in the summer of 1854 to find the Americans in highly receptive humour. Edward Barron Chandler accompanied Francis Hincks of Canada, not as a participating delegate but as a purveyor of information to the Governor General. Owing to an error in imperial protocol, Nova Scotia was not represented; and in the legislature Howe and Johnston joined in a common protest against "high-handedness." As Elgin beguiled the Americans into granting the principal objects he sought, the views of the Atlantic Provinces fell into second place. Reciprocity in natural products gave Canada everything she wanted. The placing of coal on the free list went a long way towards disarming opposition in Nova Scotia. But the shipping privileges, especially sought by New Brunswick, were conspicuously omitted. Free fish in American markets opened vistas of greater prosperity for Newfoundland and Prince Edward Island. For the Americans it was the inshore fisheries of the Atlantic Provinces that made the treaty of 1854 seem an attractive bargain. Canada had no such asset but she emerged from the negotiations with benefits equal to or greater than those of the seaward provinces which she now dwarfed. Fearing complications with France by allowing the Americans wider fishing privileges off Newfoundland, the British government insisted on an escape clause providing for the operation of the treaty with or without the inclusion of that province, but the expected difficulties did not develop. Rather too happily, Britain and France became partners in other and distant ventures in the Crimea, in 1854.

With careful regard to the susceptibilities of communities that only recently had become self-governing, Britain provided that the Reciprocity Treaty should have no effect until it should be approved in each legislature. Early in November it was quickly ratified in all except Nova Scotia, where great opposition developed, mostly owing to the alleged slight to the province in the negotiations at Washington. But William Young, brushing aside all complaints, insisted that rejection would be "a suicidal policy" and secured, on December 12, a majority of thirty-four to twelve. Those most strongly opposed were influenced towards moderation by the argument that adequate protection of the inshore fisheries, a responsibility Britain would thrust upon the province, would be difficult, expensive, and perhaps impossible.

Though it merely amplified an already high level of prosperity, the Reciprocity Treaty quickly gained popularity in all the colonies following its implementation in 1855. Year by year trade with the United States showed substantial increases, Prince Edward Island producing perhaps the greatest proportional increase of all. In record volume New Brunswick's lumber and Newfoundland's fish moved to American markets. Nova Scotia's coal found ready sale in Boston, but the export of agricultural produce from all provinces was less than might be supposed.[9] Flour in great quantities from the United States moved into the Atlantic area, much of it Canadian that was re-exported. Yet this great growth in the volume of commerce to the south did not have any important adverse effect upon the large traffic with Britain. Only in the case of New Brunswick would the figures indicate – and not very significantly – that trade moved from one orbit to another.[10]

Free trade, reciprocity, and a revival of the ancient faith in the calling of the sea created a material prosperity that was to pass as the Golden Age of the Atlantic Provinces. Political self-government was crowned by what appeared to be economic fulfilment. But the new commercial pull to the southward exercised, for a great proportion of the population, a fascination that had political overtones, and caused moralists to ruminate upon the chances of halting what appeared to be a continuous gravitation to the United States. Many years later a Father of Confederation recorded his opinion that the great movement inaugurated in 1864 was made necessary by the onset of American feeling in the Atlantic Provinces, that, during the era of reciprocity, Yankee business men exercised such a predominance in the fishing communities that annexation seemed certain to come. Each season hundreds of American vessels called at the ports of the Gut of Canso and Prince Edward Island, purchasing bait and supplies, conducting immense business with local merchants, some of whom were Americans too. They took on crews and paid high wages to local populations which seldom saw cash. "Our people were annexationist. . . ."[11]

To the outside world the Atlantic Provinces, during this era of halcyon growth, were best known for the quality of their great sailing ships which became increasingly familiar along the new trading lanes of the world to Australia and California. Ever since the War of 1812, ship construction had been an important ancillary industry, but for many years the reputation had been for vessels of low tonnage that plied the coastal waters of the United Kingdom and the eastern seaboard of North America. Almost invariably the finished product had been of cheap quality and short life. But as skills multiplied and capital increased it became possible to compete with the great builders of Britain and the United States. Saint John acquired an early pre-eminence in the new venture of constructing ships for trans-ocean routes. In 1837 William and Richard Wright commenced their career by constructing a small sealer for the Newfoundland fishery in their little shipyard at the head of Courtenay Bay. By 1855 they could build the Morning Light, 264 feet in length and of 2,377 tons, a vessel that for twenty years held the title of being the largest ever constructed in British North America.[12] By her fast return run from Britain to Australia, the Marco Polo in 1851 acquired the reputation for being the fastest sailer in the world. After 1848 the number of ocean-going vessels annually produced in Saint John alone approached one hundred, and in every little port of New Brunswick, Nova Scotia, and Prince Edward Island, ship-building was a normal feature of life. In the construction of great vessels during the fifties, Nova Scotia was far behind New Brunswick, but in the United States a Nova Scotian, Donald MacKay of Jordan River in Shelburne County, had become famous as the most skilful designer and builder of the great clippers that still essayed to challenge the unsure supremacy of steamers.

Saint John had a highly skilled labour force and the vast forests of New Brunswick to draw upon for a great variety of woods in what seemed illimitable quantity. Many vessels constructed in other ports of the Bay of Fundy were sent there for finish and rigging. Vessels of the first class were built of black birch for the keel, flooring, and lower planking, of larch for the knees and upper planking. White pine was employed for the cabins, interior finishing, and masts; black spruce for yards and topmasts. For cheaper and smaller vessels, elm, larch, cedar, and spruce were readily available.[13] After forty years of growth the ship-building industry of the Atlantic Provinces was world renowned. Visiting Scotland in 1854, Joseph Howe could boast that the shipping of British North America was in total tonnage only slightly less than that of the great proprietors of the Clyde and all the rivers of that country. In addition to the vessels that remained under the ownership of provincial merchants, there were the ships that were exported. One estimate of the average annual income from this source for Nova Scotia, New Brunswick, and Prince Edward Island is $400,000.[14]

IV

While the land question was temporarily thrust to the background, the winning of responsible government had come to the centre of the stage in Prince Edward Island. Earl Grey's scruples concerning the dangers of extending the full operation of the British Constitution to small societies were particularly relevant, but Islanders professed to be unaware of smallness and insisted on full equality with the mainland colonies. George Coles dominated the new general assembly convened in 1850 by the new Lieutenant-Governor, Sir Donald Campbell. Idealistic and hard-working, he felt that government should be reformed before education could be brought to the people, that an administration organized on the responsible principle could be the instrument of securing free land for all. Under his leadership the reform party refused supply. The disruption of the public services that followed convinced Grey there was no wisdom in resisting the demand – even from a small society. Sir Alexander Bannerman, who succeeded Campbell in 1851, arrived with instructions to put responsible government into effect and Coles became the first leader of an administration under the new and enlightened dispensation. The change was emphasized by the fact that, for the first time in provincial history, Charlottetown did not possess an overwhelming majority of members in the executive council. At the same time Prince Edward Island made itself financially independent of the British parliament by accepting the total charges for its civil list.

Making self-government work was more difficult than asking for it. In Prince Edward Island, as in the larger colonies, politicians could not easily adjust themselves to the discipline of a cabinet and in 1853 the Coles administration was broken up by a wretched quarrel about salaries. Liberal idealism and enthusiasm for the lot of the common man were casualties in the election that followed. John M. Holl and Edward Palmer, taking advantage of a host of parochial jealousies within the government, led a reorganized Conservative party to power. These erstwhile defenders of "the old system," allegedly the props of the Family Compact, followed the example of the Nova Scotian Conservatives by reviving the historic argument that salaried officers should not be members of the House of Assembly, that members of the executive council should perform their labours without financial remuneration. When they quarrelled with the legislative council, they again followed the lead of their prototypes in Nova Scotia by advocating that it should be made an elective body. Many of the men who early in life had been so well schooled to look to London for preference now became the leaders of a movement that promulgated American and ultra-democratic ideas which were opposed to the whole theory and practice of the British Constitution.

Sir Alexander Bannerman acquired a whole-hearted dislike for these unconservative proclivities of the Conservatives and inserted his own influence with telling effect. Against the advice of the Holl-Palmer administration he dissolved the House of Assembly in 1854. His justification for doing so was that a new franchise act, passed several years before during the Liberal regime, had finally received the approval of the British government and that under its terms the people should be given an opportunity to review the conduct of their representatives. Almost universal manhood suffrage gave the Liberals an easy victory in the election that followed. Coles returned to office. To make the colony more British, Sir Alexander Bannerman, having acquired the permission of the Colonial Office, resorted to an employment of his legal authority that was, under the new system of responsible government, very un-British.[15] Palmer and the Conservatives were unrepentant. They would win again on the cry of making salaried officers the servants rather than the masters of the House of Assembly and on the urge to make the legislative council elective.[16]

Even more notably than in the adjacent provinces, politicians were sensitive to public clamours and it was hard to hold a government together. Pursuing his zeal for improvement, Coles was nagged and bullied by the Sons of Temperance, who demanded prohibitory legislation for the sale of alcoholic beverages as "the Maine Law" appeared to take the consciences of evangelical Protestants by storm. During the fifties the Conservatives became more distinctively a Protestant party and echoed a rising demand for compulsory Bible reading in the schools. Catholics were satisfied with the existing feature of the education act which permitted a wide degree of local latitude. But in 1856, when a fervent Protestant principal of the new Normal School announced that the Protestant version of the Bible was to be read "with illustrations and picturing out," Catholics felt compelled to spring to their own defence. Coles supported their position, holding that in a mixed society compulsory Bible reading was impossible. He was accordingly charged with attempting to outlaw the Bible. His decision upon this question, which had been an open one since 1845, produced a great sensation throughout all the provinces, adding spark to a Protestant determination to impose religious teaching, fortifying the belief of Catholics that they should have a school system of their own, and establishing in the more dispassionate minority of the population the conviction that a system of public schools should be free of denominational influences. As the Conservatives fanned the flames of Protestant fury "the Bible question" finally brought Coles down.[17] A reform program was not enough to keep a government in power – and in Prince Edward Island it was a labour of endurance to keep a cabinet in agreement or a political party together. "Governments were either unsteady coalitions or strongholds for denominational crusaders."[18]

V

With still more reluctance the British government was to grant responsible government to Newfoundland. At St John's the return to the former mode of constitutional representative government slowly rekindled old animosities as political parties on substantially the same lines as in the 1830's experienced revival. The allocation of £14,000 for the reconstruction of the Anglican Cathedral, from funds mostly raised in England, aroused the ire of Catholics. The Assembly quarrelled over plans for enlarging the scheme of representation, Catholics insisting on doubling the members for existing constituencies, Protestants, who felt that they were inadequately represented, demanding the creation of new ones. Denominationalism flared up as St John's Academy was trisected to meet the objections that religious instruction was absent. The tractarian faction of the Church of England forced separate grants of public money to finance still more Anglican schools. Moralists were not at a loss for evidence to sustain the argument of Earl Grey that there was not sufficient wealth and independence of mind to produce a genuine public spirit.

Thoroughly wedded to the great aim of winning responsible government as the instrument for acquiring the pre-eminence they believed their due, the Catholic party acquired fresh impetus from new personalities. William Carson, their Protestant leader, was aged and enfeebled. Secure in the office of Collector of Customs, John Kent could be only half-hearted in lending his influence to the movement. Patrick Morris, the youthful tribune of the 1830's, had died, leaving in the office of the Treasurer defalcations amounting to £6,000.[19] According to Protestant accounts the new bishop, Rt. Rev. John Thomas Mullock, was responsible for the new and fiery animus that developed. Allegedly it was his influence that brought about the victory of Philip F. Little in a by-election in St John's in 1850 over a Protestant Liberal by a majority of four hundred votes. Little was a purposeful, businesslike lawyer of Prince Edward Island antecedents who had resided in the colony only six years, but he quickly rose to the leadership of the responsible government party in the Assembly.

In 1851 an address to the Queen from the Assembly requesting the grant of responsible government brought the familiar objections of Earl Grey but added another, the inability of Newfoundland to pay for the garrison of St John's, which was maintained primarily to keep peace amongst the local population. When this dispatch was sent to the Assembly on February 4, 1852, a fierce debate resulted. Transcending the example of his predecessor, Bishop Fleming, Bishop Mullock violently and openly stormed into politics and wrote a long letter to Little that was published and republished. He declaimed upon "ignorance" and "irresponsibility" in Downing Street, the general tone of his letter probably surpassing anything that had been produced in the whole story of reform in British North America. "I never knew any settled government so bad, so weak and so vile as that of our unfortunate country."[20] But the Commercial Society and the Law Society passed resolutions deploring the request for responsible government. Sir Gaspard Le Marchant scolded the Assembly for the violence of its views and was blown up in effigy, in full regalia. Not surprisingly he advocated the abolition of representative government. Sir John Pakington, the Tory Colonial Secretary, supported the views of Earl Grey. He asked the obvious question : Why should not the Protestant majority of Newfoundland organize itself to resist what was beginning to be called the establishment of a Catholic despotism?

With their central committee at St John's organizing subcommittees in the outports, the Liberals were far in front for the election of 1852. Under Hugh Hoyles the Conservatives, now forced to adopt the techniques of party organization, could merely deprecate the effrontery of their opponents and offered nothing positive. The Liberals, strongly supporting the move for reciprocity, which many Conservatives, fearful of Yankee wages and the circulation of cash in Newfoundland, opposed, adopted the slogan of "free trade" and presented vistas of future prosperity. They won nine of fifteen seats in the Assembly and the Colonial Office now had clear proof of popular support for responsible government. A delegation to London in 1853, aided by Joseph Hume, the aging radical who was still a champion of reform in the colonies, gained confidence from an interview with the Duke of Newcastle. Yet a new Lieutenant-Governor, Ker Baillie Hamilton, advised against granting the desired reform. Hoyles and the Conservatives continued to allege that the whole question of responsible government was really one of religion, that the change was advocated by a "Church-directed" party.[21] Still they relied on resistance of the Colonial Office rather than on efforts of their own.

But the British Liberals had no stamina for opposing an appeal that echoed the catchwords of their own constitutionalism and the political terminology of Durham to whom they now paid general respect. By January of 1854 Newcastle decided that responsible government could no longer be denied to Newfoundland. His dispatch of February 21 fixed three conditions for its implementation : the doubling of representation in the Assembly by the division of the larger constituencies, putting a stop to paying for private election expenses out of the public funds, and the provision of the now traditional guarantee of pensions for displaced officials. At the first two of these the Liberal majority in the Assembly baulked violently. On a bill for the fixing of representation, a long battle was fought with the legislative council, where Protestant fervour demanded a Protestant majority in the new assembly. Ultimately the council yielded on some details and the bill provided for an assembly of fifteen Protestants and fourteen Catholics that would properly reflect the three thousand Protestant majority in the colony. Fighting a strong rearguard action, Hamilton refused to call a general election until June of 1855, and delayed the formal introduction of responsible government, making good use of the time by attempting to fill up the new legislative council with Conservative nominees. But the Colonial Office, convinced that he was not the proper man to inaugurate the new system, dispatched him to Antigua.

In the contest that followed the religious pattern generally prevailed except in Burin where the Wesleyans gave their support to two Catholic Liberals. The Conservatives were unable to make advantage from the redistribution that had been made in their favour and the Liberals won eighteen seats in a house of twenty-nine. Little and his followers displayed an unconstitutional eagerness to enter office but the new Lieutenant-Governor, Sir Charles Darling, insisted on patience. At the appropriate time the pugnacious and astute lawyer became Newfoundland's first premier under responsible government, with a cabinet of four Catholics and two Protestants representing Catholic constituencies. To avoid discord, Darling appointed a majority of Liberals to the new legislative council.

There followed two years of comparative tranquillity in which traditional party lines began to disappear. With eyes upon the census returns of 1857 which showed an increasing Protestant majority, Little and his friends realized that they could not long remain in power without larger Protestant support and openly began to seek it. There were important Catholic defections from the Liberals and even Bishop Mullock was eventually to lose patience with the party he had so strenuously championed in earlier years.[22] Still greater tranquillity came with the prosperity that followed the Reciprocity Treaty. The year 1856 showed the greatest volume of imports and exports in history. Newfoundland's government was strong enough to risk its popularity by raising an ample revenue from an *ad valorem* tax on imported manufactured articles and foodstuffs.

During these years responsible government flexed its muscles and reached into a new area. Cultivating its good relations with the French Empire of Napoleon III, Britain was moving swiftly towards a settlement of the problem. of the French Shore upon which negotiations had been almost continuously proceeding since 1844. The French had had things very much their own way, pressing dangerously close towards winning a British acceptance of the doctrine of an exclusive fishery on the treaty coast. Their naval officers and fishing-admirals had imposed their authority on British settlers of the western harbours, now numbering three thousand, who had been reduced to a position inferior to that of the French fishermen, owing to the much more negligent and lackadaisical attitude of Whitehall. The promise of "not to molest," given in 1783, was being translated to mean French sovereignty over Newfoundland's territorial waters. On the few occasions when Britain took a strong diplomatic stand nothing was done to restrain local French naval commanders or to halt French poaching in waters where the treaty had no effect. French claims were now so far-reaching that, if accepted, they would deny to Newfoundlanders the right to colonize the western coastline which was beginning to be recognized as the best agricultural land in the colony. When the islanders complained of the failure of the British government to protect the rights of colonial fishermen they received the retort that the Newfoundland government should pay for the cost of additional naval patrols.

France placed great importance on the remainder of her authority in North America. In 1851 she had enlarged the bounties paid to her fishermen so that their competition with Newfoundlanders for the southern European market had become still more strenuous. St Pierre was prosperous and had established a kind of sphere of influence on the southern coast of Newfoundland where the sale of bait was a main source of livelihood to the inhabitants. Determined to legalize the French position on the treaty shore, the British government in 1856 asked Sir Charles Darling for a confidential report on the nature and extent of French legal rights. The Lieutenant-Governor gave the opinion that there was no true concurrent fishery, that ever since 1783 the French had possessed what amounted to exclusive privilege. Armed with this downright conclusion, the British government signed a convention with France in January, 1857. It secured a concurrent fishery on the western shore, except from Cape Norman to the Bay of Islands, where French right was to be exclusive, but surrendered rights to fish along the eastern littoral from Cape Norman to Cape St John. In select areas the coastal strip provided for the use of the French alone extended to the depth of one-third of a mile inland, from Bonne Bay to Cape St John to a full half-mile. Stated more simply, the convention granted to France effective ownership of the waters surrounding the northern arm of Newfoundland. It deprived the colony of effective sovereignty over great stretches of the coastline and made inoperative many acts of its legislature. Still further privileges were given to French fishermen on Labrador.[23]

Rt. Hon. Henry Labouchere, the Colonial Secretary, was well aware of the reaction that would ensue at St John's. He had taken "a chance" that the convention would be acceptable both to France and to the colony, a chance that had no hope of fulfilment so far as the latter was concerned. Indulging in the rather absurd idea that Newfoundlanders would gladly accept increased participation by the French in the fishery just as they had welcomed the Americans in 1854, he had judiciously inserted into the convention "an express stipulation" that it should take no effect until ratified by the colonial legislature. When word came from St John's of a downright refusal, of the Union Jack flying "Union down" on the Colonial Building, of the Stars and Stripes in public display, he gracefully and apologetically retreated. His dispatch in explanation, promising that "the consent of the community of Newfoundland" would be an essential preliminary to any future attempt of the British government to modify maritime and territorial rights of the colony, was hailed as a charter of liberties.

The position of the lieutenant-governor as an officer of the Crown was now embarrassing. The difficulties of the government of Newfoundland in attempting to accommodate itself to the requirements of British foreign policy and at the same time to gratify the proponents of the fishery came clearly into relief. The affair gave spur to the incipient nationalism of Newfoundland. Where the treaty rights of foreign states intruded so deeply upon the life of a colony, the assumption of Lord Durham that colonial government could be divided into two categories, internal and external, could not be applied so precisely as in the other colonies of British North America. The line between these two categories was indistinct and blurred as self-government and imperial obligations came into conflict in 1857.

VI

During the prosperous era of wood, wind, and water, Nova Scotia and New Brunswick, too, showed increasing tendencies to expand their areas of self-government. In the crisis of 1849 colonial opinion had been impelled to contemplate a career of commercial independence. Commercial independence produced an urge for greater freedom from the leading-strings of the British Foreign Office in matters of diplomacy, especially in dealings with the government at Washington where, it was commonly asserted, colonial aspirations were throttled by British protocol. This feeling became more pronounced as percentages of the native-born rose rapidly in all the provinces. By the early 1850's there was no longer important immigration from the British Isles. At the end of the decade 89 per cent of Nova Scotians were natives. Twenty years earlier in New Brunswick immigrants had considerably exceeded the number of natives, but by 1857 the latter had a considerable majority. Lieutenant-Governor Bannerman of Prince Edward Island reported in 1853 that in no colony was there a greater disposition to develop friendly relations with the United States.[24] It was fashionable and politically profitable to assume that the provinces were competent to deal with all aspects of public affairs. The more brash politicians harangued rural audiences upon the dangerous influence of alien governors from across the water, especially upon the unnecessary luxuries of gold braid and cocked hats, of frills and foibles that told heavily upon the public purse. British consent to provincial ratification of the Reciprocity Treaty gave strength to the conviction that the colonies had finally come of age; Joseph Howe enhanced the feeling of self-esteem by promulgating his "seminal ideas" of provincial representation in the Parliament at Westminster.[25]

Responsible government was in effect but in both provinces the loyal opposition was quite unprepared to admit that the constitutional problem had really been solved. In Nova Scotia the Tories deplored the strengthening of the executive council, viewing with great dismay the concentration of power in the hands of a few party leaders who had made a cipher of the lieutenant-governor and were masters of the House of Assembly. To produce a check on their authority, Johnston advocated an elective legislative council. Attempting to defeat the Liberals at their own game, the Tories were now the party of ultra-democracy. In New Brunswick the Liberal opposition, little more than a shell, whose leader was William J. Ritchie, refused to believe that responsible government was in effect while the men who had so long opposed it held office. It was not difficult to find imperfections. In the development of party discipline New Brunswick lagged behind Nova Scotia. Assemblymen continued to be mindful of their independence

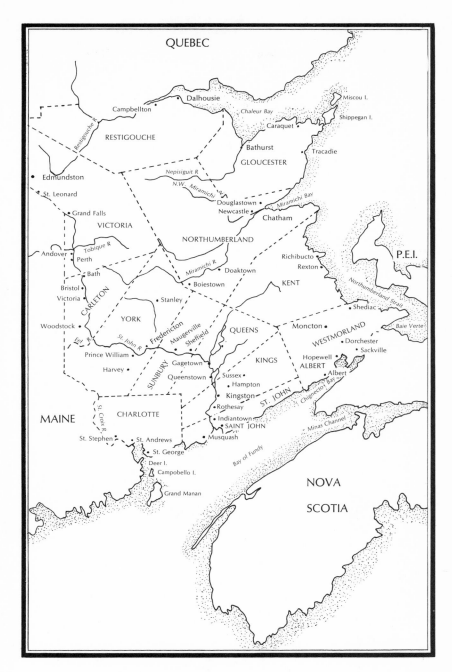

New Brunswick 1857

and the government followed, rather than attempted to control, the capricious swayings of opinion that made all legislative action uncertain. Even the members of the government refused to sacrifice the luxury of individual opinion in order to put the principle of cabinet solidarity into practice. Late in 1851, when Sir Edmund Head asked for a nomination for a new chief justice, he could extract no opinion from the members of the executive council as a body. Finally he made a nomination of his own and responsible government lost by default.[26] On this occasion Lemuel Allan Wilmot left politics for a vacant judgeship and Charles Fisher, holding high the banner of principle, resigned from the executive council and joined the Liberals, whom he had deserted in 1848, in opposition.

Fisher had his revenge in 1854 when he gathered together the fresh and green "loose fish" who had been elected to the House of Assembly to turn "the Compact" out of office. He formed what was now called, reverently and even pontifically, the Liberal Party. It was composed largely of a great number of new and young men whose principal ambition was to supplant the representatives of the older and wealthier families who had ruled for so long and who never again would be able to reform their ranks to gain an abiding hold on public support. The change of 1854 had some of the implications of a social revolution. Politics in New Brunswick became less gentlemanly and more robust, for members of Fisher's government did not pride themselves on ancestral memories and the graces of formal education. Party nomenclature remained somewhat alien, but Fisher's vociferous and half-rebellious following became known during the prohibition election of 1856 as the "Smashers," a designation applied in retaliation for the title "Rummies" which they conferred upon their opponents. Their spirit of reform was characterized by what seemed to be an irreverent and violent determination to destroy the time-honoured beliefs and vested interests of the province.

Though there were numerous advocates of the "Maine Law" in all four provinces, it was New Brunswick alone that succumbed to its dubious charms. Largely owing to the prestige in the legislature of Samuel Leonard Tilley and of the serried forces of the Sons of Temperance who were at his command, two unfortunate experiments in "prohibition" were made in 1852 and 1856. The question complicated the whole pattern of politics for two years, but after the chaos the Smashers emerged stronger than before.

Amid the prosperity of the era of reciprocity there was little relevance for schemes of political reform and the Liberal administrations of the two provinces were content to rest on the reputations earlier won for advocating the ideas of progress. Both William Young, who succeeded Uniacke as titular leader of the Nova Scotian Liberals in 1854, and Fisher in New Brunswick, resisted a franchise based on universal manhood suffrage. Johnston and the Nova Scotian Conservatives were its fervent supporters and, beneath their strong pressure, the government enacted it in 1854.[27] Fisher put into operation a ballot act, an innovation that was, however, too daring and novel for Nova Scotia to attempt.[28] Provincial finances were completely compromised by railway legislation and there was a powerful aversion to new taxation for any other purpose. Little progress was made in legislation for the public schools. Though all paid lip-service to education and some progress was made in establishing central agencies of supervision and inspection, compulsory local assessment for schools meant electoral defeat for any politician who was prepared to press for it to the point of action. Nor, in this era when reform was in great fashion, was democracy at the local level allowed opportunity to flower. New Brunswick passed legislation in 1851 to permit counties to become incorporated as municipalities, but nowhere did local improvement come from locally raised funds. Nova Scotia passed similar legislation several years later, but the great privilege of municipal incorporation generally fell into disuse.[29] Yarmouth and Moncton bravely became municipalities, but soon petitioned for the withdrawal of their charters. At Fredericton, where civic status was conferred in 1848 by Queen Victoria consequent to the creation of an episcopal see, the charter was received without enthusiasm.

All the energy of local democracies remained channelled through the multifold activities of the assemblyman. The money he acquired for local improvement was raised by the supposedly painless method of imposing customs duties. In both provinces a powerful vested interest, emanating from the provincial assembly, was opposed to the surrender of public functions and private patronage to municipal corporations. Keeping county and parish business within the assembly amplified the authority of the assemblyman. His ability to influence the nomination of magistrates to commissions of the peace and of all local officials made him the sole political factor of consequence for the area he served. Unlike Canadians, New Brunswickers and Nova Scotians were dependent for everything concerning the public welfare upon the provincial government. Visitors frequently commented upon the absence of the spirit of self-help in the small towns and rural districts of the two provinces, perhaps one of the principal reasons why Canadians and Americans held Nova Scotians "in contempt."[30] Great ships filled the harbours and Bluenose sailors were known around the world, but inland from tidewater the spectacle was considerably less imposing. The edifices that caused admiration, the gubernatorial mansions and province halls, were all monuments to the era of non-responsible colonial government. Uncontrolled, locust-like timber-cutting had destroyed the natural beauty of the forests. The low-lying mercantile establishments and ochre-painted houses of Halifax and Saint John imparted to casual travellers the suggestion of decay and unprogressiveness. Charlottetown, at most seasons of the year, was a morass, somewhat redeemed by the Colonial Building completed in 1847, that stood up "like a monument to Patience in stone," waiting for better things to come.[31]

Reformers prided themselves upon a capacity to sweep away the last vestiges of control from the Colonial Office. During the years of depression, from 1848 to 1850, there were attacks upon the civil list agreements with the British government which guaranteed to office-holders salaries that seemed inordinately high. Capitulating to the popularity of slogans for economy, the assemblies tried hard to effect modifications of the terms of the agreements that would bring public functionaries more closely under their own control. The independence of the judges of the supreme courts, who were protected by the agreements, became an important issue of principle. At election time plain men of the people spoke from the texts of equalitarianism, complimenting the electors on the freedoms that had already been won but reminding them of the shackles by which they were still bound to an apathetic or ignorant colonial secretary in London. The conduct of the lieutenant-governor and what remained of his prerogative became objects of suspicion and jealousy. In his last days at Halifax Sir John Harvey had permitted his advisers to scan all his communications, even his private correspondence, with London.[32] Sir Gaspard Le Marchant refused equal liberties; and the question of whether or not the lieutenant-governor was subject to the strictures of his advisers to the same degree as was the Sovereign in Britain became a large talking-point at the highest level of constitutional discussion. Howe and the Liberals laboured the point in Nova Scotia. Fisher took it up with aplomb in New Brunswick and persistently harried the Lieutenant-Governor, J. H. T. Manners-Sutton. Between these two a bitter feud lasted for seven years.

While Nova Scotia and New Brunswick were in no humour for self-examination and the Liberals could see no reason for altering the favourable terms on which their ascendancy rested, political experimentation was dilettante and unnecessary. When Howe returned from London in 1851 he discovered that some of his supporters, influenced by the democratic views of Johnston, favoured an elective legislative council. This reform enjoyed support from both parties in both provinces, but no administration ever summoned the energy and conviction to pass it into law. Not even that of Johnston, its most persistent advocate, did so when he came to power in 1857. It was difficult enough for a government to manage one popular assembly. Once in office, politicians shrank from the prospect of a second house armed by a direct mandate from the people which could oppose their authority and obstruct their plans.[33] The British government, though regretfully, was willing to concur in making second chambers elective.

But these senates of elderly and usually wealthy politicians remained assemblies of members who were appointed, though as time passed by they became more representative of religious denominations, commercial interests, and particular segments of the provinces.

Of reform there was little, but the great nineteenth century change in political habits of thought was expedited by the coming of responsible government. Electors sent to the legislatures men who might be described as mirrors of themselves, or of what they themselves wanted to be, merchants and tradesmen who had risen to places of affluence and respect in small communities. It is probably a fair judgement that Nova Scotia observed the proprieties of a former age to a much greater extent than did New Brunswick. That eminent editor of Halifax, Peter S. Hamilton, who visited Toronto in 1855, found the speeches in the Canadian Parliament much less prosy and soporific than those of his own assembly. In two or three hours of Canadian debate there were more violent personal attacks and insulting allusions than in an entire session at home. Every member of the Nova Scotian house, he observed, regarded himself as a Cicero who enjoyed the right to harangue his fellow-members by the hour.[34]

Hamilton might have found something more than a prototype for Canada's Parliament in nearby Fredericton, where the vocabulary of the backwoods often found parliamentary expression, where horseplay relieved the routine of legislation, and where debate was coarse-grained and abusive. While Halifax prided itself upon a tradition of Athenian eloquence, New Brunswick's Smashers were men who, representing a new dispensation, scorned tradition and the political models and mannerisms of earlier days. Strong enough to ignore the weak opposition led by John Hamilton Gray, they lustily quarrelled with one another. Fisher could not control harsh-spoken men like Albert J. Smith, James Steadman, John Mercer Johnson, "Stubtail" Charles Connell, and his leadership was constantly in jeopardy.[35] Tilley was the only member of the administration with whom Manners-Sutton felt he could deal as one gentleman to another. Halifax had a wig for the Speaker, but there was none in Fredericton. Halifax rejoiced in the erudite literary works of a host of men of whom Thomas Chandler Haliburton was probably the most conspicuous example. The Fredericton society that later produced Bliss Carman and Charles G. D. Roberts in the shadows of the Anglican cathedral was politically unimportant.

Nova Scotia may have better observed the forms of continuing tradition, but her politics were as democratic as those of her neighbour. Following the Liberal victory of 1848 a great change in the magistracies of all the counties took place. To their indignation the Conservatives, in the election of 1851, found that the official lists of qualified voters were subject to the scrutiny of Liberal party stalwarts recently raised to judicial seats. Howe did his best to halt the introduction of the spoils system but "the interests of the party" prevailed. By 1856 the degree to which party patronage dictated public appointments was still a novelty that was shocking. Sheriffs, road contractors, railway employees, all owed their places to party loyalty. When their turn came the Conservatives could be just as thorough. According to Liberal figures, 371 magistrates were removed after the turnover of 1857.[36] The full meaning of government by party came to New Brunswick after 1854 when a great many highly respected individuals who had held public office for twenty years or more were suddenly and ruthlessly expelled. Emulating the Nova Scotian Liberals, the Smashers showed no respect for ancestral memories. The introduction of the British system of responsible government to the Atlantic Provinces was accompanied by the incidental and easily understood American corollary of "the pork-barrel." At the highest level there was no doubt concerning some of the inner meanings of the political struggle. Sir Brenton Halliburton, Chief Justice of Nova Scotia, was over eighty and the strife of the parties often seemed secondary to the great rivalry of William Young and James W. Johnston for succession to the post. The Liberals amused themselves by remarking on Johnston's "wig" policy.

As they became familiar with office, an increasingly strong spirit of secularism pervaded the thinking of reformers. Nova Scotian legislators sat in judgement upon the contest for financial grants to universities and arrived at the simple solution that higher education was the responsibility of the churches. When they stopped payment of small grants to the half-dozen colleges in 1850, they evaded charges of favouritism and partiality to one denomination over another. "I will not give a shilling," said Howe, "to support divinity chairs anywhere."[37] His fond project for a provincial university could make no headway against the strenuous support that was so cheerfully given by large sections of the public to the religious foundations of their choice. In New Brunswick the legislature sought to evade its commitment by the Civil List Act of 1837 to support King's College, where the Church of England held hard to its last stronghold of privilege. A great onslaught on the college's position in 1854 was turned aside by Sir Edmund Head, who sought to make the college acceptable to all denominations by abandoning the chair of theology and introducing modern scientific and technical courses. Out of the morass of denominationalism into which higher education had fallen, New Brunswick, unlike Nova Scotia, would eventually emerge with a provincial university.[38]

These solutions, which were based upon the logical premise of complete neutrality in dealing with the demands of particular groups for public privilege, came hard, but solutions for the problem of establishing a compulsory system of public schools were of still greater complexity. In 1856, when William Young introduced a Nova Scotian bill that provided for compulsory assessment as a principal feature, it was Catholic objections that had to be answered. Rivalry for privilege among Protestant denominations gave place to a powerful Catholic demand for a system of separate schools, and Young's bill had to be abandoned. Among the Nova Scotian Liberals there developed a bitter anti-Catholic animus. In all the provinces the Catholic Church, now highly organized and militant, headed by an episcopacy very predominantly Irish, was demanding for its numerous flock what it considered to be the appropriate degree of political favour. Great changes had occurred since the early years of the century when, each November 5, the Pope had been burnt in effigy on the Grand Parade in Halifax.[39] In New Brunswick the Roman Catholics succeeded in gaining a concession that ultimately became important though at the time it was considered of little account. When, out of religious scruple, Tilley and the ultra-Protestant Smashers insisted on a clause providing for Bible reading "without note or comment" in the School Bill of 1858, the Catholics secured an amendment providing for the children of their own faith the reading of the Douai Bible.

More than anything else it was Catholic resentment that brought about the fall of the Young-Howe government in Nova Scotia. Howe's magnificent capacity for frankness and overstatement precipitated the angry reaction of the important section of the populace on which, since 1847, Liberal strength had largely rested. Ever seeking an opportunity for imperial service, he went to the United States in 1855 to secure Irish recruits for the British army that was fighting in the Crimea. His pretence that he was securing labourers for his railway in Nova Scotia failed to produce results and, for his violation of American neutrality laws, he was informed upon by William Condon, President of the Irish Charitable Society in Halifax. The Crimean War to a great many fervent Irish seemed, moreover, an appropriate occasion for avenging the alleged wrongs of their homeland. During this ridiculous fiasco, in which he moved from one American city to another under a succession of aliases, Howe was defeated in Cumberland, losing his seat in the House of Assembly to a newcomer, Charles Tupper, the verbose young medical doctor who championed the private ownership of railways.

These humiliations made Howe reckless of consequences. A riotous outbreak along the railway that was under construction, in which Irish labourers burnt the shanty of a Protestant, Gourlay, who had ridiculed them for their faith, served as inspiration for a series of articles in the *Chronicle* that commenced late in 1856. Every Protestant, Howe declared, had the right to deride the doctrine of the Real Presence. Drawing examples of Irish "crimes" from history, he went on to argue that the new basis for politics should be the exclusion of Irish Catholics from government.⁴⁰ It was not surprising that these outbursts should be accompanied by resignations of colleagues in the cabinet. In February, 1857, Johnston and Tupper sprang their trap with a motion of no confidence. Liberals and Liberal sympathizers crossed the floor of the house and the government fell, twenty-eight to twenty-two. In opposition and in anger, Howe founded the Protestant Alliance. The crusade on which he embarked produced noisy reverberations in New Brunswick and Prince Edward Island. Protestant Anglo-Saxondom was urged to rouse itself against ancient perils and to oppose a Catholic despotism of which the principal instrument was Johnston, a Baptist and the Conservative leader.

While Fisher and the Smashers were establishing a firmer control in New Brunswick, the Conservatives of Nova Scotia, in some respects slightly more radical than the Liberals, took office. They faced few problems. They could continue to advocate private ownership and control of railways, but no reputable corporation was willing to take over the half-constructed lines to Truro and Windsor. They, too, discovered that railway construction could be an effective instrument for bolstering party organization and morale. An immediate triumph was an agreement with the British government which limited the rights of the General Mining Association. The company had created a great volume of employment in Pictou and Cumberland counties as well as in Cape Breton. But, because it was monopolistic and sought extensions of its already generous leases, it was unpopular. Acquisition of control over mineral rights for the province by the Civil List Act of 1849 meant, in practice, very little if this giant monopoly, a relic of the authoritarian practice in colonial days, should stand. The British government could see reason in a provincial protest of 1855 and, two years later, the rights that had once belonged to the Duke of York were handed back to the Crown. The Nova Scotian government was willing to renew leases on properties already worked, but insisted that the Association's competitors should have the privilege of opening new coalfields. This respect for the rights of free enterprise produced no practical results that were important, for the Association was always able to undersell its competitors and to buy up new properties as soon as they showed a likelihood of yielding profits.⁴¹

VII

In 1857 the economies of the four Atlantic Provinces were riding on a high level of prosperity, a career of comparative opulence to which no limits or obstacles appeared to present themselves. The minor depression caused by the contraction of credit during the Crimean War had been shrugged away as a mere fleeting irritation. No problems that were perplexing or disquieting appeared to face their governments. Enthusiasm for railway construction had abated and there was a complacent feeling that, with or without railways, the country was doing very well. The tables of the wealthy were furnished with the wines of Madeira and the wares of English silversmiths. Each capital could boast of a social élite whose provincialisms were readily identifiable but whose attitudes were urbane and cosmopolitan. The immense volume of trans-oceanic commerce assured an educated awareness of the world outside.

For those of more moderate means there was always labour. Even in the more marginal areas of farmland there was no necessity for poverty. Extreme poverty was to be found only in the more squalid slums of the seaports. Whatever extremities might arise, the country could always produce food – and many a family lasted out the winters on a diet of potatoes and turnips, salted pork or pickled herrings. Many areas were intelligently and industriously tilled and harvested. Even in those so often regarded as more primitive, the Gaelic lands of eastern Nova Scotia and the Acadian settlements of New Brunswick, modern methods of cultivation were coming into use and literate groups were beginning to emerge. The four provinces still made up a region of pioneers, but pioneering was yielding a modest competence. The more general prosperity and sense of well-being were given emphasis by the steady increases of population which were being recorded. These, it was proudly noted, were proportionally far greater than those of the New England states and came at a time when immigration was a relatively unimportant factor.

Yet this unprecedented prosperity of the age of wood, wind, and water was something like the falling of crumbs from other tables, the consequence of the abounding expansiveness of the world economy of the 1850's. While overseas markets required fish and lumber, oats and hay, the ships of the provinces could ply the seas and reward the toil of the producers by importing the manufactured goods of other countries. Because domestic manufacturing, though remarkable for the number of hardy and small enterprises that depended exclusively on local markets, could not begin to fulfil the wants of the inhabitants, the region was highly sensitive to the state of world trade. Because all the experience of the nineteenth century had taught so many lessons of the hazards which attended commercial speculation, the nature of business enterprise was prudent rather than bold, cautious rather than expansive. The region had produced its Samuel Cunard, but others were indisposed or unable to follow his example. Its seafarers thronged the waterways of the world, but in the counting-houses of the merchants the tendency was to follow in the beaten path of former years. Scores of noteworthy commercial failures had taught that prosperity could not last, that capital, when it could be accumulated, should be conserved and not risked. Behind this conservatism was a realization that in comparison with the new lands opening to the westward the Atlantic Provinces possessed no resources that promised great riches, that they could never be much more than "a good poor man's country."

The inconclusive and unprofitable programs of railway construction inaugurated by the provinces demonstrated their incapacity to tax either their capital or their energies for the material challenges of the new age that faced them. In the highly individualistic and traditional methods by which the merchants of Halifax, Saint John, and St John's conducted their affairs there was little but stubbornness and hardihood to show that they could adjust themselves to new emergencies. A much more technical and complex organization of commerce lay immediately ahead. Competition would soon come from larger units of production and vast mergers of small interests. While the easy prosperity of widening world markets and the Reciprocity Treaty blew upon their shores they could enjoy a moderate affluence that was imparted to the rural and coastal communities whom they served. Though there were many prophecies of complete decline and fall, the sailing-ship would profitably compete with steam for many a day to come. Their world was an oceanic one. For the changes that would come with increasing industrialization and large political readjustments of the sixties and seventies they were too unco-operative, too set in the ways of small trade, for reorientation. It may have been unthinkable in 1857 but their economy was soon to be gravely injured. No longer were the great avenues of international trade confined to the oceans but were commencing, as well, to traverse the land masses of the world.

Geography and history had conspired to deny to the Atlantic Provinces the framework of any kind of unity from which strong leadership could emerge. The farmers of Prince Edward Island who built little ships to take their oats to Britain, the fishermen of Newfoundland who looked to Mediterranean markets, the lumberers of New Brunswick, the Nova Scotians who were trained to look beyond the seas for reasons that were nostalgic as well as commercial, never learned to look to a metropolis. Only the up-river countries of New Brunswick were remote from the lapping of tide-water. This isolation of regions brought by the sea had everywhere produced an intense spirit of local independence. No government, no capitalist or combine of capitalists could harness the energies of Saint John and Halifax, of the Miramichi and Pictou. Competing in trade, they opposed one another politically. What helped one could not help the other and might prove positively injurious. Even within a political boundary local interests were thoroughly schooled to grudge ambitions to others. To tax one section of a province for a railway from which it could gain no conceivable benefit was the disagreeable expedient that frequently faced governments. The strident cry for equality in the distribution of favour and patronage had the inevitable effect of halting or retarding construction everywhere. Saint John and Halifax pressed their ambitions against a dead weight of rural hostility. It was impossible to equalize progress. In comparison it was the good fortune of Canada that the way to the sea through her own territory led in only one direction, that a single line of trunk railway could benefit all, or almost all, sections of the province.

Failure was unthinkable but when the allegation was made it usually came from a context that was political. In 1784 the British government had decentralized authority, and had bidden godspeed to the hopes of many small communities that aspired to self-sufficiency. By granting responsible government while the colonies were still small it had given wings to the forces of localism and diffusion that rendered them insignificant on the vast panorama of North American material development. In their divided state Sir Edmund Head could see them as detrimental to British prestige on the North American continent. From this division strength could never flow because the colonies could not provide for themselves effective leadership. The success of responsible government, he was certain, required greater size. Because of the smallness of constituencies assemblymen could never raise themselves above the level of advocates for local improvement. "Each man sits through the Session with his eyes intently fixed on his own peculiar job." In the hurly-burly of huckstering and bargaining two or three members, by banding together, could extort great concessions – the mark of the successful politician. Horizons, both within and without the legislatures, were so limited that Head could see no opinion that properly could be called "public." His remedy for all this was union.[42]

Other observers could see alert and disputatious democracies bubbling over with local pride and completely engrossed in neighbourhood rivalries. Politicians were trained not to lead but to follow, to look back over their shoulders to the caprices of the home-folk, to the sectional and religious prejudices that provided their majorities. The secretariat at the Colonial Office, no longer in a position to dictate, was weary of dealing with "small men in small provinces." To British observers especially, the shocking realization was that there was nothing of the large public spirit that distinguished the debates of the Parliament at Westminster, where wealthy and aristocratic Whigs prided themselves on a capacity for independence of thought and a complete detachment from the more workaday features of political endeavour. The political patricians of the Atlantic Provinces bore little resemblance to those of the mother country and appeared to be in the grip of the demeaning influences of the pork-barrel that flowed in from the United States. In the eyes of one severe observer Howe and his colleagues kept their Nova Scotian supporters in line by "stooping to conquer."[43]

In 1857 the provinces could see no need for the kind of leadership desired by Sir Edmund Head, or for the intrusion of external forces that could make them over. Responsible government had brought no splendid consequences. Even in Nova Scotia where the tone of public life was probably on a higher plane than elsewhere, influential voices protested the narrowing range of governmental activity, declared that government by party had become devoid of principle, that the choice for the electorate lay not between measures but between men.[44] But there were no emergencies. The provinces could boast of low taxation and rapid growth, of the increasing independence of their legislatures, of the strength of free peoples who were producing from moderate resources something more than a bare competence. Responsible government had not made them less provincial. Provincial spirit was everywhere in the ascendancy. Always in a category by itself, Newfoundland was the most oceanic of all the colonies. Its isolated position, its eastern and southern orientations, the international connections of its great mercantile families, still denied the feasibility of including it within the plans for political reorganization that Britain's world interests were commencing to dictate. With or without justification all of the provinces were conscious of strength, feeling their way to a wider degree of self-assertion.

Whatever inklings of future emergencies there may have been, there was little disposition to abandon the common belief that the provinces could thrive in their existing state and the premise that they would remain separate from one another. The lure of Yankeeism was tarnished by the turmoils of the Union and by the monstrous effects of the Fugitive Slave Act. Unnecessarily patronizing declarations from Whitehall, occasional indiscretions of lieutenant-governors and other transient Englishmen, imposed slight strains upon the bond of loyalty to the mother country. But the continuing façade of British world power, the victories of the Crimea, Havelock's spectacular relief of the beleaguered Christians at Lucknow, stimulated self-esteem and vindicated complacency. Within the Empire their status was secure and free, their prospects bright. No future vistas excited speculation. No adventures in political reorganization were perceived on the horizon.

ABBREVIATIONS

Ad.: Admiralty.
B.M., Add. MSS: British Museum, Additional Manuscripts.
B.T.: Board of Trade.
C.H.A.: Canadian Historical Association.
C.H.R.: *Canadian Historical Review.*
C.O.: Colonial Office.
H.M.C.: Historical Manuscripts Commission.
M.H.S.C.: Massachusetts Historical Society Collections.
N.B.H.S.: New Brunswick Historical Society.
N.B. Leg. Lib.: New Brunswick Legislative Library.
N.S.A.R.: Nova Scotia Archives Reports.
N.S.H.S.: Nova Scotia Historical Society.
N.Y.C.D.: New York Colonial Documents.
P.A.C.: Public Archives of Canada.
P.A.N.S.: Public Archives of Nova Scotia.
P.R.O: Public Record Office.
S.P.: State Papers.
S.P.G.: Society for the Propagation of the Gospel.
Trans. R.S.C.: *Transactions,* Royal Society of Canada.
W.O.: War Office.

NOTES TO CHAPTER ONE

1. E. Richard, *Acadia: Missing Links of a Lost Chapter in American History* (New York, 1895), p. 1.

2. Père P. F. X. de Charlevoix, *Histoire et Description Générale de la Nouvelle France* . . . (Paris, 1744), V, 125.

3. For more detailed descriptions of the operation of the fishery and of marketing, see the opening chapter of A. H. McLintock, *The Establishment of Constitutional Government in Newfoundland 1783-1832* (London, 1941), and R. G. Lounsbury, *The British Fishery at Newfoundland, 1634-1763* (New Haven, 1934).

4. The quintal was the hundred-pound weight by which cod were marketed and sold. The quintal of cod, for want of currency, became a normal unit of exchange for all the fishing communities of the North Atlantic.

5. Lounsbury, *British Fishery at Newfoundland*, p. 239.

6. *Calendar of State Papers Colonial, 1669-74*, Capt. R. Robinson to the Board, No. 369.

7. B.M., Add. MSS, 19,071, Testimony of Moses de la Dernière.

8. *Ibid.*

9. F. Parkman, *A Half Century of Conflict* (Boston, 1897), I, 110.

10. *Collection des manuscrits contenant lettres, mémoires et autres documents historiques relatifs á la Nouvelle France* (Quebec, 1883), I, 384.

11. *Calendar of State Papers Colonial, 1697-98*, Nelson to Council of Trade and Plantations, November 2, 1697.

12. B.M., Add., MSS, 31,272, St John to Lords Plenipotentiaries, April 5, 1712.

13. B.M., Add. MSS, 22,206, Memoir, May 24, 1712.

14. Howell's *State Trials*, XV, Cols. 1025 and 1127.

15. P.R.O., State Papers Foreign, 105/28, Prior to Bolingbroke, January 8, 1713.

16. P.R.O., S.P. 78/166, Pulteney to Cragge, April 29, 1720. Papers relative to this negotiation which compre-

hended several questions arising from the Treaty of Utrecht are to be found in this volume and C.O. 218/1. The French commissaries were Marshal D'Etrees and Abbé Dubois; the British, James Pulteney and Colonel Martin Bladen.

17. This right was similarly granted to the French of Placentia and St Christopher's, in return for a concession by the French Crown that Protestants employed as galley-slaves in French ports should be released. See S.P. 105/28, Shrewsbury to Bolingbroke, May 22 and June 13, 1713, and B.M., Add. MSS, 32,273, Bolingbroke to Lords Plenipotentiaries, January 7, 1713.

18. C.O. 217/2, Caulfeild to the Board (undated), No. 8.

19. P.R.O., Board of Trade Journals, March 15, 1715 and S.P. 103/97, Report of the Board of Trade, 1715.

20. See C.O. 217/2.

21. P.R.O., Board of Trade Journals, February 5, 1719.

22. C.O. 218/1, Instructions to Phillips, June 19, 1719.

23. "Among the advantages to be given the South Sea, they are to have Nova Scotia from whence naval stores are to come, Mr. Secretary Cragge said in the House, if Law had concluded his bargain with the Czar for all the produce of Muscovy, we must have been supplied from Acadia." Historical Manuscripts Commission Reports, Portland MSS, V, Thos. Harley to Lord Harley, December 22, 1720.

24. B.M., King's MSS, 205, Report on the Colonies, 1721.

25. *Treasury Papers, 1714-1719*, Remarks on the Fisheries by Capt. William Taverner, August 21, 1718.

26. D. W. Prowse, *History of Newfoundland* (London, 1895), p. 226.

27. Lounsbury, *British Fishery at Newfoundland*, p. 274 ff.

28. Acts of the Privy Council, 1765, No. 1949.

29. S.P. 105/28, Prior to Bolingbroke, January 8, 1713.
30. Lescarbot has a description of it and it is mentioned in a memorial of des Meules of 1686, B.M., Sloan MSS, 3607.
31. C.O. 217/3, Phillips to the Board, February 8, 1720.
32. S.P. 17/166, Delafaye to Pulteney, August 3, 1720.
33. S.P. 78/166, Pulteney to Delafaye, September 10, 1720. The Latin version of the treaty gives France the islands "that are in the Gulf and mouth of the River St. Lawrence," the French, those "in the mouth of the Gulf and river."
34. B.M., Add. MSS, 38,396, Report of the Board of Trade, December 19, 1718.
35. C.O. 217/4, Phillips to the Board, November 29, 1723.
36. C.O. 218/2, Board to the King, May 10, 1722.
37. S.P. 41/10, Mascarene on the State of Canso, October 28, 1735.
38. *Treasury Papers, 1720-1728*, No. 149, Burchill to Scrope, December 19, 1724.
39. C.O. 217/7, Armstrong to the Board, E11, undated.
40. W. B. Weeden, *Economic and Social History of New England* (Boston and New York, 1890), I, 595-96.
41. B.M., Add. MSS, 35,913, Questions and Answers to the State of the French and British Fisheries, undated.
42. C.O. 217/4, Convention of Canso, November, 1724.
43. C.O. 217/5, Armstrong to the Board, September 5, 1725.
44. *Ibid.*, Armstrong to Aldridge, September 5, 1725.
45. For detailed accounts of the management of the French as well as of the British fisheries, see H. A. Innis, *The Cod Fisheries* (revised edition, Toronto, 1954), Chaps. 1-5.
46. J. S. McLennan, *Louisburg From Its Foundation to Its Fall, 1713-1758* (London, 1918), p. 226. This volume supplies excellent description of society at Louisburg as well as of military events.
47. For full description see D. C. Harvey, *The French Regime in Prince Edward Island* (New Haven, 1926).
48. McLennan, *Louisburg*, Chap. 12.
49. For further elaboration see Kate Hotblack, *Chatham's Colonial Policy* (London, 1917).
50. S.P. 78/251, Stanley to Pitt, August 6, 1761.
51. C.O. 324/21, Report of the Board of Trade, May 5, 1763.

NOTES TO CHAPTER TWO

1. *Collection des manuscrits contenant lettres, mémoires et autres documents historiques relatifs à la Nouvelle France*, III, Vaudreuil au ministre, June 28, 1713.
2. C.O. 217/4, Doucett to the Board, June 19, 1722.
3. C.O. 217/6, Council Minutes, July 25, 1731.
4. C.O. 218/1, Board to the King, May 20, 1718; to Phillips, December 28, 1720.
5. J. B. Brebner, "Subsidized Intermarriage with the Indians," C.H.R., VI (1), 1925.
6. C.O. 217/5, Dunbar and Coram to the Board, May 6, 1729. This request came to the attention of the Privy Council where it was decided that the Crown had no right to erect a new colony or to grant lands since the country was included in the Massachusetts Charter of 1691, still in force. Acts of the Privy Council, Colonial, August 10, 1732.
7. C.O. 217/6, Dunbar to Phillips, September 7, 1730; to Jeremiah Dunbar, October 7, 1730.
8. Treasury Minute Book, Order-in-Council, August 28, 1734.
9. C.O. 217/6, Phillips to the Board, November 26, 1730.
10. C.O. 217/7, Council Minutes, May 4, 1736.
11. John Knox, *Historical Journal of the Campaign in North America for the*

Years 1757, 1758, 1759 *and* 1760 (ed. A. G. Doughty, Toronto, Champlain Society, 1914), I, 98-99.

12. Belcher Papers (M.H.S.C.), Belcher to Coram, October 6, 1733, I, 392.

13. For a complete account, see J. S. McLennan, *Louisburg From Its Foundation to Its Fall.* Patriotic early American historians made a great deal of this victory, which can readily be explained in terms of military logistics, the assembly of far superior fire power against the defences at the vital point. McLennan's closely written account of the siege, never seriously challenged, calls in question both the generalship of Pepperell and the quality of the colonial troops.

14. N.Y.C.D., X, Beauharnois and Hocquart to Maurepas, September 12, 1745.

15. C.O. 5/45, Newcastle to Shirley, May 30, 1747.

16. B.M., Add. MSS, 32,808, Sandwich to Newcastle, May 30, 1747. At one stage in the Aix-la-Chapelle negotiations, the British considered that Gibraltar might be restored to Spain in return for Spanish withdrawal from the war and a guarantee that Louisburg should remain in British hands. Newcastle was not impressed by what was really a proposal to exchange Gibraltar for Louisburg. Add. MSS, 32,807, Newcastle to Sandwich, March 6, 1747.

17. C.O. 5/44, Knowles to Newcastle, January 20, 1747.

18. Reprinted in *Gentleman's Magazine*, January, 1748.

19. C.O. 5/886, Shirley to Newcastle, February 18, 1748.

20. C.O. 5/13, Bollan to Newcastle, August 19, 1747.

21. One of the traditions of the British Army dates from this incident. The 29th Regiment of Foot, whose officers and men made up this party, were long known as the Ever Sworded Twenty-Ninth because the officers were compelled, in memory of the surprise, to sit at mess with their swords belted.

22. An original copy of Halifax's plan which, to the writer's knowledge, is not in the Public Record Office, is in the House of Lords Manuscripts, Papers Relating to the Settlement of Nova Scotia, 1749-52, Bundle A. It may be of interest that Halifax's father had in 1707 urged the seizure of Nova Scotia from the French and the settlement within it of a colony of Scots. B.M., Egerton MSS, 929.

23. C.O. 217/32, Cornwallis to Bedford, June 23, 1749.

24. C.O. 217/32, Shirley to La Galissonière, May 9, 1749; La Galissonière to Shirley, June 15, 1749.

25. S.P. 78/233, Bedford to Yorke, July 6, 1749.

26. *Documents relatifs à l'histoire de la Nouvelle France*, III, Journal, October 14, 1746.

27. N.Y.C.D., VI, Capt. Stoddart to Governor Clinton, July 30, 1750.

28. *Documents relatifs à l'histoire de la Nouvelle France*, III, La Loutre to Maurepas, July 29, 1749.

29. B.M., Add. MSS, 32,821, Journal of Chignecto Expedition.

30. House of Lords MSS, Papers Relating to French Encroachments, La Jonquière to Cornwallis, April 2, 1750.

31. B.M., Add. MSS, 32,821, Pitt to Newcastle, June 19, 1750.

32. *Ibid.*, Newcastle to Yorke, June 15, 1750; to Albemarle, June 20, 1750.

33. House of Lords MSS, Papers relating to French Encroachments, Memoir of September 15, 1750.

34. B.M., Add. MSS, 32,826, Bedford to Albemarle, January 31, 1751.

35. *Ibid.*, Des Herbiers to Cornwallis, November 21, 1750.

36. B.M., Add. MSS, 35,913, Board of Trade to Bedford, March 7, 1751; 35,479, Cabinet Minutes, May 28, 1751.

37. House of Lords MSS, Papers relating to French Encroachments, Yorke to Holdernesse, October 6, 1751. It is worthy of note that of all the American problems dividing the two govern-

ments the Nova Scotian was, at this stage, the most material. See also S.P. 78/233, Newcastle to Shirley, August 10, 1750.

38. House of Lords MSS, Papers relating to French Encroachments. Privy Council Minute, March 27, 1752.

39. W.O. 34/71, Holdernesse to American Governors, August 28, 1753. Most of the diplomatic correspondence, on the British side, is found in the House of Lords MSS. The submissions of the commissaries are printed in *Mémoire des Commissaries du Roi et de Ceux de Sa Majesté Britannique sur les possessions et les droits respectifs des deux couronnes en Amérique, sur les actes publics et pièces justificatives* (5 vols.; Paris, 1756).

40. W.O. 34/71, Secret Instructions to Braddock, November 25, 1754.

41. How important such considerations were to Shirley is shown throughout his biography. See J. A. Schutz, *William Shirley: King's Governor of Massachusetts* (Williamsburg, 1961).

42. For a detailed account of operations on the isthmus, see J. C. Webster, *The Forts of Chignecto* (Shediac, 1930).

43. N.S.A.R., I, 135. Acadian petition to de Gannes, October 13, 1744.

44. N.Y.C.D., X, Hocquart and Beauharnois to Maurepas, September 12, 1745.

45. N.S. Arch., II, Mascarene to Mangeant, March 25, 1740.

46. C.O. 217/49, Mascarene to Shirley, December 9, 1745.

47. C.O. 5/901, Shirley to Newcastle, June 18, 1746.

48. C.O. 5/353, Shirley to the Board, July 8, 1747.

49. C.O. 5/901, Instructions to Shirley, October 3, 1747.

50. C.O. 5/901, Shirley to Newcastle, October 20, 1747; C.O. 5/886, To the Board, February 18, 27, 1748.

51. A *Genuine Account of Nova Scotia* (London, 1750).

52. Otis Little, *Trade of the Northern Colonies* (London, 1749) p. 46.

53. N.S. Arch., I, Council Minutes, September 6, 1749, p. 172.

54. C.O. 218/3, Board to Hopson, March 28, 1753.

55. N.S. Arch., I, Council Minutes, July 3 and 4, 1755, pp. 247-56.

56. C.O. 217/16, Belcher's Opinion on the Acadians.

57. P.A.C., *Report, 1926, Northcliffe Collection*. Lawrence to Monckton, August 8, 1755.

58. B.M., Add. MSS, 19,072, Remarks of Morris (undated).

59. The best documents concerning the expulsion are to be found in P.A.C., *Report, 1926, Northcliffe Collection*, and N.S.H.S. *Collections*, III, *Journal of Colonel John Winslow*.

60. C.O. 217/34, Lawrence to the Board, October 15, 1755.

61. *Ibid.*, Board to Fox, April 14, 1756. The Acadian expulsion has been the subject of over three hundred books, pamphlets, and articles. The most notable tendency has been to accuse Lawrence and the Council at Halifax of being the authors of a great crime from which the British government stands absolved. See E. Richard, *Acadia: Missing Links of a Lost Chapter in American History*. English-speaking writers have taken the same line, even A. G. Doughty in *The Acadian Exiles* (Toronto, 1916). The humanitarian aspect of the expulsion, taken out of context, has had an immense impact on the popular writing of Nova Scotian history. Edmund Burke denounced the expulsion in a speech in the House of Commons on February 11, 1780. But the full flood of humane sentiment was not released until the publication of Longfellow's *Evangeline* in 1839. For a spirited retort to the "history" emerging from *Evangeline*, see the papers by Sir Adams Archibald in N.S.H.S. *Collections*, V.

62. H.M.C., Stopford-Sackville MSS, Wolfe to Sackville, May 24, 1758.

63. For a detailed account, see McLennan, *Louisburg*, p. 250 ff.

64. *An Authentic Account*, cit. McLennan, *Louisburg*, p. 269.

65. Though recent writings have considerably damaged Wolfe's reputation as a general, criticism has not been extended to his tactical handling of battle while under fire. See C. P. Stacey, *Quebec, 1759* (Toronto, 1959).

66. This fort, severely damaged by storms during the following winter, was garrisoned by New England troops until 1762, and by regulars until 1768, when they were removed for the British occupation of Boston. Documentation for the St John expedition is found in P.A.C., *Report, 1926, Northcliffe Collection*, pp. 62-67.

67. Knox's *Journal*, I, 296-7.

68. It is impossible to estimate with pre-cision the number of deportees from any of the Acadian settlements. This is also the case with respect to Isle St Jean. See D. C. Harvey, *The French Regime in Prince Edward Island*, Chap. 13; also Appendix E, "The Loss of the Duke William."

69. This battle took place on what is to-day the Quebec side of the Restigouche, a little below the New Brunswick city of Campbellton. According to a letter in Knox's *Journal*, III, 400-405, there were 250 French troops, 700 Acadians, and 800 Indians involved.

70. S.P. 78/251, Pitt to Stanley, August 27, 1761.

71. For an account of the two islands, see D. W. Prowse, *History of Newfoundland*, Chap. 18.

NOTES TO CHAPTER THREE

1. B.M., Sloane MSS, 4,164, Lieut. H. Jacobs, September 30, 1755.

2. *Letter from J. B. to a Noble Lord* (London, 1756).

3. Treasury I/340, Cornwallis to Lords of Treasury, July 17, 1750.

4. C.O. 218/4, Board to Lords of Admiralty, January 14, March 6, 1752; to Cornwallis, March 6, 1752.

5. *Letter from J. B., op. cit.*

6. C.O. 217/14, Cornwallis to Board, September 4, 1751.

7. C.O. 217/13, Petition of Germans and Swiss (undated).

8. Though Lunenburg was a name chosen from the King's German dominions, the majority of the people were from south Germany.

9. C.O. 217/16, Council Minutes, May 20, 1758.

10. C.O. 217/18, Lawrence to the Board, June 16, 1760. For a very complete account of the settlement of Lunenburg and the origins of its people, see W. P. Bell, *The Foreign Protestants and the Settlement of Nova Scotia* (Toronto, 1961).

11. *Letter from a Gentleman in Nova Scotia* (London, 1756).

12. C.O. 217/15, Belcher to Pownall, January 16, 1755.

13. *Ibid.*, Murray and Lloyd to the Board, March 31, 1755.

14. C.O. 218/5, Board to Lawrence, May 7, 1755.

15. C.O. 217/16, Lawrence to the Board, December 8, 1755.

16. C.O. 218/5, Board to Lawrence, March 25, 1756.

17. B.M., Brown MSS, 19,069.

18. C.O. 217/16, Joint letter to the Board, March 12, 1757.

19. *Ibid.* (undated).

20. *Ibid.*, Petition of Paris, January 26, 1758, with Appendix to the State of Facts; C.O. 391/65, Board of Trade Minutes, January 31, February 3, 7, 1758.

21. C.O. 323/16, Hints on the New Territories, undated.

22. For a full account of these settlements see J. B. Brebner, *The Neutral Yankees of Nova Scotia* (New York, 1937).

23. N.B.H.S. *Collections*, I, James Hannay's article on Maugerville. This settlement was made in 1763.
24. C.O. 217/18, Memorial and order-in-council, April 29, 1762. An account of McNutt's career and of his work in Nova Scotia is found in the Royal Society of Canada's report for 1912. See W. O. Raymond, "Col. Alexander McNutt and the Pre-Loyalist Settlements of Nova Scotia," *Trans. R.S.C.*, 1912.
25. C.O. 220/7, Amherst to Belcher, April 28, 1761.
26. C.O. 218/6, Board to Belcher, December 3, 1762.
27. S.P. 78/260, Halifax to Hartford, January 3, 1764. In 1764 the British government strongly protested against French attempts to remove the Acadians. The Duc de Nivernois was the French minister charged with carrying out the policy. See also correspondence in C.O. 218/6.
28. C.O. 218/6, Board to Wilmot, March 20, 1764.
29. C.O. 220/9, Council Minutes, May 15, 1764.
30. C.O. 217/44, Palliser to Francklin, September 11, 1766.
31. Report on St Pierre by Joseph Woodmass, enclosed in Campbell to Hillsborough, July 5, 1769. Robin's activities were at first greatly resented by the British government. He was regarded as "a dangerous person" because of his encouragement to clandestine commerce and communication between St Pierre and British territory. C.O. 218/6, Halifax to Wilmot, May 15, 1764.
32. C.O. 217/25, Memorial of Walker (undated).
33. C.O. 218/6, Board to the King, October 5, 1763.
34. C.O. 324/21, Report, May 5, 1763.
35. C.O. 218/6, Instructions to Wilmot, November 22, 1763.
36. B.M., Add. MSS, 35,914, Petition of Egmont's supporters, Egmont to Yorke, April 26, 1766; C.O. 217/20, Memorial of Egmont.
37. C.O. 217/20, Richmond's memorial, March 26, 1764.
38. C.O. 217/45, Francklin to Hillsborough, July 31, 1768.
39. Catholic religious writings emphasize this factor. Rev. John C. MacMillan's *History of the Catholic Church in Prince Edward Island* (Quebec, 1905) refers to this as the only factor compelling emigration.
40. Frank MacKinnon, *The Government of Prince Edward Island* (Toronto, 1951), p 41.
41. C.O. 5/216, Lords of the Treasury to the King.
42. This is the considered opinion of H. A. Innis in *The Cod Fisheries* (rev. ed., Toronto, 1945) and R. F. Grant in *The Canadian Atlantic Fishery* (Toronto, 1934).
43. C.O. 217/44, Campbell to Shelburne, December 5, 1766.
44. *Ibid.*, Cawthorn to Secretary of State, October 5, 1766.
45. C.O. 217/19, Belcher to the Board, October 21, 1762.
46. C.O. 217/18, Mauger to the Board, December 2, 1762.
47. C.O. 218/7, Board to the King, April 29, 1768. For a much fuller discussion of Mauger's influence, see Brebner, *The Neutral Yankees*.
48. W. O. Raymond, "Old Townships on the St. John River," N.B.H.S. *Collections*, II.
49. Raymond, "Col. Alexander McNutt," *op. cit.*
50. See Brebner, *The Neutral Yankees*, Chap. 5, for a full and intimate account of these private transactions.
51. N.S. Assembly Journals, April 11, 1759.
52. N.S. Council Minutes, July 24, 1762.
53. For a full account, see D. C. Harvey, "The Struggle for the New England Form of Township Government in Nova Scotia," C.H.A. *Report*, 1933.
54. D. W. Prowse, *History of Newfoundland*, p. 298.
55. G. O. Rothney, "The History of Newfoundland and Labrador, 1754-83," (un-

published M.A. thesis, Institute of Historical Research, University of London, 1934), p. 75.

56. C.O. 194/18, Order-in-Council, June 19, 1772.

57. A. H. McLintock, *The Establishment of Constitutional Government in Newfoundland, 1783-1832*, p. 10.

58. C.O. 194/2,2. *Letter to Members of Parliament*, by W. Carson, 1812. Cit. McLintock, *Establishment of Constitutional Government in Newfoundland*, p. 12.

59. Rothney, "History of Newfoundland," pp. 65-66.

60. C. Pedley, *History of Newfoundland From Earliest Times to 1860* (London, 1863), p. 96.

61. Rothney, "History of Newfoundland," pp. 72-73. Newfoundland's literature of revolt is written from accounts and memories of the alleged tyrannies and injustices that stemmed from the refusal of the British government to impart a greater degree of political organization to the island. The native or resident historians, Prowse, Hatton, Harvey, and Pedley, all dwell copiously on the outrageous conduct of fishing-admirals and "naval surrogates." It might be observed that no history of Newfoundland has been written from the point of view of the West Countrymen. Even an historian like McLintock has injected into his work a great deal of humanitarian sentiment on behalf of the colonists. The editor of *The Cambridge History of the British Empire* mildly defends the imperal policy by noting the high quality of some of the convoy captains and governors, such as Lord Vere Beauclerk, Rodney, Graves, Palliser, Gambier; VI, p. 141.

NOTES TO CHAPTER FOUR

1. C.O. 5/755, cited in J. B. Brebner, *The Neutral Yankees of Nova Scotia*. For a fuller account, see same volume, pp. 157-63.

2. B.M., Stowe MSS, 264. Hinshelwood to Brittell, November 1, 1765, and threatening letter signed by fictitious names.

3. S.P.G., B.M., Add. Mss, No. 25, Anonymous letter, undated.

4. C.O. 217/51, Legge to Dartmouth, September 3, 1774.

5. C.O. 220/11, Assembly Journals, December 9, 1774.

6. H.M.C., Dartmouth MSS, Legge to Dartmouth, November 29, 1774.

7. *Ibid.*, Legge to Dartmouth, July 31, 1775.

8. C.O. 217/51, Dartmouth to Legge, June 7, July 5, 1775.

9. *Ibid.*, Suffolk to Legge, October 16, 1775.

10. C.O. 217/52, Francklin to Dartmouth, January 2, 1776.

11. H.M.C., Dartmouth MSS, Knox to Legge, February 27, 1776.

12. C.O. 217/52, Report of the Board of Trade, July 25, 1776. The charges made were in substance (1) that Legge had insulted and disregarded "the old servants of government," (2) that he had ignored the advice of the council, (3) that he had interfered with the courts of law, (4) that he had ill-treated the Loyalist refugees. They were presented by Binney and Winkworth Tonge, representing the complainants. None was, in the opinion of the Board, substantiated.

13. C.O. 217/51, Legge to Dartmouth, March 6, 1775.

14. *Ibid.*, Petition of the legislature to Parliament, June 24, 1775. It is reprinted in William Cobbett's *Parliamentary History* (London, 1813), Vol. 18, pp. 698-705.

15. Cobbett, *Parliamentary History*, Debate on the Nova Scotian petition, November 29, 1775. There was some illuminating discussion on Cooper's resolution. The Whigs argued that the same privilege be granted to the revolting colonies. Sir George Yonge's amendment was defeated in favour of another

by Thomas Pownall that nothing in the colonial act should restrain parliament from making additional requisitions in the future, avoiding any implications of a binding contract between Crown and colony.

16. G. S. Graham, *Empire of the North Atlantic* (Toronto, 1946), p. 207.

17. See, for instance, C.O. 217/52, Report of Captain Stanton, December 4, 1775.

18. *Ibid.*, Rev. Egleson to John Butler, January 27, 1776; also S.P.G., B MSS, Rev. Ellis, October 4, 1775.

19. S.P.G., B MSS, Rev. Delaroche, April 28, 1776.

20. C.O. 217/51, Memorial of eighty-two inhabitants of Yarmouth, December 8, 1775.

21. See, for instance, W. C. Ford *et al.* (eds.), *Journals of the Continental Congress* (Washington, 1904), I, 105. In appealing for support from the people of Quebec, Congress declared itself to be representative of every colony from Nova Scotia to Georgia.

22. C.O. 217/52, Memorial of the people of Cumberland, Amherst, and Sackville, and of the Acadians of the district, December 23, 1775.

23. Graham, *Empire of the North Atlantic*, p. 207.

24. W. C. Ford, *The Writings of George Washington* (New York, 1889), III, To the General Court of Massachusetts, August 11, 1775; To the President of Congress, January 30, 1776.

25. C.O. 217/53, Gorham's Journal.

26. P.A.N.S., St. John River papers, Vol. 409.

27. C. Pedley, *History of Newfoundland From Earliest Times to 1860*, p. 132; Petition of the people of Renous.

28. C.O. 217/53, Arbuthnot to Germaine, December 31, 1776.

29. C.O. 217/54, Massey to Germaine, December 10, 1777.

30. C.O. 217/53, Arbuthnot to Germaine, December 31, 1776.

31. Wharton, *Journals of the Continental Congress*, III, 58. Report of the Committee on Pacification.

32. F. C. Wharton, *The Revolutionary Diplomatic Correspondence of the United States* (Washington, 1889), III, 274, 295, 302.

33. The British asked for the Penobscot and, as a compromise, got the St Croix. See W. S. MacNutt, *New Brunswick: A History, 1784-1867* (Toronto, 1963), p. 14.

34. For an incisive and extended description of the negotiations, see F. F. Thompson, *The French Shore Problem in Newfoundland* (Toronto, 1961), pp. 14-18.

35. Rev. E. M. Saunders, "Rev. John Wiswell, M.A.," N.S.H.S. *Collections*, XIII.

36. In Carleton's dispatches from New York there is no direct evidence of an overpowering influence exerted by Watson but a great many stray scraps of evidence indicate that it must have been considerable. Note, for instance, Walter Patterson's letter from Charlottetown in 1783 in which he remarks that all the Loyalists had gone to Nova Scotia "through the influence of Mr. Watson": D. C. Campbell, *History of Prince Edward Island* (Charlottetown, 1875), p. 35.

37. Thos. H. Raddall, "Tarleton's Legion," N.S.H.S. *Collections*, XXVIII.

38. W. H. Siebert and F. E. Gilliam, "The Loyalists in Prince Edward Island," R.S.C. *Proceedings*, 1910. The estimated total of six hundred included women and children.

39. R. Brown, *A History of the Island of Cape Breton* (London, 1869), p. 392.

40. The total number of Loyalist grantees was 6,220. Of these, 408 were negroes. The proportion of civilians to soldiers was 62:38. Escheats of later years numbered 724. See Margaret Ells, "Settling the Loyalists in Nova Scotia," C.H.A. *Report*, 1934.

41. See Esther Clark Wright, *The Loyalists of New Brunswick* (Fredericton, 1955). The appendix to this volume contains lists of the Loyalist settlers, their origins and places of location.

42. *Ibid.* Mrs Wright estimates that the number of southerners who came to New Brunswick made up less than 5 per cent of the total.

43. R. S. Longley, "The Delancey Brothers, Loyalists of Annapolis County," N.S.H.S. *Collections*, XXXII.

44. R. S. Longley, "An Annapolis County Loyalist," N.S.H.S. *Collections*, XXXI.

45. MacNutt, *New Brunswick*, pp. 32-34.

46. *Ibid.*, pp. 11-12.

47. B.M., Add. MSS, 42,418, Carleton to Parr, September 5, 1783.

48. Many writers have imputed the policy of divide and rule to the partition of 1784. No real evidence exists for this point of view. At this stage of British imperial history it is difficult to find evidence of any policy in political organization. The Loyalist urgency is quite sufficient to explain the division.

49. C.O. 5/32, Order-in-council.

50. C.O. 217/56, "Plan for the Intended Province of —————."

51. A. L. Burt, "Guy Carleton, Lord Dorchester: An Estimate," C.H.A. *Report*, 1935.

52. The delegation consisted of Brenton Halliburton and Andrew Finucane, brother to the Chief Justice.

53. J. S. Macdonald, "Memoir of Governor John Parr," N.S.H.S. *Collections*, XIV, 67.

54. John Stewart, *An Account of Prince Edward Island* (London, 1806), p. 194.

55. *Ibid.*

56. MacNutt, *New Brunswick*, pp. 58-59.

NOTES TO CHAPTER FIVE

1. The proceedings of the Loyalist Commission are described in detail in L. Sabine, *The American Loyalists* (Boston, 1847), pp. 104-13.

2. C.O. 5/110, Carleton to North, October 26, 1783, with petition of Loyalist clergymen.

3. The correspondence and diary of Bishop Inglis are in P.A.C., Ottawa.

4. Page Smith, *John Adams* (New York, 1962), p. 27.

5. Samuel A. Green, "Congregational Churches in Nova Scotia," P.M.H.S., 1888.

6. C. O'Brien, *Memoirs of Right Reverend Edmund Burke* (Ottawa, 1894), p. 57.

7. Rev. J. E. Burns, "The Development of Roman Catholic Church Government in Halifax," N.S.H.S. *Collections*, XXIII.

8. B. T. Minutes 6/81, March 14, 1785.

9. Sabine, *American Loyalists*, Preface.

10. W. S. MacNutt, *New Brunswick: A History, 1784-1867*, p. 96.

11. B. Murdoch, *A History of Nova Scotia or Acadie* (Halifax, 1865-67), III, 33.

12. W. O. Raymond, "The Founding of Shelburne," N.B.H.S. *Collections*, VIII.

13. Wentworth's papers are to be found in P.A.N.S.

14. B.T. 6/20. Board of Trade Papers, February 24, 1790, with enclosure, Grenville to the Lord President, February 20, 1790.

15. Lord Selkirk said in his diary that Dorchester had influence enough to dispense with the instructions in Canada "for sake of fees." P. C. T. White (ed.), *Lord Selkirk's Diary, 1803-4* (Champlain Society, Toronto, 1958), p. 54.

16. A. H. McLintock, *The Establishment of Constitutional Government in Newfoundland, 1783-1832*, p. 24.

17. *Ibid.*, p. 64.

18. G. S. Graham, *Empire of the North Atlantic*, p. 219.

19. White, *Selkirk's Diary*, p. 7 ff.

20. According to statistics given by R. Brown, *History of the Island of Cape Breton*, p. 416, there were 3,147 chaldron extracted in 1793, 6,001 in 1800.

21. *Ibid.*, p. 402.

22. P.A.N.S., *Bulletin*, 1958, "A Letter Written at Sydney in 1789," Appendix C.

23. MacNutt, *New Brunswick*, pp. 136-37.

24. Ad. I, Vol. 495. Memorial of Joseph Freeman, November, 1799, *cit.* Graham.

25. C. Pedley, *History of Newfoundland From the Earliest Times to 1860*, p. 182.

26. D. W. Prowse, *History of Newfoundland*, p. 375.

27. McLintock, *Establishment of Constitutional Government in Newfoundland*, p. 102.

28. The most complete description of these incidents is to be found in Pedley, *History of Newfoundland*, pp. 208-17.

29. Rev. J. C. MacMillan, *The History of the Catholic Church in Prince Edward Island*, I, 90.

30. C. S. Macdonald, "Early Highland Emigration to Nova Scotia and Prince Edward Island from 1770 to 1853," *N.S.H.S. Collections*, XXIII.

31. White, *Selkirk's Diary*, pp. 54-55.

32. Burns, *op. cit.*

33. MacMillan, *Catholic Church in Prince Edward Island*, I, 156-57.

34. *Ibid.*, pp. 107-9.

35. H. L. D'Entrement, "Father Jean Sigogne, 1799-1844," *N.S.H.S. Collections*, XXIII.

36. G. E. Levy, *The Baptists of the Maritime Provinces, 1753-1946* (Saint John, 1946), p. 45.

37. *Ibid.*, p. 71.

38. T. Watson Smith, *History of the Methodist Church in Eastern British America* (Halifax, 1877), I, 46.

39. *Ibid.*, I, 181.

40. *Ibid.*, I, 343.

41. *Abstract of Proceedings of the Society for the Propagation of the Gospel, 1800* (London, 1800).

42. The entries in Bishop Inglis' diary upon the work of the Baptists and Methodists are very numerous after 1800.

43. H. Y. Hind, *The University of King's College, 1790-1890* (Cambridge, 1890), pp. 26-49.

44. I. E. Bill, *Fifty Years with the Baptists in the Maritime Provinces* (Saint John, 1880). For an account of the difficulties of Stephen Earley in King's County, see Smith, *Methodist Church in Eastern British America*, I, 268-71.

45. Smith, *Methodist Church in Eastern British America*, I, 267-68.

46. Murdoch, *Nova Scotia*, III, 61.

47. Sabine, *American Loyalists*, pp. 692-705.

48. Murdoch, *Nova Scotia*, III, pp. 66-72.

49. Sir Adams Archibald, "Life of Sir John Wentworth," *N.S.H.S. Collections*, XX.

50. *On Seeing His Excellency Sir John Wentworth Passing through Granville*, by Senex, *cit.* Murdoch, *Nova Scotia*, III, 139.

51. Archibald, *op. cit.*, p. 57.

52. Patrick Campbell's *Travels in the Interior, Inhabited Parts of British North America in the Years 1790 and 1792* (reprinted by the Champlain Society, Toronto, 1937) gives an excellent contemporary account of the life of Loyalist farmers in the St John Valley.

53. For a fuller description of Glenie and his struggle, see MacNutt, *New Brunswick*.

54. For a detailed account, see *ibid.*, pp. 123-29.

55. C.O. 188/11. Hobart to Carleton with enclosures, March 3, 1803.

NOTES TO CHAPTER SIX

1. G. S. Graham, *Empire of the North Atlantic*, p. 235.

2. *Ibid.*, pp. 233-35.

3. Thomas Carleton remained Lieutenant-Governor of New Brunswick until his death in 1817. From 1803 he was on leave of absence in England. During this time the administration was in the hands of the President of the Council.

4. G. F. Butler, "The Early Organization and Influence of Halifax Merchants," *N.S.H.S. Collections*, XXV, 6.

5. *Winslow Papers*, p. 97.

6. H.M.C., Dropmore MSS, Vol. 8, pp. 123, 142, 211. Uniacke's memorial is printed in *C.H.R.*, XVII (1), 1936, with an introduction by D. C. Harvey.

7. Jay's Treaty had expired in 1803 but most American privileges in the West Indies had remained intact until this time.

8. H. A. Davis, *An International Community on the St. Croix* (Orono, 1950), p. 94.

9. G. S. Graham, *Sea Power and British North America, 1783-1820* (Cambridge, 1941), p. 203.

10. S. E. Morison, *The Maritime History of Massachusetts* (Cambridge, Mass., 1931), p. 190.

11. Graham, *Sea Power*, p. 210.

12. See N. Atcheson, *American Encroachments on British Rights* (London, 1808).

13. Morison, *Maritime History of Massachusetts*, pp. 205-6.

14. Graham, *Sea Power*, p. 215.

15. Davis, *International Community on the St. Croix*, pp. 109-11.

16. N.B. Leg. Lib. *Sessional Papers*, 1807, petition of Robert Wood.

17. R. G. Albion, *Forests and Sea Power* (Cambridge, 1926), p. 292.

18. *Ibid.*, pp. 348-49.

19. W. S. MacNutt, *New Brunswick: A History, 1784-1867*, pp. 141-43.

20. Albion, *Forests and Sea Power*, Appendix D.

21. Wm. Wood (ed.), *Select Documents of the War of 1812* (Toronto, Champlain Society, 1920), I, 141-48.

22. *Winslow Papers*, Hatch to Winslow, April 23, 1809.

23. Louise Manny, *Ships of Miramichi* (Saint John, 1960).

24. P.R.O. C.O. 118/16, Hunter to Liverpool, November 3, 1810.

25. John Reeves, *The History of the Government of Newfoundland* (London, 1793), cit. Graham, *Sea Power*.

26. C. Pedley, *History of Newfoundland From the Earliest Times to 1860*, p. 221.

27. *Ibid.*, p. 235.

28. P.R.O. C.O. 194/43, Gambier to Hobart, December 12, 1803. This need not be taken as strictly correct if the proposals made by Reeves for the appointment of a council be taken into consideration. See A. H. McLintock, *The Establishment of Constitutional Government in Newfoundland*, pp. 152-53.

29. Pedley, *History of Newfoundland*, pp. 237-38.

30. P.R.O. C.O. 194/53. Duckworth to Bathurst, November 2, 1812.

31. D. W. Prowse, *History of Newfoundland*, pp. 398-400.

32. Graham, *Sea Power*, pp. 269-70.

33. Lieut. E. Chappell, *The Cruize of the Rosamund*, cit. Prowse, *Newfoundland*, pp. 394-95.

34. Prowse, *Newfoundland*, p. 396.

35. W. Carson, *Letter to Members of Parliament* (St John's, 1812); *Reasons for Colonizing the Island of Newfoundland* (St John's, 1813).

36. Pedley, *History of Newfoundland*, pp. 294-96.

37. P.A.N.S. *Report, 1936*. Wentworth to Bernard, May 9, 1803.

38. MacNutt, *New Brunswick*, p. 107.

39. *Ibid.*, pp. 131-33.

40. D. C. Harvey, "Uniacke's Memorial," *C.H.R.*, XVII (1), 1936.

41. B. Murdoch, *A History of Nova Scotia or Acadie*, III, 226-31.

42. *Ibid.*, p. 272.

43. *House of Assembly Journals*, January 26, 1809.

44. P.A.N.S. *Report, 1936*. Croke to Castlereagh, February 11, April 3, 1809.

45. MacNutt, *New Brunswick*, pp. 120-23.

46. P.A.N.S. *Report, 1936*. Resolution of Committee of House, April 1, 1812.

47. See W. A. Squires, *The 104th Regiment of Foot* (Fredericton, 1963).

48. For a full account, see C. H. J. Snider, *Under the Red Jack* (Toronto, 1927). This is a book written for popular consumption but it represents an immense amount of research into the documentation of the Courts of Vice-Admiralty.

49. Prowse, *Newfoundland*, p. 383.

50. Graham's *Sea Power and British North America* gives the best analysis of the considerations governing the British commercial and colonial policy during and after the war.

NOTES TO CHAPTER SEVEN

1. Norman Macdonald, *Canada, 1763-1841, Immigration and Settlement* (London, 1939), p. 154.

2. C. S. MacDonald, "Early Highland Emigration to Nova Scotia," N.S.H.S. *Collections*, XXIII.

3. C. W. Dunn, *Highland Settler: A Portrait of the Scottish Gael in Nova Scotia* (Toronto, 1953), pp. 33-34.

4. *Ibid.*, "Song to America," by the Bard MacLean of Barney's River, pp. 18-19.

5. D. W. Prowse, *History of Newfoundland*, pp. 405-6.

6. W. S. MacNutt, *New Brunswick: A History, 1784-1867*, pp. 179-81.

7. J. S. Martell, "Military Settlements in Nova Scotia," N.S.H.S. *Collections*, XXIV.

8. B. Murdoch, *A History of Nova Scotia or Acadie*, III, 270-71.

9. Prowse, *Newfoundland*, pp. 345-46.

10. J. S. Martell, "Immigration to and Emigration from Nova Scotia, 1815-38," P.A.N.S. *Bulletin* No. 6, 1942.

11. P.R.O., C.O. 217/146. Report of Committee, October 14, 1826.

12. Owing to the haphazard way in which the statistics on immigration were kept in these years the precise figures will always be "a matter for conjecture." Only Nova Scotia has attempted a close estimate. After a most careful study, J. S. Martell reckoned 39,000 immigrants to Nova Scotia from the British Isles between 1815 and 1838. Scots, Irish, and English were in the proportions of 22 : 13 : 2. See his study in P.A.N.S. *Bulletin* No. 6. A. H. Clark's *Three Centuries and the Island* (Toronto, 1959) has a great deal of material of a statistical nature on the origins of Prince Edward Island's population.

13. H. F. Wood, "The Frightful Fate of the *Frances Mary*," *Queen's Quarterly*, LXIX, 1963.

14. In Prince Edward Island the total reservations for churches and schools were 6,700 acres; in New Brunswick, 20,000; in Nova Scotia, 47,000. See N. Macdonald, *Immigration and Settlement*, p. 220.

15. G. E. Levy, *History of the Baptists in the Maritime Provinces* (Saint John, 1946), pp. 87-105.

16. T. W. Smith, *History of the Methodist Church in Eastern British America* (Halifax, 1877), I, 387-91.

17. Levy, *Baptists*, pp. 113-14. See also Rev. G. W. Hill, "History of St. Paul's Church," N.S.H.S. *Collections*, III.

18. Smith, *Methodist Church in Eastern British America*, II, 29.

19. *Ibid.*, p. 280.

20. I. F. MacKinnon's *Settlements and Churches in Nova Scotia, 1749-1776* (Montreal, 1930) has a good account of the origins of St Matthew's. See also W. C. Murray, "History of St. Matthew's Church," N.S.H.S. *Collections*, XVI.

21. Rev. George Patterson, *Memoir of the Reverend James MacGregor, D.D.* (Philadelphia, 1859), p. 215.

22. "Letter Addressed to the Rev. James Milne, A.M., 1818." Quoted in D. R. Jack's *History of St. Andrew's Church* (Saint John, 1913), pp. 67-71.

23. Rev. J. C. MacMillan, *History of the Catholic Church in Prince Edward Island*, I, 164.

24. P. C. T. White (ed.), *Lord Selkirk's Diary, 1803-1804*, pp. 313-14, 354.

25. Helen Taft Manning, *The Revolt of French Canada, 1800-1835* (Toronto, 1962), pp. 237-41.

26. MacMillan, *Catholic Church in Prince Edward Island*, I, 259.

27. Smith, *Methodist Church in Eastern British America*, II, 123.

28. Thorough reviews of the situation are to be found in K. F. C. MacNaughton's *The Development of the Theory and Practice of Education in New Brunswick* (Fredericton, 1947) and in P.A.N.S. *Bulletin No. 1*, 1937-39.

29. Legislative Debates, February 1, 1826, Murdoch, *Nova Scotia*, III, 545.

30. D. C. Harvey, *Journeys to the Island of St. John* (Toronto, 1955), pp. 170-71.

31. H. Y. Hind, *The University of King's College, 1790-1890* (Cambridge, 1890), pp. 71-73.

32. Report by S. G. W. Archibald, February 24, 1824, Murdoch, *Nova Scotia*, III, 514. For a fuller account of the history of Dalhousie, see D. C. Harvey, *An Introduction to the History of Dalhousie University* (Halifax, 1938).

33. MacNutt, *New Brunswick*, pp. 199-201.

34. See Prowse, *Newfoundland*, Appendix 7.

35. MacMillan, *Catholic Church in Prince Edward Island*, I, 269.

36. MacNutt, *New Brunswick*, pp. 173-76.

37. For greater detail see G. S. Graham, *Sea Power and British North America, 1783-1820* (Cambridge, 1941), pp. 226-31.

38. F. L. Benns, *The American Struggle for the British West Indies Carrying Trade, 1815-30* (Bloomington, 1923), pp. 70-76.

39. Murdoch, *Nova Scotia*, III, 535-36.

40. *Ibid.*, p. 500.

41. D. C. Harvey, "The Loyal Electors," *Trans. R.S.C.*, 1930.

42. Frank MacKinnon, *The Government of Prince Edward Island*, p. 37.

43. *Ibid.*, pp. 45-47.

44. P.R.O., C.O. 226/33. Bathurst to Smith, May 20, 1818.

45. For a fuller account see Harvey, "The Loyal Electors," *op. cit.*

46. *Ibid.*, p. 108.

47. A. R. M. Lower, *The North American Assault on the Canadian Forest* (Toronto, 1938), p. 77.

48. A. H. McLintock, *The Establishment of Constitutional Government in Newfoundland, 1783-1832*, pp. 139, 170.

49. C. Pedley, *History of Newfoundland From the Earliest Times to 1860*, pp. 344-46.

50. F. F. Thompson, *The French Shore Problem in Newfoundland*, pp. 23-24.

51. *A View of the Rise, Progress and Present State of the Newfoundland Fishery* (Poole, 1828).

52. P. Morris, *Arguments to Prove the Necessity of Granting to Newfoundland A Constitutional Government* (London, 1828).

53. W. E. Cormack, *Narrative of a Journey across the Island of Newfoundland* (St John's, 1822).

54. P.A.N.S. *Bulletin No. 1*, 1937-39, "Educational Report from the County of Lunenberg, May 12, 1824," p. 30.

55. R. Brown, *A History of the Island of Cape Breton*, pp. 433-35.

56. Murdoch, *Nova Scotia*, III, 437-38.

57. Proceedings of the House of Commons, June 18, 1824. See Murdoch, *Nova Scotia*, III, 521.

58. By a patent not finished until 1823 the Duke of York received the mineral rights to Cape Breton as a gift from his father, George III. To pay off his account to a jeweller, he sold them to the General Mining Association. See P.A.N.S. *Bulletin No. 1*, 1937-39, p. 43n.

59. T. C. Haliburton, *The Clockmaker*, Chap. 14, "Sayings and Doings in Cumberland" (London, 1837).

60. Murdoch, *Nova Scotia*, III, 449-50, 465.

61. Marion Gilroy, "Customs Fees in Nova Scotia," *C.H.R.*, XVII (1), 1936.

62. Murdoch, *Nova Scotia*, III, 569.

63. MacNutt, *New Brunswick*, pp. 181-84.

64. *Ibid.*, pp. 195-97, 206-8. Thomas Baillie was a brother to George Baillie, chief clerk of the North American Department in the Colonial Office. Lord Bathurst was under great personal obligation to him and relied on him to implement imperial land policy in New Brunswick.

65. Murdoch, *Nova Scotia*, III, 478-81.

66. MacNutt, *New Brunswick*, pp. 216-18.

NOTES TO CHAPTER EIGHT

1. B. Murdoch, A History of Nova Scotia or Acadie, III, 444.

2. Letters from Nova Scotia and New Brunswick (Edinburgh, 1829), p. 134.

3. P.R.O. C.O. 217/146. Report of Committee, October 14, 1826.

4. Parliamentary Papers, 1828, XXI, 359-482. "Report Laid before the Colonial Department by Lieut. Col. Cockburn on the Subject of Emigration."

5. W. S. MacNutt, New Brunswick: A History, 1784-1867, pp. 202-4.

6. J. A. Chisholm, The Speeches and Public Letters of Joseph Howe (Halifax, 1909), I, 183. Howe in the House of Assembly, April 16, 1838.

7. Ibid., p. 182.

8. L. Bliss to H. Bliss, June 18, 1832. A letter in the possession of L. M. Bell, Saint John.

9. J. M. Beck, The Government of Nova Scotia (Toronto, 1957), pp. 80-82.

10. Gene Morison, "The Brandy Election of 1830," N.S.H.S. Collections, XXX, 1954.

11. The Bank of Nova Scotia, 1832-1932 (Toronto, 1932), p. 27.

12. P.A.C. Series A, Goderich to Black, December 7, 1830.

13. On several occasions Howe remarked on the wealth of the members of New Brunswick's House of Assembly compared with that of the Nova Scotian assemblymen.

14. For a more detailed account of the struggle for the Crown Lands, see MacNutt, New Brunswick, Chap. 10.

15. Durham Report (London, 1839), p. 69.

16. Sir Francis B. Head, A Narrative (London, 1839), pp. 157-65.

17. P.A.C. Series A, Glenelg to Harvey, April 6, 1837.

18. James A. Roy, Joseph Howe: A Study in Achievement and Frustration (Toronto, 1935), p. 230.

19. Roy's book offers the best and most recent critical study of Howe's early years.

20. Very nearly a full account of the trial is to be found in Chisholm, Howe, Vol. I.

21. Chisholm, Howe, I, 104.

22. New Brunswick, House of Assembly Journals, Summer Session, 1837.

23. P.A.N.S. Akins Collection, Joseph Howe, Responsible Government: A Series of Letters to Lord John Russell (Halifax, 1839). They are republished in Chisholm, Howe, I, 221-66.

24. E. Wix, Six Months of a Newfoundland Missionary's Journal. From February to August, 1835 (London, 1836).

25. Parliamentary Debates, Vol. V (3rd Series), July 25, 1831.

26. P.R.O. C.O. 194/82. Stephen's report is dated December 19, 1831, and is printed in A. H. McLintock, The Establishment of Constitutional Government in Newfoundland, Appendix VII. See also Leslie Harris, "The First Nine Years of Representative Government in Newfoundland," (unpublished M.A. thesis, Memorial University, 1958).

27. McLintock, Establishment of Constitutional Government in Newfoundland, pp. 178-81.

28. Harris, "Representative Government in Newfoundland," pp. 32-36.

29. D. W. Prowse, History of Newfoundland, pp. 429-30.

30. C. Pedley, History of Newfoundland From Earliest Times to 1860, p. 378.

31. Harris, "Representative Government in Newfoundland," p. 61.

32. Prowse, Newfoundland, p. 447.

33. Harris, "Representative Government in Newfoundland," pp. 79-80.

34. C.O. 194/85, p. 366. Memorandum to Palmerston, July 11, 1833, cit. Harris, "Representative Government in Newfoundland."

35. Winton's account of the incident, written for the Public Ledger, is reprinted in Pedley, History of Newfoundland, pp. 392-94.

36. Pedley, *History of Newfoundland*, pp. 106-9.

37. Prowse, *Newfoundland*, p. 447.

38. Pedley, *History of Newfoundland*, p. 402.

39. A. H. Clark, *Three Centuries and the Island*, p. 95.

40. Sir Donald Campbell's recapitulatory dispatch of January 25, 1848, is a good summary of the origins of the land problem and of the political agitations of the previous ten years. See P.R.O. C.O. 226/73.

41. Robert Harris, *Some Pages from an Artist's Life*, "A Surveying Experience," (privately printed in Charlottetown, undated), pp. 30-36.

42. P.R.O. C.O. 226/71. T. W. Haviland to Huntley, July 12, 1847; enclosure to Huntley for Grey, July 13, 1847.

43. MacKinnon, *Prince Edward Island*, p. 114.

44. *Ibid.*, p. 111.

45. *Ibid.*, pp. 113-15.

46. *Ibid.*, p. 118.

47. In 1841 a committee of the House of Assembly made a report on the family connections of members of the Executive Council and Legislative Council which showed a degree of marital alliance and consanguinity that could not be approached by the government of any other province in British North America. See *Assembly Journals*, 1841, p. 151, and MacKinnon, *Prince Edward Island*, p. 38n. In No. 2 of the *Examiner* of 1847, Edward Whelan later produced another elaborate description of the connection which he called the *Black Watch*.

48. Clark, *The Island*, p. 77.

NOTES TO CHAPTER NINE

1. A. M. Payne, "The Life of Sir Samuel Cunard," N.S.H.S. *Collections*, XXIX.

2. R. D. Evans, "Stage Coaches in Nova Scotia, 1815 to 1867," N.S.H.S. *Collections*, XXIV.

3. This enterprise, commenced by six New York newspapers, is said to have had its origins in reportorial experience of the Mexican War and explains the beginnings of the Associated Press. See John W. Ryan, "The Inception of the Associated Press," N.S.H.S. *Collections*, XVI.

4. J. S. Martell, "Early Coal-Mining in Nova Scotia," *Dalhousie Review*, XXV, 1945.

5. D. W. Prowse, *History of Newfoundland*, p. 451.

6. A. H. Clark, *Three Centuries and the Island*, Chap. 6, " The Island One Century Ago."

7. MacNutt, *New Brunswick*, pp. 265-70, 308-13. From the American side the best and most easily manageable account is H. S. Burrage, *Maine in the Northeastern Boundary Controversy* (Portland, 1919).

8. J. A. Chisholm, *The Speeches and Public Letters of Joseph Howe*, I, 337.

9. James A. Roy, *Joseph Howe: A Study in Achievement and Frustration*, p. 121.

10. Chisholm, *Howe*, I, 422.

11. This famous pasquinade is published in Chisholm, *Howe*, I, 515-17.

12. MacNutt, *New Brunswick*, p. 291.

13. *Parliamentary Papers*, Select Committee, 1841, Evidence, pp. 7-9, 14, *cit.* Gertrude E. Gunn, "A Political History of Newfoundland, 1832-1861" (unpublished Ph.D. thesis, University of London, 1960).

14. Rev. Malcolm MacDonnell, "The Conflict between Sir John Harvey and Chief Justice John Gervaise Hutchinson Bourne," C.H.A. *Report*, 1956.

15. For a full account see Gunn, "Political History of Newfoundland," Chap. 7, "The Amalgamated Legislature, 1842-48."

16. Reported in *Newfoundlander*, February 8, 1844, *cit.* Gunn, "Political History of Newfoundland," p. 202.

17. Chisholm, *Howe*, I, 609.

18. MacNutt, *New Brunswick*, pp. 292-93.

19. P.R.O. C.O. 217/196, Harvey to Grey, January 25, 1847.

20. *Ibid.*, Submission of Executive Council, January 30, 1847.

21. *Ibid.*

22. *New Brunswick Courier*, January 29, 1848.

23. *Acadian Recorder*, April 12, 1845, cit. J. M. Beck, *The Government of Nova Scotia*, pp. 124-25.

24. Quoted in the Halifax *Sun*, June 14, 1847.

25. Halifax *Sun*, April 28, 1847, "The Tories and the Catholics."

26. P.R.O. C.O. 217/196, Harvey to Grey, private, August 10, 1847.

27. D. C. Harvey, "The Civil List and Responsible Government in Nova Scotia," *C.H.R.*, XXVIII (4), 1947. A full history of this controversy is given here.

28. P.R.O. C.O. 188/105, Head to Grey, January 6, 1849. For a longer account see MacNutt, *New Brunswick*, pp. 318-20. The date for the introduction of responsible government to New Brunswick has been a subject of some confusion. Owing to Howe's victory in Nova Scotia in 1848, Liberal legend has attached great importance to the change. Though the necessary technical and official adjustments were made in New Brunswick in the same year, no change of government occurred. Liberal legend in that province has chosen to follow the argument of Charles Fisher that responsible government was delayed until 1854 when he himself led a Liberal government into office. See *Debates in the House of Assembly on Mr. Fisher's Amendment . . .* (Fredericton, 1854). This partisan point of view is re-echoed in the writings of George E. Fenety, editor of the Saint John *News*

and a former apprentice of Howe at Halifax, and of James Hannay, who later wrote for Liberal journals in New Brunswick. There can be no doubt that Sir Edmund Head very literally executed the stipulations of Earl Grey's 1847 dispatch to Sir John Harvey.

29. Gunn, "Political History of Newfoundland," p. 232.

30. Rev. John C. MacMillan, *History of the Catholic Church in Prince Edward Island*, II, 44-52.

31. Frank MacKinnon, *The Government of Prince Edward Island*, p. 79.

32. *Ibid.*, pp. 78-80.

33. P.R.O. C.O. 226/71, Huntley to Grey, July 13, 1847.

34. D. C. Harvey, "Dishing the Reformers," *Trans. R.S.C.*, Sect. II, 1931.

35. P.R.O. C.O. 226/71, T. W. Haviland to Huntley, enclosure Huntley to Grey, June 19, 1847.

36. P.R.O. C.O. 226/71. This allegation that states that Coles, Mackintosh, and other reformers were present during the Belfast Riots, that they made the escheat question a part of the quarrel, is contained in letters of Haviland and other members of the Compact enclosed in Huntley's dispatch of July 13, 1847.

37. *Ibid.*, Placard enclosed.

38. *Ibid.*, Petition enclosed.

39. P.R.O. C.O. 226/73, Campbell to Grey, June 1, 1848.

40. B. W. A. Sleigh, *Pine Forests and Hackmatack Clearings* (London, 1853), Chap. 7. As a landowner, Sleigh would not be inclined to report a favourable opinion of escheat politicians.

41. Chisholm, *Howe*, II, 69.

42. P.R.O. C.O. 226/71, Huntley to Grey, June 28, 1847.

NOTES TO CHAPTER TEN

1. D. C. Masters, *The Reciprocity Treaty of 1854* (London, 1936), p. 7.

2. MacNutt, *New Brunswick*, pp. 323-24.

3. For a close study of public opinion in

Saint John during these years, see D. F. MacMillan, "Federation and Annexation Sentiment in New Brunswick, 1848-51" (unpublished M.A. thesis in the library of the University of New Brunswick, 1961).

4. MacNutt, *New Brunswick*, pp. 298-99.

5. *Ibid.*, pp. 328-29.

6. G. R. Stevens, *Canadian National Railways* (Toronto, 1960), I, 163. This volume contains a good introduction to the background of railway construction in the Atlantic Provinces. For a lengthy explanation of Howe's part, see James A. Roy, *Joseph Howe: A Study in Achievement and Frustration.*

7. J. M. Beck, *The Government of Nova Scotia*, p. 123; MacNutt, *New Brunswick*, pp. 364-65.

8. Masters, *Reciprocity Treaty*, p. 89.

9. S. A. Saunders, "The Maritime Provinces and the Reciprocity Treaty," *Dalhousie Review*, XIII, 1934.

10. See the statistics offered by Masters, *Reciprocity Treaty.*

11. "Reminiscences of Senator A. A. Macdonald," *Collier's Magazine*, July 3, 1909. This account was given by Senator Macdonald when he was a very old man and, according to the editor's comment, was "told in a somewhat haphazard way."

12. F. W. Wallace, *Wooden Ships and Iron Men* (London, 1924), p. 77.

13. M. H. Perley, *A Hand-Book of Information for Immigrants to New Brunswick* (London, 1857), p. 42.

14. Saunders, "Maritime Provinces," *op. cit.*

15. For a detailed account of Prince Edward Island politics in these years, see D. C. Harvey, "Dishing the Reformers," *Trans. R.S.C.*, Sect. II, 1931.

16. This was not until 1859.

17. For a lengthy discussion from the Catholic side, see Rev. John C. MacMillan, *History of the Catholic Church in Prince Edward Island*, II, Chap. 11.

18. Frank MacKinnon, *The Government of Prince Edward Island*, p. 93.

19. Gertrude E. Gunn, "A Political History of Newfoundland, 1832-1861," *op. cit.*, p. 246.

20. *Ibid.*, p. 256.

21. *Ibid.*, p. 277.

22. *Ibid.*, p. 327.

23. F. F. Thompson, *The French Shore Problem in Newfoundland*, pp. 33-36.

24. MacKinnon, *Prince Edward Island*, p. 94.

25. Many years later, long after Howe's death, Sir John A. Macdonald remarked on Howe's great capacity for "seminal ideas."

26. MacNutt, *New Brunswick*, pp. 350-51, 358-62.

27. Universal manhood suffrage was later repealed by the Liberals when they returned to power in 1863.

28. Nova Scotians did not vote by ballot until after 1870.

29. D. C. Harvey, "The Struggle for the New England Form of Township Government in Nova Scotia," *C.H.A. Report*, 1933. See also Beck, *Nova Scotia.* pp. 134-40.

30. H. Reid, *The American Crisis* (London, 1861), p. 289.

31. C. B. Bagster, *The Progress and Prospects of Prince Edward Island* (Charlottetown, 1861).

32. Beck, *Nova Scotia*, p. 87.

33. Prince Edward Island acquired an elective legislative council in 1862. There Edward Palmer, having put forward the design in 1852 by reason of Liberal opposition in the appointed chamber, carried his conviction into action.

34. P. B. Waite, "A Nova Scotian in Toronto, 1855," *Ontario History*, LV (3), 1963.

35. Fisher was later displaced in 1861. See MacNutt, *New Brunswick*, pp. 386-88.

36. N.S.H.A., March 18, 1858. Speech of William Young.

37. J. A. Chisholm, *The Speeches and Public Letters of Joseph Howe*, II, 15.

38. MacNutt, *New Brunswick*, pp. 349, 369-71.

39. W. M. Brown, "Recollections of Old Halifax," *N.S.H.S. Collections*, XIII, 1908.

40. Chisholm allows no detailed account of this part of Howe's career. For a documented account of the Gourlay Riots and the aftermath, see James A. Roy, *Joseph Howe: A Study in Achievement and Frustration.*

41. J. S. Martell, "Early Coal-Mining in Nova Scotia," *Dalhousie Review,* XXV, 1945.

42. Alice R. Stewart, "Sir Edmund Head's Memorandum of 1857 on Maritime Union: A Lost Confederation Document," *C.H.R.,* XXVI (4), 1945.

43. Reid, *American Crisis,* p. 289.

44. See the discussion in Beck, *Nova Scotia,* pp. 110-11.

BIBLIOGRAPHY

For the history of five colonies over a period of a century and a half the amount of source material, both in manuscript and in printed form, is literally enormous. Well over two hundred books, articles, and pamphlets have been written on the Acadian expulsion alone. The following descriptions and lists represent what the author considers to be most useful and authoritative.

MANUSCRIPTS

The Public Record Office in London is the greatest repository of original source material for this period of the history of the Atlantic Provinces. Correspondence between the governors and the Colonial Office is to be found in the C.O. Series: 188 (for New Brunswick), 194 (for Newfoundland), 217 (for Nova Scotia), 226 (for Prince Edward Island). Other documents, often of great importance, are to be found in the records of the Foreign Office, the Admiralty, the War Office, and other departments of government. The Colonial Office volumes are available both in transcript and on microfilm at the Public Archives of Canada, Ottawa. Also to be found there are transcripts of the correspondence between Paris and Quebec and Louisburg during the days of the French regime.

Other important source materials in London are to be found in the Manuscripts Division of the British Museum, notably in the Additional Series. Of these the important Newcastle Collection might be mentioned as especially useful for the diplomatic and military history between 1745 and 1763. The House of Lords Library contains manuscript material for the history of Nova Scotia between 1749 and 1755. The Library of the Society for the Propagation of the Gospel contains the records of the first English-speaking missionaries.

Important supplementary material of all kinds, such as the Diary of Bishop Inglis and the Raymond Manuscripts, is held at the Public Archives of Canada. New Brunswick does not have an archives but valuable work for the preservation of source material for provincial history is being done at the New Brunswick Museum in Saint John, the Legislative Library at Fredericton, and at the University of New Brunswick Library, the home of the Winslow and Saunders collections. Newfoundland has recently established an archives at St John's and, in spite of the losses from fires of the last century, a great effort is being made to preserve the records of provincial history. Nova Scotia is the only Atlantic province with a long-established and highly organized provincial archives. The consequence is that the details of its history can be recorded with far greater precision than those of the other provinces. As yet no archives has been established in Prince Edward Island, though certain documents can be examined in the Provincial Building at Charlottetown.

PRINTED DOCUMENTS

The volumes of the *Calendar of State Papers Colonial, America and West Indies* and of the *Journals of the Commissioners for Trade and Plantations, 1704-1782*, published by Her Majesty's Stationery Office, London, offers a good introduction to the period of the Anglo-French struggle. *Collection des manuscrits contenant lettres, mémoires et autres documents historiques relatifs à la Nouvelle France*, published by the Quebec Archives in four volumes from 1883 to 1885, does the same service for French documentation. The reports of the Public Archives of Canada frequently calendar and reproduce documents both British and French. An occasional document published in *Colonial Documents of the State of New York* and in the publications of the Massachusetts Historical Society has been helpful. The *Northcliffe Collection* (P.A.C. *Report, 1926*) contains the papers of Colonel Robert Monckton, who directed the Acadian expulsion. *The Journal of Colonel John Winslow*, his assistant, is found in N.S.H.S. *Collections*, Vol. III. A fresh and vital account of military events in the Seven Years' War is found in John Knox's *Historical Journal of the Campaign in North America for the Years 1757, 1758, 1759 and 1760* (ed. A. G. Doughty), 3 vols., published by the Champlain Society, Toronto, 1914.

For the period of the American Revolution the *Dartmouth Manuscripts*, published by the Historical Manuscripts Commission of Great Britain, offer insights into the conduct of Governor Legge of Nova Scotia. F. C. Wharton's *Revolutionary Diplomatic Correspondence of the United States*, Washington, 1889, contains frequent reference to the Atlantic Provinces. What life was like in Nova Scotia during the Revolution is vividly revealed by *The Diary of Simeon Perkins, 1766-1780* (ed. H. A. Innis), published by the Champlain Society in 1948. *The Winslow Papers* (ed. W. O. Raymond), Saint John, 1901, is still the best published collection of Loyalist correspondence. The reports of the provincial historical societies, especially that of New Brunswick, contain much Loyalist literature.

Lord Selkirk's Diary, 1803-1804: A Journal of His Travels in British North America and the Northeastern United States (ed. P. C. T. White), the Champlain Society, Toronto, 1958, presents a most detailed picture of Prince Edward Island and parts of Nova Scotia during the Napoleonic Wars. J. A. Chisholm's *The Speeches and Public Letters of Joseph Howe*, Halifax, 1909, 2 vols., is a voluminous, though one-sided, introduction to later political history.

Governmental publications of documents were few in the colonial period. The legislative journals of the colonies are available in various libraries. A few volumes of synoptic debates of the New Brunswick legislature are to be found in the Legislative Library at Fredericton.

NEWSPAPERS

All of the colonies produced many newspapers. The files that have been preserved are being reproduced on microfilm by the Canadian Library Association. For a good account of the beginnings, see *Early Journalism in Nova Scotia* by J. J. Stewart, N.S.H.S. *Collections*, Vol. VI. Of the later journals, the most important were the *Acadian Recorder*, Howe's *Nova Scotian*, the *Sun*, and the *Chronicle*, all of Halifax.

New Brunswick's newspapers are listed and briefly described in J. R. Harper's *Historical Dictionary of New Brunswick Newspapers and Periodicals*, Fredericton, 1961. Of Prince Edward Island's list, found in the bibliography of Frank MacKinnon's *The Government of Prince Edward Island*, the most significant was probably Edward Whelan's *Examiner*, though it commenced publication only in 1847. The history of journalism in Newfoundland commenced in 1806 with the publication of the *Royal Gazette* by John Ryan, who came from New Brunswick. The principal partisans in the later war of political propaganda were the *Public Ledger* and the *Patriot*. A good collection of newspaper material is to be found in the Gosling Memorial Library, St John's.

TRAVEL ACCOUNTS AND OTHER CONTEMPORARY WORKS

The Anglo-French Rivalry:

Address to the Right Honourable William Pitt. Considerations on the Importance of the American Fishery. London, 1759.

AUCHMUTY, R. *The Importance of Cape Breton to the British Nation.* London, 1746.

—— *The Ancient Right of the English People to the American Fishery.* London, 1764.

CHARLEVOIX, PÈRE P. F. X. DE. *Histoire et description générale de la Nouvelle France, avec le journal historique d'un voyage fait par ordre du roi dans l'Amérique Septentrionale.* 3 vols. Paris, 1744.

COLBERT, J. B. *The Memoirs of the Marquis of Torcy.* Translated. 2 vols. London, 1757.

The Conduct of the French with Regard to Nova Scotia. London, 1754.

La Conduite des Français justifiée ou observations sur un écrit anglais. Utrecht, 1756.

DOUGLASS, W. *Considerations on the State of the British Fisheries in America.* London, 1749.

—— *A Summary of the Present State of the British Plantations in America.* 2 vols. London, 1757.

A Fair Representation of His Majesty's Right to Nova Scotia or Acadie. London, 1756.

A Genuine Account of Nova Scotia. London, 1750.

The Importance of Settling and Fortifying Nova Scotia. London, 1751.

LITTLE, O. *A Geographic History of Nova Scotia.* London, 1749.

Mémoire des Commissaires du Roi et de ceux de Sa Majesté Britannique, sur les possessions et les droits respectifs des deux couronnes en Amérique, sur les actes publics et pièces justificatives. 5 vols. Paris, 1756. (The first volume contains the memoir on the boundaries of Nova Scotia submitted by the British commissioners, the second that by the French. The remaining volumes contain reprints of treaties, documents, and early correspondence.)

PICHON, T. *History of the Islands of Cape Breton and St John.* London, 1760.

Rélation de ce que est passé en Acadie. Paris, 1755.

SHIRLEY, W. *The Conduct of Major-General Shirley.* London, 1758.

The State of the Trade of the Northern Colonies and A Particular Account of Nova Scotia. London, 1748.

"The Use Which the French Made of Cape Breton," *Grand Magazine of Magazines,* London, 1759.

The British Colonial Period:

An Account of Nova Scotia. Two Letters to a Noble Lord. London, 1756.

ATCHESON, N. *American Encroachments on British Rights.* London, 1808.

ATKINSON, REV. M. C. *Historical and Statistical Account of New Brunswick.* Edinburgh, 1844.

BAGSTER, C. B. *The Progress and Prospects of Prince Edward Island.* Charlottetown, 1861.

BEAVAN, MRS F. *Life in the Backwoods of New Brunswick.* London, 1845.

BUCKINGHAM, J. S. *Canada, Nova Scotia and New Brunswick and the Other British Provinces in North America, with A Plan of National Colonization.* London, 1843.

CAMPBELL, P. *Travels in the Interior Inhabited Parts of North America. In the Years 1791 and 1792. . . .* Edinburgh, 1793. (Reprinted by the Champlain Society, Toronto, 1937.)

CARSON, W. *Letter to Members of Parliament.* St John's, 1812 (in C.O. 194 Series).

—— *Reasons for Colonizing the Island of Newfoundland.* St John's, 1813 (in C.O. 194 Series).

COKE, E. T. *A Subaltern's Furlough: Descriptive of Scenes in Various Parts of the United States, Upper and Lower Canada, New Brunswick and Nova Scotia, during the Summer and Autumn of 1832.* London, 1833.

DURHAM, FIRST EARL OF. *Report on the Affairs of British North America.* London, 1839.

FISHER, P. *Sketches of New Brunswick; Containing an Account of the First Settlement of the Province.* Saint John, 1825.

HEAD, SIR G. *Forest Scenes and Incidents of the Wilds of North America. . . .* London, 1829.

JOHNSTON, J. F. W. *Notes on North America, Agricultural, Economical, and Social.* 2 vols. London, 1851.

KNOX, W. *Semi-Official State Papers.* London, 1789.

A Letter from a Gentleman in Nova Scotia. London, 1756.

Letters from Nova Scotia and New Brunswick. Edinburgh, 1829.

LOCKWOOD, A. *A Brief Description of Nova Scotia . . . .* London, 1818.

MARSDEN, J. *Narrative of a Mission to Nova Scotia, New Brunswick and the Somers Islands.* London, 1816.

MARTIN, R. M. *History of the British Colonies.* London, 1834.

MOORSOM, W. *Letters from Nova Scotia and New Brunswick; Comprising Sketches of a Young Country.* London, 1830.

PERLEY, M. H. *A Hand-Book of Information for Immigrants to New Brunswick.* London, 1857.

The Present State of Nova Scotia. Edinburgh, 1786.

REID, H. *The American Crisis.* London, 1861.

Reply to Remarks in a Late Pamphlet by J. Viator. London, 1784.

SLEIGH, B. W. A. *Pine Forests and Hackmatack Clearings.* London, 1853.

A True Account of the Colonies of Nova Scotia and Georgia. London, 1780.

Vindication of Governor Parr and His Council, by a Gentleman of Halifax. London, 1784.

WIX, REV. E. *Six Months of a Newfoundland Missionary's Journal. From February to August, 1835.* London, 1836.

SECONDARY WORKS

Provincial History:

NEW BRUNSWICK

FENETY, G. E. *Political Notes.* Fredericton, 1867.

HANNAY, J. *History of New Brunswick.* 2 vols. Saint John, 1909.

LAWRENCE, J. W. *Footprints; or Incidents in the Early History of New Brunswick.* Saint John, 1883.

—— *The Judges of New Brunswick and Their Times.* Saint John, 1907.

MACNUTT, W. S. *New Brunswick: A History, 1784-1867.* Toronto, 1963.

RAYMOND, W. O. *History of the St John River.* Saint John, 1905.

WRIGHT, E. C. *The Miramichi.* Sackville, 1944.

—— *The Loyalists of New Brunswick.* Fredericton, 1955.

NEWFOUNDLAND

BONNYCASTLE, SIR R. M. *Newfoundland in 1842.* 2 vols. London, 1842.

CORMACK, W. F. *Narration of a Journey Across the Island of Newfoundland.* St John's, 1822.

GUNN, G. E. "A Political History of Newfoundland, 1832-1861." Unpublished Ph.D. thesis, University of London, 1960. This thesis, about to be published in book form by the University of Toronto Press, is the only reliable guide for the greater part of the period which it covers.

HARRIS, L. "The First Nine Years of Representative Government in Newfoundland." Unpublished M.A. thesis, Memorial University, 1958.

HATTON, J. and HARVEY, M. *Newfoundland, The Oldest British Colony.* London, 1883.

MCLINTOCK, A. H. *The Establishment of Constitutional Government in Newfoundland, 1783-1832.* London, New York, 1941.

PEDLEY, C. *History of Newfoundland From the Earliest Times to 1860.* London, 1863.

PROWSE, D. W. *History of Newfoundland.* London, 1895.

REEVES, J. *History of the Government of the Island of Newfoundland.* London, 1793.

ROGERS, J. D. *Newfoundland.* Oxford, 1911.

ROTHNEY, G. O. "The History of Newfoundland and Labrador, 1754-1785." Unpublished M.A. thesis, University of London, 1934.

NOVA SCOTIA

BECK, J. M. *The Government of Nova Scotia.* Toronto, 1957. This is the work of a political scientist and, like Dr F. MacKinnon's counterpart for Prince Edward Island, is a study of political institutions. Both draw very heavily upon historical material and have been exceptionally helpful.

BELL, W. P. *The Foreign Protestants and the Settlement of Nova Scotia.* Toronto, 1961.

BREBNER, J. B. *The Neutral Yankees of Nova Scotia.* New York, 1937. The standard work on the period of the American Revolution.

Nova Scotian Archives Bulletin No. 1 gives an excellent account of the development of educational policy. For detailed material on the early religious and educational life of Newfoundland, see the later chapters of D. W. Prowse, *History of Newfoundland.*

BROWN, R. *History of the Island of Cape Breton*. London, 1869.

CAMPBELL, D. *Nova Scotia in Its Historical, Mercantile and Industrial Relations*. Montreal, 1873.

DUNN, C. W. *Highland Settler: A Portrait of the Scottish Gael in Nova Scotia*. Toronto, 1953.

HALIBURTON, T. C. *An Historical and Statistical Account of Nova Scotia*. 2 vols. Halifax, 1829.

MURDOCH, B. *A History of Nova Scotia or Acadie*. 3 vols. Halifax, 1865. A severely chronological narrative of events that can be most useful, especially the third volume, which deals with a period given little critical study.

PATTERSON, REV. G. *A History of the County of Pictou*. Montreal, 1877.

ROY, J. A. *Joseph Howe: A Study in Achievement and Frustration*. Toronto, 1935.

SAUNDERS, E. M. *Three Premiers of Nova Scotia*. Toronto, 1909.

PRINCE EDWARD ISLAND

CAMPBELL, D. C. *History of Prince Edward Island*. Charlottetown, 1875.

CLARK, A. H. *Three Centuries and the Island*. Toronto, 1959. A very scholarly work of economic geography.

COTTON, W. L. *Chapters in Our Island Story*. Charlottetown, 1927.

HARVEY, D. C. *The French Regime in Prince Edward Island*. New Haven, 1926. The standard work.

—— (ed.) *Journeys to the Island of St. John*. Toronto, 1953.

LIVINGSTON, W. R. *Responsible Government in Prince Edward Island*. University of Iowa, 1931.

MACKINNON, FRANK. *The Government of Prince Edward Island*. Toronto, 1951.

STEWART, JOHN. *An Account of Prince Edward Island*. London, 1806.

WARBURTON, A. B. *A History of Prince Edward Island, 1534-1831*. Saint John, 1923.

General:

ALBION, R. G. *Forests and Sea-Power*. Cambridge, 1926.

ALLAN, H. C. *Great Britain and the United States*. London, 1954.

BASYE, A. H. *The Board of Trade, 1748-1782*. London, 1925.

BEER, G. L. *British Colonial Policy*. New York, 1907.

—— *The Old Colonial System*. New York, 1912.

BREBNER, J. B. *New England's Outpost: Acadia before the British Conquest of Canada*. New York, 1927. The standard work.

BURT, A. L. *The United States, Great Britain and British North America*. New Haven, 1940.

Cambridge History of the British Empire. Vols. I and VI.

CORBETT, SIR JULIAN S. *England in the Seven Years' War*. 2 vols. London, 1907.

DAVIS, H. A. *An International Community on the St. Croix*. Orono, 1950.

FLICK, A. C. *Loyalism in New York during the American Revolution*. New York, 1902.

FULLOM, S. W. *The Life of General Sir Howard Douglas, Bart*. London, 1863.

GRAHAM, G. S. *Sea Power and British North America, 1783-1820*. Cambridge, 1941.

—— *Empire of the North Atlantic*. London, 1950.

HANNAY, J. *The History of Acadia from Its First Discovery to 1763*. Saint John, 1879.

HOTBLACK, K. *Chatham's Colonial Policy*. London, 1917.

KERR, D. G. G. *Sir Edmund Head: A Scholarly Governor*. Toronto, 1954.

KIDDER, F. *Military Operations in Eastern Maine and Nova Scotia*. Boston, 1867.

LOUNSBURY, R. G. *The British Fishery in Newfoundland, 1634-1763*. New Haven, 1934.

LUCAS, SIR C. P. (ed.) *Lord Durham's Report on the Affairs of British North America*. 3 vols. Oxford, 1912.

MARTIN, C. *Empire and Commonwealth*. Oxford, 1929.

MCLENNAN, J. S. *Louisburg From Its Foundation to Its Fall, 1713-1758*. London, 1918.

MIMS, S. L. *Colbert's West India Policy*. New Haven, 1912.

PARKMAN, F. *Montcalm and Wolfe*. Boston, 1885.

—— *A Half Century of Conflict*. Boston, 1897.

SABINE, L. The American Loyalists. Boston, 1847.

SCHUTZ, J. A. William Shirley: King's Governor of Massachusetts. Williamsburg, 1961.

SNIDER, C. H. J. Under the Red Jack. Toronto, 1927.

STARK, J. H. The Loyalists of Massachusetts. Boston, 1910.

THOMPSON, F. F. The French Shore Problem in Newfoundland. Toronto, 1961.

Economic and Social:

BENNS, F. L. The American Struggle for the British West Indies Carrying Trade, 1815-30. Bloomington, 1923.

FLEMING, S. The Intercolonial Railway. Montreal, 1876.

GRANT, R. F. The Canadian Atlantic Fishery. Toronto, 1934.

INNIS, H. A. The Cod Fisheries: The History of An International Economy (rev. ed.). Toronto, 1954.

LOWER, A. R. M. The North American Assault on the Canadian Forest: A History of the Lumber Trade between Canada and the United States. Toronto, 1938.

MACDONALD, N. Canada, 1763-1841, Immigration and Settlement. London, 1939.

MANNY, L. Ships of Miramichi. Saint John, 1960.

MASTERS, D. C. The Reciprocity Treaty of 1854. Toronto, 1936.

MORISON, S. E. Maritime History of Massachusetts, 1783-1860. Cambridge, 1921.

SAUNDERS, S. A. Economic History of the Maritime Provinces. Toronto, 1940.

SHIPPEE, L. B. Canadian-American Relations, 1848-1874. Toronto, 1939.

STEVENS, G. R. Canadian National Railways, Vol. I. Toronto, 1960.

WALLACE, F. W. Wooden Ships and Iron Men. London, 1924.

WEEDEN, W. B. Economic and Social History of New England. 2 vols. Boston and New York, 1890.

Religious and Educational:

BILL, I. E. Fifty Years with the Baptists in the Maritime Provinces. Saint John, 1880.

EATON, A. W. H. The Church of England in Nova Scotia and the Tory Clergymen of the Revolution. London, 1892.

HALIBURTON, T. C. The Clockmaker. Various editions.

HARRIS, R. V. Charles Inglis, Missionary, Loyalist Bishop. Toronto, 1937.

HARVEY, D. C. An Introduction to the History of Dalhousie University. Halifax, 1938.

HIND, H. Y. The University of King's College, 1790-1890. Cambridge, 1890.

LEVY, G. E. The Baptists of the Maritime Provinces, 1753-1946. Saint John, 1946.

MACKINNON, I. F. Settlements and Churches in Nova Scotia, 1749-1776. Montreal, 1930.

MACMILLAN, J. C. History of the Catholic Church in Prince Edward Island. 2 vols. Quebec, 1905 and 1913.

MACNAUGHTON, K. F. C. The Development of the Theory and Practice of Education in New Brunswick, 1784-1900. Fredericton, 1947.

MOCKRIDGE, C. H. The Bishops of the Church of England in Canada. Toronto, 1896.

O'BRIEN, C. Memoirs of the Right Reverend Edmund Burke, Bishop of Zion. Ottawa, 1894.

PASCOE, C. F. Two Hundred Years of the S.P.G., 1700-1901. London, 1901.

PATTERSON, G. Memoir of the Reverend James MacGregor. Philadelphia, 1859. The most detailed account of the early years of the Presbyterian Church in the Atlantic Provinces.

SMITH, T. W. History of the Methodist Church in Eastern British America. 2 vols. Halifax, 1877.

See also general note bottom p. 293.

PERIODICAL ARTICLES

ARCHIBALD, SIR ADAMS. "Life of Sir John Wentworth," N.S.H.S. Collections, XX.

BREBNER, J. B. "Subsidized Intermarriage with the Indians," C.H.R., VI (1), 1925.

BURNS, REV. J. E. "The Establishment of Roman Catholic Church Government in Halifax," N.S.H.S. Collections, XXIII.

BUTLER, G. F. "The Early Organization

and Influence of Halifax Merchants," N.S.H.S. *Collections*, XXV.

D'ENTREMONT, H. L. "Father Jean Sigogne, 1799-1844," N.S.H.S. *Collections*, XXIII.

ELLS, M. E. "Settling the Loyalists in Nova Scotia," Canadian Historical Association, *Report*, 1934.

EVANS, R. D. "Stage Coaches in Nova Scotia, 1815 to 1867," N.S.H.S. *Collections*, XXIV.

GILROY, M. "The Partition of Nova Scotia," *C.H.R.*, XIV (4), 1933.

—— "Customs Fees in Nova Scotia," *C.H.R.*, XVII (1), 1936.

GRAHAM, G. S. "Britain's Defence in Newfoundland: A Survey from the Discovery to the Present Day," *C.H.R.*, XXIII (3), 1942.

GREEN, S. A. "Congregational Churches in Nova Scotia," Massachusetts Historical Society, *Collections*, 1888.

HANNAY, J. "The Founding of Maugerville," N.B.H.S. *Collections*, I.

HARVEY, D. C. "The Loyal Electors," *Trans. R.S.C.*, 1930.

—— "Dishing the Reformers," *Trans. R.S.C.*, 1931.

—— "The Struggle for the New England Form of Township Government in Nova Scotia," *Trans. R.S.C.*, 1933.

—— "The Intellectual Awakening of Nova Scotia," *Dalhousie Review*, XII, 1933.

—— "Uniacke's Memorial of 1805," *C.H.R.*, XVII (1), 1936.

—— "The Civil List and Responsible Government in Nova Scotia," *C.H.R.*, XXVIII (4), 1947.

HILL, REV. G. W. "History of St. Paul's Church," N.S.H.S. *Collections*, III.

INNIS, H. A. "Cape Breton and the French Regime," *Trans. R.S.C.*, 1935.

LONGLEY, R. S. "An Annapolis County Loyalist," N.S.H.S. *Collections*, XXXI. (An account of Timothy Ruggles.)

—— "The Delancey Brothers, Loyalists of Annapolis County," N.S.H.S. *Collections*, XXXII.

MACDONALD, J. S. "Memoir of Governor John Parr," N.S.H.S. *Collections*, XIV.

—— "Early Highland Migration to Nova Scotia and Prince Edward Island from 1770 to 1853," N.S.H.S. *Collections*, XXIII.

MACDONNELL, REV. M. "The Conflict between Sir John Harvey and Chief Justice John Gervaise Hutchinson Bourne," Canadian Historical Association, *Report*, 1956.

MACNUTT, W. S. "Why Halifax Was Founded," *Dalhousie Review*, XII, 1933.

—— "The Beginnings of Nova Scotian Politics," *C.H.R.*, XVI (1), 1935.

MURRAY, W. C. "History of St. Matthew's Church," N.S.H.S. *Collections*, XVI.

PAYNE, A. M. "The Life of Sir Samuel Cunard," N.S.H.S. *Collections*, XXIX.

RAYMOND, W. O. "Colonel Alexander McNutt and the Pre-Loyalist Settlements of Nova Scotia," *Trans. R.S.C.*, 1912.

—— "Old Townships on the St. John River," N.B.H.S. *Collections*, II.

—— "Life of Thomas Carleton," N.B.H.S. *Collections*, VI.

—— "The Founding of Shelburne," N.B.H.S. *Collections*, VIII.

RADDALL, T. H. "Tarleton's Legion," N.S.H.S. *Collections*, XXVIII.

RAWLYK, G. A. "The American Revolution and Nova Scotia Reconsidered," *Dalhousie Review*, XLIII, 1963.

RYAN, J. W. "The Inception of the Associated Press," N.S.H.S. *Collections*, XVI.

SAUNDERS, REV. E. M. "Rev. John Wiswell, M.A.," N.S.H.S. *Collections*, XIII.

SAUNDERS, S. A. "The Maritime Provinces and the Reciprocity Treaty," *Dalhousie Review*, XIII, 1934.

SIEBERT, W. H. AND GILLIAM, F. E. "The Loyalists in Prince Edward Island," *Trans. R.S.C.*, 1910.

STANLEY, G. F. G. "James Glenie," N.S.H.S. *Collections*, 1941.

STEWART, A. "Sir Edmund Head's Memorandum of 1857 on Maritime Union: A Lost Confederation Document," *C.H.R.*, XXVI (4), 1945.

STORY, N. "The Church and State Party in Nova Scotia," N.S.H.S. *Collections*, XXVII.

INDEX

A HISTORY OF CANADA IN SEVENTEEN VOLUMES

The Canadian Centenary Series is a comprehensive history of the peoples and lands which form the Dominion of Canada.

Although the series is designed as a unified whole so that no part of the story is left untold, each volume is complete in itself. Written for the general reader as well as for the scholar, each of the seventeen volumes of *The Canadian Centenary Series* is the work of a leading Canadian historian who is an authority on the period covered in his volume. Their combined efforts have made a new and significant contribution to the understanding of the history of Canada and of Canada today.

W. L. Morton, Head of the Department of History and Provost of University College, University of Manitoba, is the Executive Editor of *The Canadian Centenary Series*. A graduate of the Universities of Manitoba and Oxford, he is the author of *The Kingdom of Canada; Manitoba: A History; The Progressive Party in Canada; One University: A History of the University of Manitoba;* and other writings. He has also edited *The Journal of Alexander Begg and Other Documents Relevant to the Red River Resistance.* He holds the honorary degree of Doctor of Laws from the University of Toronto and has been awarded the Tyrrell Medal of the Royal Society of Canada and the Governor General's Award for Non-Fiction.

D. G. Creighton, Professor of History, University of Toronto, is the Advisory Editor of *The Canadian Centenary Series*. A graduate of the Universities of Toronto and Oxford, he is the author of *John A. Macdonald: The Young Politician; John A. Macdonald: The Old Chieftain; Dominion of the North; The Empire of the St Lawrence,* and many other works. He has received honorary Doctorates from the Universities of Manitoba, McGill, Queen's, New Brunswick, Saskatchewan, and British Columbia. Twice winner of the Governor General's Award for Non-Fiction, he has also been awarded the Tyrrell Medal of the Royal Society of Canada, the University of Alberta National Award in Letters, and the University of British Columbia Medal for Popular Biography.

ACKNOWLEDGEMENTS

We wish to thank the PUBLIC ARCHIVES OF CANADA for their permission to reproduce thirteen pictures used in the illustration sections; The Webster Collection of the New Brunswick Museum, and other institutions and individuals as credited in the captions.

PRINTED AND BOUND
IN CANADA BY
THE HUNTER ROSE COMPANY